National Library of Canada Cataloguing in Publication Data

Berton, Pierre, 1920–

The promised land : settling the West, 1896–1914 / Pierre Berton. — Anchor Canada ed.

ISBN 0-385-65929-6

1. Prairie Provinces—Emigration and immigration—History.
2. Minorities—Prairie Provinces—History. 3. Prairie Provinces—Social conditions. 4. Prairie Provinces—History. I. Title.

FC3209.I4B47 2002   971.2'02   C2002-902700-4
F1060.9.B48 2002

Cover photo: courtesy National Archives of Canada (PA-0010401)
Cover design: CS Richardson
Maps by Geoffrey Matthews
Printed and bound in Canada

Published in Canada by
Anchor Canada, a division of
Random House of Canada Limited

Random House of Canada Limited's website: www.randomhouse.ca

8   7   6   5   4   3   2   1

The Promised Land

The Promised

"And I am come down to deliver them
out of the hand of the Egyptians,
and to bring them up out of that land
unto a good land and a large, unto
a land flowing with milk and honey . . ."

—Exodus 3:8

Settling
the
West

1896-1914

Land

By Pierre Berton

Anchor Canada

Books by Pierre Berton

The Royal Family
The Mysterious North
Klondike
Just Add Water and Stir
Adventures of a Columnist
Fast Fast Fast Relief
The Big Sell
The Comfortable Pew
The Cool, Crazy, Committed
   World of the Sixties
The Smug Minority
The National Dream
The Last Spike
Drifting Home
Hollywood's Canada
My Country
The Dionne Years
The Wild Frontier
The Invasion of Canada
Flames Across the Border
Why We Act Like Canadians
The Promised Land
Vimy
Starting Out
The Arctic Grail
The Great Depression
Niagara: A History of the Falls
My Times: Living with History
1967, The Last Good Year
Marching as to War

Picture Books
The New City (with Henri Rossier)
Remember Yesterday
The Great Railway
The Klondike Quest
Pierre Berton's Picture Book
   of Niagara Falls
Winter
The Great Lakes
Seacoasts
Pierre Berton's Canada

Anthologies
Great Canadians
Pierre and Janet Berton's
   Canadian Food Guide
Historic Headlines
Farewell to the Twentieth Century
Worth Repeating
Welcome to the Twenty-first
   Century

Fiction
Masquerade (pseudonym
   Lisa Kroniuk)

Books for Young Readers
The Golden Trail
The Secret World of Og
Adventures in Canadian History
   (22 volumes)

Contents

ELEVEN: BOOM AND BUST

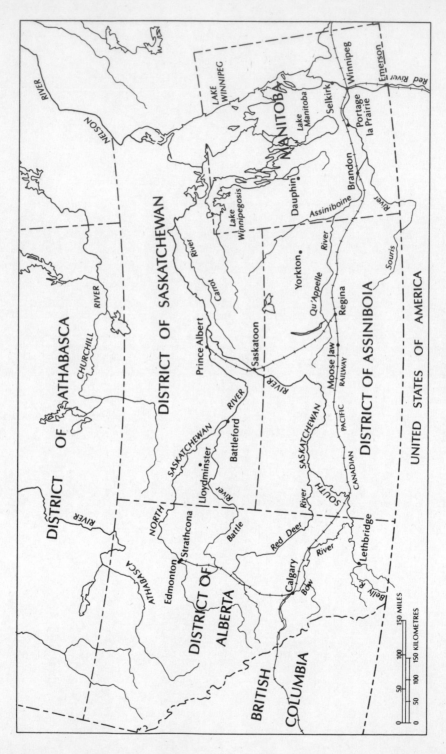

The West before 1905

DISTRICT OF ATHABASCA

DISTRICT OF SASKATCHEWAN

MANITOBA

DISTRICT OF ASSINIBOIA

DISTRICT OF ALBERTA

BRITISH COLUMBIA

UNITED STATES OF AMERICA

NELSON RIVER

CHURCHILL RIVER

ATHABASCA RIVER

LAKE WINNIPEG

Lake Winnipegosis

Lake Manitoba

Carrot River

Saskatoon

Prince Albert

Battleford

Lloydminster

Edmonton
Strathcona

NORTH SASKATCHEWAN RIVER

Battle River

SOUTH SASKATCHEWAN River

Red Deer River

Calgary
Bow River

Lethbridge
Belly R.

Moose Jaw

Regina

Qu'Appelle River

Yorkton

Dauphin

Assiniboine River

Brandon

Souris River

Portage la Prairie

Selkirk

Winnipeg

Emerson

Red River

CANADIAN PACIFIC RAILWAY

150 MILES

150 KILOMETRES

100

50

0

100

50

0

Prologue: Professor Oleskow's Vision

This is a book about dreams and illusions, escape and survival, triumph and despair. It is also a book about foolish optimism, political cunning, naïveté, greed, scandal, and opportunism. It is a book about the search for Utopia, the promise of a Promised Land, and so it treats of hope, fulfilment, and liberation as well as drudgery, loneliness, and disenchantment. What we are dealing with here is a phenomenon rare, if not unique, in history: the filling up of an empty realm, a thousand miles broad, with more than one million people in less than one generation.

This, then, is the story of the creation of a state within a state and the resultant transformation of a nation. There are grafters in this tale and hard-nosed politicians and civic boosters with dollar signs in their eyes; but there are also idealists, dreamers, and visionaries. And since these last are in the minority it is best to start with the first of them, a Slavic professor of agriculture named Josef Oleskow, who saw in the untrammelled Canadian West a haven for the downtrodden of Eastern Europe.

Let us join Dr. Oleskow in the hot summer of 1895 as he makes his way by train on a journey of discovery to the Canadian prairies. He is immediately identifiable as a stranger. His hair, dark and luxuriant, is unparted, combed straight back in the European fashion. His moustache does not droop over his lips in the North American style but turns sharply upward in two fierce points, like that of the German Kaiser. He is dressed formally and fastidiously – neat dark suit, high starched collar, heavy foulard. He is a handsome man of thirty-five with dark, intelligent eyes and regular features, and he is enchanted by the New World: the people are so clean and, equally important, so independent. There are no lords, no peasants; here, everyone is a master! Officials are not officious; they are workers just like everybody else, without special privileges. Their offices operate just like stores. You can walk in without bowing, and the man behind the desk – even a Cabinet minister – will probably keep his hat on.

But, oh, the waste! For two days, Dr. Oleskow's train plunges through the blackened forests of the Precambrian Shield. To him these vast stretches of burned timber are a painful sight – a forest cemetery. No one, apparently, bothers to extinguish the gargantuan blazes that despoil the land. In the professor's native Ruthenia, wood is the most

1

precious of commodities, to be husbanded and hoarded. But these Canadians destroy their heritage mercilessly. Why, he discovers, when they clear the land, they actually toss the stumps into the nearest ravine!

The train leaves the blackened desert of the Shield and bursts into the prairies. Here are other wonders. The Canadians have an axe with a curved handle that fits the shape of the hand. Oleskow tests it and wonders why his own countrymen have, in the course of several centuries, failed to improve the design of their own implements. As the train passes through the grain fields of Manitoba he notes that nobody uses a sickle or a scythe. Machines, not men, harvest the wheat, and if a man doesn't own a machine, he can always rent one from a neighbour. At Portage la Prairie, the professor watches these marvellous machines following one another in a staggered row across the wide fields and marvels at the horses that draw them – not the skinny miserable nags of his native Carpathians but big husky animals with real leather harnesses.

But the land is so empty! The only city of any consequence is Winnipeg. From Portage the plains roll westward, unfenced and unploughed, the buffalo grass still waist high, broken only by a thin skein of trails – mere ruts, really – and the occasional river valley bordered by cottonwood and wolf willow. Indians in brightly coloured blankets squat in picturesque groups on the station platforms. Mountains of buffalo bones line the track in the far west. But farms are few.

Strung out along the railway is a series of tiny settlements – clusters of frame buildings lining wooden sidewalks. Regina, the capital of the North West Territories, the so-called Queen City of the Plains, has fewer than two thousand people, scattered in huddles of wooden shacks that straggle for two miles across a sere plain, flat as a kitchen table. Saskatoon scarcely exists at all – a railway station and a few houses, nothing more. Calgary, with four thousand citizens, is a glorified cow town, Edmonton a glorified trading post.

These are primitive settlements. Calgary's dusty streets stink of horse manure. Regina is redolent of the stench of the hotel slops that drench the main street. Edmonton echoes with the piercing squeal of ungreased Red River carts drawn along Portage Avenue by oxen and ponies. In the smaller villages, cows, pigs, and chickens wander loose.

These islets of civilization are lost in the great sweep of the plains – wave after wave of grassland rolling west toward the foothills, so that the whole of the prairie country from the Red River to the Rockies

2

resembles a prehistoric ocean that has somehow congealed. But, as Dr. Oleskow notes, the earth is everywhere rich and black. His own countrymen are starved for land. This empty realm could be their salvation.

Josef Oleskow's journey took him as far west as Edmonton. A handful of his countrymen had preceded him to Canada, and their prosperity astonished him: Vasyl Tasiv, who came out in 1892 with only $40, now owned a house in Winnipeg, two cows, and a nest egg of $120. Yurko Paish had even managed to send home $120 – a small fortune. Dmytro Widynovich had also come with only $40 in 1893 and had been able to save $400. Credit was easy. In a town of twenty houses there were three banks, all eager to lend money. Machines could be bought on time. The problem, as Oleskow saw it, was not how to borrow money but how to avoid borrowing too much. This was an optimistic country; people talked only of success; none thought of failure.

Yet one thing bothered the fastidious professor. His countrymen in Canada were an embarrassment to him. They dressed in rags, scratched incessantly, did not appear to bathe. This offended the idealist in Oleskow. In the Promised Land, newcomers must not look and act like serfs! They must wear suits that would cover their bare chests; they must abandon hooks and ribbons for real buttons; they must scrub themselves regularly and learn to use a knife and fork. Above all, they must rid themselves of the stigma of slavery, learn to lift their heads and look squarely into the eyes of others instead of peering up from under the brow like a dog.

Like so many others who were to follow him to the Canadian West, Oleskow was looking for perfection, or, more correctly, *his* idea of perfection. It was his dream to turn Ruthenian peasants into instant Canadian farmers employing Canadian agricultural techniques, wearing Canadian clothes, speaking Canadian English. It was a magic vision that would become widely promulgated in the West.

Oleskow was shocked during a visit to one farm of Ruthenian colonists. To him, the children seemed to be clothed in filthy castoffs; and the women! Why, they didn't bother to wear blouses!

"For Heaven's sake," he cried. "How could you let yourselves go like this?"

To which one woman gave a perfectly sensible answer: "And why not? There is no one to dress for."

3

But Dr. Oleskow had never been a peasant. In his neat dark suit, he was more out of place than his countrymen. He was an academic with a doctorate in botany, chemistry, and geology. As a member of the faculty of the teachers' seminary at Lemberg, in that section of the Austro-Hungarian Empire then known as Ruthenia, he was paid six hundred dollars a year. His dream was always to better the conditions of the peasantry – partly by improving the mineral and chemical content of the soil and partly by reducing the population through emigration.

He was the leader among a group of intellectuals who made up Provista, the Ruthenian Population Society. These selfless men had two purposes: first, to stem the flow of their countrymen to the jungles of Brazil and redirect it to the Canadian prairies, and second, to prevent the exploitation of Ruthenian emigrants by unscrupulous agents working for the major shipping companies.

Brazil was tempting his people with offers of free transportation, free land, and financial assistance. The peasantry swallowed whole the Brazilian propaganda, which suggested they could loll at their ease in the new land while monkeys came down from the trees to handle all manual labour. In fact, those who reached Brazil were treated little better than slaves.

The steamship agents, who were paid a bonus for every ticket sold to a warm body, shamelessly hoodwinked each emigrant in a dozen ways, charging huge sums to exchange money, extracting fees for fake medical examinations while bribing the petty officials to ignore their swindles. No wonder Slavic peasants were arriving in Canada penniless.

Oleskow wanted to change all that. Ruthenia was so heavily overpopulated that wealthy landowners could pay their labourers only a pittance. The excess population, in the professor's belief, was more than two million. But if the remedy was emigration to Canada, it must be selective, and the exploitation of the ignorant must stop. That is why the society sent Dr. Oleskow to Canada, having persuaded the Canadian government to pay for his transportation.

Oleskow outlined his plan to T. Mayne Daly, the minister responsible for immigration in the Conservative government. He was, he explained, prepared to quit his academic post to work for Canada, to control all immigration from Ruthenia and its provinces of Galicia and Bukovina. He wanted no salary, only expenses. It would be for him a labour of love.

4

It was his plan to build a well-organized immigration movement, independent of the steamship companies and their agents, choosing his subjects carefully – farmers of adequate means whose funds would be safeguarded and who would be protected from exploitation. These people would be the best stock that Eastern Europe could offer.

But Josef Oleskow was a man ahead of his time. Daly was interested but cautious. Canada had had its share of crackpot idealists. The government recognized that Oleskow was no crackpot, but it was wary of setting a precedent.

Within a year the government changed. A new minister, Clifford Sifton, was too busy sweeping the dead wood from his department to consider the Oleskow plan. In Austria, the shipping companies and agents were opposed to any scheme that they themselves could not control. The Austrian government did not specifically oppose emigration, but it did oppose proselytizers like Oleskow. The landowning nobility was more interested in keeping the labour force high and wages low.

As Canada procrastinated, Oleskow grew dejected. His pamphlet extolling the Canadian West, describing his tour of the prairies and giving practical advice to would-be emigrants, was read by thousands. But it was the shipping agents who reaped the benefit. They slipped into the villages, disguised as pedlars and itinerant journeymen, signed up anybody they could, promised the moon, and cheated their victims. Oleskow continued to travel at his own expense, pushing the idea of emigration to the New World. In 1898 Clifford Sifton actually gave him some expense money, recognizing the professor's role in bringing to Canada the sturdy farmers he would eventually dub "the men in sheepskin coats."

But Josef Oleskow's plan was never adopted. In 1900 Sifton opted for an unrestricted settlement policy and sublet all continental immigration work to a mysterious organization known as the North Atlantic Trading Company. This suspect "company" – to this day we do not know the identity of its principals – was paid five dollars for every healthy man, woman, and child who reached Canadian shores. That was a far cry from Oleskow's carefully thought out plan. In spite of the regulations, many arrived destitute.

By this time Oleskow's little trickle of new arrivals had become a tidal wave. His report on the West had started a chain reaction, for better or for worse. The movement fed upon itself. By 1903, the Galicians as they were then called (we know them as Poles and

Ukrainians today) were strung out by the tens of thousands along the northern rim of the prairies. Long before that Josef Oleskow had wound down his activities in the emigration field. His wife was dead. He had a new post – director of a teachers' seminary – in a new town, Sokal. And he was gravely ill. On October 18, 1903, the man who helped to start it all but who would soon be forgotten, was dead at the age of forty-three.

Chapter One

The Young Napoleon of the West

1
The new broom

2
The hard sell

3
A political animal

4
The spoils system

5
The *Free Press* changes hands

6
Master and servant

1

What are we to say of Clifford Sifton? That for almost a decade he was the most powerful politician in Western Canada? That he was a visionary who changed the face of the prairies? That he enriched his closest political cronies, as well as his brother-in-law, as a result of his position? That he quit his post on a matter of principle? That he resigned not for principle at all but because of a personal scandal? That he was a ruthlessly efficient organizer? That he had no political philosophy other than the philosophy of maintaining power? That he never shrank from a battle, ignored whispering campaigns, never stooped to respond to criticism? That he was a workaholic who exhausted his colleagues? That he was an ailing cabinet minister, exhausted by overwork? That he was a political puppet master whose control extended even into the highest echelons of the Mounted Police? That he was the Pied Piper who brought prosperity to the prairies? That he was nothing less than the devil incarnate?

All these things were said of Sifton between 1896, when he took office as Minister of the Interior in Wilfrid Laurier's Liberal cabinet, and 1905, when he abruptly resigned. He was a man of impressive strength and glaring flaws who, for better or for worse, put his stamp on the times. When one speaks or writes of the West at the turn of the century one does not call it the Laurier Period. It is the Sifton Period, the Sifton Era, the Sifton Decade.

His name has become a symbol, conjuring up a series of dramatic tableaux: the grimy immigrant ships, crammed with strange, dark-featured farmers; the colonist cars, crowded with kerchiefed women and men in coats of rough sheepskin; the hovels grubbed out of tough prairie sod; the covered wagons lumbering across the border from Utah and Minnesota; the babel of tongues in Winnipeg's immigration hall; the bell tents of the Barr colonists whitening the plains at Saskatoon; the straggle of barefooted Doukhobor fanatics, tramping down the frosted roads of Saskatchewan; the remittance men holding up the long bar of the Alberta Hotel.

So it is appropriate to look at Sifton on the threshold of his federal career, recently sworn into the Laurier cabinet, and about to return triumphantly to his home town, where he knows he will shortly win his federal seat by acclamation.

It is the night of November 25, 1896, and we have joined the boister-

ous crowd of Liberals on the CPR platform at Brandon, Manitoba, braving the bitter thirty-below weather, waiting to greet the city's favourite son. D'Alton McCarthy has been persuaded to relinquish the riding; Sifton is slated to take it unopposed.

The train is an hour late. The faithful stamp their feet and beat their hands together. Moustaches are frosted; eye glasses mist up. It is eleven-thirty before Sifton steps down from the sleeper to acknowledge the crowd. Cheers break out. Fireworks explode. Two hundred torches are lit. As the new minister is escorted to a waiting carriage, a brass band strikes up a lively march. It is so cold that the valves in the trumpets freeze and the music dies as we all shuffle off up Ninth Street and across Rosser Avenue toward Princess, where a roaring bonfire lights up the city hall.

Here Sifton is greeted by an old political crony, the Mayor of Brandon, James Smart, bulky and balding. A reporter for the local Sun scribbles away in his notebook. "Never was a homecoming more cheerful," he will write. "Never was a citizen received with such heartiness." The hyperbole will surprise no one, since Sifton and his friend the Mayor both own a piece of the paper. According to the Toronto Mail, Sifton himself writes half the editorials, which have recently been eulogizing the Young Napoleon of the West.

In the flickering light of the bonfire, we all enter the city hall, whose chambers have been decorated for the occasion by the young Liberals. Smart, as chairman, praises Sifton in what the Sun will call "a masterly manner." Then the man of the hour rises to his feet to address the cheering throng.

He is a strapping figure, six feet tall, glowing with health and energy, his cheeks plump with good living. But there is something forbidding about Sifton, even at thirty-five, something about his mien that says: Do not approach too close. A sparse moustache droops downward over his lips; but it is the eyes that are his most notable feature. They are small, close set, and chillingly cold. Not an easy man to know, one would say; not an easy man to cross.

Tonight, however, he is all warmth. These are his friends, his neighbours, his political supporters. There isn't a Tory in the hall.

Sifton speaks modestly about his Brandon connections and the greeting he has been tendered. "I had not the slightest idea when I left Ottawa for home that I would receive such a royal welcome and warm homecoming," he declares.

Cheers punctuate these remarks, even though everyone must know

9

that the details of the welcome have been public knowledge for several days and that Sifton himself, if he has acted true to form, had a hand in the planning. But now he is all humility. "I will not forget the people who sent me down," he says. Nor will he. Dozens of old comrades in this audience will benefit from the new minister's personal orchestration of the political spoils system.

A modest promise follows: "When I go I will do my work just as a plain Brandon boy would do his on Rosser avenue." And then a boast: "The magnitude and prospect of the work before me does not disturb me." Nor does it. There isn't a lazy bone in Clifford Sifton's body. He is prepared to work throughout the night if necessary to clear the two-year backlog in his new department.

Finally, Sifton turns, as he must, to "the troublesome question – the school question – no speech in Manitoba would be complete without it." He reveals that he has reached a compromise with Wilfrid Laurier: there will be no separate schools in the province, but in the predominantly Roman Catholic areas the Prime Minister has agreed to half an hour of religious teaching by Catholic teachers at the day's end. At that there are more cheers: it has taken several weeks for Sifton to reach this accommodation with his leader. Now the way is cleared for his acclamation. It will be nearly a decade before the school question, like an unwanted relative, again lands on his doorstep.

Eight days later, Sifton returned to Ottawa to do battle with the most powerful bureaucrat in the government service, A.M. Burgess, the deputy minister he had inherited from the previous administration. Sifton was determined to shake up the department, on whose officials, he said, "the pall of death seemed to have fallen." He would start at the top. Burgess, a haughty Scot and former newspaperman, had been having his way with a series of weak ministers since 1882. But Sifton was no weakling. Somebody once said of him that he had a mind like a steel trap, the memory of an elephant, and the hide of a rhinoceros. Sifton made it clear that "instead of the deputy running the minister, the minister would run the deputy." Burgess would have to go.

Sifton's elephant-like memory went back a long way to a day in 1884 when, as a young Brandon lawyer, just twenty-three, he had sought an audience with Burgess on behalf of the newly formed Manitoba and North West Farmers' Union, an organization concerned with the handling of public lands. The arrogant Burgess had kept him waiting for seven hours while he remained closeted with his Tory friends, and then dismissed him and a colleague contemptuously as self-serving Liberal hacks who knew less about the West than he did. Sifton did not forget the insult. And now he was Burgess's boss.

For a cabinet minister to dislodge a veteran deputy was unthinkable in the bureaucracy of that day (and almost unthinkable in this). But Sifton wanted to fire *two*: not only Burgess but also Hayter Reed, the Deputy Superintendent General of Indian affairs. In Sifton's view both men were incompetent – Easterners who didn't understand the West, masters of red tape and bureaucracy who made any sensible dealings with the department impossible. It was, Sifton found, "a department of delay, a department of circumlocution . . . a department which tired men to death who undertook to get any business transacted with it."

The two civil servants fought back. They had powerful political connections; but Laurier had promised Sifton a free hand, and he meant to use it. In addition, he had the support of the West. Even the arch-Conservative Calgary *Herald* wanted to see Burgess ousted. The paper reflected the general impression in the West that Burgess considered settlers a nuisance and even a menace. "Whenever the opportunity occurred to give it to the settler in the neck . . . the deputy minister did not fail to deliver the blow."

The battle dragged on into February. The civil service was aghast. Joseph Pope, the very proper Under Secretary of State, who had once served John A. Macdonald, thought it "a bad business [which] creates general disquietude." In Pope's eyes, this act of surgery by a bumptious Westerner destroyed "the feeling of permanence and stability, which attached to the office in the past."

But Sifton was less interested in stability than he was in action. He wanted his own men in the department, men he could trust and with whom he had worked before – Liberals, of course. In the end he won. Reed and Burgess were brushed aside, and one man assumed the duties of two – the same Jim Smart who had greeted Sifton on his return to Brandon, twice mayor of that city, a former member of the Manitoba cabinet, and an old friend of the Minister.

Smart, noted the Governor General, Lord Minto, was Sifton's alter ego. The two men were contemporaries – Smart was just a year older – and had grown up in Brandon politics together. In 1885, when Smart was president of the local reform association, Sifton was vice-president. The ex-mayor was known as an able administrator; even

T. Mayne Daly, Sifton's Tory predecessor, had a good word for him: "A man of integrity and worth and of great personal character." It would be some twenty years before a Tory investigation was to undermine that assessment.

That same month, March, 1897, Sifton wrote to a correspondent in British Columbia about the evils of the spoils system in the department during the Conservative regime. "The most guilty and rascally officials have been kept in place by political influence," he reported. But Sifton himself was not averse to hiring political rascals if they did the job. In the months that followed, he fired twenty-three members of the staff, six for "active political partisanship," but the men who replaced them were just as partisan for the Liberal cause. In fact, those who worked for Sifton really had two jobs: to push immigration, of course, but also to organize and canvass for the party.

That was the practice of the time. Like his colleagues, the Minister filled the key jobs in his department with close friends and political supporters. These included W.F. McCreary, the Mayor of Winnipeg, who became Commissioner of Immigration, resident in that city; William J. White, editor of the Brandon *Sun*, who was put in charge of press relations in the United States; and C. Wesley Speers, who was made general colonization agent. Speers had been put up as a dummy opponent to Sifton at the Liberal nominating meeting in Brandon the previous fall and had gone through the charade of graciously stepping aside in favour of his future employer.

There was of course no possibility that Sifton could have hired a Tory had he wanted to. Even the appointment of Mayor McCreary, a johnny-come-lately in the eyes of veteran ward heelers, was controversial. Sifton was forced to disappoint hordes of loyal party men who expected jobs in his department and complained when he overlooked them. The Minister ignored their pleas. He certainly wanted Liberals, but he wanted Liberals who were efficient, hard working, and personally loyal. These conditions did not apply, however, to Canadian immigration officials serving in the United States. In the Outside Service, as it was called, defeated candidates, former Liberal members, relatives of cabinet ministers, and friends of Sifton and Smart had no difficulty finding jobs. Scarcely one had any immigration experience. But Sifton defended the practice, declaring in the House that any man who was regarded as valuable to the Liberal party must also be valuable as a public servant.

In Ottawa he was determined to run an efficient department. Salaries would be raised on merit, not on seniority, and commissions rather than straight salaries would be paid in the field. He wanted to get the most out of his people.

Sifton's goal was clear. He intended to fill up the West with farmers. To do that he must force the Hudson's Bay Company and the Canadian Pacific Railway to place on the market the lands that had originally been reserved for them. Since these lands were not taxed until patented, neither of the two historic companies was in any rush to claim or to sell them, preferring to wait until prices rose with the demand. By 1896, the railways alone had been granted 24 million acres but had held off obtaining title to most of them. Sifton was determined there would be no more land grants, and he was equally determined that the railway lands be opened for settlement. It took him most of his term of office to achieve these results, but by 1905, 22.5 million acres of railway land were on the market and the Western land boom was gathering speed.

2

John Wesley Dafoe, Sifton's biographer as well as his employee, *The* purported to believe that the various hard-sell methods used by the *hard* department to settle the West originated with the Minister of the *sell* Interior. This wasn't true. Almost every technique had been developed some years before by American railroads, land companies, and the CPR. Sifton borrowed these techniques, improved on some of them, and through superior organization and efficiency made them work.

But they would not have worked had the times been different. Dafoe and others credited the Liberal government with filling up the plains. But the Liberals were lucky, as they have been in more recent times. They rode into power just as the great depression of the nineties was ending.

In fact, 1896 was a turning-point year. The crippling droughts of 1892, 1893, and 1894 were over. After 1895 grain prices began to rise. The cost of rail and steam transportation dropped. Red Fife wheat with its superior milling and baking properties came into its own — by 1900 it had replaced some fifty lesser varieties. Steel reduction rollers transformed the milling process. The chilled steel plough was ideal for turning the tough sod of the Canadian prairie. The chain ownership of elevators changed the face of the prairie landscape. Improvements in binder twine accelerated the automation of farming.

Yet none of these technological and agricultural advances fully explains the rush to the Canadian West that took place during the Sifton period. Far more significant was the growing scarcity of free land – especially humid land – in the United States and indeed in Canada. Experiments in the techniques of dryland farming had already proven the efficiency of summer fallowing. But dry-farming methods had to await the end of the depression. Once Canada was seen to contain the last frost-free, sub-humid areas of the continent, it required only an educational program to bring in the farmers.

The Liberal government's plan for Western Canada was simple and specific. The prairies were to be settled by practical farmers; nobody else was wanted from overseas. City people, clerks, shopkeepers, and artisans were not to be considered.

"We do not want anything but agricultural laborers and farmers or people who are coming for the purpose of engaging in agriculture, whether as farmers or farm laborers," Sifton told his deputy. The Liberals, in short, had espoused John A. Macdonald's National Policy and made it their own. The West would be a gigantic granary, tied to Central Canada by a ribbon of steel. The wheat would move east in ever-increasing quantities; the manufactured goods required by Western farmers would fill up the empty freight cars on the return journey. The concept of an industrialized West had no place in this scheme.

Sifton was convinced that certain races had the character to become farmers while others did not. "Northernness" was the key. The Scots, Scandinavians, Germans, and British would make excellent citizens. Even the northern English, in Sifton's view, were preferable to the southern English; in fact, a higher bonus was paid to steamship agents for those who emigrated from northern England.

The northern Slavs were welcomed. Mediterranean people were not. Italians, especially southern Italians, and Jews were taboo. "I don't want anything done to facilitate Italian immigration," Sifton told his people. He feared the infusion of "undesirable persons." When in May, 1898, the CPR hired a carload of Italians from New York to work on the construction of the Crow's Nest Pass line, Sifton sent them all back. At one point the department had looked favourably on a plan to bring in a small number of Rumanian Jewish farmers. Laurier put a stop to it. "I do not favour this movement," he told Sifton, who, in redrafting the department's memo, declared that "ex-

14

perience shows that the Jewish people do not become agriculturalists." Given the anti-Semitism of the time, this attitude caused scarcely a raised eyebrow.

The Canadian policy was more pragmatic and certainly more cautious than that of the United States, which, in its idealism and self-confidence, had welcomed the masses of Europe to its shores, serene in the belief that once established in America they could not help but flourish. But Canada wanted only those who it believed would not become a burden on the public purse. The Americans saw their country as a haven for the downtrodden; at least that was the rhetoric, and the rhetoric was often as important as the reality. Canada didn't really want the downtrodden unless they could contribute to the nation's wealth. It could be argued that while most emigrants set off for the United States in *search* of something vaguely called the American Dream, the ones who came to Canada were *escaping* from something that might be called the European Nightmare. The Americans offered an ideal: liberty. The Canadians offered something more practical: free land.

Every immigrant who arrived in the North West was entitled to choose 160 acres of public land on the payment of a ten-dollar registration fee. He must be prepared to live on his land and do a stipulated amount of work on it for three years. If he could stick it out, the land was his. But before anybody could be convinced to take up the land, some facts about this strange and unknown realm at the top of North America would have to be broadcast.

The first and most important task was to dispel the image of the West as a snow-covered desert. Sifton had hardly taken hold before his own paper reported that the *Nation*, a respected Dublin journal, was warning people away from Canada, declaring that Manitoba was "a kind of Siberia." One of Sifton's first moves was to try to ban the daily publication of Manitoba temperatures, but since that might prove even more alarming, he dropped the idea. Nevertheless, snow was never mentioned in the blizzard of pamphlets his department issued. "Cold" was another taboo word. The accepted adjectives were "bracing" and "invigorating." Why, it was so mild, one pamphlet declared, that "the soft maple" could grow five feet in a single season! And if prospective immigrants confused the Manitoba maple, a weed tree, with the Eastern hardwood – Canada's symbol – too bad.

In this anti-cold campaign, Sifton had the enthusiastic support of the CPR's ebullient chairman, William Van Horne, who never lost an

15

opportunity to suggest that the prairies were close to being subtropical. In one public statement in Europe, Van Horne announced that the coldest weather he had ever known was in Rome and Florence. "I pine for Winnipeg to thaw me," he declared, maintaining the same straight face that allowed him to bluff his way through innumerable all-night poker games. "The atmosphere in the far west intoxicates you, it is so very invigorating."

There were better lures than the weather. Canada was touted not only as a free country but also as an orderly one: no one needed to carry a gun in the Canadian West; the Mounted Police, who were establishing an international reputation in the Yukon, would see to that. And the land was free. More, you could usually pick up an adjoining quarter-section for a song. And there was money to be made in the West by anybody willing to work. The titles on the pamphlets trumpeted the story: *The Wondrous West*; *Canada, Land of Opportunity*; *Prosperity Follows Settlement*.

In 1896, the Immigration Department sent out sixty-five thousand pamphlets. By 1900, the number had reached one million. The best-known and most successful appeared just after Sifton left office and was directed at immigrants from south of the border. In thirty-three pages of large type *The Last and Best West* (later simplified to *The Last Best West*) cunningly played on the American agrarian myth beloved by the readers of Horatio Alger, extolling the farmer as the finest type of citizen and echoing the ingrained belief that the most successful men "have as a rule been those whose youth was spent on a farm. . . ."

Sifton took personal direction of this propaganda. One highly successful pamphlet entitled *A Few Facts about Canada* consisted of a series of letters, carefully culled from thousands solicited by the department, from former British farmers praising the West. At Sifton's suggestion, these letters were printed in the handwriting of the correspondents rather than in cold type "to impress the ordinary farmer with the idea of reality." Sifton also insisted that the editors of the pamphlet avoid exaggeration and select "fair samples, not too favourable."

Nonetheless, other pamphleteers indulged in hyperbole. "The kindest thing to say about it is that the literature was a little on the optimistic side," one British immigrant recalled. "Canada was said to have a healthy climate guaranteed to be free of malaria. One has to admit that this was true. It was said that while the prairie summers were hot, the heat was delightfully invigorating and while it got cold in the winter the cold was dry and not unpleasant. I used to recall those glowing words as I pitched sheaves with the temperature at 95 in the shade, and as I ran behind the sleigh at 30 below to keep from freezing."

To alter the international image of the Canadian prairies, Sifton curried favour with American newspapermen and farmers as well as with British politicians. Thousands were wined, dined, and shuttled across the prairies at government expense. Lloyd George, then an up-and-coming Member of Parliament, was one of those brought to Canada and persuaded that his Welsh countrymen who had emigrated to Patagonia should be advised to move north.

As a newspaper publisher himself Sifton had a cynical attitude toward the press. Reporters, editors, and small-town publishers could be purchased with flattery and a few free whiskeys. Sifton went further. Entire trainloads of editors from south of the border were conducted in luxury across the plains, lubricated by strong drink. Those too lazy or too inebriated to write their own stories were fed specially composed articles, which often appeared without a comma changed.

The venality of the newspapers played into Sifton's hands. If a publisher wanted government advertising he had better not run any anti-Canadian material. On at least one occasion, the members of a journalistic junket assured the department that any negative articles would be censored and their authors banned from future trips across the West. One editor (of the Shelby, Kentucky, *Sentinel*) actually apologized for not getting his story into type quickly enough, explaining that "when I arrived home I found my office in an uproar, with every member of the force drunk except my lady stenographer."

The Minister's purpose was to saturate the world with propaganda about the Canadian West. Sifton, the one-time lay preacher, saw himself as a new kind of missionary for his country, proselytizing the unconverted and never letting up. "Just as soon as you stop advertising and missionary work," he told the Commons, "the movement is going to stop." In 1902 alone, 465 American farmers' "delegations" crossed the prairies at government expense. These delegations were made up of civic leaders, municipal officials, and former legislators, elected by local farmers and encouraged to write and lecture about the wonders they had seen in Canada.

The statistics suggest the extent of the Sifton campaigns: tens of thousands of pamphlets and exhibits at state fairs, 200,000 pamphlets distributed at the St. Louis world exposition in 1904 alone; seven thousand newspaper advertisements for "Free Land Clubs" (the name told the story); one thousand lantern-slide lectures in England in a single year; one thousand inquiries a month at the High Commissioner's office in London; and a thirty-five-thousand-dollar arch at the coronation of Edward VII, trumpeting the advantages of immigration.

When Sifton took office in 1896, the department had six agents operating south of the border. By 1899 it had three hundred. The Minister liked to tell the story of one such agent who quit his job after six months "on the plea that no one thought of Canada." Sifton brought him back to Ottawa, gave him a holiday, and persuaded him to go back. Six months later, the agent had finally managed to convince one family to emigrate. But between 1900 and 1903 he brought five thousand American settlers into the Canadian West.

There were other, more exotic, ventures. In 1902, M.V. "Mac" MacInness, the department's portly and jovial agent in Detroit, began to cultivate James Oliver Curwood, soon to become the best-known outdoor novelist in the United States. Eventually, as a result of this connection, the Canadian government hired Curwood for eight hundred dollars a year plus expenses to tour the Canadian North West in search of material for his novels. The gamble paid off. Curwood, in a series of best-selling books, coined the name "God's Country," a phrase that is still in use.

In 1896, about 17,000 immigrants arrived in Canada. In 1899 the figure approached 45,000. Bill McCreary, the bulky, black-browed Irishman whom Sifton had made Commissioner of Immigration in Winnipeg, was overworked to the point of breakdown. The immigration hall could not accommodate the flow of newcomers, and the government was forced to pitch tents to handle new arrivals. Yet this was a comparative trickle. "I confess it makes my head swim trying to keep tab on the development that is going on," John Dafoe of the *Free Press* wrote to Sifton in 1902. Long queues were forming at every land office. One weekend in 1903 at the Prince Albert office, men sat on camp stools from Friday night to Monday morning waiting to file on the homesteads they had selected. One such was a German-born farmer from Neustadt, Ontario, named William Thomas Diefenbaker, whose son, a future prime minister of Canada, kept him revived with innumerable pots of tea, rustled up between snatches of sleep caught under a billiard table in a nearby pool hall.

By 1905 when Sifton left office, the annual intake of immigrants was pushing 150,000. Every board of trade in the West was copying the government propaganda, and the prairie country was in the throes of a boom. "It roars in . . . [one's] ears like the race of machinery in a factory," one travel writer exclaimed. "Maps, pamphlets, diagrams, reports, books, photographs swish around him like a tornado. They are handed to him on the railroad car; they are by his porridge bowl at breakfast in the morning. You go into a drugstore to buy a cigar, and the eye is fascinated by a brochure. . . . Being an ordinary hum drum individual . . . you read and you learn and are amazed at your own stupendous ignorance. . . . Every ten or twelve miles a town is springing up like a mushroom. . . . The chief product of many of these places is the pamphlet about their own virtues. . . ."

3

Sifton took office with the reputation of being an iron man. In the words of an admirer, "he never gets tired, works like a horse, never worries, eats three square meals a day and at night could go to sleep on a nail keg." During the Manitoba provincial campaign of 1896 he would climb off the train at Brandon at eleven at night, sit up until morning talking politics with friends, entertain at breakfast, and then take off in the winter's cold by sleigh, speaking at Souris, say, in the afternoon, and Hartney at night before heading off to the railhead at Oak Lake to catch the train back home. "All he needed," one of his companions recalled, "was to pull the buffalo robe around him to sleep in the rig." In Ottawa he had the reputation of staying all night at his desk, leaving behind a pile of work for his clerks at 6 a.m. and returning at ten o'clock looking as fresh as ever. It was not that he had an iron constitution; his secret was an iron will power.

A political animal

But as Sifton's work load increased, his health began to suffer. His years in office were punctuated by periodic breakdowns. After only a few months, the long office hours began to take their toll on him. By the end of July, he had reached a point where he could "neither eat, rest nor sleep"; yet he could not consider a holiday until he had wound up the last remains of the backlog of business – his legacy from the Conservatives.

Plagued by high blood pressure and "insomnia, my old enemy," he suffered a nervous collapse but bounced back after a one-month

19

seaside vacation. Two years later he was again in a state of near exhaustion. "I would as soon spend life in the treadmill as carrying the load of work I have to do now," he wrote to a Winnipeg friend. In February 1902, his nerves were so badly upset that Laurier insisted he take a fortnight's holiday. Yet the iron man reputation remained. Even today it is difficult to think of Sifton as a sickly, nervous insomniac. His image was always that of the man who could catnap on a nail keg.

The strain and overwork were exacerbated by Sifton's chronic deafness, an affliction he suffered as the result of a fever contracted at fifteen. In 1900, he set off to Europe to see a Viennese specialist in an attempt to alleviate "the nightmare which has been hanging over me." That *cri de coeur* in a letter to a close friend is one of the rare times that Sifton reveals himself as an ordinary mortal, subject to human frailty and tormented by it. Relief, alas, was only temporary. He used an ear trumpet, but that didn't help. By 1905 Clifford Sifton was almost stone deaf. His deafness was not without advantages. It stimulated his lifelong habit of reading and probably helped develop his photographic memory – the uncanny ability to quote long passages verbatim from the books he so eagerly devoured. His responses to Opposition attacks could not be hasty or ill-considered because in his later years he could not hear his detractors. He was forced to pore over the Hansard reports and thus construct a more deliberate but often more effective reply.

His inability to hear properly and thus communicate has been given as one reason for his public reputation as a cold, aloof, even ruthless politician. Yet it is hard to imagine anyone being truly intimate with Clifford Sifton, deaf or not – not even his sons, perhaps not even his attractive and outgoing wife, Arma, the daughter of a socially prominent Ottawa family whom he married when he was twenty-three. She was, so tradition has it, a gifted clairvoyante, the direct antithesis of her unmystical, pragmatic husband.

Sifton, in his lifetime and after, was called abrasive, exacting, distant, abrupt, and impatient. He did not suffer fools. He was ambitious and outwardly self-assured. He made enemies easily but did not deign to recognize them. He never complained, never explained. One suspects there were more facets to this icily formal politician than deafness can account for. Did he ever suffer from self-doubt or unfulfilled yearnings? Did he ever acknowledge his weaknesses or his regrets to an intimate? We have no record of it. Was he ever the victim of unbridled passion, jealousy, or infatuation? Here the curtain parts momentarily, on the eve of his resignation – he is caught in a dalliance – and then closes tantalizingly. It is not possible to feel the kind of familiarity with Sifton that we sense when we study some of his contemporaries – John A. Macdonald, for example, or William Cornelius Van Horne, or George Stephen, who poured out his heart in his letters. But Sifton, even when he wrote to his father, was chillingly formal. He did not sign his correspondence with the elder Sifton "Affectionately, Cliff" or "Love, Clifford" or even "Your loving son, Clifford." It was always "Yours faithfully, Clifford Sifton," as if he were addressing a chance acquaintance or a constituent seeking favours.

Yet he was his father's son, the younger of two boys. (His easy-going brother, Arthur, would eventually become Premier of Alberta.) Like his father, he was a political animal and a staunch Methodist who passed the plate on Sundays in Brandon and for all of his life took part in the ritual of family prayers. As a Methodist he was a fervent advocate of temperance. Strong drink never sullied his lips, though he did not shrink from passing out gallons to the faithful at election time.

He had a deep-seated suspicion of Roman Catholics and French Canadians. He did not employ Quebeckers in his department, nor did he mingle with his French-Canadian colleagues. There was no love lost between Sifton and Israel Tarte, the Minister of Public Works from Quebec, and there was a real dislike for Charles Fitzpatrick, the pious Irish-Catholic Solicitor General and later Justice Minister, with whom he would publicly tangle in 1905.

These attitudes sprang out of the traditional Methodist Clear Grit tradition of southern Ontario in which the Siftons had been nurtured. Clifford's father had been a neighbour and close political ally of Alexander Mackenzie, the dour Liberal M.P. from Lambton who later became Prime Minister. Like every other successful officeholder, Mackenzie rewarded his friends. In 1874, J.W. Sifton managed to wangle a $100,000 government contract to build a telegraph line out of Fort Garry, in spite of the fact that there were lower bidders and that his tender was so ambiguous nobody could understand it. He was paid an inflated price for the work, constructed the poles out of cheap poplar, allowed them to rot away in spite of his contractual obligation to maintain the line for five years, and pocketed a substantial profit, to which a subsequent royal commission said he wasn't entitled.

None of this had the least effect on the elder Sifton's political career. He soon became a leading Manitoba politician, rising to Speaker of the legislature. His son Clifford graduated in 1880, a gold medallist from Victoria College, a Methodist institution in Cobourg, Ontario. Unlike so many of his political colleagues, Clifford Sifton had the advantage of a classical education. A serious student who exhibited none of the frivolity or bonhomie of his brother, Arthur, he was for all of his life an omnivorous reader. His interest in newspapers also went back to his days at Cobourg, where he had helped to found and edit the college paper.

With his brother, Clifford hung out his lawyer's shingle in Brandon. Later he liked to boast that he made $428 that first year and lived on it. But his father's political connections, and before long his own contacts, brought him business and, undoubtedly, inside information that aided his considerable speculation in prairie lands.

He learned the political ropes working on his father's election campaigns in 1883 and 1886. In 1887 he himself ran successfully for office. Three years later he was Attorney General of Manitoba. He quickly established a reputation as a skilled political organizer and a hard and tenacious campaigner who loved politics for the joy of the battle. They called him the Young Napoleon of the West.

The title fitted, for Sifton ran his campaigns like a field marshal. His generals were the key civil servants in the Immigration and Indian departments. Below them were the field officers: the local Members, the constituency workers, the friendly journalists, all kept in line by the glue of patronage. And like any great military strategist, Sifton had his own intelligence and espionage departments. He planted spies in the opposition camp to report back on the enemy's tactics, especially if those tactics were seen to be illegal or improper. Later he could use them to unseat a successful opponent or, perhaps, defend himself from similar charges, thus preventing the Conservatives from taking a successful Liberal to court for bribery or ballot-box stuffing. In addition, he sent watchdogs to Conservative meetings to take down statements that could later be nailed as lies or produce subsequent libel actions.

These tactics paid off. After the 1896 campaign, for example, Sifton was able to gather enough evidence to unseat two Conservative winners including John A.'s son, the powerful Hugh John Macdonald. It turned out that the Tories were giving their people courses in the fine art of ballot-box stuffing, even to the extent of introducing their rural supporters to a professional gambler and card sharp from Winnipeg, a master at the kind of sleight-of-hand required for such sure-thing

22

games as three-card monte. In the by-elections that followed, the Sifton forces were victorious.

In the political donnybrooks of prairie elections, Sifton's early training as a Methodist lay preacher served him well. His platform style was an extension of his personality—crisp, logical, forceful. He did not engage in rhetoric or bombast; instead, he mastered his subject and attacked his audience with clear, direct prose, "delivering his arguments in such continuous and aggressive sequence that they seemed to batter down all opposition."

But he wasn't content to batter the Opposition only at election time. The battering continued in Parliament, when a more conciliatory attitude might have been more effective. In the course of a debate, when he himself was not speaking, Sifton was in the habit of passing belligerent notes across the floor of the House: "How do you like that?" or "Take your medicine!"

He made enemies, not only among the Tories but also among members of his own party. By 1899, when he was firmly ensconced in the federal cabinet, there were in Winnipeg twenty members of his own party who he said "hate me . . . like the devil hates holy water." He seemed to rejoice in this acrimony and had his own explanation for it: "I suppose I might size it up by saying that . . . I occasionally wear a silk hat and a dress coat and do not drink whiskey in the bar of a third class hotel. . . ." There was something of the patrician about Sifton. One could not describe him as a hail-fellow-well-met. One cannot imagine a ward heeler daring to put his arm around Sifton's shoulder any more than one could imagine Sifton slapping a fellow Liberal on the back.

Sifton's wealth, his lifestyle, and his personal ostentation were a source of criticism throughout his career. The young lawyer who had started life on a pittance arrived in Ottawa with two suitcases and a trunk crammed with securities, including a batch of first mortgages worth $100,000. He never attempted to conceal his wealth; indeed, he flaunted it. The Calgary *Herald*, which hated him, gleefully described his appearance during a campaign rally in the Lyric Theatre in 1904: "A great diamond flashed on his left hand, a handsome pin of precious stones peeped out from his natty tie and a massive gold watch chain was looped high on his vest from which dangled a big locket and a charm."

The veteran Grit Sir Richard Cartwright, who blamed Sifton for the loss of a cabinet post in the Laurier government, watched the young Napoleon step from his carriage and warned him, "Young man do you note this display of affluence on the part of a minister so new and young? Do you note those spirited horses, that silver mounted harness and the magnificent chariot behind? Shall I tell you what Sir John Macdonald would have said to one of his ministers if he'd appeared thus? Sir John would have said: 'My dear fellow, it is bad enough to do it, but for Heaven's sake, don't advertise it!'"

But Sifton *did* advertise it. Opposition members and opposition newspapers harped on his vast wealth and hinted darkly at crooked dealings within his department. It is certainly true that several of his key people, including James Smart, enriched themselves as a result of their positions. It is equally true that his closest political cronies in Brandon profited by their friendship with the Minister and that Sifton handed out timber leases on a platter to his brother-in-law, Theodore Burrows. If he had personal tracks to cover, he covered them carefully, for there is no direct evidence suggesting that he shared in any of the booty. Yet, given the loose morality of the times, it is difficult to believe that he did not profit financially from his position. The Governor General himself was suspicious. In 1902, Lord Minto told Laurier that "Mr. Sifton's reputation was not above reproach" and added, "the opinion of the man on the street was certainly not favourable to Mr. Sifton in respect to his apparent wealth, his yacht on the Lakes, etc. etc."

Sifton didn't give a hoot. The *Winnipeg Daily Tribune*, whose editor, R.L. Richardson, was an anti-Sifton fanatic, loved to point out that the Minister never travelled anywhere "whether on public or private business, without a couple of private secretaries, a retinue of servants, refreshments for the boys, all stowed away in a luxuriantly furnished private car paid for out of the pockets of the people."

Sifton's salary as minister was $7,000 a year plus a sessional indemnity of $1,500; yet, as *Le Journal* of Montreal reported in 1902, he lived on a scale that would require twice that income, "a scale which none of his colleagues can imitate; indeed there are few millionaires who live as well as he." The paper listed some of Sifton's assets: a house assessed at $23,000 and maintained at a cost of $90,000; shares in the Bank of Ottawa valued at $42,000; a steam yacht worth at least $25,000; and a "magnificent villa in the west," value unknown. *Le Journal* clearly underestimated Sifton's wealth. He was then in the process of building one of the finest racing stables in the country. He entertained lavishly at private dinners and society balls. In his top hat and hunting pinks, he was a figure of ducal opulence.

24

He revelled in it, made no apologies, and never replied to his critics, some of whom accused him of outright theft. When he died in 1929, his will was probated at $3 million, a sum equal to almost $20 million in 1984 values. How did he get it? Through shrewd investment, wild speculation, inside knowledge, political manipulation, or a combination of all these? No one will ever really know.

4

In the words of Beecham Trotter, a Brandon pioneer and a chronicler *The* of his times, Sifton was "the greatest combination of cold blooded *spoils* businessman, machine politician and statesman our country has pro- *system* duced." He was more than a mere cabinet minister; he was the political monarch of the West, in charge of the Liberal machine in Manitoba and the North West Territories. From the Ontario border to the Rockies, from the forty-ninth parallel to the Arctic coast, Sifton was boss – totally in control of party propaganda, party patronage, and election tactics. The key members of his department were also his political vassals. One of their tasks was to make sure the European immigrants voted the right way at election time. The Liberal government had brought them to Canada; the Liberal government expected gratitude.

The Doukhobors must be brought alongside, and who better to do the job than another Liberal stalwart, J. Obed Smith, Sifton's new commissioner of immigration in Winnipeg? (The overworked but popular ex-mayor McCreary, his predecessor, had been promoted to Member of Parliament.) "I think the Doukhobours should all take out naturalization papers, get their names on the voters list and vote," Sifton wrote to Smith in 1903. "There is no necessity for anyone except themselves to know what is going to be done. It will be enough for the opposition to find out they are going to vote after they have voted." The vision of Conservative candidates suddenly faced with long queues of unbribable Doukhobors at the polling booths must surely have caused a brief smile to play over that sober countenance.

Sifton left nothing to chance, watched over every detail where matters of political tactics were involved. He virtually dictated the text of political pamphlets designed to convince newcomers to vote Liberal: "In the Galician pamphlet . . . it should set out that a few of the

25

Galician people who were brought in before the change in '96 were neglected and in a miserable condition and that immediately after I took office they were looked after and work found for them. . . . Point out that they were neglected and deprived of the franchise and indicate that the Party which has deliberately broken all political traditions by depriving them of the franchise would be equally ready to deprive them of a right to homestead, in fact their rights of any kind would not be safe. . . ."

In 1903, one Immigration Department employee, J.B. Harkin, was ordered to devote himself almost entirely "to attending to the Galician business." And when the anti-Sifton *Winnipeg Daily Tribune* attacked the government for making the West "a dumping ground for immigrants," Sifton made sure that fact was brought to the attention of all foreign voters.

Even the smallest ethnic groups received his personal attention. There were about forty Icelandic voters in Manitoba in 1900, but Sifton went after all of them, bringing in speakers of Icelandic descent to spread the Liberal gospel and even putting one Icelandic youth in the local post office after learning that the incumbent clerk, unable to tell one Icelander from another, had been blindly handing out Liberal campaign literature to Conservatives.

The oil that lubricated the Sifton machine in the West was patronage. Party stalwarts and political cronies expected to be rewarded with fat contracts and good jobs. If anybody wanted to do business with the government he must be seen to be a party wheelhorse. In his first month in office, Sifton discovered that the North West Mounted Police were buying their harness, saddles, and leather goods from E.F. Hutchings of Winnipeg. Hutchings, he told Laurier, was "the most uncompromising and violent opponent of the Government, and perhaps the most offensive to our Liberal friends of any Conservative in the City of Winnipeg." The contract should go to Sifton's friends and supporters, the Adams brothers of Brandon, one of whom sat as a Liberal in the Manitoba legislature.

The NWMP had been formed under the Conservative administration of John A. Macdonald; thus its leadership was Conservative. Now it found itself dominated by an aggressive politician from the opposing party. Laurier apparently did not realize the extent to which Sifton controlled the police. In 1902, he told Lord Minto that the force was totally in his own hands under its comptroller, Fred White. "I did not think it advisable to contradict him," Minto wrote in a memorandum of the conversation, "but Fred White has assured me on more than one occasion most positively that the manipulation of the N.W.M.P. is absolutely in Sifton's hands – that Sifton takes no advice whatever – and that he himself has almost despaired of being able to carry on control of the Force. In fact Fred White has expressed to me his utter despondence at the consequences of Sifton's unjustifiable interference. . . ."

Sifton had a short list of Brandon and Winnipeg supporters who were to receive departmental patronage. These were the key men who had organized his torchlight procession in Brandon and who ran his campaigns. The largess did not stop at the Department of the Interior. When, for instance, Sifton discovered that an Ottawa firm "not a friend of ours" had done business with the Militia Department, he wrote to the Minister and again urged that all further leather business be directed to his friends, the Adams brothers.

The biggest supporter of the Conservative party was, of course, the Canadian Pacific Railway, John A. Macdonald's creation. The company poured money into Tory election campaigns, persuaded its employees to vote Tory, and on occasion trucked them into town on election day with clear instructions on how to cast their ballots. When Sifton discovered that the company was giving contracts to a Tory supporter to supply beef for the navvies building the CPR line through the Crow's Nest Pass, he struck hard at its president, Thomas Shaughnessy. "No better way could be devised," he wrote, "of making the Liberals in Manitoba hostile to the Railway Company, to the contract and to anybody who has anything to do with it myself included." The threat was naked: if the CPR wanted any further government aid it had better toe the line. And Sifton would tell the company exactly which Liberal would benefit. "If there is any beef to be supplied, I would rather see the contract go to Mr. J.D. McGregor of Brandon than to anybody else. He is a practical stock man and perfectly competent to handle it satisfactorily."

McGregor – "Big Jim" as he was sometimes called – was Sifton's campaign manager. He headed Sifton's list of Brandon cronies, which also included A.C. Fraser, who had replaced Sifton as provincial member for North Brandon (dry goods), J.W. Fleming, an old Brandon Liberal and unswerving Sifton supporter (drugs), and, of course, the Adams brothers (harness and leather goods).

Sifton preferred to dispense patronage himself or else through James Smart, his deputy, but sometimes also on the advice of the local

27

Member of Parliament. When he learned that Bill McCreary had bought uniforms for his immigration officials in Winnipeg without consulting Richard Jamieson, the local Member, he rapped the commissioner's knuckles: "The rule is perfectly explicit that in purchasing any goods or supplies of this kind you must either purchase from the persons to whom you are directed by myself or Mr. Smart, or when you have no such directions and have not the time to write . . . you must consult the member. This is a rule that cannot in any case be overlooked or neglected. . . ."

But Sifton's real patronage problems centred around jobs, not contracts. Once the party gained power it seemed that every minion who had toiled in the Liberal vineyards wanted a job for himself, his brother, or his sons. Sifton had no intention of hiring incompetent party members, no matter how fierce the pressure.

"I understand," he wrote to the Minister of Customs early in 1897, "that the Collector of Customs is pressing for the appointment of a man named Jones. The Collector of Customs at Winnipeg is a drunken reprobate. He is a disgrace to the Government service and his opinion in regard to the matter is of no value whatsoever, in fact I would myself consider it sufficient to indicate that a man was unfit for a position if the Collector recommended him. . . ."

"I cannot take every active Grit in the West on my immigration staff," he wrote in exasperation to Obed Smith in 1901. To another colleague, he tried to explain that "if we are going to accomplish anything in immigration we will have to make use of men who know how to do the work and they are not always the men we would like to give political rewards to."

This attitude got him into trouble in Winnipeg. "I am a good deal put out by the kicking that has taken place about the appointments," he told his friend and former colleague Isaac Campbell, a Liberal lawyer in Winnipeg, in August 1897. "I have done everything I possibly could to meet everybody's wishes, but I only had five loaves and two fishes and what are they among so many?"

Nonetheless, the Winnipeg situation didn't calm down, and within a year the anti-Siftonites, led by R.L. Richardson, M.P., the ambitious, cranky editor of the *Winnipeg Daily Tribune*, gained control of the annual meeting of the party. "They are unfriendly to me because, to put it shortly, they are all for boodling and they do not see any chance for success so long as I am here," Sifton explained to John Willison, editor of the *Globe*, Toronto. That was certainly one of the reasons for the anti-Sifton dissent among Manitoba Liberals. Sifton was a man who liked to run his own show. He did not brook disagreement; he did not always listen to advice; he was never one of the boys. But there was another reason for the disaffection of Richardson, a fellow Liberal (for Lisgar) and one-time Sifton supporter. The Member for Lisgar was also proprietor and editor of a Winnipeg newspaper. When it dawned on him that Clifford Sifton had for some time been the secret proprietor of the rival *Manitoba Free Press*, he felt he had been stabbed in the back. From then on, he became one of Sifton's bitterest enemies.

5

On October 14, 1898, the *Manitoba Free Press* in a lavish editorial *The* showered praises upon the Sifton record: "There is not a man in public Free Press life on the continent who would not be envious of such a record, but *changes* Mr. Sifton, with a modesty that is new in the political life of Canada, *hands* has not even claimed that credit for himself to which he is justly entitled. . . . No man could have worked harder or thought more of his duties and responsibilities than Clifford Sifton."

Since the *Free Press* was widely believed to be under the control of the pro-Tory CPR, this seemed high praise indeed. The paper had not always been so complimentary. It had once called Sifton "the most slippery customer Manitoba politics has yet developed" and "the greatest of all ministerial hypocrites." Why this startling change of heart?

What was not known was that the paper was no longer a CPR organ. It was, in fact, under the direct control of Sifton. He had bought it the previous January from Sir William Van Horne, the CPR's chairman, and Donald Smith (Lord Strathcona), one of the railway's major shareholders.

For all of that year Sifton categorically denied, publicly and privately, that he had any control over the newspaper – quite the contrary. Even his close friend Campbell was kept in the dark. "My own judgement," Sifton wrote to him on November 9, "is that it is an extremely injudicious thing for any man in public life to own a newspaper. I do not own the Free Press or any interest in it directly or indirectly . . . I have . . . no financial interest whatever in the paper, it is in perfectly independent hands."

This was, of course, a bald lie, but Sifton kept it up: to a correspondent on November 14, "At the present time as in the past I have no interest or control over the Free Press"; to a friend on November 16, "I have . . . no interest whatever in the paper . . ."; and in another letter on January 19, as the news began to leak out, "The statement that I was the owner of a controlling interest in the Free Press of Winnipeg was made by interested persons for the purpose of injuring me politically. There is no truth whatever in the statement. I have no control over the editorial utterances of the Winnipeg Free Press. . . ."

The "interested persons" were R.L. Richardson and the dissident Liberals. The week before, Richardson's *Tribune* had challenged its rival to "withdraw the veil of mystery from its ownership." If the CPR didn't control the paper, Richardson wrote, "then the control is in the hands of the minister of the interior."

Sifton bought the paper partly because he needed to neutralize Richardson, the defecting Liberal, partly because he needed a strong government organ in Winnipeg, and partly because he thought it was a good business proposition. The previous August he had stripped the *Tribune* of all patronage under his control and shifted this lucrative government advertising to his own paper. In November he further pulled Richardson's political teeth by ordering that the Member for Lisgar no longer be consulted in matters of local patronage.

In Richardson, Sifton had a tough and uncompromising opponent. R.L., as he was called, was a big, ruggedly handsome man, raised on a pioneer Ontario farm – an ex-boxer and wrestler and an enthusiastic and indefatigable outdoorsman. He had an enviable reputation. As a reporter, one colleague recalled, he was "one of the ablest in Winnipeg's history." He had worked for the *Montreal Star*, the Toronto *Globe*, and as city editor of the Winnipeg *Sun* until its absorption by the *Free Press*. After three weeks on the latter paper he decided to buy the old *Sun* equipment and start a paper of his own, the *Tribune*. An independent Liberal (the worst kind!), a populist, a believer in public ownership and government by referendum, an enemy of the political spoils system, he was everything that Sifton was not. Impetuous, quirky, a lover of the classics, a student of history, a political gadfly ever in hot water, he gave as good as he got in the pages of his personal organ.

In those days there was no such thing in Canada as an objective press. Most of the major dailies were controlled by active politicians or by the railways. Of seventeen city dailies in the West in the early days of the century, twelve were owned, edited, or controlled by sitting members of Parliament or the legislature. If they supported the government they expected to get government advertising, knowing that they would lose it if the government fell. In their news columns and headlines they made no pretense at objectivity. News stories, when they dealt with political issues, read like editorials. Reporters thought nothing of inserting their own opinions (or, more realistically, their employer's opinions) into reports of political meetings. And it was not difficult to buy an editor. Smaller papers could easily be persuaded to change their political thrust under the promise of government patronage. Sifton, it was said, controlled nineteen or twenty papers in Manitoba alone through the judicious dispensation of advertising.

A headline on a news story from the rabidly Conservative Calgary *Herald* reporting one of Clifford Sifton's political speeches in the 1904 campaign gives the flavour of Western journalism during the period:

OIL THE MACHINE THAT HAS GROUND OUT
A COLD MILLION FOR ME – CLIFFORD $IFTON

It was the *Herald*'s regular device to employ a dollar sign whenever Sifton's name appeared above a major news story. This kind of headline, which would cause a scandal today, was accepted by newspaper readers as part of the game.

In today's context, reports of political meetings at the turn of the century are hilarious, and it is difficult to believe that anybody but the faithful took them seriously, if, in fact, they read them at all. The newspaper's candidate – who was so often its publisher – was praised to the heavens. He invariably spoke to a large and deliriously enthusiastic crowd, who, it was reported, greeted his every statement with prolonged cheers. Incisive, clear headed, totally convincing, he demolished his opponent, who was portrayed as a pathetic puppet, dancing to the tune of his party's machine. The day before the election each paper announced unreservedly that the candidate of its choice would sweep the polls and decimate the opposition. If he lost, the paper would explain that he had never had a chance because of rampant bribery on the part of the winner. Name calling was part of the game. In the provincial election of 1910, the *Tribune* was able to point out that of ninety candidates only seven had not been called liars, boodlers, or crooks. Scores of elections were challenged because of election day irregularities (Richardson was one who lost his seat). If bribery was proved – and it often was – the election was declared null and void. As a result, each party would challenge a number of elections on the

31

thinnest of evidence in order to arrange a saw-off with the opposition, who were chary of expensive and long-drawn-out court cases.

The amount of newspaper space devoted to politics was awesome. Speeches were reported verbatim and often ran to several columns. Banner headlines, otherwise reserved for an earthquake or a railway disaster, trumpeted each candidate's qualities and his opponent's short-comings. A newcomer reading the Regina *Leader*, the Winnipeg *Telegram*, or the *Edmonton Bulletin* might easily have concluded that politics was a game that obsessed every man, woman, and child on the prairies.

This was far from the truth. As the British magazine *Nineteenth Century* reported late in the nineties, "the mass of the people do not pay enough attention to politics to care much what individual gets in." Everybody, save for a small coterie of heelers and hacks, was far more concerned with clearing the land, ploughing the new fields, working a homestead, and making a living. The Machine got out the vote, but it was a five-dollar bill, a bottle of whiskey, or the promise of a job that brought an apathetic public to the polls.

But to the politicians and their hangers-on, each campaign was a life-and-death contest. To Sifton, the Conservatives were more than the Opposition; they were "the enemy." At election time he talked of putting on his war paint, and he entered the lists as a battler who genuinely enjoyed a scrap. He asked for no quarter and gave none. He was subjected to the most vicious calumny, especially by Richardson, but he never complained and never sued. The *Tribune* called him "unsavory," – "a grafter," "a crook," "a coward," and "a thief." Richardson charged that the *Free Press* was controlled by "financial grafters" and that the Department of the Interior was "a paradise for partisan hangers on . . . a bribery agency." "MR. SIFTON'S CROOKED CAREER LAID BARE," one of its headlines declared in 1902. During the federal election campaign of 1904, Richardson wrote that "no man in Canada now in public life has done more to smash ideals of public righteousness and promote public wrong doing and political corruption, to bedevil the public interests, to enslave the people and to debauch the politics of the country. . . ."

The *Free Press* was under Sifton's orders not to attack Richardson personally except in its reports of political meetings. Instead, its job was to boost the Liberal party in general and the Minister of the Interior in particular.

32

MR. SIFTON DISPOSES
OF AIRY OPPONENT
Richardson Gets Severely Worsted at the Joint Meeting at Brandon – His Braggadocio and Abuse Fails – The Minister's Clean-Cut, Facty Reply Scored Hard – Political Record of Opposition Candidate Exposed

This *Free Press* report of November 1, 1904, which described Richardson's remarks as "tawdry and commonplace in comparison with the weighty, earnest utterances of the minister" was no more shameless than the report of the same meeting the same day in the *Tribune*:

GREAT TRIUMPH FOR
PUBLIC OWNERSHIP
Mr. Richardson, Candidate of the Great Cause, Carried the Mammoth Mass Meeting at Brandon – Mr. Sifton, Apologist for Private Corporations, Clearly Worsted in the Joint Debate

The accompanying story described Richardson's speech as "a nail in the coffin of the Young Napoleon," claimed that Brandon "failed to give the minister one spontaneous cheer," and reported that "it was apparent at once that the sympathies of the great majority of the audience" were with Richardson.

With commendable optimism Richardson was forever announcing the complete disarray of the dark Siftonian forces aligned against him, only to be forced into an apologetic editorial the day after each election – as in the 1904 federal election, in which Richardson decided to take on Sifton in Brandon.

Tribune news story, *November 2, 1904:* "The forces of the Sifton party are shattered.... The total rout of Sifton and his boodle gang is only a matter of hours.... Sifton is a gonner [*sic*].... That Richardson will be elected by the will of the people tomorrow is an indisputable fact.... Opinion in the Conservative and Independent ranks is...that Richardson will have a clear majority of 500...."

But Sifton beat Richardson handily, and in an editorial on November 4, Richardson blandly pretended he had expected a Sifton win all along: "In view of all that Mr. Sifton had at stake in the election, The Tribune hardly expected that Mr. Richardson would defeat him. We hoped, however, a much closer run would have been made...."

Richardson continued gamely to run for office and continued to be defeated. Thirteen years passed before he regained a seat in Parliament.

6

Sifton, the cynical pragmatist, realized that slanted news stories were far more effective than opinionated editorials. In 1901 he told his business manager, E.H. Macklin, that the government wasn't hurt by opposition editorials nor much helped by friendly ones. "What actually injures the Government is some carefully concocted piece of alleged news. . . . The simple-minded farmer swallows it and a great many people who are not farmers and ought to know better. I am quite convinced however that the damage is done by the news columns and not by the editorial columns. . . ."

But he needed a strong voice, and the following year he hired a new editor in the person of John Wesley Dafoe, the big, dishevelled genius who would rise to become the most respected journalist in Canada. Like so many other Manitobans of that time, Dafoe had his roots in pioneer Ontario. There was always something of the backwoods boy about him. He was tall and thickset, with a shock of red hair, a shaggy moustache, and a long, flabby face with a nose to match. In his photographs he always seems to be peering downwards through his pince-nez at some obscure and mysterious document. As a youth he was something of a prodigy and something of a rebel. Although he had no more than a high school education, he was a schoolteacher at the age of fifteen. His parents were Conservative farmers and doctrinaire Methodists. But a single speech by the great Liberal orator Edward Blake turned Dafoe into a Grit; and as for fundamentalism, he shucked that off in his early years – it was, to him, "a damnable doctrine."

As a token Anglican, a passionate Liberal, and a sometimes cynical journalist, Dafoe seemed to be at war with his upbringing, yet his philosophy was deeply influenced by his agrarian background. In the one instance in which he broke with his employer he took the Western farmers' side against the Eastern industrialists.

He was never comfortable in what he called a "plug hat." Even in his later years when he had achieved an awesome prestige he looked like a farmer – a "rube," to use the expression of the day. That stood him in good stead when with no experience he got his first job on the *Montreal Star*. The teenaged tyro looked enough like a hick to be disguised as one in the newspaper's exposé of a clothing store that was cheating country bumpkins by substituting cheap suits for expensive ones. In one year he rose to be the paper's Ottawa correspondent. At the age of nineteen the new Ottawa *Journal* hired him as editor, surely the youngest in history. It was too much for him. Three weeks later he bounced west to the *Free Press*, and there he learned his craft. In 1892, the Montreal *Herald* offered him its editorship and he grabbed it, flinging himself into the task, working fourteen hours a day, tripling the circulation in his first year, then moving to the companion *Weekly Star*, which he edited for six years, doubling *its* circulation from fifty thousand to one hundred thousand.

It did not seem to bother Dafoe, the Liberal convert, that he was working for a Tory organ. But Sifton knew he was a Liberal. "I do not think we can afford to let you work for the Tories any longer," he told Dafoe, who seized the offer, moved back to Winnipeg, and proceeded to put Sifton's stamp, and his own, on the one-time CPR organ. Richardson attacked his editorial style almost immediately as "a sort of cheap imitation, Macaulayese, stilted, tawdry and ranting." But it was Dafoe's style, not Richardson's, that would influence a future generation of editorial writers. To Dafoe, Richardson was "a blather-skite."

For decades, the name of Dafoe has had a godlike ring to young journalists. The myth, still believed in some quarters, was that the young editor was granted, almost from the outset, the ideal arrangement that every journalist seeks from the publisher but few attain — absolute independence and freedom to express opinion.* The myth stems entirely from Dafoe's celebrated break with his employer over the issue of reciprocity during the 1911 election. But for the first decade of his career, and indeed with that one exception for some time after, Dafoe was Sifton's willing and compliant servant. He wrote what he was told.

In those early years, he was as much a party hack as an editor. He addressed political meetings, attended Liberal conventions, advised on patronage, wrote party pamphlets, and published propaganda for the Liberal government in general and Sifton's department in particular. His job was to drive the Conservatives in Manitoba out of office, a task that took fifteen years. In 1903, for instance, Dafoe thought nothing of devoting more than half the paper to attacks on Rodmond Roblin, the Premier. Dafoe was as much a Liberal back-room boy as

---

*Arthur Irwin, the former editor of *Maclean's*, told me in 1983 that he had always believed the story that Dafoe had a contract with Sifton guaranteeing editorial independence. No such contract existed.

some of Sifton's Immigration Department employees – and with more power. The *Free Press* operated as a kind of clearing house for party patronage. And when Sifton gave an order, Dafoe jumped.

When, for example, R.S. Mullins, a prominent Manitoba Conservative, bolted the Tory ranks, Sifton seized the opportunity to exploit the defection in the *Free Press*. He did not leave the task to his editors; instead, he had a former Brandon crony prepare an interview, which he sent to Dafoe with specific instructions. The story was to be vetted, not by the newspaper, but by another old Sifton hand, J.D. Cameron, and then turned over to the paper. Dafoe was ordered to give it a great deal of prominence and to accompany the news story with an editorial. There was never any question but that Dafoe would go along with what many journalists would today consider front office meddling.

The same year – 1904 – Dafoe was ordered to write or have written a "first class" introduction to a special election edition that was to appear as a *Free Press* supplement. The introduction was to occupy half of the front page. The supplement itself was not written in the *Free Press* offices but in those of the Toronto *Globe*. Some seventy thousand were to be sent out. "My organizer tells me that the people, strange to say, read these sheets better than they do carefully prepared and well printed pamphlets," Sifton told Dafoe, "so we will give them both."

Sifton, who was not one to overestimate the intelligence of the electorate, saw his paper as a political tool. Dafoe, the loyal Grit, did not demur in this assessment. During election campaigns, Sifton's people would prepare lists of doubtful voters who were to receive the *Free Press* free until voting day. The paper was also used as a cover for partisan political activity. In 1901, for instance, Sifton suggested that one of his organizers travel about the province, ostensibly as a *Free Press* reporter but actually to devote his time to visiting Orange lodges and proselytizing Protestant voters.

If Dafoe didn't know Sifton's views on a subject, he asked for them before committing an editorial to print. What, for instance, should be the *Free Press* policy on the Crow's Nest Pass rail extension? What line should the paper take on the coming visit to Winnipeg of Israel Tarte, Minister of Public Works, who had little love for Sifton? When Dafoe prepared an editorial critical of the Governor General he sent a copy to his employer before printing it. Sifton "suggested" more than he ordered, but to Dafoe these suggestions were law. "I was glad to get your letter giving me your views on some of the subjects now attracting public attention," he wrote to Sifton in December 1902, adding, "I had already taken much the same ground on most of the points; and have since worked them over again. . . ."

Dafoe, of course, was more than a passive political servant dancing to Sifton's tune. He had always been an activist, even under a Conservative publisher. When, at the outset of his editorship, a public outcry washed over the West because of the absence of enough freight cars to handle grain shipments, he saw in it a prime opportunity to erase the pro-CPR bias that had stained Sifton's new organ. His articles on the subject, he told his employer, "were written very carefully to . . . serve notice on the railway officials that the Free Press was quite prepared to criticize them [and] to satisfy the farmers that the Free Press is quite free from railway control."

At times Dafoe seems to have spent as much or more time working as a politician than as a journalist. When he discovered a new German language paper was about to be launched at Rosthern in the District of Saskatchewan, he managed to bring its editor at least part way into the Liberal camp and "to say a good word for the Liberal government in its record of settling the west." To sweeten the deal, Dafoe urged Sifton to throw the paper some government business.

On another occasion, he prepared a blatantly pro-Liberal pamphlet to be distributed among Galician settlers containing photographs of all the Liberal candidates who had Galicians in their constituencies. "Under every cut," he told Sifton, proudly, "we will put the name and then some legend as this – 'This is the Government Candidate for such and such a constituency, all Galetians [sic] should vote for him.' We are also arranging to include a small map of western Canada showing the projected G.T.P. [Grand Trunk Pacific] line and branches in bold relief. Under it we will put some such words as these, – 'This is a railway the Liberal government intends to build. If you want this railway vote for the Liberal Candidates.'"

It is true that Sifton – after considerable argument (the two men wrangled for a week) – allowed Dafoe to go his own way during the 1911 election campaign. It was an odd reversal of roles. Sifton, the leading Westerner, was now an Eastern capitalist. Dafoe, whose family roots in Ontario went back for several generations, had become a fervent Westerner. Sifton moved in the same social and financial circles as the industrial power brokers of Ontario and Quebec who wanted to maintain the protective tariff on Eastern manufactured goods. Dafoe saw himself as the spokesman for the Western farmer, who was tired of paying a premium on agricultural implements and other goods, which would be cheaper if the tariff were reduced or dropped.

But Sifton was ever the businessman. For his newspaper suddenly to change its advocacy of reciprocity would be embarrassing and damaging; the *Free Press* would lose not only its hard-won prestige in the West but also circulation. So Dafoe was allowed to continue his support of the official Liberal platform. As a result, the paper gained credibility among the Western farmers, Dafoe went down in history as a fighting editor who was no man's servant, and Sifton's own image was immeasurably polished as a man of principle, broadminded enough to give a great journalist his head.

The fact that one editor had actually been permitted to take a different line from his political master was so startling in those days that it became a *cause célèbre*. Nothing like it had ever happened before, certainly in Western Canada. And, in Dafoe's case, nothing like it happened again. A year after this indulgence Sifton was again giving orders to Dafoe, and Dafoe was following them. Here is Sifton, gently rapping his editor's knuckles on the matter of the Grand Trunk Pacific, at that time the Liberal party's pet railway but certainly not Sifton's: "Now I want to be perfectly plain with you. So far as I can remember you have sheared off of making any attacks on or serious criticism of the Grand Trunk Pacific. You have always been ready enough to strike the CPR or the CNR [Canadian Northern Railway] but apparently for political reasons you are very loathe to say anything about the GTP. That policy will have to be dropped." And Dafoe dropped it.

None of this is in the least surprising. Editors were hired because their publishers knew in advance what political opinions they held. Dafoe's views rarely differed from those of Sifton. Some journalists who professed to know said that Dafoe did not care for his employer, but there is no documentary evidence of that. His biography of Sifton, in fact, borders on the sycophantic; in it Dafoe was not above glossing over certain disagreeable facts and inflating favourable ones to put his publisher in the best possible light. But that, too, was the way of politics and journalism in the early years of the century.

Dafoe was not the first editor, nor the last, to jump with both feet into party politics. The difference was that his subsequent stature as a leading Canadian editor and an international figure made his close political ties seem acceptable to others who followed. The link between

1

In the mountain trenches of Galicia, the land was too precious to be wasted. The furrows of the strip farms ran to the very edges of the houses. Cows and sheep dotted the pasture land on the lower flanks of the mountains. Oats, rye, and potatoes sprouted up from the valley floor. Above the huddle of thatched roofs the great peaks rose, clothed in oak, beech, and fir, each ridge effectively sealing off one village from the next, maintaining a peasant culture that was frozen in time.

Since there were no fences – only corner stakes to identify personal holdings – each fertile Carpathian valley resembled one gigantic farm under a single management. Appearances were deceptive. Each peasant required fourteen acres to provide for himself and his family, yet 70 per cent of the farms were no more than half that size. Some families, in fact, tried to subsist on a single acre.

Wages were as low as five cents a day, but the price of land for those who could afford it was high. The mean was eighty dollars an acre, but some land fetched as much as four hundred dollars. Taxes were among the highest in Europe. Under these depressing conditions thievery was common and alcoholism endemic. The wealthy *pahns* (lords) owned not only the forests, meadows, and villages; they also owned the taverns, of which there were more than twenty-three thousand in Galicia. It was in the interests of the ruling class to keep the peasants drunk and underpaid. The consumption of liquor was stupendous: twenty-six litres a year for every man, woman, and child. One of the commonest words in the language was *beeda*, meaning misery. To the question "How is everything?" the usual reply was "Beeda."

No wonder, then, that Josef Oleskow's pamphlets were so successful. Across the ocean lay a promised land where 160 acres of fertile soil could be had for the asking. Thus was initiated the great emigration of Poles and Ukrainians from Austria-Hungary. Until the Great War, Canadians lumped them together as Galicians because so many – 150,000 – came from that region. To save confusion, that is what we will call them in this book. It was these people that Clifford Sifton was describing when, more than twenty years later, he talked of "a stalwart peasant in a sheep-skin coat."

It is a spring morning in 1897, and in the Galician village of

the Liberal party and a new generation of respected journalists surely begins with the Dafoe example. Such partisan newspapermen as Grant Dexter, Blair Fraser, and Bruce Hutchison were to carry it forward into the mid-century. Fraser, for one, was so close to being an apologist for the Liberal party during his years as Ottawa editor for *Maclean's* that, when the government changed, he found his sources had dried up.* And Bruce Hutchison, while editor of the *Vancouver Sun* and Winnipeg *Free Press*, actually wrote speeches for Lester B. Pearson. Thus, like so much else that happened in the West during those yeasty years, the pact that was sealed in 1901 between the ambitious young newspaperman and his hard-headed publisher created a ripple that was not without effect half a century later.

---

*To *Maclean's* editors, Fraser played down the rising importance of John Diefenbaker, referring to him as "a lightweight, not destined for power." It was almost certainly his influence that prompted the then editor, Ralph Allen, to commit to type in 1957 an editorial on another Liberal win before the actual election took place. To Allen's embarrassment, the Liberals lost.

Chapter Two

The Sheepskin People

Ghermakivka the Humeniuk family is packing to leave for Canada on money borrowed from relatives and friends. Everything they own takes up no more than twenty cubic feet and will be carefully stored away in a green wooden trunk built by Nykola Humeniuk himself. His wife, Anastasia, puts the winter clothes, blankets, and bed sheets at the bottom; next come the holy pictures, packed between pillows; and on top of that the family's dress clothes for Sunday church (for surely there will be a little church with an onion-shaped spire in whichever community they reach). Then, another covering, and twenty-five little cloth bundles of garden seeds – onions, garlic, horseradish, dried ears of corn – and above that some religious articles: candles, chalk, a bottle of holy water. Four precious books will also be taken: a prayer book, a history of the Ukraine, a school primer, and a collection of Bible stories. And finally, Nykola's carpentry and farm tools: hammers and planes, axe and draw-knife, saws, bits, chisels, sickles, scythes, hoes, rake, and flail.

Great excitement! The task is done. Anastasia ties up some food for the trip in a cloth bundle as the neighbours and relatives pour into the house to say goodbye. What a commotion, with everybody talking at once! There are smiles at first; then, suddenly, some of the women begin to cry. They hug and kiss Anastasia, apologizing for things left undone, past offences real and imagined. The children start to cry, too, and then some of the men are seen to wipe tears from their eyes.

Somebody shouts for silence and then, as all bow their heads, he begins to recite a prayer, asking God to bless the Humeniuks and their two small children, Petryk and baby Theodore, and give them a safe voyage, prosperity, and good health in the strange land across the ocean. Write soon, everybody cries, write as soon as you arrive!

The wagon and team are waiting for the journey to the station. Four men hoist the big trunk onto the back as the family climbs aboard. But Anastasia Humeniuk stops and turns back, her baby in her arms. She walks to the doorway, makes the sign of the cross, kisses the frame, and then, in one last gesture, picks up a small lump of Galician earth, wraps it in a rag, and puts it in her hand valise, a memory of a land she will never see again.

Professor Oleskow's plan had been to bring to Canada only the best farmers, the most productive and educated elements of the population – those who owned enough land to finance the long journey overseas and the first hard years on a Canadian homestead. But

Oleskow's plan was never acted upon. The steamship agents, to whom each peasant paid a fee, and their myriad subcontractors wanted to sign up as many as possible. It was the ignorant and the innocent who came to Canada, their naïveté exploited shamelessly by those who stood to make a profit from emigration.

We have on record a graphic example of the kind of exploitation suffered by the peasants as a result of the machinations of an agency in the Galician town of Oswiecim, now part of Poland. Its operators, Jacob Klausner and Simon Herz, were masters of the art of bribery and corruption. They fixed all the local officials, including both the police and the railway conductors, in order to achieve maximum emigration. They overcharged shamelessly for ocean passage, cheated on the exchange rate, and sold worthless advertising cards in lieu of tickets. If a man was of military age, subject to conscription and thus legally unable to emigrate, they charged double to smuggle him out of the country, even though the advertised risks had been eliminated by bribery. And whenever anybody was incautious enough to object, he was locked in a barn and beaten.

One Polish agent, Abraham Landerer, invented a fake telephone on which he received spurious "information." It was only an alarm clock, but when it rang, Landerer claimed it was an inquiry about passage. Later, when the clock rang again, he would charge the peasant a special fee for its use. Sometimes he would use the alarm clock to ask "the American Emperor" whether he would allow the prospective emigrant to enter his country. That, of course, involved another fee.

One swindler dressed as a doctor invariably "failed" prospective emigrants for reasons of health but was happy to accept a bribe and pass them at a subagent's suggestion. Another had a store full of clothing that he sold to peasants at inflated prices, claiming that they would not be allowed to wear their native dress on the other side of the water. At ports of departure, especially in Germany, scores were told they would have to wait for a boat and were deliberately held in boarding houses, hotels, and taverns where they were cheated for lodgings and food.

In order to increase their commissions, the steamship agents peddled fantastic stories that were generally believed by their unworldly victims. One group from Bukovina arrived at Winnipeg's immigration hall in May 1897 protesting bitterly that misrepresentations had been used to induce them to come over. They had been told that the "Crown

Princess of Austria" was in Montreal and would see that they were given free land with houses, cattle, and farm equipment. All they had to do was telegraph her if these promises went unfulfilled. Many of the newcomers, therefore, refused all offers of employment in Winnipeg and sat tight in the crowded hall. With five hundred more newcomers arriving, the police attempted to move them out, and a small riot ensued. Many of the newcomers flung themselves on the floor until they were dragged or carried off, the women "yelling, crying and shrieking" in the words of the long-suffering immigration commissioner, William McCreary, ex-mayor of Winnipeg, who narrowly escaped being felled by a boot flung at his head.

McCreary, who had been working from six in the morning until nine at night, had managed to negotiate a special low rate on the railway to Yorkton, Assiniboia. In addition, he had arranged for fifty days' work on the same line for those who were destitute. That did not suit the new arrivals, who were still intoxicated by the steamship agents' promises and so refused to board the train. Some upset the baggage carts. Some, with their goods on their backs, started marching north. Others squatted on the street or seized vacant houses near the track. In the end they capitulated. McCreary supplied them with some sacks of flour and a few bushels of potatoes and finally settled them on homesteads in the vicinity of Saltcoats, Assiniboia, where, eventually, they forgot about the non-existent Austrian princess. It was exactly this kind of fraud and exploitation that Professor Oleskow had sought to avoid.

If some immigrants were disillusioned and rebellious when they reached Canada, it was understandable. Apart from the false promises, there was the long journey across Europe from their home villages, then the stormy ocean voyage in the holds of immigrant ships, and finally the trek first by rail and then by ox cart to their prairie homesteads.

The first stop in Europe, usually after a twenty-four-hour train journey, came at a control station between Galicia and Germany, where men, women, and children submitted to a medical examination before being allowed to proceed. These stations – there were thirteen – had been established as a result of the cholera epidemic in Hamburg in 1892. They were maintained by the steamship companies as the result of a compromise with the German authorities, who had blamed the epidemic on emigrants from Russia and originally wanted to seal off the border. Now, everybody entering Germany from Austria-Hungary or Russia en route to North America was subjected to a medical inspection.

We have arrived at the control station at Myslowitz at the junction of the German, Austrian, and Russian borders. A uniformed official leads us from the Krakow train through a long hall to a desk behind which stand three more officials: a steamship agent and, in uniform, a Russian policeman and a German officer. We give up our rail and steamship tickets to the agent; then, clutching our baggage, we are led into two large halls, where the Galicians and Russians are separated.

Our hall has a tiled floor, painted walls, a high ceiling, and windows of coloured glass. It is ringed by wooden benches, under which we stuff our baggage. As many of us as can find space sleep on the benches; the rest stretch out on our baggage or on the floor — men, women, and children all crammed together. The walls are alive with vermin.

We are prisoners. No one is allowed to leave the building until the next train arrives. The only available food is sold at a canteen, but the canteenkeeper is drunk (as are the watchmen and porters), and, in spite of a long price list on the wall, the stock consists mainly of beer, wine, and liquor, tobacco, bread, and sausage. Neither tea nor coffee is available.

More officers arrive with more immigrants. We demand breakfast but are told only the canteen can supply our wants. At nine, the wife of the canteenkeeper turns up and makes some coffee. At noon, for twenty-five cents we get a dinner of soup, boiled beef, potato salad, and bread. (To Galician peasants this is an exorbitant price; many cannot afford it.) Even as we eat, the price goes up. Indeed, prices continue to fluctuate without reason in three currencies. Getting correct change is entirely a matter of luck.

A Russian lays a half-mark on the counter, orders a glass of beer, and waits for his change. He gets none. An argument follows. The waiter insists he has been given a different coin and pretends he cannot understand the language. More arguments follow. For three hours customers and canteenkeeper keep up a constant verbal battle over coinage.

At two in the afternoon a doctor arrives. We have been waiting almost twenty-four hours to be inspected, others much longer. We are driven into another room, pass in single file before the doctor, and wait for our clothing and baggage to be disinfected. Then our tickets are returned and we are packed aboard the train. (By this time most of the passengers are drunk. Liquor is the one thing that is available for the journey.)

We are faced with a twenty-hour journey across Germany. The third-class coach is so crowded that many have to stand for all of that time. At Hamburg another medical examination takes place. But now, all of us who have paid steerage fees are told there is no more room on the ship; we must wait another ten days or pay an additional thirty marks for a third-class ticket. Some can afford neither the additional fare nor the expense of waiting: cheated by agents who lied to them that their rail fare had been prepaid, they have already been forced to part with their meagre funds; they cannot even afford the expense of a telegram home. Now a flurry of counting, consulting, borrowing, and lending takes place. At last we all decide to pay the extra fare and go on across the angry ocean, gambling that we will not be rejected on the other side for lack of funds.

For most emigrants, the ocean voyage was a nightmare. Jammed into tiered bunks in the stifling holds of ancient vessels, vomiting from seasickness, half starved, terror stricken by hurricane-force gales, men, women, and children were flung together under conditions that made a mockery of privacy. One woman agent of the American immigration service made such a journey disguised as a European emigrant with a counterfeit passport and described her voyage out of Hamburg:

"During these twelve days in the steerage, I lived in a disorder and in surroundings that offended every sense. Only the fresh breeze from the sea overcame the sickening odors. The vile language of the men, the screams of the women defending themselves, the crying of children, wretched because of their surroundings ... irritated beyond endurance. There was no sight before which the eye did not prefer to close. Everything was dirty, sticky and disagreeable to the touch. Every impression was offensive. Worse than this was the general air of immorality. For fifteen hours each day, I witnessed all around me this improper, indecent and forced mingling of men and women who were total strangers and often did not understand one word of the same language. People cannot live in such surroundings and not be influenced. . . ."

These were the words of an American civil servant. Undoubtedly, the Slavic peasants, long used to cramped quarters, were less fastidious. To them, the real horror of the ocean crossing was not the lack of privacy but the storms that raged across the North Atlantic. One of these emigrants, Theodore Nemerski, has left a graphic account of his own experiences aboard the ancient vessel *Christiana* in the spring of 1896. Nemerski was one of the first Galicians to be influenced by Professor Oleskow's pamphlet *O Emigratsii*. He got a copy fresh from the press and with eight other members of his family boarded the ship at Hamburg in April. At first, the journey was bearable, but four days out of port, the storm broke:

"Good Lord! What fear grips one here. You look, and here from the side there appears a great opening. The water has drawn back and the whole ship simply flies into that void, turning almost completely over on its side. And here all of a sudden a huge mountain with a great roar and clatter of the waves tears into the ship, spilling over the top onto the other side. This is no place to be! . . . escape inside.

"Inside you find complete panic . . . all are silent . . . whispering prayers . . . awaiting the end. . . .

"Some tied their eyes so as not to see this terror, while they hung onto the bed so they would not fall out. Suddenly water is coming in to the inside from the top, splashing from wall to wall. The people are in lament. Some cry, some complain: Did we need this? It was good for us to live in the old country. This is all on account of you . . . I listened to you and now we shall all perish. . . ."

On the *Arcadia*, another ancient sailing craft with an auxiliary engine, the crew herded the passengers below and locked the hatches when the storm struck. Fifteen hundred Galicians clung to the four tiers of iron beds, praying and vomiting, the stench so ghastly that those stewards who ventured in were themselves taken sick. An old man and a child died before the storm abated, but that was not the end. The ship struck an iceberg, and when the hole in her side was repaired, the captain discovered he was beset – locked in the grip of the frozen ocean. All of the passengers were herded back up on deck and required to race from side to side – back and forth, back and forth – on signals from the ship's whistle until the *Arcadia* was finally shaken free from her icy embrace. By this time, most of the baggage was soaked and ruined. One month after they had left their home villages, the hapless passengers finally landed at Quebec City.

For those who were able to eat, the steerage food was generally execrable: filthy water, rotten herrings, dirty potatoes, rancid lard, smelly meat, eaten from unwashed dishes and cutlery. The staple meat was pork – not the best remedy for a queasy stomach. Thirty years after his ordeal, one immigrant wrote: "To this moment I cannot face the warm smell of pork without sweat starting on my forehead."

48

Another, who travelled steerage on the *Bavaria* in 1904, claimed that he was served pig's feet three times a day and "had visions of millions of pigs being sacrificed so that their feet could be given to the many emigrants leaving Europe."

The more fortunate travelled third class, which was a notch better than steerage, although it did no more than provide decently for the simplest human needs. As one woman put it, "to travel in anything worse than what is offered in the third class is to arrive at the journey's end with a mind unfit for healthy, wholesome impressions and with a body weakened and unfit for the hardships that are involved in the beginning of life in a new land. . . ." Yet tens of thousands of sturdy men, women, and children, who quit their tiny Carpathian farms to make a new life in a world of strangers, endured it all and somehow managed to survive and prosper.

2

The Galicians who arrived at Halifax or Quebec City after a month of hard travel presented a sorry and bedraggled appearance. Few had any conception of distance. Until this voyage, scarcely any had ventured farther than twenty-five or thirty miles from their home villages. Thus they had not realized the need for changes of clothing; everything was packed away in trunks, boxes, and valises to be opened only when they reached their prairie homes. These were a people obsessed with cleanliness, used to scrubbing themselves regularly, but now, suffering from a lack of washing facilities on train and steamship, they looked and felt unclean.

"Dirty, ignorant Slavs"

Maria Olinyk, a nine-year-old girl from the western Ukraine, remembered how the crowd on the dock at Halifax stared at her and her shipmates, some out of curiosity, some out of contempt. Here were women in peasant costumes, and men in coats of strong-smelling sheepskin wearing fur hats, linen blouses, and trousers tucked into enormous boots, their long hair greased with lard. The Canadians, Maria noticed, stopped their noses. These first impressions helped to encourage the wave of anti-Galician feeling that was fed by the anti-Sifton newspapers.

Thus Sir Mackenzie Bowell, a former Conservative prime minister and leader of his party in the Senate, was able to write in his newspaper, the Belleville *Intelligencer*, that "the Galicians, they of the sheepskin coats, the filth and the vermin do not make splendid material for the building of a great nation. One look at the disgusting creatures after they pass through over the C.P.R. on their way West has caused many to marvel that beings bearing the human form could have sunk to such a bestial level. . . ."

To many newcomers, the new land, at first glimpse, seemed equally appalling. Dmytro Romanchych, who came out from the mountains of Bukovina as a result of reading Professor Oleskow's pamphlet, never forgot his first sight of Quebec City—streaks of dirty grey snow lying in the ravines. The sad, uninviting landscape made him feel that Canada was sparsely settled and inhospitable. Dmytro felt depressed, for he had left a land whose meadows and glens, three weeks before, had been green with the promise of early spring. Ottawa with its granite Parliament buildings was more impressive, but across the river the land seemed wild, with the bare rock banks and sickly trees making an unpleasant impression.

But these vistas were cheerful compared to the despair that seized the newcomers when the colonist trains rattled and swayed across the Precambrian desert of the Canadian Shield. Theodore Nemerski, barely recovered from the storm that tore at the *Christiana*, was shaken by the possibility that this gnarled expanse of granite ridges and stunted pines might in fact be the actual promised land that Oleskow had described. His companions "turned grey with fear." What if there were no better soil than this in Canada? they asked. "Here the heart froze in not a few men . . . the hair on the head stands on end . . . because not a few think, what if they get into something like this?"

This was not an isolated instance. When the Humeniuk family came out the following year, 1897, the women in their car began to sob and cry out that "it would have been better to suffer in the old country than to come to this Siberia." Two years later Maria Olinyk felt the same shock of apprehension. "The heart of many a man sank to his heels," she remembered, "and the women and children raised such lamentations as defies description."

There were other problems. In Montreal, the Galicians were met by hordes of small-time entrepreneurs trying to separate them from their funds, charging exorbitant prices for food, hawking useless goods, and urging them not to venture farther west. The situation became so serious in the spring of 1897 that immigration authorities were forced to call in the police and confine the new arrivals to sheds until they could be put into railway cars with their final destination clearly marked and the tickets in their hands.

The exploitation resumed in Winnipeg, the jumping-off spot for the prairies. Here, a group of Winnipeg real estate agents collared six Galicians, discovered they had twelve thousand dollars among them, and talked them out of leaving Winnipeg, saying it was too cold in Alberta and that the very horns on the cattle froze in the winter. The real estate men were a little too persuasive. Four of their victims immediately bought tickets and returned to Europe.

There were other disappointments. Maria Olinyk and her family were among those who took one of the special trains to the Yorkton area where hundreds of their fellow countrymen were homesteading. A friend who had come out the year before had written to them, boasting of his prosperity, describing his home as a mansion, telling of his immense cultivated fields and how his wife now dressed like a lady. He depicted Canada "as a country of incredible abundance whose borders were braided with sausage like some fantastic land in a fairy tale."

The family hired a rig and after a thirty-mile journey north through clouds of mosquitoes finally reached their destination. What they found was a small log cabin, partially plastered and roofed with sod, a tiny garden plot dug with a spade, a woman dressed in ancient torn overalls "suntanned like a gypsy," and her husband, his face smeared with dirt from ear to ear, "weird, like some unearthly creature," grubbing up stumps. Maria's mother broke into tears at the sight, but, like so many others, the Olinyk family hung on and, after years of pain and hardship, eventually prospered. Maria became Dr. Maria Adamowska, a noted Ukrainian-Canadian poet, who, when she died in 1961 at Melville, Saskatchewan, left behind a literary legacy that included her vivid memories of those lean, far-off years.

The Galicians did not care to settle on the bald southern prairie. They preferred the wooded valleys of the Saskatchewan. This baffled the immigration authorities. "These Galicians are a peculiar people," McCreary wrote to James Smart in the spring of 1897. "They will not accept as a gift 160 acres of what we consider the best land in Manitoba, that is first class wheat growing prairie land; what they particularly want is wood; and they care but little whether the land is heavy soil or light gravel; but each man must have some wood on his place. . . ."

There was reason for this. Wood was precious in the Carpathians –

so scarce that it was bought by the pound. In some areas the harvesting of wood was a monopoly: it was a crime to cut down a tree. Thus in Canada the Galicians were allowed, perhaps even encouraged, to settle on marginal lands while other immigrants, notably the Americans, seized the more fertile prairie to the south.

It is June of 1897, and the Humeniuk family has arrived in Winnipeg. In the colonist car, they and the others sit quietly in their seats as they have been told, peering curiously out of the windows at the equally curious crowd on the platform peering in. Suddenly they spot a familiar figure – a Galician searching about for acquaintances. His name is Michaniuk, and he soon spies his old friends.

"Neighbours!" Mr. Michaniuk shouts, "where are you going?"

There is a commotion in the coach. Where are they going? Nobody seems to know.

"Don't go any farther," cries Mr. Michaniuk to his former towns-people. "It is good here!"

One of the men in the coach rises to his feet and addresses the assembly.

"There is our neighbour, Mr. Michaniuk. He came to Canada last year. He says it is good here. Let us get off the train."

A stampede follows. Men seize the doors, but they are locked. They try the windows, but these too are fastened. Several, in a frenzy, pick up their handbags, smash the glass, and begin to crawl through the openings, throwing their goods ahead of them. The Humeniuk family is borne forward by the press of people onto the platform.

Up runs the conductor, accompanied by an interpreter.

"What are you going to do now?" the interpreter cries out. "We have good land for you near Yorkton. There are no free good homesteads for farming left in Manitoba."

But the newcomers cannot be convinced. A spokesman replies: "We are not going any further. Our Old Country friend has been here one year. He says it is good where he settled."

No one can persuade them to go on to Yorkton. The dissidents are moved to the immigration hall where the women begin to cook food, launder the clothes, and tend to the children. The men follow Mr. Michaniuk to the Dominion Land Office to file for homesteads near Stuartburn on the Roseau River, where thirty-seven Galician families are already located. It turns out that some land is still available, and it is there that they settle. Most will still be there more than half a century

*later, when Nykola and Anastasia Humeniuk, surrounded by grand-
children, celebrate their golden wedding anniversary on the farm they
filed for back in 1897.*

The sheepskin people made do with essentials. Their houses were
constructed of timber and whitewashed clay, the roofs thatched with
straw. Entire families slept on top of the vast stove-furnaces, six feet
square. Gardens were dug with spades, since better equipment was
beyond the financial reach of most families. Benches and tables were
hand hewn. Plates were hammered out of tin cans found in garbage
dumps. Drinking glasses were created by cutting beer bottles in half.

Browbeaten for centuries, the Galicians did not find it easy to throw
off old habits. W.A. Griesbach, the young mayor of Edmonton, found
them timid and frightened and noticed that when a uniformed policeman approached they drove right off the road, removed their caps,
and waited for him to pass. If a well-dressed Canadian gave them an
order, they would immediately obey. This made them ripe targets for
exploitation.

Ely Culbertson, who later devised the famous contract bridge bidding system that bears his name, worked as a bookkeeper on the
Grand Trunk Pacific, where most of the labourers were Galicians –
"naïve, trustful, bearded giants [who] worked like elephants, laughed
like children and asked no questions" but were subjected to a "ruthless,
brazen robbery." The food was meagre and barely edible; better fare
was available in the commissary but "for prices that New York night
clubs would be ashamed to ask. . . . Those who didn't like it could get
out (at their own expense) for there was a never ending stream shang-
haied by the mass-procurement agencies of the East. . . . The Ukrainians were held in check by the small Anglo-Saxon element present in
every camp, who, being decently treated, were always ready to put
down with fists, clubs, and even guns, any outbreak of the 'Bohunks.'"

But the Galicians were changing the look of the prairies. Carpathian
villages with neat, whitewashed houses and thatched roofs sprang up.
Onion-shaped spires began to dominate the landscape. Mingled with
the starker silhouettes of the grain elevators and the familiar style of
the prairie railway stations, they helped create a profile that was
distinctively Western.

To those public figures who had no axe to grind, the Galicians were
an attractive addition to the prairie mix. Van Horne found them "a
very desirable people." Charles Constantine, the veteran Mounted

Police inspector at Fort Saskatchewan, used the same adjective. The immigration agent in Edmonton, R.A. Ruttan, reported to Ottawa that "they are good settlers and I should like to see more of them." James Dickson, a Dominion Land Surveyor who had had some doubts, changed his mind and expressed himself as "agreeably surprised" at the Galicians' progress in the Dauphin district of Manitoba.

Van Horne, in 1899, was astonished to discover that those Galicians who had been given railway transportation on credit actually paid the debt! "We had little hope of ever getting what they owed us but they have paid up every cent." In such cases, familiarity bred the opposite of contempt. Dr. R.H. Mason of Saltcoats, originally a bitter opponent of Slavic immigration, described his visit to a Galician colony as "a revelation" and went on to describe the colonists as "worthy, industrious, sober, and ambitious to make homes for themselves." Another who had a change of heart was W.M. Fisher, manager of the Canada Permanent and Western Canada Mortgage Company. After visiting the Edmonton district he reported that "the Galicians against whom I was prejudiced before my visit . . . I found to be a most desirable class of settlers, being hard working, frugal people and in their financial dealings honest to a degree."

The newspapers' attitude to the newcomers was predictable. The government press thought they were wonderful; the opposition papers thought the opposite. The first wave of Galicians had scarcely stepped ashore when the Conservative newspapers mounted a virulent attack. To the Belleville *Intelligencer* they were "disgusting creatures," to the Brandon *Independent* "human vermin." The Ottawa *Citizen* objected to Canada "being turned into a social sewage farm to purify the rinsings and leavings of rotten European states." In Edmonton, the *Bulletin*'s Frank Oliver, an independent and generally wayward Liberal, pulled out all the stops. The Galicians were "a servile, shiftless people . . . the scum of other lands . . . not a people who are wanted in this country at any price." Oliver coveted Sifton's job; eventually he got it.

The attacks were entirely political. In the pro-Sifton newspapers, the Galicians could do no wrong. Sifton's Winnipeg organ was so laudatory that Oliver's *Bulletin* referred caustically to "the Galician editor of the *Free Press*."

In Parliament, the Conservative outcry over Sifton's policy of unrestricted immigration was so violent that the Minister was finally forced to put a damper on Galician immigration into Canada. The general Opposition contention was that the influx of Slavs would dilute and muddy the purity of Canada's Anglo-Saxon heritage. Hugh John Macdonald, the son of Canada's first prime minister, actually referred to the Galicians as "a mongrel race." Premier Roblin of Manitoba went further. He called them "foreign trash" and proceeded to deny them the provincial franchise in order to "defend the 'old flag' against an invading foe."

The Conservatives harped on the belief that the Galicians were sub-humans with violent criminal tendencies, subject to avarice and uncontrollable passions. Mackenzie Bowell wrote of "tales of murder, arson and brutality, more horrible than anything ever dreamed of by the wildest disciple of the school of realistic fiction." These were not the words of a street-corner bigot; they came from the pen of a former prime minister.

The tales of murder and brutality were just that — fiction. When, in February, 1900, the Shoal Lake *Star* wrote of murder, robbery, wife-beating, and other crimes being committed among the Galicians of that area, Bill McCreary sent his best agent, Wesley Speers, to investigate. Speers tracked down every story, found all to be untrue, and forced an apology and a correction from the offending reporter.

Yet the concept of the Galicians as potentially dangerous criminals persisted in the public mind, largely because every Galician who got into trouble was identified as such in bold headlines. "GALICIAN HORROR" is the way the *Winnipeg Daily Tribune* headlined a local murder in June, 1899, convicting the accused out of hand long before he went to trial. Another Galician, charged with murder, was castigated as an "inhuman wretch." Trial by newspaper was far more common at the turn of the century than it was several decades later.

The following month the pro-Conservative Winnipeg *Telegram* reported the murder of Mrs. Robert Lane of Brandon and identified her assailant as Galician. The real culprit, of course, in the *Telegram*'s eyes, was the man who had brought the "foreign scum" into Canada.

ANOTHER SIFTONIAN TRAGEDY

Another horrible crime has been committed by the foreign ruffians whom Mr. Sifton is rushing into this country. The tragedy took place in Mr. Sifton's own town, Brandon. A foreign tramp goes to the door of one of Brandon's most prominent citizens and demands provisions; the lady of the house tells him she has no time to bother with him; he draws a revolver and brutally shoots her before the eyes of her little children! . . .

In order that Mr. Sifton may keep his Liberal party in power by

55

the votes of ignorant and vicious foreign scum he is dumping on our prairies, we are to submit to have our nearest and dearest butchered on our door-steps.

This account was a total fabrication. The murderer was not a Galician but an English woman, Emily Hilda Blake. Later she confessed to the crime and was hanged for it. But the impression of Galician madmen murdering defenceless Canadian women was hard to erase.

As for real Galician crime, it was virtually non-existent. That very year the chief of police in Winnipeg released annual figures showing the ethnic origins of convicted prisoners. Of 1,205 criminals, 1,037 were Canadians and 168 were foreign born. Of these latter only nine were Galicians.

3

The Galician vote
In 1904, the attitude toward the Galicians began to change, and for a very practical reason. Suddenly, the newspapers and politicians who had attacked "Sifton's dirty Slavs" reversed their strategy. The violently Tory Winnipeg *Telegram* for instance, which had vilified the immigrants as "ignorant, superstitious and filthy," now discovered that they were "industrious," "thrifty," "progressive," and "prosperous."

How to explain this sudden and astonishing about-face? The answer was that a federal election was called for 1904, and the editor of the *Telegram*, among others, was a candidate. The Conservatives were scrambling for Galician votes, and even the Tory premier of Manitoba was having second thoughts.

Roblin, who had once called the newcomers "dirty ignorant Slavs" who lived on rats and mice, now rose in the legislature that February to praise "their diligence, their intelligence, their sobriety, their generally estimable character." In 1899, Manitoba had denied the Galicians the provincial franchise. Now the Premier scrambled to redeem himself. He had been receiving Galician delegations, he announced, "and in every case they used English with fluency and betrayed a comprehension of the rights of citizens that showed that no disqualification was longer needed or could fairly be retained."

This, too, was nonsense. Few Galicians yet spoke English or cared about the Canadian political process. But the Premier had to do something to thwart the federal Liberal campaign, which was making great headway among all the immigrant groups in the West. Dmytro Romanchych explained in his memoirs why the Galicians in the Dauphin district of the province voted for the Liberal candidate, who happened to be Sifton's brother-in-law, Theodore Burrows. Some did it, he said, because it was felt the Conservatives were the party of the rich, some because the Liberal program resembled that of the radical party of Galicia; but the main reason lay in the fact that it was the Liberal party that had opened the doors to Galician immigrants and granted them free lands. In the provincial election of 1908, however, the same people voted for the Conservatives because it was the Tories who had established bilingual schools and a college in Brandon for the training of Ukrainian teachers.

It's doubtful whether many Galicians really understood the Canadian electoral system, at least in the early years. In Eastern Europe they had voted for "electors" – one for every five hundred voters – who, in turn, went to the political centre of their district and voted for the actual candidate, usually a big landowner. That system made the newcomers suspicious of all politicians. Their cynicism was reinforced when they discovered that in Canada a vote could be sold for a dollar. Some sold their votes twice – once to each opposing candidate – and then voted as they pleased.

In spite of Roblin's contention that "they used English with fluency," most could not understand a word the politicians uttered when they toured their villages. Both parties were forced to use interpreters chosen from among those leading Galicians who spoke some English. Illia Kiriak has left a lively account of one local interpreter warming up a crowd of potential Liberal voters: "I am going to call upon the local candidate to speak and I want you to listen carefully. When I start clapping I want all of you to do the same. And when he finishes I want all of you to give him a great ovation. You won't regret it and neither will I." To such men, the Liberal party extended the expected patronage. After the election they went on the government payroll as weed inspectors, game guardians, fire wardens.

In Edmonton in 1904, Frank Oliver woke up to discover that his own riding was so crowded with Galicians that they could, if organized, defeat him. The newcomers had known no enemy more deadly than Oliver, who had called them scum and had declared a Galician was "only a generation removed from a debased and brutalized serf." Westerners, he insisted, "objected to having this millstone of an alien

Slav population hung about their necks." A more sensitive or less determined politician might have had some reservations about attempting to solicit the Galician vote after these attacks, but Oliver had no such qualms. He intended to collar that vote and put his considerable party machine into high gear for that purpose. Surprisingly, he succeeded.

J.G. MacGregor, Alberta's best-known social historian, has an amusing account of Oliver speaking to a group of Galicians in a small general store in his riding. Except for the local party interpreter, none had any idea what the candidate was saying, and if they had would have had little interest in the subject, for Oliver was ranting on about the Department of the Interior, about high tariffs, about British preference and the Alaska border dispute.

"What's he say?" one listener finally asked the interpreter.

"He's glad we're here. Canada was lucky to get us. . . ."

"What about the stupid fire regulations?"

"He'll fix them."

"What's he say about the railroad?"

"I forgot to tell you that – he's got it started for sure."

"What about the mudholes around Whitford Lake?"

"He'll fix them – he'll do all he can for our area. . . ."

Griesbach, the so-called boy mayor of Edmonton, who was backing the Conservative candidate, Richard Secord, attempted to set up local organizations in every township to secure the Galician vote. Oliver bested him at every turn. A week before the election, parties of three or four men dressed as surveyors and carrying transits began appearing in areas organized for Secord. These men drove into the Galician farmyard, set up their instruments, and pretended to run a line directly through the barn, explaining to the worried farmer that they were locating Frank Oliver's new railway. *Disaster!* When the despairing immigrant begged for a change of route, the pseudo-surveyors suggested he get in touch with the local Liberal agent who might just be persuaded to switch the direction of the line. In every case, of course, the Liberals agreed and the grateful farmer gave Frank Oliver his vote.

The Galicians were vague about voting dates, since they read no English, and an effort was needed to get out the vote, or, in some cases, to keep it away. Oliver had his organizers swarm over the Galician communities asking each man for whom he intended to vote. Those who were voting Liberal were told the proper date of the election, Monday. The Conservative voters were told it was Wednesday.

Oliver always got out the vote. In the 1904 election, 352 out of 458 Galicians turned up at the polls. Of these, 278 voted for the man who had called them "debased and brutalized." As a result, Oliver was swept back into office and the following year replaced Clifford Sifton as Minister of the Interior. Not surprisingly, under Oliver the concept of unrestricted immigration was tossed aside.

4

"Ethnic" has become a peculiarly Canadian word, but it belongs to a later era. At the turn of the century there were no discussions about "roots," no talk of "multiculturalism," little pandering to national cultures, and certainly no reference to a Canadian mosaic. The key word – the *only* word – was "assimilation." Assimilation meant conformity: in dress, in language, in customs, in attitudes, in religion. It meant, in short, that every immigrant who arrived in the West was expected to accept as quickly as possible the Anglo-Celtic Protestant values of his Canadian neighbours. These attitudes were held almost universally and at every level of society, espoused by such diverse public figures as William Van Horne of the CPR; by the Reverend J.S. Woodsworth, the Methodist reformer; by John Wesley Dafoe of the *Manitoba Free Press*; by Nellie McClung, the suffragette and temperance activist; and by Clifford Sifton himself.

The melting-pot syndrome

Everybody agreed that certain races could not be assimilated and had no place in Canadian society. Orientals, East Indians, and Blacks were not wanted. Anti-Semitism was universal, as the stereotype caricatures in the newspapers and periodicals make clear. And the press did not engage in racial niceties: Negroes were niggers; Orientals were Chinamen; Jews were sheenies.

Could the Galicians be assimilated, or would their presence mongrelize the nation? That was the crux of the controversy from the moment of their arrival. It was generally held that they were an inferior race; that was not the argument. The question was whether or not they could be turned into "white" Canadians. The anti-Sifton newspapers – Oliver's *Bulletin* was the worst offender – did not believe it possible. "They have withstood assimilation in the country from whence they come for many generations. What reason have we to expect their ready assimilation here?" Others, such as the Hamilton *Times*, were

59

grudgingly optimistic: "They may never develop into such perfect Canadians as the Scotch or the Irish but the chances are they will turn out all right."

That was the general sentiment. Everything would turn out all right. The prevailing attitude in the West was one of heady optimism. A new century was dawning – Canada's century, Laurier called it – and the country was capable of working miracles. The men in sheepskin coats would quickly be transformed into well-cropped, bowler-hatted Canadians. As the *Manitoba Free Press* put it in the fall of 1897, "the land is here and the Anglo-Saxon race has great assimilating qualities." Already William McCreary was reporting to Sifton that the Galicians were "dressing in a more civilized garb" and that the majority were "accepting Canadian customs and ways."

It was widely held that those immigrants who did not come from northwestern Europe were inferior to others in terms of religion, education, and political outlook. Germans and Scandinavians were not really aliens. As John Dafoe put it in 1907, in an article for an American publication about the influx of immigrants, "a considerable percentage of those recorded as foreigners are of Teutonic and Scandinavian stock *and therefore akin* [my italics]. . . . The only alien race represented at all strongly is Slavic." Dafoe went on to reassure his American readers that there was no chance of "a mongrel race and a mongrel civilization" springing up in Western Canada because the Slavic peoples were "being Anglicized with a rapidity which sometimes results in startling transformations. . . . The Galician youth of five or seven years ago is now, in many cases, not easily distinguishable in speech or manners from his neighbour of Canadian birth and lineage."

J.S. Woodsworth in his book *Strangers within Our Gates* was happy to quote an American view that a line drawn from northeast to southwest across Europe separated the "superior" races – Scandinavian, British, German, and French – from the "inferior" ones – Russian, Austro-Hungarian, Italian, and Turkish. Like almost everybody else, the future founder of the CCF was convinced that the Galicians must be assimilated to a uniform standard, which was the Anglo-Celtic norm. He went along with the view that "the Galician figures, disproportionately to his numbers, in the police court and penitentiary. Centuries of poverty and oppression have to some extent animalized him. Drunk, he is quarrelsome and dangerous. The flowers of courtesy and refinement are not abundant in the first generation of immigrants."

One of Canada's leading churchmen, J.W. Sparling, principal of

Winnipeg's Methodist Wesley College, in his introduction to Woodsworth's book urged everybody to read it: "*For there is a danger and it is national!* Either we must educate and elevate the incoming multitudes or they will drag us and our children down to a lower level. We must see to it that the civilization and ideals of Southeastern Europe are not transplanted to and perpetuated on our virgin soil." To Sparling, these ideals were, of course, those of the Catholic religions.

To a generation that views Woodsworth as a socialist saint, his acceptance of these sentiments in a book that bears his name may seem shocking. But he was very much a man of his time, a Methodist activist who staunchly believed in the virtues of radical Protestantism and the civilizing effect of the British Empire. His motives were pure enough. In the All Peoples' Mission in Winnipeg's North End, he saw it as his duty to minister to the immigrant poor. His book was designed to familiarize Canadians with their problems and to help make his fellow countrymen more responsive to them.

The Methodists were proselytizers and therefore in the forefront of the active movement to assimilate the Galicians. Men like Woodsworth did not believe the process would work without a strong nudge from the church. That was very much in the Methodist tradition. Unlike the Anglicans, they did not wait for communicants to come to them; their circuit riders went out into the villages to spread the Word. Behind this activism lay the fear of the growing power and influence of the Roman Catholic Church. The move to assimilate the Slavs was bound up with the desperate battle in Manitoba over religious education. The Methodists were in the vanguard of the fight against parochial schools in the province. The leading politicians were Methodists. Sifton was a Methodist and so were many of his political cronies. Dafoe had been born a Methodist, and though he rejected dogma and became a nominal Anglican, he could not reject the tenets of Methodism's social creed. The cant of the day was that while Catholicism bred ignorance, suspicion, and autocracy, Protestantism brought freedom, initiative, industry, and democracy. To a very large extent, this Methodist credo helped form the Western ethic.

In June 1908, the Methodist publication *Missionary Outlook* summed up the Methodist point of view: "If from this North American continent is to come a superior race, a race to be specially used of God in the carrying on of His work, what is our duty to those who are now our fellow-citizens? Many of them come to us as nominal Christians, that is, they owe allegiance to the Greek or Roman Catholic

61

churches but their moral standards and ideals are far below those of the Christian citizens of the Dominion. . . . It is our duty to meet them with an open Bible, and to instill into their minds the principles and ideals of Anglo-Saxon civilization."

In this crusade, the Methodists had the help of both the Presbyterians and the Baptists. The Reverend Dr. James Robertson, superintendent of home missions for the Presbyterian Church, was on record as early as 1898 in declaring that "the interest of the state lies in its doing all it can to assimilate these and other foreigners and make of them Canadians. They should be put into the great Anglo-Saxon mill and be ground up; in the grinding they lose their foreign prejudices and characters."

The Methodists had no intention of poaching on the territory of these other Protestants. After all, the ideal of a United Church was less than two decades away. When Woodsworth talked of "independence," he clearly meant independence from Greek or Roman Catholicism: "Independence means that people are taught to think for themselves; it means that the Bible is placed in their hands; it means that their children attend the Public Schools instead of the parochial schools; it means that people ally themselves with Protestants rather than Catholics. *Independence offers the opportunity for reformation*."

Things did not work out as Woodsworth hoped. Nobody had asked the Galicians whether or not they wished to be ground up in the great Anglo-Saxon mill. They clung tenaciously to their religion; indeed, the presence of Roman Catholic and Greek Orthodox churches in the rural Prairies acted as a spur to the retention of language and culture. Certainly, many were anxious to learn English and even more anxious that their children learn it. It is ironic that in this desire they were often frustrated by the lack of good teachers in their communities. But they also wanted to retain their original language, and this they did to a remarkable degree, producing an impressive body of prose and poetry in their own tongue.

In a sense Oliver was right when he said that the Slavic peoples had withstood assimilation for many centuries and would also withstand it in Canada. But the fears of mongrelization were groundless. The newcomers and their children managed to become Canadians while retaining a pride in their heritage, as the Scots did, as the Icelanders and others did. By the First World War, when immigration ceased, the talk of assimilation began to abate. By the 1920s, the term "Galician" had died out. By then most Canadians were beginning to understand the difference between Poles and Ukrainians, for by then Polish and Ukrainian social and political clubs were scattered across the West. The time was coming when Canadians of every background would be referring to the Canadian Mosaic and indeed boasting about it as if it had been purposely invented as an instrument of national policy to preserve the Dominion from the conformity of the American Melting-Pot.

Chapter Three

The Spirit Wrestlers

1

The touching and often tragic drama of the Doukhobor migration to the Canadian West is animated by a singular cast of characters. The leading actors (setting aside the Spirit Wrestlers themselves) form a unique international brotherhood, perhaps the most remarkable ever assembled to make common and selfless cause in the interests of one immigrant sect. They were poorly organized; they often quarrelled with one another; and they only vaguely understood the nature of the communities they proposed to settle in the West. But they were idealists, men of quality and rank in most cases, who were prepared to devote their time, energies, money, and reputation to a project from which they could not personally benefit and which some would live to regret.

Look at them! There were, first, those indomitable Russian nobles with the tangled beards who seem to have stepped out of a Tolstoyan novel: Kropotkin, Hilkoff, Tchertkoff, and the saintly count himself – the author of *War and Peace* – who had, often at considerable cost, rejected the crasser values of their homeland. There were the Quakers on both sides of the Atlantic, stubborn pacifists who dressed in funeral black and peppered their conversations with the archaic second-person singular. There was Aylmer Maude, hard-nosed businessman turned Tolstoyan disciple, prickly, dedicated, often impractical. There were those quirky anarchists from the doomed Utopian colony of Purleigh in Essex. And last, but not least, there was the eccentric professor of political science at the University of Toronto, the remarkable James Mavor.

On September 22, 1897, there arrived in Winnipeg the most exotic member of this group, Peter Aleksevich Kropotkin, who was – or had been – a Czarist prince. An exile from his native land, an escapee from a Siberian cell, expelled from Switzerland, imprisoned in France, this one-time royal aide and army officer had an international reputation among scientists as a geographer, zoologist, sociologist, and historian and among his friends and enemies as a radical, an anarchist, and a revolutionary.

Prince Kropotkin spent an hour dashing about at full speed on one of Winnipeg's electric tram cars, marvelling at the city, which was already being compared with Chicago. Substantial buildings of masonry and brick lined the downtown streets, where the pavements were of solid stone blocks. Here was the dazzling city hall, flamboyantly baroque — Western enthusiasm expressed in pink brick and spikey domes. Here were grand hotels with grander names flanking the two-hundred-foot-wide expanse of Main: the Oriental, the Cosmopolitan, the American, the Brunswick, and, at the busy intersection of Main and Water, the eight-storey Manitoban with its curved façade and conical cupola. By the time he took the train west, Prince Kropotkin was properly impressed. Why, Winnipeg was only twenty-five years old! In Russia, a city of that size and quality might go back for centuries.

We have boarded the train with the Prince. He is a bulky man with a great naked dome and a monstrous square beard. As the train rolls heavily out of the city limits and enters the prairie, he takes everything in with the eyes both of a geographer and of a poet. They are blue and intelligent, those eyes, peering out from behind a pair of tiny, wire-rimmed spectacles, and now they sparkle with astonishment as he contemplates the flatness of the prairie. Ahead, he sees the straight line of the railway — a ruler laid across the level surface of the plain; behind him is another steel ruler leading back to Winnipeg. The land is so flat that even after miles of track have clattered beneath him, he can still spot the silhouette of the elevators on the city's outskirts.

He notes the black earth, the extraordinary absence of a single tree or shrub, and, on the horizon, a sunset such as he has not experienced since he left the steppes of southern Russia. We, his travelling companions, including his fellow members of the British Association for the Advancement of Science, find it all very monotonous, but the Prince is thrilled. "What an infinite variety of life in these steppes!" he thinks to himself. These Western Europeans have no concept of the poetry of the steppes; even his own people in middle Russia are ignorant of it. One cannot find any reference to it in the geographical works with which he is so familiar. One must seek for it instead in Russian literature — in the souls of men born on the steppes, in the poetry of Klotsoff or the novels of Oertel. One must have lived on the steppes, rambled over them on horseback, inhaled the perfume of mown grass, spent the night in the open, crossed the boundless prairie in sledges behind a trio of galloping horses to realize the real beauty of a country which, in Kropotkin's poetic vision, is so like this Manitoba prairie. This is his kind of country; mountains and valleys are not for him — they make him feel like a bird in a cage.

The prairie, though almost empty of humans, is bursting with life.

Flocks of wildfowl blacken the sky. Gulls rise screaming from the lakelets. Ducks speckle the prairie ponds. Gophers and squirrels scamper about by the thousands. The wild grasses, tinted red, yellow, and brown, make a Persian carpet of the plains.

As the prairie unfolds the Prince continues to be amazed by the similarities between Canada's geographical features and those of his native land. When he first reached Manitoba the illusion was complete; he might as well be in the prairies of South Tobolsk at the foot of the Urals: the same aspect, the same black soil, the same dried-up lake bottoms, the same character of climate.

Now, as the train rolls westward toward the high sub-arid prairie, he can easily imagine himself upon the higher level steppe, which the Trans-Siberian railway enters beyond Tomsk. The little Siberian towns, he tells us, could be described as sister growths of Medicine Hat, Calgary, and Regina were it not for the Americanized aspect of the Canadian communities. Even the vegetation is similar. Suddenly the expatriate feels at home again. And, with his help, the day will come when actual Russian villages, indistinguishable from those of the Caucasus, will spring up here in this strangely familiar land.

There was another reminder of home, here in the Canadian West — the presence of the Mennonites. These were also followers of Leo Tolstoy, with whom the anarchist prince felt more than kinship. To escape military service, these industrious, God-fearing people had left Russia in the 1870s. Visiting a Mennonite village, Kropotkin once again found himself in a replica of his homeland, a small Russian community, complete with thatched houses, broad streets, manured plots, and lines of little trees. These people, too, were anarchists in the sense that "they never have anything to do with justice or law." Kropotkin found it remarkable that in the midst of a capitalist civilization some twenty thousand people had been able to continue to live and thrive under a system of partial communism and passive resistance to the state, which they had managed to maintain for more than three centuries in the face of almost continual persecution.

He was, of course, aware that in the valleys of the Caucasus Mountains, between the Caspian and Black seas, there was another religious group in some ways similar to the Mennonites, who lived communally, rejected military service, and refused to take an oath of allegiance to the Czar. They called themselves the Christian Community of Universal Brotherhood, but their tormentors jeered at them as Doukhoborski, or Spirit Wrestlers. The name stuck and, in the end, was accepted with pride, in the same way that the Society of Friends accepted the epithet "Quaker."

Among these simple people, until he fled the country, lived another of those curiously attractive Russian noblemen – one who, like Kropotkin, had been driven to reject his aristocratic heritage by Czarist excesses and his own conscience. Prince Dmitri Alexandrovich Hilkoff came of one of the oldest of the noble families – older, in fact, than the ruling Romanovs. The family was still powerful; Hilkoff's uncle was a member of the Czarist cabinet. But Hilkoff himself subscribed to the pacifist philosophy of Leo Tolstoy. As a colonel in the Russian Army during the war with Turkey in 1878, he had slain an enemy soldier in battle and suffered such pangs of remorse that he quit both the army and the Orthodox Church. Appalled at the condition of the serfs on the family estate, he gave up his legacy upon his mother's death and divided all his lands among them.

Banished to the Caucasus (where he encountered the Doukhobors), broken hearted because his children had been removed from him forever by the Czar's decree, he at last received permission to exile himself from Russia, but not before he had brought the plight of the Doukhobors to the attention of his hero, Tolstoy. Doukhobors were being plundered, raped, tortured, imprisoned, beaten, and starved by Cossack troops because they refused to bear arms or take an oath of allegiance to the Czar. Tolstoy, whose own philosophy was remarkably similar to theirs, brought the details of their plight to the world.

In March, 1898, a few months after Kropotkin's Canadian tour, three events took place that were to lead to the most bizarre chapter in the history of the shaping of the Canadian West. First, Kropotkin published in the *Nineteenth Century* a long article about Canada and the Mennonites, which he had written in the Toronto home of his friend Professor James Mavor. Second, the Empress Alexandra of Russia, prompted both by Tolstoy's importunings and by those of the Society of Friends of England, had persuaded the Czar that the Doukhobors might leave Russia if they did so immediately. Third, Tolstoy's personal representative, another exiled noble named Vladimir Tchertkoff, arrived at Purleigh in England. Here a Tolstoyan community had been set up by J.C. Kenworthy, a disciple of the Russian author and an anarchist colleague of Kropotkin. It was to be a "part of a world wide movement toward a better and truer life for humanity." The spirit there was one of tolerance, of encouraging others "to wake up to the real meaning of life. . . ."

At Purleigh, Tchertkoff, the one-time St. Petersburg aristocrat, and his wife lived a life of absolute simplicity, eschewing all meat and proclaiming that "as long as there are starving men in the world we hold that luxury is wrong." Prince Hilkoff also turned up at Purleigh, another exotic figure to visiting journalists who goggled over the spectacle of the scion of one of Russia's noblest families working with a spade in the garden while his wife, the Princess, chopped wood and hauled water "in true Tolstoy fashion."

Here, too, was Aylmer Maude, a former businessman who had spent seventeen years in Russia. While acting as director of the Russian Carpet Company, Maude had encountered Tolstoy's work and presently became a regular visitor at the author's home in Moscow and at his country villa at Tula.

Tolstoy's influence on nineteenth-century thought cannot be overestimated. Here was Maude, the English carpet salesman, about to toss aside those values that had sustained him into middle age. Early in the 1890s, under Tolstoy's influence, he found his conscience could no longer allow him to continue as a tool of the capitalistic world; after all, his mentor's whole philosophy was an indictment of the industrial system. He quit his job and proceeded to devote himself to the translation of Tolstoy's works into English. Tolstoy's *What Is Art?* would shortly be published by Purleigh's founder, Kenworthy, through his own Brotherhood Press. Meanwhile, the members of the Purleigh community busied themselves with efforts to save the Doukhobors.

Tolstoyism was the glue that held all these people together. Tchertkoff had been sent to Purleigh by Tolstoy in the hope that the community, aided by Maude's business acumen, would raise funds to pay for the Doukhobors' passage to another country. But time was of the essence: the Czarina might withdraw her permission for the sect's departure at any moment.

A variety of destinations was discussed: Texas, Brazil, Argentina, Hawaii, Cyprus. The last was finally chosen because it was the closest refuge to the Black Sea port of Batum, from which the Doukhobors would embark. Plans were laid and money raised to move eleven hundred Doukhobors to Cyprus at once. Prince Hilkoff was dispatched to the island to prepare for their arrival. Then, on the eve of

70

his departure, Tchertkoff came across Kropotkin's article about Canada and the Mennonites.

Canada! To most Europeans it hardly existed. Certainly no one had considered it as a new home for the Spirit Wrestlers. Yet Kropotkin made it clear that this oddly attractive country would welcome Russian religious refugees with farming experience as it had the Mennonites, and that the conditions were remarkably similar to those in Russia.

Kropotkin was invited to come to Purleigh to discuss the Doukhobor problem. From there he wrote a long letter to his closest friend in Canada, Professor Mavor, whom he had known since 1884 and who had arranged the cross-Canada tour of the British association, which had sparked the Prince's article on the Canadian West. In his letter Kropotkin asked if Mavor thought Canada would accept twelve thousand Doukhobors and what advice the professor could give about the mechanics of such a venture.

Here was another remarkable figure. At forty-four, Jimmy Mavor had already acquired a reputation as an eccentric and a Bohemian – a man who dazzled his students with his broad range of knowledge and the brilliance of his teaching. With his vast, rumpled beard, his high, balding forehead, and his long, greying hair, he was said to be Toronto's "most picturesque academic personality." He seemed to know a little about everything: indeed, his colleagues tended to look askance at him because he peppered his lectures with anecdotes! He had held the chair of political science at the University of Toronto since 1892, but his bents were also literary and scientific. He had once studied informally under the future Lord Kelvin, the inventor of the absolute temperature scale that bears his name. His correspondence was wide and eclectic, including such exotic figures as Oscar Wilde and Aubrey Beardsley. He had once been a Fabian reformer but was now in the process of reforming himself. He believed, however, that "there must be a constant effort to correct the prevailing tendency of things." He was an admirer of Tolstoy, of course (he would shortly visit him in Russia), and was also a Russophile who had wintered in St. Petersburg. And he knew a good deal about the Doukhobors.

This was the man who would act as the catalyst to bring the Spirit Wrestlers to Canada – the go-between who linked the American and British Quakers, the Purleigh community, the Russian expatriates, and Clifford Sifton's Department of Immigration. Without Mavor, the Doukhobor immigration to Canada would not have been possible.

He knew he must act quickly. "They must leave at once," his friend Kropotkin wrote to him; "there is not a moment to be lost." Mavor plunged into his task with characteristic enthusiasm. He wrote at once to Sir William Mulock, the Postmaster General, whom he knew, and to Clifford Sifton, whom he didn't. He wrote to Tchertkoff, to Kropotkin, to Tolstoy. This was the beginning of a voluminous correspondence on the Doukhobors by Mavor – some five hundred letters in all, of which sixty were written that late summer and fall of 1898 when Mavor was also busying himself with the autumn semester.

The emigration was already moving with precipitate and (to Mavor) alarming speed. On September 2, long before he had any word from the Canadian government, Mavor learned that eleven hundred Doukhobors had landed at Cyprus, which was to prove unsuitable, and that a delegation from Purleigh, consisting of two Doukhobor farmers together with Aylmer Maude and Prince Hilkoff, had embarked for Canada. They expected to meet Mavor at Quebec on the tenth and proceed to Ottawa to arrange matters with the government.

They paid their own way, the penniless prince and the Doukhobors travelling steerage while Maude, who was now in charge, took a first-class cabin, "feeling much ashamed of myself for such un-Tolstoyan self-indulgence." The Doukhobors were rarely consulted since they spoke a dialect of their own, which Hilkoff understood imperfectly and Maude not at all. Nor were they ever party to the deals that were subsequently made on their behalf with the Canadian government.

Among these well-intentioned but often naïve idealists, personality conflicts were beginning to develop. Maude, the nominal leader, unable to speak the language, found himself a mere supernumerary. Hilkoff and Tchertkoff had had a flaming row over Cyprus arising from the fact that one controlled the money – £1,100 contributed by the Purleigh community – while the other organized the emigration. They no longer spoke to one another. Maude was also cool to Tchertkoff, who he felt entirely lacked any business capacity. His own prickly letters irritated Mavor. Eventually Maude and Mavor became such bitter antagonists that in their respective books on the Doukhobor migration they scarcely mentioned one another. Similar tensions were to cause the break-up of the anarchist colony at Purleigh.

The situation was ripe for the misunderstandings that followed. The Doukhobors, "like a Queenless hive of bees," were leaderless, their acknowledged helmsman, Peter Verigin, an exile in Siberia. Their friends and supporters were not only at odds with one another but, and this was equally serious, also appeared to believe that once the Doukhobors were landed in Canada they would be able to fend for themselves without further aid. No one, apparently, understood the rigours of the Canadian winter.

For Mavor, with the university year about to begin, the next two weeks were hectic. Sifton was in the West, but a letter from his deputy, James Smart, finally indicated the government was interested. Indeed, the Doukhobors represented exactly the kind of tough, experienced peasantry that Sifton felt could withstand the appalling conditions on the empty plains. Mavor rushed to Ottawa to talk with Smart. Here, as he had in his previous correspondence, he tried to make clear the terms under which the Doukhobors were prepared to come to Canada. They expected exemption from military service. They wanted to hold land communally. They wanted some help in getting established. They wished to be consulted about the education of their children.

Nothing, apparently, was said about the Doukhobors' refusal to take an oath of allegiance to the sovereign. Their only allegiance, they insisted, was to God. When Maude, behind Mavor's back and to his considerable annoyance, finally signed a contract with the Immigration Department on behalf of the Purleigh community (neither Mavor nor the Doukhobor representatives were present) the oath was never mentioned. Nor was another significant condition: the right to hold land in common rather than individually. These omissions would eventually force the Doukhobors out of Saskatchewan at great financial sacrifice.

Nobody, it seemed, wanted to take responsibility for the Doukhobors, yet more and more of them, it appeared, were preparing to leave Russia. Besides the Purleigh community, the Quakers on both sides of the Atlantic and Leo Tolstoy himself were raising funds for their passage and subsequent establishment in the West. Tolstoy, for one, contributed seventeen thousand dollars in royalties from *What Is Art?*

But who would look after all this money? And was it sufficient? Many of the Doukhobors were destitute. Eleven hundred pounds had already been squandered on the abortive voyage to Cyprus.

Queries began arriving: could Canada accept another two thousand, then four thousand, then an additional three thousand, as well as the Cyprus exiles? Mavor was appalled. As he wrote to Smart, "Their idea that they might as well be frozen to death in Canada as flogged to death by the Cossacks, is natural enough, but no one would venture to induce the Government to receive a greater number of them than can be reasonably well sheltered and fed during the winter."

Maude rushed off to Philadelphia to raise money from the Quakers there. Then, by-passing Mavor, he left for England, turning over all responsibility for the Doukhobors in Canada to Hilkoff. For Mavor this was the last straw; his breach with Maude was complete.

The government, eager to get farmers on the empty Western lands, found a way to subsidize the Doukhobors without actually having to admit to it. Since no shipping agents were involved, why not pay into a special Doukhobor fund all the public money that would normally have gone into bonuses? Thus one pound for every Doukhobor man, woman, and child landed in Canada went toward settling the new immigrants. The money, however, could not be paid out until the Doukhobors actually arrived – in instalments. This subsidy was legalized in a new contract with Hilkoff, a contract that guaranteed the Doukhobors exemption from military service and gave them a block of 750,000 acres in northern Assiniboia. But again, in this contract there was no mention of exemption from the oath of allegiance or from the homestead law, which prevented the holding of land in common.

The government was in a dilemma. It wanted these immigrants. And whether or not it wanted them, they seemed determined to come anyway. Some twenty-one hundred were already preparing to embark at the Black Sea port of Batum. But Sifton was already under extreme criticism from the Conservative press over his "coddling" of the Galicians. He could not be seen to give anything more to the Doukhobors than was the rightful due of any immigrant. On the other hand, he could not leave them to starve and freeze when they left the train at Winnipeg. The government agreed to pay out ten thousand dollars of the bonus money on the arrival of the first group of twenty-one hundred in Winnipeg. A second party, under the leadership of Tolstoy's son, Sergius, was not expected until May. In addition to the bonus money, the Doukhobor trust fund had reached $200,000, one-fifth of it contributed by the Doukhobors themselves.

The Immigration Department now faced a superhuman task.

Nothing like this had ever taken place before, and nothing like it has ever taken place since. This was the largest single immigration ever organized in Canada. Somehow, more than two thousand men, women, and children, scarcely any of whom understood a word of English, had to be trundled half way across Canada, immediately after disembarkation.

With winter (the worst in decades) about to strike, the hard-pressed Commissioner of Immigration in Winnipeg, Bill McCreary, would have to have warm accommodation and food waiting for all of them. Somehow he would have to get them aboard other trains and dispatch them to northern Assiniboia. And there, on the treeless snow-swept prairie, frozen hard as granite, they would have to survive until they could begin tilling the land in the spring. They were slated to arrive in mid-January. McCreary had no more than six weeks to get ready.

2

At 4 p.m. on January 20 – a perfect winter's day – the S.S. *Lake Huron* steamed into Halifax harbour with twenty-one hundred Doukhobors on board – the largest single body of emigrants ever to have crossed the Atlantic in one ship. She had travelled for twenty-nine days from Batum, manned by a skeleton crew (to save money) assisted by ninety-four untrained emigrants. Ten persons had died during the voyage; five more couples had been married in the simple Doukhobor ceremony. The new arrivals had also survived a dreadful tempest that blew unceasingly for eight days, causing all to give up hope of ever reaching Canadian shores. In spite of this, the ship was spanking clean, scrubbed spotless by the women. The chief health officer remarked he had never known so clean a vessel to enter Halifax harbour.

We have joined the small knot of dignitaries boarding the steam tug Henry Hoover *as she chugs off to meet the incoming steamship. These include James Smart and William White of the Immigration Department; Prince Hilkoff, already dubbed by the press "the 19th Century Moses"; a representative of Canadian labour; several newspapermen; and two saintly and venerable Quakers in the dark clothing and broad black hats of their sect – Joseph Elkington of Philadelphia and Job Gidley of North Dartmouth, Massachusetts.*

"Greetings, Dou-khobors!"

Across the water comes the hum of human voices raised in song. Two thousand and seventy-three Doukhobors are chanting a psalm. Hilkoff translates for us: "God is with us; he has brought us through." Job Gidley raises his hat. "Welcome, Doukhobors!" he calls across the water.

High above us now, crowded along the deck rail, bowing their heads in greeting, are the "peculiar people" as the newspapers have called them – the men in high boots, fur leggings, sheepskin coats, and fur hats, the women in embroidered blouses, vests, red sashes, shawls, red plaid skirts, and woollen comforters, all staring down at their first view of Canadians and Canada.

We all clamber on board. Joseph Elkington closes his eyes, moistens his lips, and utters a prayer. The peculiar people bow. With Hilkoff translating, J.T. Bulmer, the labour man, follows with a fervent and declamatory speech on behalf of "the peaceful workmen of this country." As he finishes, the entire multitude, in an astonishing gesture, fling themselves to their knees and press their foreheads to the deck. Bulmer looks baffled. Why this fawning display of servility in free Canada? Hilkoff hastens to explain. They are not bowing to the welcoming committee but to "the spirit of God in their hearts, which has made them take us as brothers in their own homeland of Canada."

The *Lake Huron* steamed on to Saint John, with the Doukhobors gossiping among themselves about the marvels they had witnessed. No policemen had come to meet them! The government doctor did not wear gold braid nor did the immigration agent. The governor of the country was a Frenchman, but the English didn't seem to mind! And it was even said there were no soldiers in this governor's palace!

Five passenger trains, each eleven cars in length (one entire car carrying food), awaited the newcomers at Saint John. Since there was no room in the passenger cars for baggage, every trunk and box had to be relabelled. To avoid congestion, the newcomers were held on board ship until each train was ready to roll westward. On the dock, waiting for the Doukhobor children, were barrels of candies, donated by a group of Montreal wellwishers.

By the time the Doukhobors entrained, the commissary cars were loaded with 1,700 two-pound loaves of bread, 1,700 pounds of baked beans, 850 pounds of hard tack, 80 gallons of milk, 55 pounds of salt, 6 bushels of onions, and 50 pounds of coffee. By the time the trains reached Ottawa, it had all been devoured. Twice that amount was waiting on the station platform for the next leg of the journey.

76

In Winnipeg, meanwhile, McCreary had been struggling night and day to find accommodation for the new arrivals. Where was he going to house twenty-one hundred people? The immigration shed at Winnipeg could handle no more than six hundred. The shed at Brandon could hold another four hundred; but it was not insulated, and blowing snow was pouring through the cracks in the walls. Calgary might handle two hundred, but that, clearly, was not enough.

Nor was the department equipped to feed such an army. McCreary figured that even if the two ranges in the immigration hall ran day and night, they couldn't boil enough vegetables or bake enough bread to feed more than one hundred. He could, of course, buy bread, but at twenty-five loaves for a dollar the price was prohibitive. He would need to have a dozen big cauldrons, again working night and day, to boil enough soup for six hundred people. Prince Hilkoff, who had arrived in town to help, suggested erecting clay ovens in the yard. He could not realize that when his compatriots arrived, the temperature would be colder than forty below with a blizzard blowing.

By early January, with the deadline fast approaching, McCreary was managing to untangle the problem of accommodation. Calgary was too far away, but he was planning to throw up a frame shed at Yorkton, which he hoped would be ready by January 16. There would be no time to paint it, but he thought he could cram three hundred into it, and in a pinch an extra one hundred. There was also a shed at Dauphin, Manitoba, that could hold another three hundred, mainly women and children (the men would be sent out at once to put up houses of timber). An additional hundred could perhaps be squeezed into the immigration shed in Brandon, another hundred at Birtle, and upwards of fifty at Qu'Appelle. That would still leave another hundred who would have to be shoe-horned into the overtaxed hall in Winnipeg.

At Selkirk, north of Winnipeg, there was an ancient railway round-house capable of holding between fifteen hundred and two thousand souls; but it needed to be repaired, and Sifton's department was getting nowhere with his adversary, Israel Tarte, of the Department of Public Works. McCreary was beside himself from overwork, and on the verge of breakdown. That midwinter he had worked every holiday, every Sunday, and almost every evening until shortly before midnight. The only meal he was able to enjoy with his family was breakfast. He wolfed lunch and dinner in twenty-minute breaks at a restaurant next door to his office. "I do not think I could stand it more than a couple of years longer," he told Sifton. A reformed alcoholic, he had fallen off the wagon at Christmas, got himself entangled in a public quarrel, and almost lost his job. He blamed this fall from grace on overwork. "I have been completely prostrated at times," he wrote, "and hardly felt able to draw one foot after the other from the severe strain that has been on me. . . . I have not a blessed moment that I can call my own." A year later McCreary quit his job, ran for federal office as a Liberal, and was elected. Three years after that he was dead.

In Winnipeg he felt powerless to cope with the Doukhobor influx. It was easy enough, he told Smart, to ship 2,073 people by train from the East, "but to take hold of 2073, house and feed them, look after the sanitary arrangements and prevent them from being frozen to death is not an easy task. Our weather here has been from twenty to forty below zero for two or three weeks with a bad blizzard blowing. . . ."

He had no authority to make purchases. No committee had been organized to handle Doukhobor funds and no line of credit issued. He needed to buy wood, water, harnesses, oxen, sleighs, flour, and vegetables. He could not find sixty-gallon cauldrons in the West; these would have to be shipped by freight, and that would take a week or ten days or even longer, should there be a blizzard. "It will then take twenty-four hours to set them up," McCreary reminded Smart, "so I should know now more particulars of what my powers are." In the end he did the only thing possible: he dipped into his own departmental funds and endured a tough reprimand from Ottawa for doing so.

The five trainloads of Doukhobors began arriving in Winnipeg at 12:30 on the afternoon of January 27, 1899. The first train, delayed by weather at White River, was destined for Yorkton. But the shed there was not yet complete, and with the temperature now at forty-five below, McCreary did not feel it safe to house anybody there until the stoves and cauldrons had been going for at least twenty-four hours. He crammed 296 into the Dufferin School in Winnipeg – "forty more than its capacity" – and kept the rest in the immigration hall.

This was the coldest winter in the memory of the city's oldest inhabitants. The third train did not pull into the station until one o'clock in the morning; by then it was so cold on the platform that McCreary froze his nose and fingers. Train No. 4 was an hour behind, en route to Brandon and making slow time, being forced to stop periodically to make steam when the engines froze. The fifth train arrived at 5:30 a.m. and collided with a yard engine just as it pulled out for Dauphin. Two cars were damaged and had to be replaced.

But the Doukhobors were in a state of near ecstasy. To them, McCreary's makeshift arrangements were little short of Elysian. Hot dinners awaited them the moment they stepped off the train: the women of Winnipeg had spent hours peeling potatoes, chopping cabbage, making soup. Thousands turned out the following day to greet them. An address of welcome was offered by R.G. Macbeth, a local minister heading a committee especially organized for that purpose. As Wasil Papsouf stood up to reply, his face wreathed in smiles, there were tears of emotion in the eyes of the onlookers.

"God has been good to us," Papsouf said. "We have come to a country where oppression does not exist. The kindness of your people has deeply impressed us all, and we are thankful. Everything has been first class." As the spectators applauded, all the Doukhobors dropped to their knees and bowed their heads to the ground. That night, one of the leaders, Leopold Soulerkitsky, wired to Count Tolstoy: "*Safe. Doukhobors obtained grand welcome from Canada. All are free.*" As far as the Spirit Wrestlers were concerned, their problems were over.

McCreary's were just beginning. He had managed to house two-thousand-odd Doukhobors in temporary quarters. Now he was faced with four new concerns: clothing his charges, moving food out to the various accommodations, providing more permanent housing, and doing all this before the next two thousand arrived. These were already aboard the Beaver Line's *Lake Superior*, due to reach Halifax in a fortnight's time.

The Doukhobors were ill prepared for the forty-five below weather. The men wore hard leather boots with pieces of blanket around the feet in lieu of socks. The women wore only a half-slipper with a leather sole. None had mitts. Several froze their toes trying to work out of doors. McCreary bought two hundred pairs of moccasins, four hundred pairs of socks, and a mountain of warm clothing for the men he was dispatching to prepare the new colonies for the others.

The staple food was simplified. Cheese, molasses, and fish, which some had been fed at Brandon and Portage la Prairie, were cut off because the Doukhobors themselves insisted that they all get the same provisions. The regular diet would be potatoes, onions, cabbage, tea, and sugar. But it soon became impossible to move the vegetables by sleigh because of the weather. "To try to keep vegetables warm by putting a stove in a sleigh would be impossible as they will quite likely meet with some upsets." Nor was there any place to store perishables. Early that fall, Aylmer Maude had spent two thousand dollars on vegetables. All had rotted in Winnipeg. When McCreary finally received the government advance in February for the first group of Doukhobors it was two thousand dollars short of the promised ten thousand because of this unfortunate purchase.

Luckily for McCreary, the next contingent was held for twenty-eight days in quarantine because of an outbreak of smallpox aboard the *Lake Superior*. But the long delay was costly. The new arrivals still had to be fed, and the CPR had to be paid a stiff price for holding its trains at Saint John.

Meanwhile, McCreary had managed to outfit and supply gangs of ten men from each of the three colonies planning to settle in the West, who were cutting timber for houses. By February 9, one gang had erected three buildings in the settlement, each twenty-four-feet square and large enough to hold fifty or sixty Doukhobors. Food was still a problem. No teamster would go out, even for additional pay, in the face of the biting cold.

It was essential that the roundhouse at Selkirk be refurbished before the new trainloads arrived. McCreary had thirty Doukhobors working on the building, which had to be plastered and papered before it would be habitable.

And so it went, with McCreary shuffling thousands of people by train and ox team off to Yorkton to make way for the new arrivals, while gangs of men on the new village sites kept cauldrons of water bubbling to warm the plaster for the partially built homes. By February 9, the government payment of eight thousand dollars was gone and the Treasury Board was vacillating because of the quarantine delay. McCreary was told he would not receive the second payment of sixteen thousand dollars until June. A final payment of about eight thousand dollars was not made until the last contingent of Doukhobors reached Canada in the fall, many of whom were forced to live in caves for a portion of the winter. At that point the government was relieved of all payments based on the bonus of $4.87 for each immigrant settled in the West.

Much of the sum raised by the Quakers and Purleigh community had gone to pay transportation costs; the rest was not available until late in the summer. Thrown on their own resources, the Doukhobors rose to the challenge. Out went the men from Selkirk, Brandon, and Winnipeg, taking any job they could get from shovelling snow to chopping wood. The older men set up cottage industries, making wooden spoons and painted bowls for sale. The women responded to the local demand for fine embroidery and woven woollens. The younger girls took jobs as domestics. Rather than purchase shovels and harnesses, the Doukhobor farmers bought iron bars and leather, built forges to produce implements, and fashioned Russian-style gear that was superior to the mass-produced Canadian harnesses.

Meanwhile, James Mavor had persuaded William Saunders of the Dominion Experimental Farm to visit the villages and give advice on crops. He had also talked the Massey-Harris Company into selling the newcomers equipment on credit. By the summer of 1901, the Doukhobors had 40 binders, 70 mowers, and 120 ploughing machines in operation. Thus, with the help of a number of dedicated and generous friends, these extraordinary people were well on the way to self-sufficiency.

In spite of all the problems, the Doukhobor resettlement was a remarkable feat. In a little more than a year after Prince Kropotkin wrote his original letter to Mavor, Canada had managed to settle seventy-five hundred persecuted and poverty-stricken Russians on the black soil of northern Saskatchewan. Within another year, their villages had been built and their future, it seemed, was secure. Yet the seeds of future trouble had already been sown – by the government in its eagerness to complete a vague and ambiguous contract and by a small but fanatical group of Doukhoborski to whom the true promised land was not in Saskatchewan at all but in the dreams and visions of their leaders.

3

Who were these "peculiar people" now struggling to build their communal homes and villages in three colonies in Saskatchewan? They were not nearly as monolithic as the naïve Tchertkoff had believed and as McCreary came to realize: "They are not by any means Universal Brethren, from the fact that they do not altogether agree on every point; they have their dissensions like ordinary mortals, so that a little difficulty may arise at times of this nature. Some of them, too, I understand, at Portage la Prairie, especially, are calling for fish, so that they are not all strictly vegetarians."

This was a prescient assessment. In 1886, the death of their passionate leader, Lukeria Vasilevna Gubanova, and the disputed choice of her selected heir, Peter Vasilivich Verigin (rightly or wrongly believed to be her young lover), had caused a split in the sect, which was further

The "peculiar people"

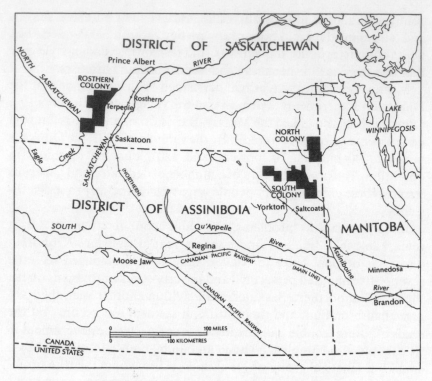

Doukhobor Settlements in Saskatchewan

divided geographically by Russian persecution. Some Doukhobors were vegetarians; some were not. Some were comparatively wealthy; some were destitute. Some believed in independence, others in conformity. In Canada, the divisions continued. The Georgian group went to Thunder Hill, seventy miles north of Yorkton; it became known as the North Colony. The refugees from Cyprus went to Devil's Hill, thirty miles north of Yorkton, the "South Colony." The people from Kars went to the "Prince Albert" or "Rosthern Colony" between Saskatoon and Prince Albert.

In general, the Doukhobors believed that Christ lived in every man and thus priests were unnecessary and the Bible obsolete. They rejected churches, litany, ikons, and festivals. Their only allegiance, they insisted, was to Christ; they could take no oath to temporal power. And yet their subservience to Peter Verigin seemed almost total.

Since 1886 Verigin had been in exile in Siberia, where he too had come under the influence of Tolstoy's teachings. His directives, sent secretly to the community's headmen, had been partly responsible for

82

bringing about the persecution of the Doukhobors under Czar Nicholas II. Verigin advocated a form of Christian communism, vegetarianism, abstinence from alcohol and, in times of tribulation, sex. He issued a ban on killing of any living thing, including human beings – hence the refusal to serve in the Czar's army. But Verigin's directives were often subtle and ambiguous, causing dissension within the sect.

When all of Verigin's flock was settled in Canada, another directive arrived from Siberia. It was permissible, the leader said, to learn to read and write. All essential goods, all shops, smithies, storehouses, granaries and the like should be held in common. Villages should not contain more than fifty houses, each capable of sheltering an extended family. Trees should line the streets; windbreaks must be planted and orchards cultivated.

By the end of 1900, a total of fifty-seven villages had sprung up in the three communities, most containing fewer than twenty houses. James Mavor, who was sent out by Sifton in April 1899 to report on the Doukhobors, spent three weeks in one of these one-room buildings with Prince Hilkoff. The house was built of logs, caulked with clay, and heated by a single stove. On two sides of the big room were double tiers of bunks, fourteen in all, each seven feet long and five feet wide. In each bunk an entire family slept together. Mavor and Hilkoff had one to themselves. The remaining thirteen accommodated fifty persons.

In that first summer there was scarcely an able-bodied man left in any of the villages. While they worked on the railway, the women broke the sod. Since the few horses available were needed to bring supplies from Yorkton, the women hitched themselves to the ploughs – twenty-four women to each team, guided by one of the old men of the village. A photograph of one of these teams appeared in the Conservative newspapers, which reviled the Doukhobor men as inhuman beasts who forced their womenfolk into harness.

By 1900, the men themselves were back at work in the fields. Life was hard, yet there is an engaging quality to the descriptions of Doukhobor society – the choir chanting in the streets each morning to wake the workers; the men, divided into gangs, singing as they marched toward the fields; the town meeting or *sobranie*, where a rough democracy prevailed; the antelope and deer foraging unmolested among the cattle; the family dipping their wooden spoons into the communal bowl of borscht.

Those officials who came into contact with the Doukhobors were impressed. "I never saw a more orderly lot of people," the Mounted Police inspector at Duck Lake wrote in August 1899. One immigrant agent aboard a Doukhobor train wrote: "I take the greatest pleasure in stating that during my many years travelling with passengers of so many different nationalities, I never came across a more clean, respectable, well behaved lot of people." The veteran Mounted Police Inspector Darcy Strickland was astonished to note that they never passed one another on the village streets without removing their caps and bowing. Old men bowed to children, and the children bowed back. It was explained to him that they were not really bowing to each other but to the spirit of Jesus within them.

It is a crisp March morning in 1902 and we are driving west from Rosthern in a two-horse cutter along the wedge of land that lies between the two branches of the Saskatchewan. Dawn is a lemon-coloured streak on the horizon, and the lower edges of the purple clouds are tinged with rose. This is new country, the haunt until recently of Métis, Indian, and fox. Five years ago, Rosthern did not exist. Now the prairie is dotted with homesteads and diapered with fields broken by the plough – a land of hollows and crests, of poplar and willow saplings and the occasional gnarled oak. The scattered buildings tell the story of Western settlement: the original homestead shacks have been turned into henhouses and the first log cabins are used now as granaries. Beside the cabins, more substantial frame, and even brick, dwellings signal the progress of the German and Scandinavian settlers who came here in '96, '97, and '98.

As we approach the great river, the homesteads are scattered farther apart. At some points we can see no sign of human life in any direction. Far out of the north the Blue Hills rise gracefully – a golden saffron in the morning light, striped with white snow and brown belts of timber, intersected by purple ravines. Before us lies the great trench of the North Saskatchewan with the frozen ribbon of the river at its bottom, fringed with birch, elm, and poplar. Here the trail is scarcely more than a rut. Soon it becomes a three-hundred-foot toboggan slide as our team hurtles down into the valley. But two miles away on the far horizon we can spot the Doukhobor village of Terpenie, thirty miles from Rosthern, the object of our visit. It lies at the top of a ravine on the opposite side of the valley, at the end of a well-kept trail leading up from the river. A short time later we arrive.

The village consists of a single street, half as broad again as Winnipeg's Portage Avenue, lined with long, low yellow buildings, gabled and roofed with sod or thatch. The gable ends face the road and are separated from it by neatly railed gardens. Each building is fifty feet

84

long, divided equally – the front half for humans, the rear for animals. The thick mud walls are smooth as plaster; the sods on the roof are laid like shingles; each yard is raked clean of debris.

We enter one of the houses; a single room, fourteen by twenty feet, its floor of hard-packed earth smooth as a tabletop, the walls white-washed. Two windows, each three feet square, are thick with house plants, some brought all the way from Batum.

A large stove and oven dominate one corner. A bench runs round three sides of the room, broadening into a sleeping shelf big enough for entire families. Coloured lithographs adorn the walls. Here in the rolling Saskatchewan prairie, a little corner of Russia has been successfully transplanted.

Terpenie is a prosperous village. In the rear of each house stands a neatly scrubbed granary with an adjoining implement shed stocked with harnesses, ploughs, mowers, and rakes. Most of the people here come from the alpine meadows of Kars, once part of the ancient kingdom of Armenia. The last to arrive in Canada, they are better off than the others, having had funds of their own. They are also more independent, less entranced by religious communism. Yet generalizations are impossible. For even here, where the trend is toward individual ownership, there are those who hew to the old ways and who listen to the words of Tolstoy and Verigin as interpreted by that uncompromising zealot Nicholas Zibarov, who calls himself John the Baptist and who will shortly lead his Sons of God barefoot across the frosty stubble of the prairie on a pilgrimage to nowhere. So powerful is the call that 80 members of this community of 280 will leave these prosperous, comfortable homes to join the multitude crying out for Jesus.

Across the country the general attitude toward the Doukhobors was one of curiosity and good nature. After all, these were a persecuted people, refugees from a tyrannical government, and the sympathy of the general public was with them. The presence also of noblemen like Hilkoff, who had practised what they preached at considerable personal sacrifice, impressed Canadians. In Winnipeg, a delegation of leading citizens had arranged a welcome for the newcomers. In Yorkton, the crowd cheered their arrival, and local women helped with the feeding arrangements. In Toronto, Mary Agnes Fitzgerald, who wrote for the *Globe* as "Lally Bernard," organized a national women's committee to aid the Doukhobors.

Not everybody was so benevolent. Real estate speculators resented the huge blocks of land granted to the sect. Some labour leaders objected to the low wages paid them by the railway companies. Local retail merchants did not like their practice of buying land in communal packages. And there was general opposition among the Conservative party regarding their exemption from military service.

The Opposition press fed these political flames, as it had in the case of the Galicians. Conservative newspapers sneered at the Doukhobors as "Sifton's paupers" and claimed the government was subsidizing indigent immigrants with public funds, an attack that forced Sifton's department to watch every dollar spent by McCreary.

The virulence of some of these attacks was remarkable even for those freewheeling times. To the London *Free Press*, the Doukhobors were "a mass of ancient dunnage from the filthiest regions of Asia." The *Halifax Herald* implied that they were "illiterate, unprogressive, lazy and criminal." The *Ottawa Citizen*, which called them "the most backward and ignorant people in the back concessions of Europe," went so far as to suggest that their initial well-scrubbed appearance aboard the *Lake Huron* had been carefully stage-managed by Sifton's minions: ". . . the horrid suspicion grows . . . that the little entrance was rehearsed . . . it looks just a little bit as if some enterprising person wiped the Doukhobours' noses, put on their Sunday clothes, lined 'em up at the bulwarks, and told them to 'make a joyful noise' when it would do the most good . . . the universal belief that no one ever saw a clean Muscovite gives color to the suspicion regarding such ostentatious cleanliness."

The Doukhobors themselves quickly dispelled such calumny. By 1902 most of the opposition to them had ceased, and it was generally agreed that these strange people were excellent and frugal farmers helping to bring prosperity to the prairies.

And then, that fall, a stunning series of events occurred that would put the Spirit Wrestlers back on the front pages and for the rest of time made the name Doukhobor a synonym for terror, fanaticism, and lunacy.

4

The In all his years on the prairies, Wes Speers had never seen anything like
Sons it, and knew he would never see anything like it again.
of God   He was standing on the open prairie, some thirteen miles north of Yorkton — a tall, rangy figure, Sifton's appointee as colonization agent for the West — waiting for the Doukhobors.

They came upon him slowly like a black cloud, low on the prairie, densely packed, thirty to forty abreast. There were 1,160 in the first group, stretched out for three miles; six miles behind, another group advanced, 730 strong. The procession was headed by an old man with a flowing white beard, chanting and waving his hands. Behind him, two stalwart Russians led a blind man, followed by men bearing stretchers of poplar branches and blankets carrying the sick, and behind them a choir, three hundred strong. The chanting, doleful and sonorous, never stopped, the multitude repeating the verses of the Twenty-second Psalm over and over again: *My God, my God, why hast thou forsaken me?*

The date was October 27, 1902. In the weeks to come, this and similar spectacles would haunt the dreams of Charles Wesley Speers, the quintessential Westerner, the supreme optimist, the genial back-room raconteur. Years of service to the Liberal party had not prepared him for the extraordinary events of this month, but Speers was equal to them. A man of quick decision and awesome efficiency, he had been given the job by Sifton as a political reward; after all, it was Speers who had lent his name to the charade of a nomination meeting in Brandon in 1896, and it was Speers, following the script, who had graciously stepped aside in favour of his future master – but not before delivering a eulogy to the Young Napoleon of the West. This did not mean that Speers was unsuited for the post. His years as a Liberal wheelhorse and organizer had not been wasted; his engaging personality, his natural bonhomie, his physical energy, and his tact had made him a valuable member of the Manitoba Liberal hierarchy. He was, as the saying went, "a good mixer." Now these talents were to be channelled into a different course.

For the next fortnight, Speers would come head to head with the most stubborn, dedicated, and recalcitrant group of fanatics in Western Canada – the splinter group who called themselves the Sons of God. These people seemed intent on killing themselves in the name of the Saviour, not by any sudden action but simply from hunger and exposure on the frostbitten prairie.

The government faced a dilemma: it could not allow the demise of close to nineteen hundred souls; neither could it be seen to thwart the religious aspirations of a devout and inoffensive religious sect. When the Doukhobors come, Speers told his people, treat them with firmness but also with kindness. There must be no violence: after all, they are intent on harming nobody but themselves.

Methodically, the army of men, women, and children advanced on the colonization agent. He knew it was useless to reason with them. They required nothing of him, they said. "We are going to seek Christ," they told him vaguely. Christ, apparently, was somewhere in the southeast, somewhere in the land of the sun, far from the windswept prairie, in a country where the fruit hung thickly on the trees and vegetables were cropped the year round, where it was not necessary to use a single animal for labour, food, or clothing.

The pale prairie afternoon would soon turn to dusk. Speers knew that he must find immediate shelter for these people who believed, with a Gibraltar-like conviction, that God would look after them, feed them, protect them from the elements. Back he rode to Yorkton to arrange for accommodation in the immigration hall, the Orange Hall, an implement warehouse, a pool hall, a grain elevator. Some of the children were crying with hunger. The people were living on dried rose-hips, herbs, leaves, and grasses. The women of Yorkton would have to feed them — if they agreed to be fed.

Speers was saddened by what he had seen. He liked and admired the Doukhobors, knew scores of them personally. Like most of his political friends he was a fervent Methodist (after all, his middle name was Wesley); his father had been a lay preacher in Ontario. It is not too much to say that Wes Speers had an obsession with the destiny of Western Canada. He was one of a growing breed who, watching the West prosper, were convinced that the nation's future lay here in the rich soil of the prairie country, which Speers himself had farmed before this new job stole all his waking hours. Speers's feeling for the West amounted almost to a religion. In his eyes, the Liberal party's God-given duty was to fill the plains with people — stalwart vigorous men, like the Doukhobors, like Speers himself. Now that laudable policy was threatened by the aberrations of a fanatical splinter group.

Speers had picked up the first rumours of trouble at the end of June when he got wind of a report that some of the Doukhobors in the Yorkton area were acting strangely. By August these reports were confirmed. Certain members of the community were freeing all their animals — actually turning their cattle loose on the prairies — burning their sheepskin vests and leather boots, making sandals from plaited binder twine, refusing to eat eggs, butter, or milk, abandoning their horses and hitching themselves as teams, and making no provision for the coming winter by putting up hay for their stock.

What on earth was going on in these seemingly placid, squeaky-clean villages? All that Speers knew was what he was told: some of the

Doukhobors had come to believe that it was a sin to exploit animals in any way. The government corralled the stray beasts – 120 horses, 95 sheep, 285 cattle – and sold them at auction, realizing sixteen thousand dollars for the Doukhobor trust fund. But why this unexpected and eccentric turn of events?

The problem had its roots in the complex mind of Peter Verigin, languishing comfortably in Siberian exile and daydreaming of a pure Tolstoyan society, an ideal world, a paradise on earth – unattainable, no doubt, but pleasant to speculate over – a world in which the sun would always shine, where men would live on fruit and never exploit their animal brethren, where money would not be needed, and metal, the symbol of an industrial society, would be outlawed.

Verigin did not transmit the specifics of his impossible dream to the brethren in Canada; his correspondence was more practical and pro-saic. But he did communicate his ideas in high-flown letters to the idealists at the Purleigh community in Essex, where the expatriate nobleman Tchertkoff, without a by-your-leave, had them printed in a booklet in the Russian language. When, early in 1902, copies finally reached the literate elders of the Doukhobor communities in Canada, they caused a sensation.

For more than fifteen years members of the sect had been without a pope to guide them. They were hungry for leadership, especially by 1902, when the Canadian government began to press upon them demands they could not accept. Canada wanted them to file individual titles to each 160-acre homestead. Now that the land was surveyed, the government was insisting on a resolution of this impasse. In addition, it wanted every Doukhobor to take an oath of allegiance to the state. Now, out of the blue, came an exhortation from the one man who could stand up for them against the same kind of authority that had forced their exodus from Russia.

There was more, surely. There must also have been a longing for the kind of sunny paradise that Verigin dreamed of, where frost never fell, winds did not blow, and prairie white-outs were unknown. The exiled leader had talked of warmth and energy from the sun: "Man employing food raised by an abundance of solar heat, such as, for instance, raspberries, strawberries ... tender fruits, his organism will be formed, as it were, of energy itself. ..."

Slowly, a sect within a sect was forming. Its members called them-selves the Sons of God. Self-appointed apostles began moving through the villages, spreading the new gospel. And when one of the most respected elders, Nicholas Zibarov, a huge bear of a man with a tangled mass of beard and hair, joined the movement and threw away his shoes, more than a quarter of the whole Doukhobor population was prepared to follow wherever he led. If Verigin was the Doukhobor Messiah, Zibarov was his John the Baptist, and that is how he began to refer to himself.

On that night of October 27, the pilgrimage halted three miles north of Yorkton. Men, women, and children huddled together in a poplar bluff without a fire to warm them. The next morning, Wes Speers, who had arranged accommodation, rode out to reason with the leaders. Shortly after, to the astonishment of the townspeople, the entire assembly straggled into the village.

"What is it you want?" one of the Yorkton men asked.

"We are going to a warmer climate where we can live on fruit and will not need to use horses or be under any government," a Doukhobor woman replied, neatly summing up the three main reasons for the pilgrimage.

Speers confronted the leaders and vainly tried to persuade them to go back to their villages. They refused. "We are searching for Christ and will seek till we find him," he was told.

But Speers had no intention of letting the women and children go on. Almost every woman was carrying a child, and their cries of hunger threatened to drown out the endless chanting of the men. With the help of the Mounted Police, the colonization agent herded the resisting women into shelter. Some townspeople arrived with gifts of milk and biscuits, but these were refused, being the products of the labour of animals. When several hungry children tried to seize a biscuit, their mothers removed it, slapped their faces gently, and chided them for eating prohibited food.

With the women under shelter and guarded by three Mounted Policemen and fifteen special constables, the men were free to continue their march. They spent the cold night outside the town, standing up, praying and chanting. The following day they set off once more.

On they went, through Saltcoats, unaccountably throwing away the clothes they had bought in Yorkton, leaving behind a trail of boots, cloaks, and hats. They slept in ditches, lived on grasses and raw potatoes until their faces grew gaunt and their eyes feverish. Yet they still managed to walk twenty miles a day, their feet torn and bleeding from the frost-covered stubble. Six yards in the lead trudged their John the Baptist, Nicholas Zibarov, he of the burning eyes and flowing beard, a man who could neither read nor write but who had memorized great chunks of scripture in the Slavonic tongue. On his followers he exerted an almost magical effect: "The Christ!" he cried. "The Christ! I see him. He is coming to us. There, do you not see him? He is beckoning to us. Follow, follow on, children of the Lord."

Speers, like an ineffectual shepherd, trailed closely behind, trying to get Zibarov and the other leaders to listen to reason. But the answer was always the same: "Jesus will look after us."

On November 6, when the mob reached Shoal Lake, Manitoba, Speers, looking worried, worn, and exhausted, tried again to offer free train transportation home for the pilgrims. Again he was refused. Zibarov, who had walked for four days with scarcely any sleep or food, seemed near collapse. Many of his followers were reluctant to sleep because they feared missing the Messiah when he came. They bought small amounts of dry oatmeal and salt from local merchants along the way, but little else.

They seemed to have no fixed destination in mind. A few collapsed. A handful accepted Speers's offer and returned home. Some listened to the blandishments and entreaties of other Doukhobors who had not joined the Sons of God but had followed behind to reason with their brethren. But when the pilgrimage reached Minnedosa on November 7, there were still 450 hard-core believers, temporarily housed in the town's skating rink, determined to continue on, though none knew quite where.

Speers had no intention of allowing that. The thermometer was dropping and a fine snow was again falling. Two nights before, shivering in a cottonwood bluff, they had slept in six inches of snow. If they kept going, Speers knew, they would all die, and their deaths would be laid at the government's door. His fears were not only political. He was genuinely concerned with the fate of "these misguided people." To him they looked like hunted animals. They must be persuaded to go home – with force, if necessary, but with a minimum of violence.

Out from Ottawa came Frank Pedley, Superintendent of Immigration, a bulky Liberal lawyer and the only man of Sifton's department who was not a Westerner. Pedley was a Newfoundlander who had practised law in Toronto for the best part of a decade before joining the department. Now he and Speers tackled Zibarov and the other leaders in the skating rink. There would be no more leniency, they declared; the Doukhobors must return to their villages.

They made an interesting trio, these three pugnacious, determined men – the tall, stalwart Speers of the rugged features and firm jaw; Pedley, with his formidable moustache and heavy jowls; Zibarov, tall and haggard like an Old Testament prophet, his beard flecked with crumbs of dried oatmeal, his eyes flashing with the fervour of evangelism.

Pedley, the Toronto lawyer, was no match for the eloquent Zibarov. They talked into the night for two hours through interpreters and got nowhere. In a shrewd and impassioned speech Zibarov defied the government forces. He and his followers would go on, he said, even if they froze to death on the prairie. Speers shook his head. They would go back to Yorkton the following day, he told the Doukhobor leader. An impasse had been reached.

All night long, the Sons of God prayed and sang while the townspeople, expecting trouble, waited outside the rink. Early that morning the Doukhobors tried to rush the doors. Four escaped, but the Mounted Police forced the others back. At 4:30 that afternoon, a special train with twenty-three police arrived. At five, with dusk falling and a fine snow blowing, Speers stood up on a box and, through an interpreter, addressed the gathering: "We have shown you a lot of consideration. You must go with us now. Get your wraps and blankets and march."

One of the leaders – probably Zibarov – tried to interrupt. Speers was on him in an instant: "It's men like you that have caused this trouble. If you don't keep quiet, I'll deal with you in a way you won't like. All of you get ready to come."

About 150 followed Speers out of the rink but immediately turned from him and started to head east.

"Head them off. Don't lose a man!" Speers cried, seizing Zibarov by the neck. The Doukhobor leader struggled to free himself, at the same time starting the familiar weird chant, which was taken up by the others.

Speers now called for help, and about fifty of the townspeople answered. The resisting Doukhobors linked arms around each other and were pulled for yards across the frozen ground. A Herculean grain merchant named Arkwright broke the knot, and the squirming, kicking Russians were carried bodily to the waiting train. Zibarov struggled desperately, exhorting his followers to resist. Speers hailed a passing wagon, picked him up bodily, and hurled him into it.

Soon the space between the train and the station was filled with flailing bodies. The entire town turned out to watch the struggle – 150 townsmen against 450 fanatics. The Sons of God refused to strike a blow against their captors. Instead they tried to turn their faces eastward and resume their march. It took forty minutes to pack them into the waiting cars, and then "the bloodless battle of Minnedosa," as the press called it, was over.

That broke the back of the pilgrimage. The women and children had already been taken back to the railhead near their villages. They refused to ride the rest of the way and insisted on walking the full twenty-seven miles. Within two hours of their return they had their furnaces going, vegetable soup on the stove, and were hard at work scrubbing and cleaning their homes.

For the Doukhobors, the pilgrimage left a bitter legacy. It turned public opinion against them just as the original criticism had died down and the country was beginning to applaud their energy and resourcefulness. The opposition press began again to rail against them, rarely bothering to make any distinction between the Sons of God and the majority of the newcomers.

The Conservative party felt itself vindicated for the original attacks on "Sifton's Pets." As the *Montreal Star* said: "At the time they were imported, the Conservatives protested against such indiscriminate immigration, without investigating in a rational way the causes of their leaving Russia . . . but the Liberals have acted like men demented in their frenzy to get certain lands taken up."

One of the underlying reasons for the Sons of God demonstration had been the fear that the sect would shortly be forced out of the communal holding of land and that the government would insist upon individual titles as well as an oath of allegiance to the state. This fear was well founded. The urge to assimilate the Doukhobors – to turn them into carbon copies of Canadians – was just as strong as it was in the case of the Galicians. But the demand for what Zibarov's followers insisted were their "rights" caused widespread irritation, making it even less likely that the Doukhobors would be granted any special consideration.

The *Edmonton Bulletin*, which believed that the difference between the fanatics and the majority was "only a difference of degree not of kind," wrote: "The pilgrimage is the limit. It puts them outside of reasons or excuse. The authorities will not hereafter be justified in dealing with them otherwise than as ordinary citizens." The Doukhobors would get the same treatment as the Mennonites and the Dunkards: "Beyond that, not a step, not a line." These were significant words, for they sprang from the pen of Frank Oliver, who as Sifton's replacement, would within three years have total control over the future of the Spirit Wrestlers.

For the moment, however, the villages were at peace. Exhausted by their long travail, the Sons of God rested quietly, awaiting the imminent arrival of their leader, Verigin, released at last from his Siberian confinement.

Wes Speers, too, was exhausted. After the events of the month just past, he found it almost impossible to sleep. He could not lay his head upon his pillow, he declared, without having frightful dreams of unwashed hordes of the fanatics dancing before his vision.

5

Peter the Lordly

It is a crisp winter afternoon in Winnipeg, three days before Christmas, 1902. We are standing on the CPR platform, waiting impatiently for the eastern train, which is three hours late. A small knot of people has been here since noon and one, a woman, has waited since early morning. The anarchist Herbert Archer is here – that strange graduate from Purleigh who has dedicated his life to the Doukhobor cause and whom Wes Speers believes has had as much to do as anybody in stirring up the fanatics earlier this autumn. Crerar, the immigration agent from Yorkton, is here too. Three Doukhobor elders, an interpreter, and one reporter (from the Free Press, *of course) make up the delegation.*

At last the train hisses in. A crowd of holidayers surges forward to meet another crowd of holidayers pouring from the cars, their luggage stuffed with Christmas parcels. We crane our necks vainly for the object of our long wait. At last we spot him, towering over the throng. He alights from the coach and starts down the platform – a big man, half a head taller than his fellow passengers, with a luxuriant black beard and dark, thoughtful eyes. He is not dressed like the others: under his short gabardine coat we can see leggings, close fitting, dark grey, piped with black. He wears a black fedora, and around his neck, on a long cord, dangle a silver watch and a gold pencil.

The woman rushes toward him, followed by her Doukhobor companions. He drops his black nickel-studded valise, removes his hat, stretches out his arms to embrace her, and cries: "Anna!" She is his sister. He is Peter Verigin. They have not seen each other for fifteen years.

She clings to his arm as he walks quietly on toward the rest of the reception committee. We all repair to the immigration building where the acting commissioner, Moffat, who has replaced the ailing McCreary (now enjoying a well-earned rest as Member of Parliament for Selkirk), greets him warmly.

"You'll be glad to be in a country where there is religious and individual freedom," says Moffat.

"I haven't looked around yet," replies Peter Verigin in his soft voice, "so I cannot yet tell whether this is a free country or not."

Both the Doukhobors and the Immigration Department viewed Verigin as a saviour. The sect was convinced he would stand up for their rights. The government was hopeful he would calm the fanatics before further political damage was done.

The Russians had released him suddenly—no one really knew why—on the understanding that he would go at once to Canada. Even his wife and son, who had loyally waited for him in the Caucasus, were not allowed to see him. He stopped off in Moscow to visit Tolstoy, who, having expected an illiterate peasant, found him much too poised and smooth to fit the stereotype. He visited Tchertkoff at Purleigh in England, then came directly to Canada.

He wanted no ceremony, for he was impatient to be on his way. His first desire was to visit his mother, who lived in a village north of Yorkton. Much to his dismay, he was greeted at the Yorkton station by a crowd of one hundred. Delegates from the various villages shoved and elbowed their way toward him. He cut the reception short, moved on to his mother's village, and there, as his followers chanted psalms of welcome and bowed to the ground, he accepted the homage of his people.

For the next three days, from early morning until late in the evening, Peter Vasilivich Verigin received deputation after deputation from each of the fifty-seven villages. Archer, the anarchist, was impressed. He found him "a man of remarkable intelligence and power [whose]... endurance is remarkable." Verigin talked on and on with the delegates "without any apparent diminution of energy."

They called him Peter the Lordly, and the title fitted. Off he went on a tour of all the villages, seated in a six-horse sleigh, with a choir of maidens chanting psalms. This casual employment of animals as beasts of transport did not go unnoticed. Verigin was conveying a subtle message to the malcontents.

The authorities were delighted by Verigin's immediate assumption of power and his apparently conciliatory attitude. "A great change has taken place in the Doukhobor situation in this district," Corporal Christian Junget of the NWMP reported. "Peter Verigin has succeeded in convincing them of their foolishness. . . ."

Early in January, Verigin met with immigration officials and quickly grasped the problem of the Doukhobor lands. The registration demanded by the government was no more than a formality, he realized. His people could comply with that and still hold property in common. The time might come when the government would demand that each Doukhobor settle and build on the 160-acre homestead to which he technically held title, but that was at least three years away. Verigin had time to plan.

He impressed everybody, including the railroad men with whom he bargained for those of his people who worked for wages. When one contractor offered 25.5 cents a cubic yard for grading, Verigin insisted on 27.5. The contractor told him that was the price the railway paid him; therefore he couldn't make a profit.

"No company will profit by our work," Verigin told him. "I have known all along that you were getting twenty-seven and a half from the railway. Now you can take it or leave it." Workmen were hard to find. The contractor took it.

Speers was delighted by the changes that Verigin wrought. When the Doukhobor leader arrived in Winnipeg with his committee to purchase stock, the colonization agent noted that Nicholas Zibarov was a member and a willing follower: *Zibarov!* the very man who had once advocated giving up the use of animals!

"These people are dressing like ourselves, they have expressed a desire also to conform to our customs, they are observing our holidays, they are accepting our calendar . . ." Speers reported to Ottawa. "Peter Verigin is a man of superior judgement and his influence is very great among the people."

On this occasion Verigin told J. Obed Smith, the new immigration commissioner, that his people were now all Canadians and that spirit marches were a thing of the past.

"Well," Smith retorted, "if you are going to be a Canadian, why don't you wear Canadian clothes and set your people an example?"

Without a word, Verigin headed for the door. When he returned two

96

hours later, he was all but unrecognizable in a tailored suit with a white shirt and turned-down collar, his long hair close-cropped, and his face clean-shaven except for a bristling moustache. He would, he said, give his children Canadian names such as Thomas, John, and William.

Verigin made it a point to visit James Mavor in Toronto. The professor's impression was also favourable. Verigin, he noted, had a shrewd and able mind, understood his people's faults and weaknesses, and was determined to serve them "to the limits of his own powers. . . . He must often have been provoked and discouraged by the bêtises of his people, yet he never revealed to me any impatience of them."

There was reason for provocation, for the community was split into three factions. The well-to-do farmers of the Rosthern Colony were opting, more and more, for independence and free enterprise. The radical Left, especially in the South Colony, nearest Yorkton, were activists who believed that only by overt demonstrations could the sect achieve its ends. In the centre was the great mass of Doukhobors whose main concern was to retain the communal system of central villages where personal possessions were all but unknown. This was Verigin's desire, but he became more and more unsure of achieving it in Saskatchewan.

He travelled about like an Oriental potentate, in a six-horse sleigh in winter and a phaeton in summer, a silk hat on his head, accompanied by the inevitable choir of chanting maidens, with, at his side, a plump, blue-eyed brunette of eighteen, Anastasia Golubova, whom he called his wife. Yet in spite of this pomp, he must have felt his power dwindling. In May, 1903, the first of a series of small but highly visible protest marches began again, engineered by some of the same fanatics who had led the pilgrimage of 1902. These people – there were only about fifty – refused to register their lands and began to travel from village to village urging their fellows to resist temptation, turn their animals loose, and seek the sun. Verigin's fanciful description to Tchertkoff of a sunny Doukhobor utopia had returned to haunt him.

To this latest protest the Freedomites (*Svobodniki*), as they now called themselves, or "Sons of Freedom" as the press nicknamed them, added two new rituals: first nudity, and later arson. The results, for Verigin, were catastrophic. The press was intrigued by men, women, and children who burned their clothes and marched naked on the chill prairie. The authorities stamped out all efforts to photograph the unclad demonstrators; one Saskatoon photographer was fined for taking their pictures and had his plates destroyed, while a luckless

Mounted Police constable who actually posed with a dozen naked Doukhobor women (hoping, he claimed, to jolly them into quitting their demonstration) was given a month in jail.

Why the nudity? The indefatigable Speers, who rode day and night for forty hours to break up the demonstration, asked that question and was told it was part of the Freedomites' religion — that they wanted to go to a warm country and live like Adam and Eve. Yet nudity, which was to dominate the Freedomite demonstrations for decades to come, was a new manifestation. Even though the numbers involved were always small, this and future spectacles received banner headlines in the newspapers. Perhaps that was the Freedomites' purpose. If so, it did not endear the Doukhobors' cause to the Canadian public. Some of the demonstrators went to jail, where they lived on raw potatoes and oatmeal. Others followed on charges of arson. Two were judged insane. One died in prison of malnutrition. And the headlines continued.

The Doukhobors had no political power because, having refused to swear fealty to Canada, they could not become citizens and vote. But the squatters who moved onto unregistered Doukhobor lands, as well as the real estate men, had clout in Ottawa. In 1899 these lands had been unattractive; now, with tens of thousands of settlers moving into the West, the Doukhobors' holdings were positively alluring. As the pressures began to mount, an event occurred that doomed Verigin's last hopes of maintaining a communal Christian brotherhood on the prairies. Sifton resigned and Frank Oliver replaced him as Minister of the Interior.

Backed up by the inevitable commission of investigation, Oliver made his move in 1906. The Doukhobors were to be treated like any other landowners, just as Oliver's editorial had once promised. They must, in short, conform to Canadian customs. There would be no exceptions in the West to the rigid regulations of the Homestead Act: each must obey its stipulations; each must build his house on his free quarter-section and farm it individually. As a result there could be no villages, no common tilling of the soil; houses would be scattered about, four to a section, in the Canadian fashion. If any Doukhobor continued to live in the villages, his land patents would be extinguished. James Mavor was one of the few who protested this violent attempt at assimilation. But the Canadian public didn't care.

Verigin had seen it coming, and Verigin had no intention of submerging his people's religion and lifestyle in an ocean of Canadian

98

conformity. The short haircut, the clean-shaven face, the Western clothes had lulled the authorities into believing that the Doukhobor leader was just like everybody else. He was a far more complicated, determined, and farsighted man than outward appearances suggested. Already he had secured a massive war chest by sending male members of his flock out to earn money working on the railways. With these funds he determined to buy other lands, privately, in another province – in the Kootenay district of British Columbia – and start all over again. For the first and only time a substantial immigrant body rejected the Canadian dream *en bloc* and turned its back on the promised land.

It was an incredible sacrifice. Everything the Doukhobors had slaved for since 1899 was to be abandoned: the neatly ploughed fields, the well-kept villages, the stacks of hay, the lofts bursting with grain. Not everybody agreed with Verigin's decision. Two thousand independent Doukhobors, members of the Rosthern community, took the oath and settled on their individual homesteads. Another thousand in the two colonies north of Yorkton also decided to remain. The rest – more than five thousand – followed their leader to the new province.

Suddenly, in June 1907, a quarter of a million acres of prime farm land, abandoned by the Doukhobors, came onto the market – free homesteads for any man who could fight for a place in the queues forming at the doors of the land offices. This was not raw land. Some of these homesteads, it was said, were worth from three thousand to ten thousand dollars. And so the stage was set for the last great land rush in North America.

In Yorkton and Prince Albert, the scenes of mob violence exceeded in fury any of the demonstrations of the Sons of God. Line-ups formed daily at the land offices as township after township was opened for settlement. In Yorkton over the weekend of June 1 and 2, men waited for forty-five hours in the cold and rain for the office to open on Monday morning at nine. The town itself was crammed with real estate speculators. Hotels were bursting, and out-of-towners paid ten cents a night to sleep in haystacks.

Far more people queued up each night than there were homesteads available. In Prince Albert on Monday, June 3, one group of thirty exhausted and shivering men, bone weary after more than twenty-four hours in line, found themselves muscled from their positions by a fresher party, who crushed them so tightly that some were shoved through the glass panes of the land office. Five policemen helped restore order with fists and batons.

In Yorkton, Mrs. Jessie Harper of Westbourne, a farm woman well over seventy, flung herself repeatedly at the line of men being admitted to the land office until one finally allowed her a place. It turned out she already had a farm worth ten thousand dollars. By the first week in June the police estimated that five hundred strangers, the representatives of real estate men, were in town with orders to break into the queue at any cost. During one night, a group of these entrepreneurs charged the line and struggled with the Mounted Police. "Mob the police! Mob the police!" they cried until the sergeant in charge called out the fire department and turned a hose on them. Even that did not deter the determined. Still dripping wet in the wan light of dawn, they clung stubbornly to their places in the queue.

In this way the reign of Peter the Lordly came to an end on the prairies, with fists and truncheons, cries and catcalls, and the jarring cacophony of human beings in collision — a stark contrast to the soft chanting of the choir of maidens, now only an echo in the empty villages scattered along the verdant valleys of Saskatchewan.

Chapter Four

Isaac Barr's Lambs

1

Barr's   *It is the last day of March, 1903, just before nine in the morning and we*
dream   *are standing at the Liverpool dockside in the midst of a jostling crowd,*
watching the spring sun dappling the waters. Out in the harbour,
waiting for the tide, is the Beaver Line's Lake Manitoba, a Boer War
troopship, built to hold seven hundred souls but now chartered by the
Reverend I.M. Barr to convey 1,960 British men, women, and chil-
dren – "the flower of England," to quote a local paper – to Canada.

There must be at least five thousand people here on the landing
dock, all bidding one another goodbye. Great lorries arrive by the
minute, loaded with luggage labelled "Saint John, N.B." Grandmothers
are crying and praying, for they realize they may never see their
families again. Handkerchiefs flutter, children sniffle, dogs destined
for the passage scuffle and whine. Whole families arrive by carriage to
the cheers of friends and strangers, toting baskets of food, shotguns,
umbrellas, birds in cages. The band of the King's (Liverpool) Regiment,
resplendent in scarlet and gold, strikes up a military air. The crush on
the landing stage becomes unbearable.

What a crowd this is – a cross-section of the British Isles (one
hundred from Scotland, another hundred from Ireland); men from the
coal pits, cotton mills, stores and offices; fifty clergymen's sons, five
offspring of one Irish peer; families from John o' Groats to the Tweed;
Boer War veterans; butchers and bakers and even a few farmers –
although these are in the minority – all turning their backs on Merrie
England to start again in an unknown land. Scores are dressed for the
new world – or for their romantic vision of it – in riding breeches,
puttees, and broad-brimmed Stetsons, with bowie knives at their hips
and pistols at their belts. They are off to the great North West, the
domain of the Red Indians, where they will become gentlemen farmers,
living the countrified life. The Reverend Mr. Barr has assured them
that their neighbours will be others like themselves: no sweaty Slavs,
German dirt farmers, or grubbing Yankees in the all-British colony
west of Battleford – only proper Britons.

At last the little black-and-white tug pushes the liner toward the
dock. Great heaps of baggage bearing brightly coloured Beaver Line
labels are hoisted aboard. The tide waits for no man; there is no time
for slings. Trunks and boxes are hauled onto the deck by hawsers, and

if some break open, spilling their contents into the sea, that is too bad.

Now the gangway is lowered. Two thousand souls rush towards it, eager to start for the land of promise. For a few minutes the crush around us is stifling. Then the band strikes up "Auld Lang Syne" and "Till We Meet Again." Up goes the gangway, and the ship moves out into the harbour stern first. The dock becomes a sea of waving handkerchiefs. We rush with the others toward the prow of the vessel to shout our last goodbyes. With this movement forward, the Lake Manitoba *lurches alarmingly. The captain roars out to the mate: "Get these people topside!" The long, irritating voyage has begun.*

We have all encountered men like the Reverend Isaac Montgomery Barr: dedicated enthusiasts with a missionary's zeal – likeable, earnest, utterly believable. Their credentials seem impeccable, their dreams and visions bold, imaginative, convincing, their enthusiasms infectious. We warm to them, for these are selfless men, disinterested in personal gain, willing to give their all in the interests of the Great Plan. We defend them against their critics and place ourselves with total trust in their hands. Only later does it begin to dawn on us that they are not what they seem, that their dreams are gossamer, their plans impractical, their promises unfulfillable, their abilities wanting, their organization hollow, their dedication suspect. They are charlatans, though they do not know it and cannot admit it, confidence men who have conned themselves. They are the Kings of the Gullible. In the end, the scales fall from the eyes of their followers; but they never fall from their own. They continue on through life, leaping from project to project, convinced after each collapse that they have been sabotaged by sinister forces not of their making. But they themselves are the saboteurs; and the innocent and the naïve suffer for it.

Such a one was the Reverend Mr. Barr, who arrived in England from North America in January, 1902, after a career that can only be described as chequered. A son of the rectory, raised in Hornby, Ontario, he had in his early years served as a Church of England priest in a series of posts – but seldom for long. At both Woodstock and Exeter, Ontario, when he argued over the size of his salary, his parishioners made no real effort to seek his retention. His contract as minister to an Indian reserve at Brantford was terminated for the same reasons. In 1875, he accepted an appointment as missionary in Prince Albert but abandoned that charge after a few weeks on the excuse that his wife and son were both ailing – a defection that irritated the Bishop of

103

Rupert's Land. Back in Ontario, at Teeswater he lost his job after denying the doctrine of the fall of man. He recanted, tried again to get a job in the North West Territories, but did not succeed. The next two decades were spent in the United States, where he held half a dozen posts, the last being in Whatcom County, Washington State. At this point he had been, by his own account, married and divorced three times, a fact that he apparently had been able to hide from the church.

Barr was fifty-three when he arrived in London. His son had died of enteric fever while serving in South Africa, and the senior Barr had "a strong desire to take up my abode again under the old flag which I love so well." He had come to England to arrange for transportation of potential emigrants from Washington State who wanted to become farmers in South Africa after the Boer War ended. The Colonial Office was cool to that scheme, and Barr abandoned it. Instead he applied for a job as Canadian immigration agent in Washington, having "had some successful experience in locating people on land and have for years taken a deep interest in immigration and colonization." These vague credentials did not commend him to William White, the inspector of emigration from the United States, who met Barr in London; nothing more came of it. Instead, Barr embarked on a scheme of his own: the establishment of an all-British colony of emigrants from the Old Country somewhere in the North West Territories of Canada.

Barr had all but abandoned the church, but he received a licence to preach during the summer at St. Saviour's, London, and so was able to wear his clerical collar, a considerable asset, since it put the odour of sanctity on his project. He was a short, thickset man, with a broad moustache and plump, bland features. Although he was blessed with the voice of a bull he could, on first encounter, be soft spoken, courteous, and convincing. As one of his future colonists put it, "You could not help but trust him." But there were serious flaws: a lack of any sense of humour, an inability to accept criticism, a quick Irish temper, an autocratic bent. He was not able to delegate authority, and he had a tendency to gloss over unpalatable truths. Yet he had an imaginative mind, and he certainly had a way with words.

Barr was intoxicated by words, and he knew how to use them to the best advantage. As far as he was concerned, once a plan took shape on paper it was half way to completion. As he scribbled away that spring and summer of 1902, churning out articles for no fewer than thirty-two publications, the grandiose scheme of an all-British colony in the Canadian West began to balloon in his mind. What a coup it would be!

To place hundreds, even *thousands* of stout British yeomen and tradespeople, the finest stock in the world, in a colony all their own! No foreigners – no Slavs or Germans or Swedes, and certainly no Americans – would be allowed to creep in. This would be an Imperial undertaking.

Barr had already built a town in his head, complete with shops, churches, schools, and post office grouped around a central park, with the homesteads of the settlers encircling it for miles. His enthusiasm was infectious. By August, having received two hundred written inquiries and one hundred personal calls, he was ready to produce a small pamphlet outlining his scheme. Building materials would be cheap because they could be purchased wholesale and in quantity. Horses, oxen, cows, implements, and seeds would all be arranged for in advance and available at the new colony for purchase. There might even be co-operative ownership of property and animals. And yes! There would be openings for tradesmen and teachers in the new settlement.

Barr's hyperbole flowered like the daisies of summer. "Agriculture on the prairies is simple," he wrote enthusiastically, "the work not very hard. . . ." He would welcome inquiries: prospective emigrants could write to him or even turn up on his London doorstep in person. He would be home Monday and Wednesday mornings and Saturday afternoons and evenings.

If he could get some kind of official sanction for his scheme the all-British colony would be well on its way. He shot off a draft of the pamphlet to the Canadian immigration office in London, asking for approval and also for a year's contract "at a very moderate salary" as well as an office, expenses, and free transportation to Canada to choose a site for the proposed venture. Most of those who had called him, he claimed, were either practical farmers or the sons of farmers. That was scarcely true, as events were to prove; as for his statement "I know the North well having labored as a missionary at Prince Albert in the North Saskatchewan in 1874," that was totally misleading.

C.F. Just, the deputy commissioner, could not give Barr what he wanted; that was up to his boss, W.T.R. Preston, who was that month in Canada. But Just thought there would be no difficulty getting free transportation from the Beaver Line and the CPR for Barr to visit Canada. In fact, Just was charmed and impressed by Barr. He wrote to Preston that he found him "a masterful kind of man" . . . "quite a 'hustler'" . . . "evidently a very capable fellow."

105

Barr didn't waste a minute. In September, he produced a second, longer pamphlet, which suggested that he was a man with wide farming experience in the Canadian North West and that he had something resembling an official seal of approval from the Canadian Immigration Department:

"Modesty suggests that I should not say anything of myself, but it seems necessary that I should. . . . First, then, before taking action I conferred with the Canadian Emigration Commissioner here in England, and I keep in constant touch with the Emigration Office, although this is a perfectly independent movement. I was born on a large farm in Canada, and learned all branches of agriculture. With me, farming has always been an enthusiasm – I might also say a passion, and I have farmed both in Canada and the United States. I have been interested in Colonization for many years, have done some fairly good work as a colonizer, and am now anxious to build up my native Land, and keep it as much as possible in the hands of people of British birth. . . ."

Nobody in the government bothered to check into Barr's background. No one took the trouble to find out how much time this particular clergyman had spent in the North West. No one bothered to investigate his background as a colonizer. No one looked over the list of applicants for the all-British colony to see how many were bona fide farmers. No one really *wanted* to know. The British took Barr at his face value; how could a cleric of the Established Church treat them dishonestly? As for Preston and Sifton's deputy, James Smart, awaiting the promoter's arrival in Ottawa with Just's enthusiastic recommendations in their hands, Barr provided a heaven-sent opportunity for Clifford Sifton to get the Liberals out from under the blanket of criticism directed at them for bringing in the Galicians and the Doukhobors.

The opposition papers had been in full cry, demanding to know why impecunious Slavs were being imported instead of well-to-do British farmers. It did no good to explain that well-to-do British farmers were perfectly content where they were and that, for the most part, the British who did want to emigrate were artisans, office-workers, and slum dwellers, city people unfit for the rigours of the Canadian prairie. Now here was an imaginative man – a Canadian *and* a man of the cloth – prepared to bring in thousands of Britons, "very generally men of sufficient means," as he put it, men who would not be a burden on the country and who would not water down Canada's sacred Anglo-Saxon heritage.

Events began to take on a velocity of their own. Buoyed up by enthusiastic press comments and an equally enthusiastic response to his pamphlets, Barr was planning to leave for Canada on September 30 (both the Beaver Line and the CPR had come through, as Just predicted). Now, a few days before his departure, he was joined by another enthusiast – a man who could handle the details of his plan during his absence from Britain. This was the Reverend George Exton Lloyd, a tall, cadaverous Church of England cleric who knew a good deal more about the Canadian North West than Barr and who had just returned to England after an absence of two decades. One of the "muscular Christians" so typical of the late Victorian era, Lloyd rejoiced in a background romantic enough to entice the most phlegmatic Briton to the new country.

A born Londoner, Lloyd had gone out to Canada at the age of twenty, a zealous young missionary dazzled by the example of the great David Anderson, first Bishop of Rupert's Land, whose son was vicar in Lloyd's London parish. Lloyd spent his first years in a poverty-stricken backwoods Ontario community. In 1885, while a divinity student at Wycliffe College, Toronto, he rushed to the colours the instant the Saskatchewan rebellion broke out. At the Battle of Cut Knife Hill, with his last cartridge expended and a bullet piercing his side, Lloyd and a fellow Wycliffian* were saved by a last-minute rescue from certain death at the hands of Poundmaker's Crees.

This episode brought Lloyd the chaplaincy of the Queen's Own Rifles and later a position as minister at St. George's Anglican Church, Winnipeg. In 1891 he founded a boys' school near Saint John, N.B. Now, at the age of forty-one, he was back in his native London as assistant secretary to the Colonial and Continental Church Society.

Like Isaac Barr, George Exton Lloyd was a dreamer with Imperialist stars in his eyes. He believed implicitly in the rightness of the Imperial cause, whatever that cause might be (even when it involved killing Boers, Métis, or Matabele), just as he believed in the evils of alcohol or the revealed truth of the Gospels. Upright, tenacious, relatively humourless but dedicated, he was a born leader, a good if dictatorial organizer, and, as it developed, an impractical businessman. He could and did inspire great affection, a quality Barr lacked; he could also drive people to paroxysms of frustration.

---

*Lloyd's companion, Edward Campion Acheson, later became Bishop of Connecticut and fathered Dean Acheson, Harry Truman's Secretary of State.

A confirmed jingoist, Lloyd had penned several letters to the press, decrying the mongrelization of the Canadian West. To *The Times* he wrote: "Might not the English newspapers do more than they are now doing to keep the magnificent area of wheat land in Western Canada thoroughly British by encouraging the emigration of English people to their own territories? . . . It grieved me to see what is now a fine British province being settled so largely by Americans and foreigners. I am not a capitalist, or I would take a few thousand of good British blood to settle upon these fine farming lands – I mean take some of those who are now treading on each other's heels in the old country, scrambling for a living. But why do they not go on their own account? Are they afraid they would be going from civilization to barbarism in a wild unknown land?"

Lloyd had struck a nerve. When he offered to answer any questions that prospective emigrants might have, he was not prepared for the deluge of letters that swamped him. At this point Britain was overcrowded. With the end of the Boer War thousands of veterans had returned home, seeking new horizons. The Victorian Age had reached its zenith, and the urge to bring British ideals to the untamed corners of the globe was inherent in every Englishman. In London, jobs were scarce; firms were failing; vacancies had to be made for sons coming into family businesses; but fewer and fewer vacancies existed. And with trade decreasing, labour was cheap, wages low.

It was not the farmers who looked across the Atlantic but the huddled masses in Shelley's "populous and smoky" cities, who yearned for a return to the pastoral life of pre-industrialized Britain. In the open spaces of Canada, surely, that dream could come true; or so they wanted to believe. Charles Tweedale, one of those who responded to Barr's siren call, wrote that "most of us pictured our homesteads as picturesque parkland with grassy, gently-rolling slopes interspersed by clumps of trees, a sparkling stream or possibly a silvery lake thrown in, the whole estate alive with game of all kinds." But the Canadian North West was not the Cotswolds.

Unable to reply to the flood of mail personally, Lloyd contrived a circular letter answering the forty-two questions most frequently asked and had it printed and mailed to correspondents. A few days later Barr knocked on his door, and the two joined forces. Lloyd and a secretary manned the small office that Barr had set up and began to take applications for the Britannia Colony. Barr himself left on September 30 for Canada.

No one could argue with C.F. Just's description of Isaac Barr as "quite *Quite*
a hustler." He had produced his first pamphlet in mid-August and *a hustler*
rushed out his second in mid-September. By early October he was in
Ottawa and by the end of that month he was one hundred miles west of
Battleford selecting homesteads for his prospective colony. He was
back in Ottawa in mid-November and after a fortnight's discussions
with Sifton's staff returned to England in time to produce a third, more
detailed, pamphlet before Christmas. It was his intention to bring out
a shipload of settlers in early March – not much more than a year after
his original arrival in Great Britain.

James Smart was impressed by Barr and agreed to hold the odd-
numbered homesteads in eight townships until February or later if
Barr sent him a list of prospective emigrants with fees for their
homestead registrations. Barr had also persuaded the CPR to reserve
additional even-numbered homesteads in the same area for sale to the
British. Smart, after meeting Barr, felt that "he is most enthusiastic
and is also very clever and I am inclined to think that he probably
stands a good chance of making a success of his work." Smart, the civil
servant's civil servant, never totally committed himself to anything. He
was invariably "inclined" to an idea, and he sprinkled his correspondence with "probablys."

Others were less enthusiastic. W.J. White, then Acting Superintendent of Immigration, didn't think Barr would be successful. Barr's
"propaganda has assumed such a magnitude and the many schemes he
has in connection with it are so great and multifarious, I am afraid
very little will come of it." Seymour Gourley, a Tory M.P., who
encountered Barr at the Russell House in Ottawa, dismissed him as a
"sharper." T.G. Pearce, a successful colonization entrepreneur who
had brought out three trainloads of immigrants to the North West in
1892, read about Barr's scheme and thought him inexperienced. After
some correspondence with Barr in which he tried to offer suggestions,
he came to the conclusion that Barr was an impractical man who
didn't like criticism. In spite of Smart's controlled enthusiasm, the
government remained cautious. It would not employ Barr, give him
any expenses, or set him up in an office. But the press on both sides of
the Atlantic had been captured by Barr's eloquence. The government
was prepared to give him the benefit of the doubt.

Smart himself became nervous at the speed with which Barr was moving in London. The reverend gentleman was actually talking about bringing his people out early in March! Pearce, the colonizer, had pointed out that when he had brought people to Alberta in April the weather was so bad the women and children all came down with flu. March was a month of storms, the worst possible time to impress prospective settlers. Smart was dismayed. The vision of the Doukhobors' disastrous wintertime arrival was still etched on his memory. He rushed a letter off to Preston, who was back in charge in London, urging him to delay the departure of the colonists to May or June. Preston tried to reason with Barr. The clergyman, who disliked anybody tampering with his plans, grudgingly agreed to postpone the sailing date, but only until the end of March.

Barr had moved so quickly that the government, even if it wanted to, couldn't wash its hands of him. He had arrived in Canada at the height of the Doukhobor troubles, a propitious moment for him. With the Conservatives demanding more Anglo-Celtic immigrants and fewer Slavic paupers, his enthusiastic interviews with the press were exactly what the Liberals needed. To have cut him off would have invited a public outcry.

White, however, was right. Barr had let his fancy run away with him. In his new pamphlet, he proposed a variety of ancillary enterprises: a "Stores Syndicate," which would operate retail outlets at the colony; a hospital syndicate, which would look after the community's health; a transportation syndicate, which would convey the colonists and their effects comfortably from the railhead to the site.

Was Barr in it for the money? "I am not on the make," he declared. Certainly profit was secondary to the Grand Scheme. On the other hand, he did not view the enterprise as philanthropic. He got $1.50 a colonist from the steamship company and commissions also from the CPR for the sale of railway lands, which the company agreed to withhold from the market until the scheme was under way. He also planned a five-dollar charge on homesteads for those prospective settlers who could not come out with the first group but who wanted land reserved for themselves. Under the Homestead Act, that was illegal.

In England, enthusiasm was building as a result of Barr's newest and longest pamphlet, which described his journey to Canada, outlined the areas reserved for the Britannia Colony, and explained that "those who wish to join us must decide at once and deposit passage money." Much of what Barr wrote was sensible and accurate. Some of it, however, was misleading. He managed to give the impression that fruit trees – apple and plum – would grow easily in northern Saskatchewan; that the Canadian Northern Railway would reach the settlement "within a few months"; that timber was easily available because it could be rafted down river from Edmonton; that a good road existed between the railhead and the colony. These were wild exaggerations.

Barr fudged on distances, intimating that a factory for producing sugar from beets was close by when it was actually three hundred miles from the settlement. He agreed that it was "sometimes very cold" but made much of the "invigorating and enjoyable climate" (as, indeed, the government itself did) and the "dry and highly exhilarating atmosphere." He did not say how long the winters were, nor did he give any details on the kind of sod, log, or frame houses the newcomers would have to build. He promised that "at Saskatoon there will be provided horses, waggons, harness and provisions for the journey, also coverings for the waggons, camp stools and other necessary things" and that for the women and children there would be a covered-wagon stage service all the way to Battleford, "where they would be suitably housed and cared for until the men could establish homesteads."

These were paper promises, but they were believed. It was not possible, in England's green and pleasant land, to conceive of a country where a road was nothing more than a rut, a village a huddle of shacks, and a homestead a vast expanse of unbroken turf stretching off to the horizon. Englishmen were knowledgeable enough about settled Canada: cities like Halifax and Saint John, Montreal and Toronto – even Vancouver – were not unfamiliar. These had streetcars, six-storey brick buildings, banks with marble pillars, theatres, even opera houses. Had not Jenny Lind sung in Toronto? Was not Madame Albani a Canadian?

Thousands of Britons knew of Canada from relatives or friends, or knew of somebody who had a relative or friend in Ontario, Quebec, or the Maritime Provinces. The CPR with its palace cars and its burgeoning string of château-style hotels was advertised throughout the country. And Winnipeg! Traveller after traveller wrote of its miraculous growth, of its electric railway, its brick buildings, its block pavement. Winnipeg was the West, wasn't it? Few Britons realized that after Winnipeg, civilization came to a stop; that Canada was split in twain, one half sophisticated, the other as wild and empty as the veld. In a country where it was rarely possible to travel without seeing a cluster of homes, it was difficult to imagine a realm where one's nearest

111

neighbour was a quarter of a mile away. Who in crowded England could conceive of the vast distances west of Winnipeg? No map could convey the emptiness, the loneliness, the desolation. To most of Barr's prospects, the Britannia Colony was just around the corner from the nearest metropolis.

By the end of January, Barr's scheme had, in his words, reached "immense proportions." He could, he told Preston, bring out as many as six thousand settlers in March, but since he couldn't handle that number he was closing off the movement. He would have some two thousand members for the colony; only the previous fall he had contemplated no more than a few hundred. But by this time Preston, too, was disillusioned with Barr; he no longer believed the clergyman had the qualifications to carry through an undertaking of such proportions. In Canada enthusiasm was snowballing to the point where Clifford Sifton realized he would have to step in and take hold to prevent a catastrophe.

Smart was in London in February, still inclined to believe the Barr plan was likely to be a huge success. The pragmatic Sifton was less easily impressed. Barr had sent advance agents from England to the West with instructions to scout out supplies but with no money or authority to buy anything. Several Englishmen, members of the so-called Stores Syndicate, arrived in Winnipeg with grandiose plans to start businesses in the new colony but with scant funds. None had experience, and the leader, in the assessment of Obed Smith, the Commissioner of Immigration at Winnipeg, didn't appear "to be a practical man in any respect." It was quite evident, Smith reported, "that this Stores Syndicate is *non est*."

That was March 10, two weeks before the Barr party was due to leave for Canada. Meanwhile, Charles May, Barr's advance agent, who had been sent to Battleford ostensibly to buy supplies, turned up in Winnipeg and revealed that he had no money to purchase anything. Barr cancelled May's authority and turned the responsibility over to W.S. Bromhead, who sailed from England, arriving in Winnipeg on March 18, to find that he, too, had had his authority cancelled. By March 19, he had been replaced by a third agent, John Robbins, another Church of England clergyman, who had, however, not yet reached Canada. As far as Smith could figure out, Barr up to this point hadn't spent a dollar in Canada.

Sifton's frustration with his deputy in London can be seen in the cables he fired off, day after day, to Smart: *March 14*: "... see Barr and

112

bring him to his senses"; *two days later*: "Barr evidently misleading you." Finally, on March 18, a desperate cable came from Smith in Winnipeg: "Those out here must act now regardless of him. Time too limited for further delay." The sailing date was just one week away.

Sifton now did take personal charge. He wanted two top farm instructors on hand to teach the newcomers practical agriculture. None but "absolutely first class men" would do, and he was prepared to pay top wages of one hundred dollars a month. He wanted at least three land guides on hand to help the newcomers locate their home-steads. He had no faith in Barr's arrangements. Wes Speers would go immediately to Saskatoon to see that marquees, firewood, and fodder were spaced at regular intervals along the trail that led from Saskatoon to Battleford and on to the colony.

Smart, meanwhile, had been vainly trying to push back the sailing date. Getting nowhere with Barr, he wrote to Sir Alfred Jones of the Elder-Dempster shipping company, owners of the Beaver Line, and urged a fortnight's delay. Sir Alfred met him half way. "Slight repairs," he revealed, would justify a delay until perhaps April 1. An angry Barr, who was bombarding his clients with circulars, sent out a special one explaining the delay was not of his making.

But, in spite of all these difficulties, Barr's enthusiasm had not lessened. On March 21, in an interview with *The Times*, he managed to give the impression that all of his projects were thriving. Nor could he leave it at that: "Lumber yards, creameries, mills, grain elevators, schools, post office, a newspaper . . . will be established without delay." It was enough for Barr to say something would be done to make it an accomplished fact in his own mind.

The truth, as reported by Obed Smith from Winnipeg, was bleaker. The Indians could not furnish lumber for the colony until mid-May, when it would be too late. The Battleford contractor charged with providing portable sawmills had refused to do so because Barr's plans were so indefinite. Barr's agent, Robbins, with his limited funds, was making purchases "which were altogether inexcusable from a business point of view." There was no provision for hay or oats at the settle-ment. And finally – the last straw – Barr's brother, Jack, who had gone to Calgary to buy two carloads of broncos for the so-called trans-port service, discovered that one carload had suffocated to death in transit.

Yet even as his house of cards was collapsing in Canada, Barr and two thousand British colonists were on the high seas heading for Saint

John. Somehow this idealistic if incompetent clergyman had managed to pull off a coup. He had slithered around the cautious Canadian bureaucrats, bedazzled two thousand generally unromantic Britishers with his wild vision, shocked the Canadian government into precipitate action, and bamboozled everybody into taking part in an adventure whose outcome was uncertain and, for some, would be horrific.

3

Stormy A young Belfast Irishman stood at the deck rail of the *Lake Manitoba*
passage with three newfound Irish friends, looking down at the waving crowd and, as the ship inched out into the harbour, thinking of the remarkable chain of events that had changed his life.

Ivan Crossley was one of "Barr's lambs," as the colonists would soon call themselves. He was just eighteen years old but not without experience, for he had spent the previous year working on a fruit farm in Florida. Back in Belfast in January he had been kicking up his heels, wondering what to do with himself, thirsting for adventure, planning to seek his fortune somewhere in the Empire – South Africa, perhaps, or Australia.

And then his mother had received a letter from a relative in England, and a pamphlet had dropped out of the envelope describing the wonders of the Canadian West. So Ivan Crossley had written to Isaac Barr and received an enthusiastic letter by return mail and sent in his ten dollars and got his receipt, and here he was with the ship's horn blasting and the band playing "Auld Lang Syne" and the people on the dock waving goodbye with tears in their eyes. Just twenty-four hours before, he remembered with a pang, he had been part of a similar scene before boarding the channel steamer at Belfast, his mother praying and crying and singing "God Be with You Till We Meet Again." But they would not meet again, though Ivan Crossley could not know that at the time. He had said goodbye to her forever.

Farther along the crowded ship's rail, young Robert Holtby felt a lump in his throat as he too realized that he and his family were bidding goodbye to Leeds and that, in all probability, he would not see his school friends again. The thought was too much for him; he could not bear the spectacle, and so turned away and made his way down to one of the holds. When dinner came, the food was so awful he forgot one misery and replaced it with another.

The *Lake Manitoba* was a reconverted troopship from the South African war. According to the British Board of Trade, it was supposed to carry seven hundred passengers, but there were close to two thousand crowded on board. The steerage passengers were divided into sections, each with its own cook: single men in one hold, married couples in others. The more affluent travelled in second-class cabins. There was no first class.

Paul Sylvester Hordern, the thirteen-year-old son of a drygoods merchant from Coalville, Leicestershire, scrambled about with his father looking for their bunks. They finally found themselves in the forward hold with seven hundred others. At first sight, as they made their way downward, the setting seemed shipshape, the walls painted gleaming white. Only later, when the big waves hit and the whitewash peeled off the walls, revealing a layer of manure, did the Horderns realize this had been a cavalry ship.

The holds, dark, smoky, and fetid, had two or three tiers of bunks. A second-class passenger, Stanley Rackham, a younger brother of the famous English illustrator Arthur Rackham, visited one of the holds to locate his vast array of luggage — he was travelling with 350 pounds — and thanked his Maker he didn't have to spend much time below. Rackham had crossed the Atlantic before on an earlier trip to Canada. What would it be like, he thought, when the weather grew rough and the people crammed into these bunks grew seasick? He shuddered to think of it and decided never to go below again.

Almost everybody *was* seasick. Paul Hordern was overcome so suddenly in his upper bunk that he didn't have time to shout a warning below. Fortunately somebody across the way shouted, "Duck!" and the man below jumped aside, reproaching Hordern.

"Why the devil didn't you holler?" he asked.

"How can I with my mouth full?" Hordern replied. There was a six-inch layer of sawdust below his bed to handle such emergencies.

Robert Holtby was so sick he wished somebody would come along and pitch him overboard. When, after a few days, he recovered enough to swallow solid food, he found he could not face eating in the hold, with its smell of soup, potatoes, and sour sawdust and with a foot and a half of bilge water slopping back and forth. He shovelled some food into a plate and went up on deck where he found a hundred people like himself, sniffing the salt air and trying to balance their plates on their knees. And here, when the weather was fine, they could hear the strains of a portable organ and youthful voices piping familiar hymns. *Choirboys?* A close approximation, certainly. For here was Miss

Laura Sisley, a banker's daughter from London, and her charges, a dozen underprivileged boys from the church club she ran in the inner city. She had come into a small fortune on her father's death and was using the funds to bring them all out to the new land, where she hoped to settle them together in their own community near the Barr reserve.

Miss Sisley's organ was a welcome diversion from the sombre side of shipboard life. For now, during this voyage, the disillusionment with Barr began. He was the least diplomatic of men, and by the time the ship reached Saint John he had managed to antagonize a good percentage of the passengers, especially those in steerage. One of these, Harry Pick, may have been exaggerating when he wrote that "it speaks well for British love of law and order to record that only eleven fights, seven incipient mutinies, three riots and twenty-two violent interviews with Barr . . . occurred during the voyage"; nonetheless, it was a stormy passage.

Much of it was Barr's own fault. He had painted the rosiest possible picture; now, faced with reality, his flock turned on him. He did not mix with the passengers as Lloyd did but kept to himself in his cabin. Lloyd gave regular lectures on Canada, complete with question and answer sessions. In his dealings with scores of complaints from passengers he was tactful, clear, and forthright. More and more, as the voyage progressed, they turned to him as their natural leader. It was Lloyd that most of them had seen in London, not Barr. The latter seemed to have an aversion to contact with strangers.

They made an odd pair, the squat, heavy-set Barr and the reed-thin Lloyd with his cadaverous features and his long side-whiskers. Lloyd was leaving England forever. With his wife and five children he would make his home in the new colony that would one day bear his name.

When Barr did meet with the colonists he often lost his temper. Once, in a fury, he fled to the bridge and threatened to turn a firehose on the malcontents. No sea voyage in those days was a pleasant experience, but this vessel was so badly overcrowded that whole groups of families were squeezed together below decks, with little privacy. There were far more passengers than the lifeboats could accommodate, and there was not nearly enough fresh water. The colonists were forced to get along on partially distilled salt water, so brackish it ruined the tea.

The food in steerage was dreadful; but then it always was – the British colonists probably fared better than the Galicians. The difference was that they were not used to it. The potatoes were rotten, the meat tough, the cutlery dirty. There was no butter and no bread, only ship's biscuit. In Ivan Crossley's words, "We didn't die but we damned near starved to death." Crossley and his Irish comrades sat at a long table in steerage; when the steward arrived with a basket of hard-boiled eggs he would roll them down the table, the diners grabbing at them as they whirled by.

Many of the stewards who had signed on for the voyage quit before the ship sailed when they heard the *Lake Manitoba* was carrying immigrants. Barr was forced to hire replacements from among the passengers, but not before some ugly scenes occurred. Lloyd was called to one dining room to settle a fracas between a group of Boer War veterans and a covey of stewards. One of the ex-soldiers had thrown a pot of jam at a diminutive red-faced waiter, and the two were spoiling for a fight.

"Sure, I threw the jam tin at him," the veteran barked. . . .

"What, a little fellow like that?" said Lloyd mildly. "You might at least help him to scrape the jam off."

Without further ado, the soldier complied and the two shook hands.

Barr was the kind of man who always ran from trouble. Driven half crazy by passenger complaints, he shut himself up in his cabin and refused to see anybody. Ivan Crossley and a group of friends went to his cabin and demanded that he come to the dining room to see how bad the food was. Barr agreed, and that night in the hold he stood up on a wooden box and tried to explain that he was doing his best to improve both the meals and the conditions aboard ship. At that point somebody threw a ship's biscuit at him. It was three inches thick and the size of a saucer, and it hit Barr squarely on the nose, knocking him from his box and touching off a mêlée. When the ship's crew finally rescued the hot-tempered clergyman, he retired to his cabin for the rest of the voyage, crying out that his charges were nothing but a bunch of savages.

The Sunday service conducted by Lloyd on April 5, when the ship was twelve hundred miles out of England, provided a contrast to the hurly-burly of the dining rooms. William Hutchison, a twenty-seven-year-old colonist from Southey Green, near Sheffield, thought it the most interesting and impressive service he had ever attended. It was held in one of the holds, with the men sitting on their cots or leaning on the rails of the bunks, smoking their pipes and listening as three violinists accompanied the hymns. Looking about him, Hutchison could not help observing the incongruousness of the surroundings: the gun cases, coats and hats, kit bags hung on nails, boxes, trunks, bundles of rugs and bedding strewn about – an improbable setting for an impromptu evensong.

Few of these men were farmers, in spite of what Barr had told the Canadian government. But then one of Barr's problems was that he was inclined to tell people what they wanted to hear. That flaw lay behind the hyperbole in his pamphlets and the rosy interviews he continued to give to the press. Those few colonists with farming experience were surrounded by a knot of men eager to learn the fundamentals of agriculture. As one remembered: "Very few had the remotest conception of what conditions actually were or what difficulties would have to be overcome, but trusted blindly to our leader and all his promises. . . ."

During the voyage Barr urged his people to pick out their homesteads, sight unseen, from a large map. It would, he said, save time and confusion, and besides, the terrain was so uniform it didn't matter where they settled: every quarter-section was like every other one. This was a bald lie. When one man, a stonemason, asked for a homestead with "enough rocks on it to build a house," Barr cheerfully agreed. "I've got just the thing for you," he said, marking out a quarter-section on the map. But Barr had earlier told Lloyd that "not a stone would be found in the new colony that was bigger than a walnut," a remark that Lloyd had reason, later, to curse.

The *Lake Manitoba* reached Saint John harbour on April 10, 1903. To the passengers' dismay, it could not dock, for this was Good Friday, a sacrosanct holy day. That was not Barr's fault; he had made it clear that the delay in sailing was the Beaver Line's doing.

Now a group got together and raised a purse of three hundred dollars to buy Lloyd a buggy and two ponies, but for Barr there was no gift. The passengers' tempers flared when it was learned that Barr had had eight thousand loaves of bread baked and intended to sell them at double the going price. "The old rogue is trying to make some money out of us," Robert Holtby wrote in his diary.

On Saturday the distraught immigrants found they faced days of waiting while customs officers inspected a mountain of luggage. And what luggage! Few had conceived of a country where vans and lorries did not shuttle back and forth between communities. Barr had promised a transport service; Barr's lambs took him at his word and brought their worldly goods to Canada; one colonist brought a ton of baggage. There were at least half a dozen pianos, heaps of furniture, cases of books. There were bathtubs, jewellery, banjos, bicycles, gramophones, sewing machines. There were vast wardrobes of clothes, including formal wear. There were parrots and canaries in cages, and, these immigrants being English, well over a hundred dogs, all tied up on the afterdeck and howling to be exercised.

At this juncture, Barr vanished; he simply couldn't take the responsibility. Lloyd went directly to the CPR, which was as eager as anyone to get the trains moving, and managed to have the customs inspection waived. The ship docked at 5 a.m. on Easter Sunday. At nine the first of four trains left for the West.

It was not possible to sort out the luggage. Piles of boxes and trunks jammed the freight shed to the point where the owners could not squeeze between them. Everything was trundled onto the baggage cars to be identified later at Saskatoon; that included the blankets the passengers had brought. A pile of blankets purchased for sale by the Stores Syndicate, however, was on the dock. Lloyd proceeded to dole these out to his shivering charges, keeping a careful record of those distributed. Just before the last train left, at midnight, Barr turned up, apparently drunk, and got into a screaming altercation with his partner, implying that Lloyd was stealing the blankets. He even tried to sell some at four dollars apiece but in his fuddled state had difficulty counting the money. Ivan Crossley watched in amusement as Barr tried ineffectually to make change. When Barr gave him back two dollars too much, Crossley returned it. "You're the first honest man I've seen in the community," Barr told him. Typically, Barr did not travel with his charges but left for Saskatoon on the regular CPR train.

The two Horderns, father and son, refused to buy Barr's bread and stocked up instead at local grocery stores, having learned that food was difficult to get aboard the trains. They bought cheese, beans, and canned goods, which they ate cold because the one small stove on each of the crowded colonist cars was in constant use by women brewing tea. The train swayed so badly one night that young Paul, in the top bunk, was thrown directly across the passageway onto two sleeping colonists.

"Where did you come from?" one asked.

"Leicester," said Paul Hordern sleepily.

For once the newspapers, whose reporters greeted the trains at every major stop, had no reservations about the new arrivals. The Americans, still burning with the idealism of the revolution, might make a virtue of welcoming the huddled masses and downtrodden of Europe, but Canadians preferred their own kind. The *Ottawa Citizen*, so vicious in its condemnation of the Galicians and Doukhobors, was delighted that everyone spoke English. The *Globe* found them "a splendid class," the *Winnipeg Tribune* "a fine looking lot, above the average." To the *Manitoba Free Press* they were "strong, manly, clean, well dressed, intelligent." The Toronto *News* pulled out all stops in describing the women of the party: "Rosy-cheeked English farmers' help, sinewy and graceful, and with a glitter of gaiety and intelligence about their eyes, they filed through into the platform yard, to carry with them into the unknown West the destiny of a nation. The hands that rock the West's cradle will be strong enough to rule the world of Canada in a few years."

Sifton's people, determined that there should be no further bad publicity as a result of Barr's dereliction, watched over them like shepherds. In Winnipeg the party was astonished to discover that the immigration offices had been kept open all night to greet them and that Obed Smith was actually at work at four in the morning when one section pulled in. Here, two hundred bachelors left the trains to seek work.

But in spite of the diversions the journey offered – a herd of five thousand antelope crossing the tracks and barring the passage, sportsmen potting gophers, prairie chickens, and rabbits from the train windows – Barr's lambs were uneasy. Stanley Rackham, climbing back onto his car after a tram ride through the streets of Winnipeg, noted a general feeling of unrest among his countrymen. What lay ahead, after Winnipeg? Disquieting rumours began to circulate. At Brandon during a twenty-minute stop Rackham cheered up a little after talking to an old settler who, after describing the hard times he'd had, explained that he'd come through all right and told the colonists they'd do the same if they just stuck to it.

But after Portage and Brandon, the real West began to unfold. The colonists gazed out at the limitless prairie, the coarse brown grass covering the tough sod – flat, treeless, hedgeless. For many, this was their first inkling of the future; at last they began to comprehend the dimensions of the land of promise. Here, in this dun-coloured realm, the villages, mere clusters of log shacks or hovels of corrugated iron, were dumped down as if by chance – not perched on a hillside or nestled in a valley as in England, but stark on the level plain. It was not what they had expected, but then what *had* they expected? Barr had never told them that the Canadian West was a replica of the English countryside; like the Canadian government's own pamphlets, his had ignored that kind of descriptive detail and discoursed instead on the promise of the future. He had let the colonists dream their own dreams, conjure up their own visions. Like all good con men, Barr had allowed them to con themselves.

4

The bulk of the Barr contingent arrived in Saskatoon on the morning *Indig-* of April 17, a steaming hot day with the temperature at 85°F. The *nation* Reverend Dr. Robbins, Barr's agent, was on the platform to greet them *meetings* and to introduce them to a big, broad-shouldered man with a weather-beaten face and a brisk moustache. This was C. W. Speers, veteran of the previous fall's Doukhobor pilgrimage. The colonization agent chose the occasion to indulge in a morale-building address, which Stanley Rackham thought was more than a little flowery. "I have a vision of teeming millions in the great valley to the West where you are going, and you are the forerunners," he cried in his deep voice. "You will not be disappointed. The valley contains the richest land in the Dominion and the Government has provided you with shelter here and will see you safely settled. March westward ho! There are your tents, march!"

The government had not waited for Barr to supply shelter. Speers had arranged for additional bell tents and marquees – a wise precaution, because most of Barr's tents were on the baggage cars, running more than a day behind the main trains.

To the newcomers, used to cosy English villages with ivy-covered cottages, Saskatoon presented an unprepossessing appearance. Young Paul Hordern was bitterly disappointed. He had heard a lot about Saskatoon from Canadians at the various station stops. "Oh, that's some town," they told him. "That's a big town!" But a big town in Canada was not like a big town in the Old Country. There wasn't even a cobblestone on the wet and muddy main street down which Hordern splashed his way.

Saskatoon was scarcely a year old: another huddle of shacks with two small hotels and a few stores, "large boxes rushed up without regard to architecture or comfort," as another colonist commented. A single stone building, the Windsor Hotel, stood out incongruously. A

121

year before, fewer than one hundred people had lived here; now the town harboured six hundred permanent residents and close to two thousand transients. This was the West, raw and new – a few houses clustered around a grain elevator and a railway station, the core of a community no different from scores of others springing up along the line of prairie steel.

But Saskatoon, like so many other Western villages, was on the verge of a boom that would see entire streets constructed in less than three weeks. Now, with tents blossoming everywhere, with cowboys, Mounted Police, Indians, and Englishmen in broad sombreros crowding its single wooden sidewalk, it took on the atmosphere of a carnival.

The new arrivals had other matters on their minds. Those who had paid Barr four dollars for a tent found for the first time that they must pay an extra dollar for shipping costs from Saint John. That Saturday they held the first of a series of indignation meetings. Because Barr had not yet arrived in camp it came to nothing, and so they paid the surcharge reluctantly and scheduled a second meeting for Sunday.

By then the protestors were in another frenzy about their luggage, which finally arrived, jammed into eighteen cars, with nobody to sort it out. Some was still on the train, some lay in heaps dumped alongside the tracks. The protest meeting lasted two hours while Barr, now on hand, pleaded for patience. But he made the mistake of warning the crowd that the Mounted Police would fire on any who tried to rush the baggage cars. From this point on, the wretched clergyman could do nothing right. A brief, wild rush for the baggage cars destroyed the Sunday quiet, blows were struck right and left, and goods captured and retaken, even as other colonists prepared for the morning service.

We are kneeling, this hot April Sunday, among the crush of suppliants beneath the filtered sunlight in Barr's big restaurant marquee, listening to the drone of an Anglican service. Saskatoon has never seen anything like this. A sea of dainty hats meets our eyes as the neatly gloved women in their tailored suits bow their heads. Beside them, their menfolk mumble the responses, sober in broadcloth and tweed with fresh linen, white ties, and neatly polished boots.

The text of the lesson seems appropriate since it deals with the rebellion of the children of Israel against Moses: "Thou hast not brought us into a land flowing with milk and honey, to kill us in the wilderness, except thou makest thyself a prince over us," the curate reads and goes on to describe how the rebellious ones were blasted by fire and swallowed by the earth—a passage not calculated to soothe the rebellious colonists fresh from their altercation with Barr.

Now a cheerful little man, bearded and sunburned, gives us the text for his sermon: "The wilderness and the solitary place shall be glad for them; and the desert shall rejoice and bloom." This is Archdeacon Mackay, veteran of twenty years in the North West, whose diocese includes all the Saskatchewan district. He welcomes his temporary congregation, warns against faint-heartedness, counsels perseverance, talks of the pluck and grit needed to wrest a fortune from Saskatchewan's soil.

The service ends. On go the sombreros, fedoras, and bowlers. There is even a silk hat in evidence. Who but an Englishman would bring a silk hat into the West? We might be walking out into the green and manicured English countryside rather than the yellow prairie.

But this is not England. On the west side of the tracks, one hundred acres of white canvas greet our eyes—close to five hundred bell tents and marquees, a flapping of flags, a labyrinth of pegs and guy ropes over which men and women trip and stumble. The tents are pitched every which way in the elbow of the South Saskatchewan, a river red with mud and barred from access by the gigantic blocks of blue ice thrown up on its banks. Scores are chopping away at these blocks, for they are the only source of fresh water in this overcrowded community.

Others are struggling to erect additional canvas with more energy than craft, for many have never seen a tent before; many more do not know how to use an axe. A group of Boer War veterans helps the former, a handful of townspeople the latter. And so this Lord's Day rolls along, the air alive with the sounds of axe and hammer, of wagons creaking and oxen lowing, children crying, men cursing, dogs yapping.

Then, as dusk falls, an ominous glow lights up the sky. This is not the sunset but a prairie fire, the flames leaping higher and higher as it roars toward the camp. We gape and wonder, for we have not imagined anything like this. Are we, too, to be immolated like the rebellious children of Israel? But the old-timers reassure us: the village road will act as a firebreak. For the moment at least we will be spared the ravages of nature in the great North West.

The colonists were impatient to get moving toward their new home, but Barr was not yet ready. All that week the indignation meetings continued. There was anger over the prices charged for food and equipment, although this was not entirely Barr's fault. He had no

123

control over the merchants of Saskatoon who, hearing tales of the newcomers' enormous wealth, were determined to make a good thing out of them. Again Barr showed he could not face criticism. He tried to evade a mass meeting but was forced to attend by the indomitable Wes Speers. Here he was assailed on all sides. Why was he now trying to charge the colonists a guinea each for the privilege of joining the party? Why was he trying to take money from late arrivals for holding their homesteads for them? Why was he charging young girls ten dollars each for future homesteads? Why was he taking a commission from the leading Saskatoon merchants? Barr made little attempt to be conciliatory. He told the meeting it was nobody's business, flung out of the tent, returned to the platform, cried out that he wasn't making a cent of profit, and called one man a liar. These outbursts increased the pandemonium. Some wanted to toss Barr into the river, others to kick him out of the camp.

Not all the colonists attended these meetings and not all were equally incensed with Barr. Some of the malcontents were tenderfeet, unused to rough conditions, who tended to magnify the smallest troubles and were seeking a convenient scapegoat. Barr was an easy target. It is doubtful that he made much money out of his project. On the other hand, there is more than a little evidence to show that he tried. Some of the Saskatoon merchants showed a *Toronto Star* reporter letters from Barr demanding a 10-per-cent commission on goods sold to the colonists. Barr himself admitted as much. Much was made of the fact that he bought up all the oats in town for 40 cents a bushel and sold them for a dollar when the going rate was only 23½ cents. The Calgary *Herald* published a comparison of Barr's charges for horses, livestock, wagons, and equipment with those in the *Canadian Handbook* and found Barr was getting between 20 per cent and 100 per cent more than the established rate.

On the other hand, J.A. Donaghy, a student missionary with the party, thought the colonists' troubles were often of their own making, pointing out that when Barr put up a team of horses for sale, rival purchasers bid up the prices unnecessarily. Lloyd's statement the following year that Barr suffered from inordinate greed and "wanted to make a dollar out of everything he sold them" was undoubtedly coloured by Lloyd's bitter enmity toward his erstwhile partner.

Barr himself made little effort to come to terms with his critics. On Thursday, 140 colonists petitioned James Clinkskill, the Member of the North West Legislative Assembly for the district, to discuss the

124

situation. The meeting was held in the Barr restaurant tent with the government's permission, the government having supplied the tents. But Barr would have none of it. He shook his fist in Clinkskill's face, called him an "infamous scoundrel," told him that the meeting was being held for political purposes, and ordered him off the premises. The meeting broke up.

> Barr, Barr, wily old Barr [the colonists sang]
> He'll do you as much as he can.
> You bet he will collar
> Your very last dollar
> In the valley of the Sask-atchewan.

In the midst of this "constant turmoil and excitement" (Speers's words), two things were being made abundantly clear to the government agent: first, that most of the colonists had no farming expertise, and second, that many did not have enough money to run a homestead. Something would have to be done or the Liberal government would end up with a political black eye. Having received no co-operation from the leader, who warned him to "kindly leave my people alone," Speers took matters into his own hands and called another meeting to determine who was destitute, who required more funds to continue, who needed work to earn more. Close to fourteen hundred people turned out. Two hundred men, Speers discovered, had less than ten pounds left apiece. He went to work immediately, setting up an employment bureau which secured jobs for 135 in Moose Jaw and 50 more in Prince Albert. He placed the remainder with local surveying parties. For the others he arranged practical talks on farming from government instructors.

The major Canadian newspapers by this time had reporters in Saskatoon. The correspondents were astonished by the naïveté of some of the colonists. Thus, the Toronto *News* reported: "Women who spend their time in dressing and kissing ugly little pug dogs talk of going out to earn money the first year by working in the cornfields, quite blind to the fact that there can be no 'cornfields' there until they sow the first crop in 1904. A pork packing factory is projected while, as a Westerner points out, there isn't a hog nearer the colony than Battleford."

J.J. Dodds, a Western farmer in charge of the government horses, was scathing in his criticism. Not one man in twenty, he discovered, knew how to hitch a team; Canadian schoolboys could learn the work faster.

125

Paul Hordern was convinced that the number of bona fide farmers could be counted on the fingers of one hand. The Horderns were preparing to quit Barr. A few days after arriving in Saskatoon they packed their goods and located on a homestead near Dundurn, south of Saskatoon. Mrs. Hordern, who was handling the drygoods store back home in Coalville, sold the business in 1904 and brought the rest of the family out to join her son and husband. Half a century later, when Saskatchewan celebrated its fiftieth jubilee, Paul Sylvester Hordern was still in Dundurn to join in the festivities. He died in Saskatoon in 1983 in his ninety-fifth year.

But not all were as practical as these. The government and, indeed, the country were beginning to wake to the fact that Barr's rosy promises about stout English yeomen were so much eyewash.

It is Tuesday, April 21, 1903. Wes Speers is working in his tent, planning his employment agency, when a thirty-five-year-old Englishman enters, obviously in distress. Behind him comes his wife, slender and dark-eyed, cuddling a tiny fox terrier in her arms. Speers recognizes her at once, for she has been the talk of the camp, gambolling about, caressing her dog, crooning to it as she would to a child. She is a romantic, sees herself as a brave pioneer's wife, a heroine helping her husband to ultimate fortune.

Her husband is not so sanguine. He has sunk his money in Barr's stores syndicate. If he buys a yoke of oxen, a wagon, and a breaking plough he will have no more than seven pounds to his name.

"I cannot live on seven pounds for a year and a half," he tells Speers. "What am I going to do for food, for a house, for barns and horses?"

"Why, hire yourself out to Mr. Barr to break sod," says Speers. "Mr. Barr says he will give you three dollars an acre for the work."

"But I cannot break sod, dontchaknow. I never did it before."

"You can learn."

"And where will I live?"

"Build a sod house."

"What's that?"

"A house of sod, built in a ravineside."

"I don't think I could possibly do it."

"Yes, you could. Go ahead and buy your oxen and take your stuff out there. Make some money carrying another man's goods along with you."

"Whom shall I get to drive these oxen?"

126

"Drive 'em yourself!"

The Englishman looks dumbfounded.

"Come on down tomorrow and we'll pick out your cattle for you,"
says Speers.

She will be kind to the oxen, the wife says. They will be like
household pets. She will feed them bread and butter.

Did she say bread and butter? Yes, she did! A reporter for the
Toronto Star *who has been viewing the scene scribbles the words in his*
notebook.

Speers suppresses a smile. His mind goes back to the day when he
chased a yoke of oxen up a furrow with a cordwood stick.

"You'll have enough to do to feed yourself bread and butter," he
snorts.

"And we shall have some delightful little piggies," she burbles. "I
shall go out and bustle in the harvest field with my dear husband."

It is all too much for Wes Speers.

"Go and buy those oxen and your plough," he says shortly. "And go
ahead if you haven't got a loaf of bread left. The Government of this
country isn't going to let anybody starve."

In the hurly-burly of the great tent city, as each family bought its
equipment and its animals and prepared for the long trek to Battleford
and the Britannia Colony, a few bizarre incidents stood out. Here were
a dozen women cooking for their husbands, and all wearing gloves.
Here was a six-foot Englishman bathing a fox terrier in a dishpan.
Here was one wretched woman, half drunk, rescued from the open
prairie by the Mounted Police, rushing through the camp shrieking
that Indians had been trying to abduct her.

There was more: a crush of three hundred crammed into the tent
post office waiting for mail; when it arrived, there were just forty-three
letters. . .an Englishman spotted invading the male preserve of the
local bar and calling, vainly, for an "arf an' arf". . .and another, struggling with an ox, striking it in a sudden fury, then begging the animal's
pardon, saying he didn't mean it.

By Friday the first of the colonists were ready to move out. The news
was not propitious. Barr's transport service had collapsed. There
would be no wagon stages for the women and children. Charles May,
Barr's former agent at Battleford, admitting the failure of advance
arrangements, had quit and was taking up a homestead of his own.
And Barr's pioneer party, sent out to prepare the new site, had

returned in disarray, its members having lost their way on the prairie, lost their transport cattle in the muskegs, and starved for three days before reaching civilization.

5

Trekking to Britannia Barr's original scheme had called for convoys of twenty or thirty wagons to cover the two-hundred-mile distance between Saskatoon and the new colony, with the women and children travelling separately. Now the colonists were forced to strike out individually, without guides or freighters. Each had to find his own way, work out his own salvation in slough or muskeg, and care for his family at nightfall.

Many would be driving horses and oxen for the first time. Some had pocket charts showing that part of the animal's anatomy where the harness should be attached. Others actually used marking chalk to sketch diagrams directly on the horses' hides.

Most colonists spent the best part of a week searching out and bargaining for animals, wagons, harnesses, farm equipment, and supplies. The first party managed to get away on April 23, but the last stragglers didn't set off until May 5. Thus, for the best part of a month,

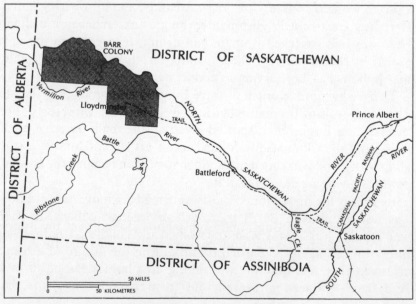

The Trail to the Barr Colony

the trail that led to Battleford and then westward to the Britannia Colony was dotted with wagons.

Stanley Rackham planned to leave on the twenty-third but found the wagon he had chosen had been sold to someone else. By then no more wagons were to be had, and Rackham had to wait until the CPR freight arrived with more. He got away at ten o'clock the following morning, a blistering hot day, found his oxen very soft after an idle winter, indulged in a long rest at noon (as much for the animals as himself), and by four was stuck fast in a bog. A Russian immigrant turned up and helped haul him out.

Rackham's experience was repeated again and again that Friday. Even before they found themselves out of sight of Saskatoon, a dozen wagons were mired. Matthew Snow, one of the experienced farm instructors hired by Sifton, helped pull them out. But this was only the beginning. Barr's "road" wasn't anything more than a deeply rutted trail through the scrub timber made by the Red River carts of the Métis freighters, bringing in furs from Battleford. The entire country in spring was a heaving bog, dotted by sloughs, little streams, and ponds left by the rapidly melting snow.

William Hutchison of Sheffield, whom we last met attending Lloyd's church service on the *Lake Manitoba*, took the advice of old-timers and delayed his departure until prices came down and the ground was firmer. A day's delay in Saskatoon, he was told, would mean a gain of two days on the trek. As a result, he and his brother Ted reached Battleford without mishap in a fast five days. Just five miles out of Saskatoon he came upon four teams of oxen, all stuck fast in the mud, exhausted from trying to pull themselves out and now, having given up the struggle, "looking around with wistful eyes for something to eat." A local farmer took time off from his spring seeding to pull them out. Hutchison's own ordeal was yet to come.

The colonists had been warned not to carry more than a thousand pounds per wagon; a team of oxen could manage no more. But cart after cart was overloaded — a ton, a ton and a half, even, on occasion, two tons. Some looked like gigantic Christmas trees, hung with lamps, kitchen chairs, oil cans, baby buggies, plough handles, bags, parcels, tools, women's hats, dogs, and even pianos. Jolted over the uneven terrain, flour sacks burst and coal oil spilled into the foodstuffs. Because of the heavy loads, the women and children could not ride and were forced to walk the entire distance. A bitter wind sprang up; half an inch of ice formed on the ponds; after the heat of early April, it was the worst spring weather in the memory of the oldest freighters. The women trudged numbly onward; the children cried with the cold.

Wagon after wagon sank to its axles in the white alkali mud of the bogs and sloughs. When that happened, the entire load had to be taken off while the drivers, wading through the gumbo, found a dry spot. Then the team was rehitched to the rear axle and the wagon hauled out with a logging chain. These frustrating delays gobbled up the best part of a day. There were other problems: the horses, up to their knees in mud, would often lie down and die in the swamps. Many more succumbed from lack of feed and overwork at the hands of men who had never handled a team. One freighter counted eighteen dead horses on the trail to Battleford. As J.A. Donaghy, the student missionary, put it, "some never seemed to realize how much a horse must eat to live, and the whole country was full of the finest pasture along the trail. It was painful to see horses staggering under the weight of the harness until they dropped." There was at least one runaway a day. Some settlers were so fearful of losing their horses that they tied them to trees, but with such a short rope that they could not graze properly and so starved slowly to death.

Barr's plan to have marquees with fresh baked bread and newly butchered meat all along the route had also collapsed. Now Sifton's foresight in arranging for large tents at regular intervals saved a great deal of misery. The early birds crowded into these marquees, wolfing tea and porridge, the main provender on the trail. Latecomers had to unload and pitch their own tents nearby.

It was spring in England, but here in this drab land, blue patches of old snow could still be seen in the bluffs of naked poplars. The settlers grew homesick. Robert Holtby, trudging along, mile after mile in the drenching rain — twenty-five miles a day behind the family's wagon — thought nostalgically of the cricket field at home, green as emerald. Stanley Rackham stared at the brown grass, bleached by the frost, and at the gaunt, lifeless trees, and realized that it was May Day back home; into his mind came a familiar vision of primroses, violets, and cowslips surrounding the japonica-covered cottages in his native Mayfield.

Yet spring was on its way, a fact made terribly clear by the water gurgling down the slopes and coulées and into the swelling sloughs that barred the route. For latecomers, there were purple anemones poking out of the grasses and in June the sweet perfume of briar rose in the night air. Frogs chorused after dark and wildfowl burst from the willow groves. The crack shots feasted on rabbit, duck, and prairie chicken.

Suddenly, in the heart of this wilderness — rolling brown hills, white alkali, scrub willow — an astonishing spectacle greeted the trekkers. William Hutchison could scarcely believe his eyes: here, surrounded by furrowed fields, was a Russian village, the houses of trim logs, carefully plastered, neatly arranged along a wide street, their verandahs all gaily painted. This was a Doukhobor settlement, and here the travellers rested. The hospitable Slavs took the women and children into their homes and fed them on fresh eggs and butter.

Hutchison came upon a party of children walking two by two to Sunday School. In their brightly coloured dresses they looked like a living rainbow, and he was reminded, not without a tremor of nostalgia, of a children's ballet at a Christmas pantomime. He and his brother were impressed by the Doukhobors' progress: solid buildings and barns, droves of fat cattle, piles of equipment. If these people could make it, so could they! Before they left they took careful note of what they had seen, storing it in their minds for the day when they might benefit from the lesson.

Not far ahead lay the dreaded Eagle Creek ravine. Here was a vast chasm, five miles from rim to rim, with a raging torrent at the bottom, and sides that seemed to be as steep as the wall of a house. Robert Holtby, gazing at it in awe, thought it must have been torn up by a gigantic earthquake. Down this dizzy incline ran the semblance of a track at an angle so steep it seemed impossible to negotiate. Few wagons had brakes. Some tenderfeet actually hobbled their oxen before attempting the descent. As a result, the careering wagons rammed into the rumps of the terrified beasts, overturning the whole and scattering the contents on the slope. The more experienced drivers locked their rear wheels with chains and stood by with long poles to sprag the front wheels should the wagon get away.

The upward ascent was equally dismaying. Some wagons required four horses or three teams of oxen to haul the heavy loads up to the rim. Here Holtby and his family came upon a pitiable sight: a horse had struggled to the top only to drop dead of exhaustion, the ants and hawks already transforming the cadaver into a skeleton. By the time the family reached the government tent at ten that night, Robert was so tired he could scarcely finish his tea, but the incessant squalling of young children kept him awake.

At last Battleford, the midway point on the trail, came into view. Here, in this historic community, the colonists got a glimpse of the old West, of fur traders and Indians, now vanishing before the new invasion. Here were the Mounted Police barracks, white and trim, the

Hudson's Bay post with its pink roof, and the native school across the river. The little community, untouched until now by successive immigrant waves, sat on the flat tableland between the North Saskatchewan and Battle rivers. A government marquee was already in place; the overflow was quartered in the nearby agricultural hall. Some of the colonists did not venture farther, preparing to homestead in the neighbourhood. The others caught their breath, reorganized their loads, and pressed onward to the colony, nearly one hundred miles distant.

Now they entered wilder, emptier country, the haunt of Indians and animals. Forty miles out of Battleford lay the farm of Peter Paynter, an ex-Mounted Policeman. From that point west there was no white settlement (save for the new colony) for three hundred miles – only undulating hills, little lakes, scrub willow, prairie grass, and pea vine.

Barr reached Battleford on May 2, the day a large contingent of colonists took off for Britannia, one hundred miles to the west. He spent four days in Battleford, harried constantly by indignant colonists, many of whom flew into a violent rage at the mere mention of his name. Barr was now perceived as a dictator who wanted the absolute right to assign each man a homestead and compel him to accept it. Few now believed his shipboard assurance that all the land was of equal fertility. That was clearly fantasy. Some was flat, some rolling; some was wooded, some bald; some was fertile, some stony. Barr had insisted that all settlers wait until he personally reached Britannia to dole out homesteads. But R.F. Chisholm, the Dominion Lands Agent, told them to ignore Barr, move on to the settlement, contact George Langley, his sub-agent there, and choose their own land. Barr was furious. "If there is bloodshed and destruction of the colony as a result I throw the whole blame on you," he shouted. Chisholm told Barr he had no authority to tell anybody where to settle.

On May 6 the embattled clergyman, accompanied by Lloyd and travelling light, left for Britannia, and reached it on May 9. But Lloyd, dismayed by the number of his charges returning to Battleford in disgust, began working back along the trail to encourage the trekkers and trying to dissuade them from quitting the project and going home to England.

These people were bitterly disappointed. They had reached the colony ahead of Barr and found nothing except three large marquees, two of them government tents, the other occupied by Barr's Stores Syndicate. There were no buildings and not a stick of lumber to be had. Contrary to his promises, Barr had made no arrangements to

132

supply doors and sashes and float them down the Saskatchewan. There was no post office; the mail had been dumped on the floor of the Stores tent. And the prices Barr's advance party was charging were so prohibitive that many packed up and left. They had bought oats from Peter Paynter at a quarter of the Barr price.

For the hundreds of outfits strung out along the dreadful trail between Battleford and Britannia, the Paynter farm, which employed a dozen hands, was an oasis. Here were herds of horses and cattle, flocks of turkeys, grunts of pigs. The Holtby family stayed at Paynter's for two days to give an exhausted horse time to rest. Mrs. Paynter, whose kitchen was full of women and children warming themselves, let Mrs. Holtby use her oven to bake bread while the men put up the tents.

Ahead lay devastation. Fires had charred the land, leaving a wilderness of ruin, a monotony of blackness. No sliver of green could be seen through the ashen world that greeted those travellers who had the good fortune to escape the flames. Some lost everything – tents, wagons, horses, supplies – everything but their lives.

We have stopped with the Tweedale party beside a shallow slough several days out of Battleford. It is the second week of May. Hot weather and strong winds have turned the prairie grass to tinder. A heavy pall of smoke has blotted out the sun and is driving toward us; it has been growing in intensity all day, and now we find ourselves choking and gasping in the fumes.

There is no time to be lost. We drive the team and wagon into a foot of water, unhitch the oxen, tie them securely to the wheels, cover their heads with wet sacks, soak the wagon's canvas covering, and then build a backfire to create a guard, beating it out at the edges with a spade.

Dusk falls before we finish our task. Now the horizon ahead is rimmed with flame – a great flickering line moving towards us. The air is thick with smoke and sparks; birds go shrieking past; gophers, rabbits, even antelopes dash by in panic. Now the fire is almost upon us. We wade into the slough, covering our heads with wet sacks as it reaches us, roaring and crackling. The heat is so intense we can scarcely breathe. Our oxen bellow and tear at the ropes. In minutes the fire has raced past us and on to the far horizon, but we must wait until the blackened grass has cooled and the smoke died down before we can remove our covering and crawl out of the slough.

In the eerie light of the retreating flames we can view the havoc the fire has caused — mile upon mile of charred, smouldering prairie. Next day we travel through an ocean of ash. There is scarcely any feed left for the oxen, only a few patches of dead grass left behind in the fire's mad haste. Emaciated horses lie dead on the trail as we pass, starved for lack of fodder. And all because a carefree settler — one of Barr's lambs — did not have the sense to extinguish his campfire.

In this glum terrain, the sloughs and bogs were the worst the colonists had yet encountered in spite of the hot weather. The Hutchison brothers, who had managed to avoid every swamp on the trail from Saskatoon, were stuck fast on three occasions. With their wagon mired to the axles and tilted on its side in the muddy bank of a small torrent, they were struck by a blizzard that blocked their passage for four days. In all that time the brothers were never dry, their clothing, greatcoats, and blankets drenched and encrusted with mud. From Saturday night to the following Thursday they lived on starvation rations: a plate of boiled rice and one pancake made from flour, water, and snow per meal. When they were able at last to push forward at a leaden pace, very little else was moving. They passed scores of tents pitched in the snow beside the trail, their occupants depressed and sick, many of them trying to sell their ploughs and equipment to earn enough to pay their passage home.

At the settlement, Barr was the focus of every complaint. Ivan Crossley watched while one group demanded to know what had happened to all the fresh meat he'd promised. Barr seized an axe and knocked down one of his own oxen. "There's fresh meat for you all now!" he cried. "Help yourselves." And they did.

Barr left the colony on May 13, taking with him the three nurses brought out for the abortive hospital syndicate. On May 15 he was back in Battleford, where he encountered more angry demonstrations. Two Boer War veterans lit into him over their purchase from him of CPR land in the colony. The railway's Battleford agent had no record of the transaction; the homesteads in question had already been sold. Barr blustered, but when threatened with violence he gave them their money back.

It was obvious to all that he *had* been on the make. He had not only tried to sell supplies at exorbitant prices and collect money for CPR land without authorization, he had also charged absentee Englishmen five dollars apiece to reserve their homesteads; he had extracted ten dollars from single girls in England, promising to settle them later; he had tried to collect a premium of five dollars or more from every settler; and he had taken another five dollars from each member of a hospital syndicate that he knew was collapsing.

It was the end for Isaac Barr. On May 16 in Battleford, a mass meeting took away any control he had left and appointed Lloyd in his place as head of a twelve-man committee, quickly dubbed the Twelve Apostles. Barr, in a final moment of bluster, shouted that they were all ruffians and brandished a revolver. Then he meekly gave in, surrendered his accounts, resigned all claims to a homestead for himself, and turned over everything of value to the community which, all agreed, would be named Lloydminster.

Barr returned to the settlement, where he spent most of his time returning money to those indignant colonists who felt they'd been cheated. He left forever in mid-June, narrowly escaped being pelted by eggs by some of his former charges in Regina, and tried in Ottawa to get the bonus the government paid to all colonizers. The department turned him down on the grounds that he had not only caused it more expense than the total payments would allow but had also tried to squeeze money illegally from the British settlers.

That was the end, in Canada, of Isaac Barr. He married his secretary (his fourth wife, thirty-five years his junior), became an American citizen, and for the rest of his life dreamed unfulfilled dreams of settling people in the far corners of the Empire. He died in Australia in his ninetieth year, still scribbling away in the endpapers of a book he was reading, building more paper communities in non-existent promised lands.

Chapter Five

The Problem of the English

1
No Englishmen need apply

2
Remittance men

3
Lloydminster

4
The odyssey of Ella Sykes

5
Don't come back, Dad

1

No Englishmen need apply When the Liberals took office in 1896, it was generally agreed in the West that the ideal immigrant was a white Anglo-Celt with farming experience, preferably English or Scottish. Outside of Quebec, the people of Central and Eastern Canada thought of themselves as British first and Canadian second. Few took issue with the common cant that Britain was not only the greatest nation on earth but also the greatest nation that had ever *been* on earth. The British were colonizers and civilizers. They were "just like us." With the British there could be no future problem of assimilation; how could there be, in a British colony? Only the presence of large numbers of English farmers would prevent the destruction of the national fabric. As Dr. George Landerkin declared in the Senate in 1903: "Take the Englishman and place him where you will, he is equal to the immigrant from the United States and superior to the immigrant from any other nation in the world."

No wonder then that Sifton's department strained every effort to attract English and Scottish farmers. By 1897 immigration agents in the United Kingdom were delivering a thousand lectures a year in small farming communities in England and Scotland. One agent reported that he had held meetings in one hundred small towns, attended fifteen summer fairs, visited farmers, blacksmiths, and cartwrights in seventy-three communities, and turned up at twenty-one hiring fairs, distributing pamphlets, guidebooks, and reports and giving lantern-slide lectures.

Posters proclaiming the wonders of Canada were on the walls of every English post office. The CPR and other steamship companies advertised Canada in the newspapers and with posters and pamphlets. English reporters were invited to visit Canada. And those English farmers who had emigrated earlier were induced to send back testimonials and newspaper articles to convince others to come over.

Yet few came over. In its campaign to pull Englishmen off their farms, the department found itself up against a stone wall. There was no mystery about the English farmers' refusal to emigrate; they had no need to. They were well off in the Old Country and becoming better off every year. Because they were a diminishing class, their profits were constantly increasing. By April 1899, Sifton had despaired of attracting British or Scottish farm labourers to Canada and was quietly turning his attention to the American midwest.

138

For it was farmers Sifton wanted: not the clerks, the shopkeepers, or even the artisans who were emigrating to the United States in quantity. The country, however, was up in arms. Why was the government bringing in Galicians and Doukhobors instead of British farmers? A note of panic crept into the press reports when the United States was mentioned: with its polyglot immigrant masses, it was seen as a mongrel nation. Why on earth would any Englishman want to go there in preference to a British colony? Was Canada purposely rejecting the English in favour of a less desirable immigrant mix, to become (in the words of the *Canadian* magazine) "as rude, as uncultured, as fickle, as heterogeneous, as careless of law and order and good citizenship as the United States?"

This attitude, fostered by the Conservative press, explains the genuine enthusiasm with which Barr's immigration scheme was greeted and also the letdown that followed when it was realized that few of his charges were farmers. Nor did the extreme newspaper examples of the colonists' foolishness and stubbornness help the stereotype of the typical Englishman as a comic figure and a snob that was beginning to form in Western minds. After 1903, the year of the Barr onslaught, demands for increased emigration from the United Kingdom began to abate, and Canadians adopted a curious kind of doublethink where the English were concerned: at a distance they were admired, even venerated, but on a personal level they came to be cordially disliked.

Basil Stewart, an Englishman who worked in railway construction camps and later as an assistant engineer on the Grand Trunk Pacific, wrote how shocked his countrymen were "to be told that, in a country which flies the same flag, the Englishman is held of less account than the lowest type of immigrant from Europe." Even the despised Galicians, Stewart found, were preferred on the land to his fellow countrymen. In Winnipeg, a man applying for a job with the Associated Charities was kicked right out of the office when it was learned he was English.

The words "No Englishmen Need Apply" attached to newspaper advertisements became a kind of slogan in the West. One advertiser, Stewart reported, explained that he excluded the English "because those who were capable were too good for the work and would soon throw it up and go elsewhere to better themselves; the others would too soon give in." Stewart thought the explanation "a little 'thin'" but recognized that it was a symptom of Canadian disgust with the English that couldn't be ignored.

139

If the English were blind to Canadian conditions, Canadians were equally myopic about England – Shakespeare's jewel-like nation supposedly populated by the finest stock in the world – and about the English. It was not easy to separate the myth from the reality because the myth was part of the cultural baggage of most native-born Canadians. They were beguiled by the image of the gallant Englishman – upstanding, courageous, adaptable – planting the standard of justice and freedom in the soil of less cultivated nations, civilizing the world from Mombasa to Hong Kong, harvesting coffee in Kenya, tea in Ceylon, sugar in Jamaica, coconuts in Fiji, cocoa on the Gold Coast. Then why not wheat in the Canadian West? (But it was not English farmers who planted the rice or tapped the rubber trees; they left that to the natives.)

Settled Canada owed a debt to the English. With the French and the Scots they had founded and formed the Canadian nation. In Ontario, where British soldiers had twice saved the country from the Americans, theirs was the dominant bloodline. Schoolchildren memorized the names of all the British monarchs, and all the English heroes from Hereward the Wake to Cecil Rhodes. Indeed, as much English history as Canadian – perhaps more – was taught in the schools, while American history was ignored. The Union Jack formed the frontispiece of more than one elementary reader, with the accompanying Imperial slogan, "One flag, one fleet, one throne." Every map proudly showed the world bespattered with Imperial red.

What had gone wrong? Why didn't the English who arrived in Canada live up to their Kiplingesque billing? Surely they were not, *could* not be, typical! The general feeling in Canada was that somehow the country was getting the wrong *kind* of Englishman, that somewhere in that land of neat hedgerows and country lanes there existed a different breed: stalwart yeomen, the very backbone of Empire. Was there an English plot to jettison the ne'er-do-well younger sons of the gentry, the lazy, snobbish aristocrats, and the unreliable clerks and office workers by shipping them off to Canada?

Worse yet, was Canada being used as a wastebin for convicts and paupers, the offscourings of the London slums? Suspicion deepened in 1905 when charitable societies in Britain began to pay passage to Canada for an increasing number of English while others were subsidized by public funds under the Unemployed Workmen's Act of that year. In one case, it was revealed, the master at a workhouse received twelve shillings for every inmate he sent to Canada. By 1908, when 70

140

per cent of all deportations from Canada turned out to be British, the government enacted an order-in-council refusing entry to anyone whose way had been paid by a charitable organization it had not officially approved.

The belief that Great Britain was dumping her undesirables in Canada is inherent in J.S. Woodsworth's book *Strangers within Our Gates*. Woodsworth told the story of an English magistrate reprimanding a youthful criminal: "'You have broken your mother's heart, you have brought down your father's gray hairs in sorrow to the grave. You are a disgrace to your country. Why don't you go to Canada?'" "England," Woodsworth declared, "has sent us largely the failures of the cities."

In his book, the same man who was to occupy the pinnacle of the pantheon of socialist saints showed a harsh pragmatism: "We sympathize with these poor people, but we are glad the Canadian government is taking steps to prevent the 'dumping' of these unfortunates in Canada." He was equally firm in his opposition to the emigration of Dr. Barnardo's destitute children. "Children from such surroundings with *inherited tendencies to evil* [my italics] are a very doubtful acquisition to Canada."

But it was not the slum dwellers who couldn't adjust to life in Canada. It was the middle and upper classes who, Woodsworth believed, stubbornly refused to adapt to Canadian conditions and suffered from "a certain arrogant superiority and exclusiveness." The English were seen as snobs who criticized everything in the West because it wasn't like the Old Country. In 1905, the London *Standard*'s reporter, H.R. Whates, covering the immigration boom, was bluntly told: "The Englishman is too cocksure; he is too conceited, he thinks he knows everything and he won't try to learn our ways." Almost every English writer who visited the West during that period found the same thing. The Scots, and to a lesser extent the Irish and Welsh, were welcome. The English were not. Basil Stewart's advice, arrived at after he worked on the railway, was that prospective immigrants should keep their opinions to themselves, never tender advice unless asked, and try to show a willingness to learn.

But the English – or some of them – did not find it easy. Seduced by the roseate literature of the steamship companies and the immigration agents, they expected too much of Canada. English girls were told they could get wages of twenty dollars a month as domestic servants. Clerks were told they could get good positions in stores and factories.

Prospective labourers were enticed with tales of forty-dollar-a-month wages on Western farms at all seasons. None of these promises held much water. As a result, many English men and women were disillusioned and openly scornful of their adopted country.

They felt themselves entitled to better treatment; after all, they had been brought up that way. Every newspaper, every book, every hour of schooling had drilled it into them: the English were superior, the colonists were inferior. These people brought the English class system with them, or tried to. Reporters who visited the Barr tent town in Saskatoon were taken aback to discover that even under those conditions the English had separated themselves into distinctive groups based on class.

Everybody had talked of the need for assimilation and the ease with which the English could melt into the Canadian ethnic landscape. Now it dawned on Canadians that the Englishman was no more assimilable than the Galician, perhaps even less so, given his native stubbornness and his general air of superiority. This should have come as no surprise, since for all of the Victorian era English colonists from Kenya to Kashmir had refused to conform to local customs and to learn local idioms, preferring instead to create a little bit of Old England, walled off from native contamination in the jungles, velds, and coral strands of Empire. In short, they *weren't* all that different from Kipling's empire builders who had worn wing collars in the South Pacific and kept clear of the natives in Poona and Shanghai. Now the Canadians were being treated as wogs and fuzzy-wuzzies, and they didn't like it.

It was only natural that they should retaliate by scoffing at the Englishman, turning him into a comic figure. The "green Englishman," the remittance man, the aristocratic snob, caricatured and satirized from Montreal to Calgary (by Arthur Racey, the cartoonist of the *Montreal Star*, for instance, or Bob Edwards in the Calgary *Eye Opener*) contributed to the stereotype. There was some truth in it. In Britain, paperback manuals, endorsed by colonial outfitters who had an interest in selling outlandish gear to emigrants, pictured Canada as a foreign nation full of wild animals and wilder Indians; some emigrants fell for it and arrived armed to the teeth, to the amusement of the natives. Other would-be farmers contributed to the folklore of the country with incredible gaffes.

"Some Englishmen who come out are terribly green," one homesteader wrote home in 1907. "Did I tell you the story about one living

THE ENGLISHMAN IN CANADA.

Clarence, the Younger Son and Dead Game Sport of the de Brown Jones Family, Decides to Go to Canada. His Parents Sorrowfully Give Their Consent.

143

THE ENGLISHMAN IN CANADA — 2

He Straightway Secures a Number of Canadian "Souvenir" and "Guide" Books Compiled by Authors With More Imagination Than Patriotism.

144

not far from us who thought that bran was very good food for cattle, so he bought three bags of it and SOWED it in the ground; he also SOWED three bags of oatmeal, so as to grow his own porridge. This is not romance, for it actually happened."

In spite of this calumny there is strong reason to believe that the stereotype of the immigrant Englishman as a snob and a greenhorn was highly exaggerated, in much the same way that the stereotype of the Galician as a dirty, lazy subhuman bore little relation to reality. Between the two census years of 1901 and 1911, more than 150,000 English immigrants made their homes in the West. The largest number settled in Manitoba, where the anti-English feeling was strongest. Could it be that, in Canadian eyes, their crime was the same as that of the Galicians and Doukhobors? Like them, the English resisted the pressure to assimilate, to conform, to become "real Canadians." For they too were strangers; they too were "different": they dressed funny and they talked funny and, like so many others who came to the West in those years, they refused to reject the roots of the culture in which they had been nurtured. The extremists among them clung desperately to the old ways; the wonder is that so many others adapted themselves to the new.

2

In the summer of 1905, two young Welshmen, Evan Davies and David James, newly arrived in Canada, were strolling down the main street of Winnipeg, disconsolate because they could find no work, when they fell into conversation with a young Englishman. His name was Jack Ball. He was just twenty-four, tall and thin, fair of complexion, and wearing, of all things, a pince-nez. The eyeglasses made him stand out in the crowd, made him seem a little more distinguished. "I swear that only an Englishman would dare emigrate in such a thing," is the way Evan Davies put it. *Remittance men*

They were glad to know him, for on board the boat the other English had tended to treat the Welshmen as foreigners. Ball was well educated and likeable. In London, he'd been a civil servant. Fed up with the sedentary life, he'd emigrated to Canada two years before, had worked on a farm at Estevan, and had now decided to homestead for himself. After he'd explained to his two new friends the method of obtaining free land, the trio decided to throw in their lot together.

145

Off they went to Saskatoon, endured the crush at the counter of the land office and, with the amiable Jack Ball's initiative, found a teamster to take them to their homestead — a stony patch of prairie so unlike the green and hilly country they had imagined before leaving Wales. They were the first settlers in the township, and the loneliness, "so grim, so terrifying," brought the three together. They built their sod house, fought prairie fires, broke turf to the plough. Evan Davies's young brother joined them, and all four became close friends as well as partners.

Yet there was a gap between the three Welshmen and Jack Ball that had nothing to do with racial differences. "We had one thing against him — he was a *remittance man*." In his memoirs, Davies italicized the epithet as he might had Jack Ball been a homosexual or a convicted felon. "He regularly received money from his mother. She sent it to him in a parcel, which usually included books . . . and a ball of wool. That was all. The ball of wool was the important item, for inside the wool Jack invariably found a fiver. It is difficult to explain why we should have held this gift against him. I suppose we felt that, because of it, he was not obliged to struggle for his living as we were. The anxiety, which bred a determination to see it through, was one stage removed from him by comparison with the rest of us. In spite of his amiable qualities, we never quite felt he was one of us."

The interesting thing about this account is that Jack Ball wasn't really a remittance man. He did not — *could* not — live on the pittance his mother sent him. Moreover, unlike the stereotyped remittance man, he was a worker, not a wastrel. Yet so strong was the feeling against the English remittance man in the Canadian West that even this young farmer, receiving an occasional fiver from the Old Country, could not escape the stigma. There were many like him.

The remittance man is part of the enduring mythology of the Canadian West, a kind of human artifact, as significant as the Red River cart or the sod house. There were remittance men in most British colonies at the century's turn — the name was coined in Australia — but in Canada, more than in any other country, the spectacle of the English black sheep eking out the final days of each month with borrowed funds until his remittance arrives from home forms part of the folklore of every committed Westerner.

He was a figure of fun and also of scorn, in the words of the *Manitoba Free Press* "a useless incumbrance [*sic*] to the country not to be mentioned in the same class with the average Galician or Doukhobour, whom he no doubt regards as inconceivably inferior. . . ."

146

The remittance men gravitated naturally to the ranching country of Alberta. "Ranching" had a glamorous upper-class ring; "farming" did not. Here the remittance men could be seen in the lounges and bars of the hotels, clad in riding breeches and Norfolk jackets and wearing round, soft felt hats with enormous brims. These were the superfluous sons of well-to-do English families who, in the words of an English reporter, had "neither the capacity nor the will to make for themselves acceptable careers in the Old Country."

Bob Edwards, the irrepressible editor of the Calgary *Eye Opener*, took a sardonic pleasure in skewering the remittance men. For this purpose he invented a character, Albert Buzzard-Cholmondoley, whose letters home were a popular feature in Edwards's weekly. Albert was seen each week contriving another ingenious trick to squeeze money out of his father in England:

"I am married to a half breed and have three ornery looking copper colored brats. We are all coming over to visit you at Christmas when you will be having the usual big house party at Shootingham Hall. I shall so like to see the dear old place again and my wife is most anxious to become acquainted with her darling husband's people and obtain a glimpse of English society. The Hall will be quite a change for her from the log shacks and tepees she has been used to all her life.

"If I had only about a thousand pounds just now with which to start afresh, I would invest it all in cattle right away, settle down to business and forego the pleasure of a trip home and remain here. But I do not know where to lay my hands on that amount. . . ."

Edwards's satire was not so farfetched. The West abounded in stories of how English ne'er-do-wells schemed to squeeze extra funds out of their families back home. For instance, there was the tale of Dickie Bright, grandson of the scientist for whom Bright's disease was named, who squandered his entire remittance on riotous living in Calgary instead of investing in a ranch and livestock as his father supposed. Bright kept sending home florid stories of the profits his ranch was making until he received an alarming dispatch that his father was on his way to Canada to visit him. In desperation, it was said, he persuaded a neighbouring rancher to lend him a thousand head of cattle for a single night. When the elder Bright arrived, his son assured him that the visible stock was only a sample of the thousands he had roaming the range. Bright senior was so delighted he gave his son $10,000 to increase his business and boasted of how the boy had built up one of the biggest stock ranches in the Canadian West.

It is hard today to understand the antipathy and scorn reserved for the English remittance man. It can be explained only by reference to the Western work ethic, the Western concept of a classless society, and the Western rejection of Imperial and colonial attitudes.

The Westerner was already beginning to think of himself as a new breed of Canadian, freed of Eastern prejudices and concepts, breathing the pure air of the prairies where every man was equal and success depended on hard work. The West was peopled by self-made men who had started from nothing and prospered. They had little time for those who, born to privilege, lived on a stipend, refused honest toil, and looked down on their fellows. As one English traveller discovered, "There is only one class on the plains, and that is the working class."

Hard work was the criterion by which newcomers were judged in the West. Time and again, British writers advised their readers that they must be prepared for backbreaking toil during their early years in the new land. But the remittance man was not capable of work – or at least that was his image – and it was this that raised the hackles of editors like Bob Edwards:

"Were he good at even ONE thing he would be all right. His dilettante training precludes all idea of his getting a job in a store or in a bank – he does not know even enough for that. With machinery or mechanics he naturally is unfamiliar, only knows live stock from the saddle of an Irish hunter, couldn't hold a job in a newspaper office longer than ten or fifteen minutes, has not had sufficient savvy to go breaking on the railroad, is too gentlemanly to canvass books and finally has to seek aid from the local English clergyman as a preliminary to going on to a farm to work for his board.

"What can you expect from young men brought up in a hunting and shooting atmosphere?"

These cultured but improvident Englishmen often lived in abject poverty. Frank G. Roe, who came to Alberta in 1904, worked on the railways, and eventually became a distinguished Western historian, visited two remittance men – one the son of a mayor of Crewe, the English railway town, the other of a distinguished officer of the Indian Army – who had "sunk to an unimaginable depth of squalor and filth, physical and moral." They lived in a shack built of pieces of stolen scrap lumber, roofed with a jumble of shingles, pieces of tarpaper, and kerosene cans hammered flat. It looked, Roe said, like a great square packing case dumped on the prairie, "truly . . . a thing of shreds and patches," unswept and filthy with coal dust.

Yet many hid their penury behind a masquerade of sartorial bravado. Some kept wardrobes of formal clothes and dressed for dinner; others hired tailcoats for an evening and were photographed with their cronies, the pictures to be sent home to England as "a few friends I entertained at the ranch recently." Roe remembered men who could not ride anything "but the most docile sheep of a horse" who ventured into town on a wagon, parked it on the outskirts, then donned Stetsons, chaps, and neckerchiefs "to camouflage the degrading contamination of wheels and harness."

The calumny heaped upon the remittance men belongs to another era. These eccentric hangers-on formed a tiny minority in the great mass of British immigrants, but, like the Sons of Freedom, they were highly visible. As such they became convenient targets, the focus for much of the anti-British antipathy in Canada, their reputation blown up out of all proportion to their numbers. Many an innocent Englishman, genuinely seeking work, suffered from the stigma.

In retrospect it's hard to view the remittance man without a certain affection as a colourful footnote to the saga of the opening of the West. For the remittance man, more than any other, refused to conform. In the great scramble to adapt to the Western style and the Western spirit, he stood apart. It is difficult not to admire the eccentricities, the ingenuity, and the panache of a man like Robert Dixon, who lived near Edmonton as Rattlesnake Pete, who did indeed carry a live rattlesnake, defanged, inside his shirt, who dressed the part sometimes in buckskin jacket, chaps, and moccasins, sometimes in derby hat, checked suit, and spats, whose cuffs were prominently and fashionably displayed two inches below the edges of his sleeves, and who, when prospecting in the bush, insisted on fashioning an instant set of them each morning out of toilet paper. He was nothing if not dramatic. When faced with a girl who refused his advances in a canoe, he knew just how to conduct himself. Without a moment's hesitation, Rattlesnake Pete the remittance man flung himself into the chilly waters of Cocking Lake.

3

All the qualities of the British in general and the English in particular – *Lloyd-* their amateurism, their clannishness, their endurance and stick-to- *minster* itiveness – can be seen in the microcosm of Lloydminster's formative years. For Lloydminster was unique; it was the only colony in the West that was 100 per cent British—its leadership entirely English, its outlook Imperial. Lloydminster and the Britannia Colony started out with every disadvantage: an incompetent and dilatory leadership; an utter lack of practical farming methods among its people; a refusal and an inability to learn from other immigrants. And yet, in the end, Lloydminster prospered. There were many reasons: the richness of the Saskatchewan Valley; the coming of the Canadian Northern Railway; the general growing prosperity of the Canadian West. But not the least of these reasons was the peculiarly English habit of being able to hang on and muddle through.

In exchanging the leadership of Isaac Barr for that of the Reverend Mr. George Exton Lloyd and his twelve-man committee, the colonists weren't out of the woods. Lloyd was a likeable but hopelessly incompetent leader and businessman. George Langley, the land agent, called the Twelve Apostles "one of the most incapable bodies of men ever got together." Donaghy described Lloyd as "the blind leading the blind." Speers reported an absence of all business methods among Lloyd and his council. The hospital plan collapsed; the Stores Syndicate went out of business, paying its investors twenty-five cents on the dollar. Free enterprise replaced co-operative effort. Power went to Lloyd's head, and like Barr, he became autocratic. The Mounted Police inspector at the settlement thought he would have made a Grand Inquisitor in an earlier age.

One problem was Lloyd's jingoism. He and his committee insisted that nobody other than Englishmen be allowed to locate in the colony, a policy originally established by Barr, who had declared: "We hope to keep the colony free from any foreign admixture, even of American people. . . . I think it not wise to mix that people with this colony. I hope to keep it British in actuality as well as in sentiment." As a result, the English tenderfeet had no practical farmers from Iowa or Nebraska as neighbours to help them by example and advice but only novices like themselves. The colony's doctor, who had stayed behind when the hospital syndicate folded, found that his work was constant but pretty monotonous. His biggest daily chore was stitching up axe wounds. Scores of colonists had never before had an axe or hatchet in their hands.

This lack of experience and of knowledgeable neighbours held up the development of the colony for at least a year and caused untold hardships. Langley reported that the buildings being erected on the new homesteads were some of the poorest in the North West. Some were almost useless, and many were so badly built there was danger of the roofs collapsing.

To comprehend the magnitude of the problem facing these green arrivals, let us go out onto the empty prairie with Ivan Crossley and see what he and his three friends were up against.

The land agent has brought them here, located the survey posts, and left them standing beside their wagon on their new homestead — 640 acres of unbroken prairie some twelve miles southeast of the colony.

It is a lonely scene — not a sign of human habitation, nothing as far as the eye can see, save for the prairie, blackened by fire, and a few skeletal copses of charred cottonwoods.

The scene is not unique. It has already been repeated thousands of times in the open country that lies between the Red River and the Rockies. It will be repeated thousands of times more before the plains are broken and fenced. And it will remain engraved on Ivan Crossley's memory for all of his life, as well as on the memories of thousands of others — British, American, German, Scandinavian, Slav, and Dutch. None will ever forget these first despairing moments on the limitless ocean of the prairie. This is home. This is where we must live. This hard turf on which we stand, as tough as human gristle, will be our building material. Before we can prosper, before we plant a single grain, we must attack it, break it, turn it over, rip it apart, and finally nurture the black soil beneath. This is the folk memory of the West, the glue of prairie nationalism.

Crossley knows that some of their compatriots, faced with the magnitude of the challenge, have already packed up and fled. He and his partners are almost broke; but they are unencumbered by wives and children, and they have the enthusiasm and energy of youth. They pitch their tent, unload their walking plough, and go to work.

They have a sketchy idea of how to build a sod house, thanks to the government's farm instruction in Saskatoon. So they set to work ploughing long strips of various lengths and dragging them to the site on a stone boat built of fire-killed trees. They learn by trial and error. Their house is to be sixteen feet by twelve. They simply mark out a space, lay a row of sods around it, and continue to build until the walls are eight feet high.

There will be no windows; glass is unobtainable. But they make a door out of split poles and cover it with blankets. They fashion a roof of sorts out of small poplar poles, laid close together and shaped to

*shed the rain. They pile more sods on top of the poles and chink them
with earth. That will have to do, even though it is not watertight; no
sod house is. There is a saying in the West that if it rains three days
outside, it rains for two weeks inside. They must get used to that.*

*They install their stove, build bunks out of more poles, make
mattresses of branches. It would, as Crossley says, take a lot of
imagination to call this hovel a house. But it will be their only shelter in
the winter to come, and before many weeks have crept by they will
start to think of it as home.*

It was one thing to throw up a house of sorts, quite another to begin
practical farming. Crossley and his friends tried to plant a garden in
the bare spot where the sods had been stripped away, only to discover,
too late, that they had also removed the best soil. The vegetables
withered and died, and the men were forced to go to work for wages.

Scores left the colony to seek jobs. Scores more would have gone
had Lloyd and his committee not persuaded them to stay, promising
jobs in the town itself; alas, these never materialized. Others sat on
their homesteads, attempting to break the land, with little success.

Matthew Snow, the government farm inspector, had great difficulty
getting the colonists to move quickly to break the land and prepare it
for the following year's crops. The breaking season was quickly passing,
yet 70 per cent had no chance of getting a crop in the following year, let
alone in the summer of 1903. Teams stood idle, some animals straying
away because their owners were so lackadaisical. They did not seem to
realize that the prairie could be broken only in the summer. Many
thought, in their ignorance, that they could work late into the fall, after
their houses were finished.

In fact, these middle-class Englishmen from Leeds and Birmingham,
London and Manchester had no comprehension of the harshness of
the prairie climate. They had never experienced a Western winter,
never faced a blizzard or a white-out, never felt their eyelids freeze
together or their skin peel off when pressed against icy metal. The
Slavs and Scandinavians, the Nebraskans and Iowans were used to
such conditions. The English weren't. By fall it was apparent that the
average amount of farmland broken to the plough, let alone planted,
was less than two acres a homestead.

That winter, in the course of a snowshoe patrol, Sgt. D.J. McCarthy
of the Mounted Police happened upon a curious spectacle some miles
southeast of the community. Here was one of the Barr colonists,

crouching in his shack with the door partially open, sitting close to his stove, wearing all his outer clothing including his cap and mitts, and calmly reading Shakespeare. The door would not close because he had pushed a long tree from the outside into the door of his stove. When the fire died down he simply pushed the tree farther in. He seemed quite cheerful, invited the policeman in for "a spot of tea," and revealed that he was the son of the former British ambassador to Turkey.

In sharp contrast was the example of those who *had* farming experience. These people prospered. By July 22, for instance, William Rendell, whose family had farmed in England for two centuries, managed to break and plant three acres of oats, an acre and a half of barley, another acre and a half of potatoes, and a quarter-acre of vegetables. His family bungalow, the largest in the settlement, was within two weeks of completion, even though Rendell had to haul the lumber thirty miles. But Rendell was one of the few who knew his business. He had refused the homestead Barr offered, chosen another one, and started to plough the day after he arrived. That winter his wife, Alice, wrote her friends in England an enthusiastic letter: "I would never advise anyone to come out here who is afraid of work. They are better off at home. There is room to breathe in this country and if the work is hard the freedom, which is the indispensable attribute of the life here, makes one far less susceptible to physical fatigue. . . . Here, one feels that each week's work is a step forward, whilst in the old country oftentimes a year's hard work brought nothing but disappointment. . . ."

The Rendells were in a minority. Less than 10 per cent of the community had farming experience. By October, Wes Speers was concerned at the prospect of serious hardship and destitution that winter. He called a meeting to try to discover who would require government aid but was hampered by the pride and reserve of the English. As one woman told him: "I will not become the object of charity."

Speers was appalled at the conditions among some of the destitute families. The worst example was that of J.G. Bulmer, whose ailing wife was the mother of eighteen children, one no more than three weeks old. While Speers was visiting the family, she fainted dead away. Bulmer had a fine piece of land, but he hadn't broken a foot of ground. Speers packed the entire family off to Battleford.

An equally pathetic case was that of Alexander Carlyle-Bell, who

153

had somehow dropped his wallet, stuffed with two hundred dollars in cash, on the prairie, and then lost an endorsed bank draft for five hundred dollars. The wretched Carlyle-Bell could do nothing right. He had managed to break seven acres on a quarter-section of land only to discover it was the *wrong* quarter-section. The last straw came when his wife fell off the wagon and broke her arm. "Unaccustomed to work," Speers wrote against his name, and that was the last the colony saw of the Carlyle-Bells.

E. W. Thomson, a special correspondent for the Boston *Transcript*, visited the settlement in November and reported on it as he might a strange colony in the wilds of Africa. The inability of the colonists to prepare for the Canadian winter both dismayed and charmed him: "It is impossible not to like their curious, dauntless demeanour. Going about among them one is strongly affected by their spirit. He half believes all will come right in the end – that once again the English will 'muddle through.'"

And so they did. Somehow they made it through the winter. Some of the men had taken jobs during the cold weather, not always successfully. One group, which took a contract to grade twenty-five miles of the Canadian Northern roadbed, had managed to complete no more than two miles by April.

Speers was frustrated at the evidence of the settlers' ineptitude. Very little of their land was yet broken by June, 1904, three-quarters of their horses were dead of exposure, and the rest were spavined and mangy. He was by this time fed up with Lloyd and his town-bred committee, who thought in urban rather than rural terms. Speers was convinced that Lloyd and his council were wasting the colonists' time at planting season with endless meetings, organizations, and subcommittees, all planning in the most optimistic fashion for a glorious future – discussing taxes, lot sizes, and all the petty details of municipal organization, "troubling about small things that should give them no concern . . . trying to build up a commerce without cultivating their good lands. . . ."

The rugged Speers – practical farmer, apostle of the West, committed Liberal – had his patience sorely tried that winter. Like all Canadians he had welcomed the idea of British immigration, a politically popular strengthening of the Protestant Anglo-Celtic mix that had, in his view, built Canada. But now these people, in their own way, were proving as maddening as the Doukhobors. What were these English doing organizing musical societies, tennis clubs, theatrical enterprises, and literary

154

circles in the town when they ought to be out in the fields, building up their quarter-sections? In Speers's view, pioneers could not afford such indulgence. What these people lacked, he thought, was not culture but common sense.

And yet they were beginning to prosper. The impossible cases had been weeded out; those left behind were learning slowly, by trial and error, to meet the demands of the Canadian prairie. In 1905, the colonists broke more land than they had during the two previous years combined, though many, in Speers's opinion, were "sticking too closely to Lloydminster, listening to the dreams and prophetic forecasts of the leaders of the community." But by November, with Lloyd out of the way – promoted to Archdeacon of Prince Albert – Speers was able to announce a decided improvement. It was spurred by the arrival in the area of Americans and Canadians with farming experience and in the fall of 1905 by the coming of the Canadian Northern Railway (two years later than Barr's prediction).

By February 1907, W.R. "Billy" Ridington, the local immigration agent, was able to report that Lloydminster had surpassed all expectations. In 1908, the Lloydminster Board of Trade felt justified in putting out a pamphlet boosting the town as "The Banner District of the West." By then all the heartache and controversy that had marked the settlement's early days were forgotten. E.J. Ashton, late of Norfolk, a bank teller turned Boer War veteran, was to recall at the end of his life that "strangely enough, as the years rolled by, it was apparent that several among the most successful settlers were men who had no previous farming experience."

This was true of William Hutchison, who by 1905 was able to write on "How to Become a Farmer" for his home town paper, the Sheffield *Weekly Telegraph*. Stanley Rackham did so well that he was able to make regular trips home to the Old Country. But he never left the site of the Barr colony and was still in Lloydminster in 1937 when, at the age of sixty, he died.

Like many others, Ivan Crossley alternately farmed his homestead and supplemented his income by taking temporary jobs. When he needed money he'd go to work ploughing another man's acreage or taking a winter mail contract from Battleford or Saskatoon. In between he'd go back to his homestead, break ground, work on his shack, put up a barn, until he owned the land outright. In 1906 he ran into Robert Holtby, bringing a load of hay into town for sale. Robert Holtby's pretty sister was sitting astride the load. Crossley took her to lunch and soon became a regular visitor at the thriving Holtby homestead seven miles out of town. They were engaged that fall, married in Lloyd's log church the following spring, and enjoyed forty-eight years of married life, the memories of those early struggles on the long trail from Saskatoon slowly fading as the years wore on and Lloydminster prospered and the grandchildren of that pioneer union began to arrive.

4

The odyssey of Ella Sykes In the fall of 1910, Miss Ella Constance Sykes, a high-born English-woman of redoubtable energy and enterprise, was struck forcibly by a letter to *The Times*, which reminded her of the hard future faced by so many of the million surplus women in the United Kingdom. Too often, the writer suggested, educated women found themselves a drug on the labour market; indeed, it was almost impossible for any English working girl to support herself comfortably let alone put anything aside for her old age. The answer? Surely it lay in the Overseas Dominions.

Miss Sykes, in spite of a sheltered upbringing, was by middle age no delicate Edwardian flower. She was one of a small but distinguished company of adventurous ladies, so typical of the late Victorian era, who thought nothing of dashing off to the far corners of the Empire on voyages of adventure and inquiry. In 1899 she had been the first woman to ride from the Caspian Sea to India and the first to visit Persian Baluchistan, where her brother, a Sandhurst-trained officer in the Dragoon Guards, was British consul. It was an invigorating experience. In her book *Through Persia on a Side Saddle* she revelled in the "sense of freedom and expansion which quickened the blood and made the pulse beat high."

Now Miss Sykes determined upon a second adventure: she would set off for the Canadian West to try to assess the prospects for an educated Englishwoman working as home help in the new world. She outlined the plan to a friend, who made a blunt suggestion: if she *really* wanted to find out how the English were treated in Canada, wouldn't it be more effective if she disguised herself as a potential job-seeker?

Miss Sykes demurred; the idea was not only distasteful but also she, who had grown accustomed to the attention of twelve servants in Persia, had no experience of being a servant herself.

156

"Ah," said her friend, "evidently you wish merely to dip your fingers in the water; you shirk at taking a plunge that might prove of real service to the women you say you want to help!"

That did it. Ella Sykes determined to take the plunge even though she saw herself, like so many others of her class, as "an incompetent amateur, trained to do nothing properly the country wanted."

On shipboard, she met several English families returning to their Western Canadian farms after a winter spent in the Old Country. "We could never live in England now, after having been in Canada," she was told over and over again, but when she talked to the women she began to understand the dimensions of the problems that even the wives of successful homesteaders faced. One woman told of her first experience when her fiancé wrote that he had a home at last and she went out to Winnipeg, loaded down with household goods, to marry him.

"I remember asking him what was the colour of our bedroom paper, as I wanted to get a toilet-set to match it. He didn't say much then, but I shall never forget my feelings when I found our new home was just a one-roomed wooden shack, divided in two with a curtain, and not papered at all. It was an *awful* shock to me. . . ."

"But now that you are well off your life is much easier isn't it?" Miss Sykes asked.

The reply astonished her: "I had less work when I began my married life as a poor woman than I have now." It was, she said, the farmer's passion to buy more and more land: "They will sacrifice everything to that and the house and its comforts have to come last. My husband buys every acre he can get and of course has to engage hired men to work his farms; and the more men there are, the more work it is for a woman. . . ."

Miss Sykes understood the problems, but she also realized that the life her shipboard companion described would be far harder on an Englishwoman fresh from a comfortable home than it would be on a Canadian or on a European peasant.

In Winnipeg Miss Sykes checked into the Home of Welcome. In this government-subsidized frame house as many as fifty single women could be packed. The first night's lodging was free, courtesy of the Immigration Department. After that Miss Sykes paid five dollars a week for a single room. The matron who registered her and listened to her background looked at her sadly. "What a pity it is that English-women are taught to do nothing properly," she said. Miss Sykes agreed.

At the YWCA, where she went for information, she was advised to put a classified ad in the *Free Press*:

Educated Englishwoman, inexperienced, wishes to assist mistress of farm in housework.

Job offers came in immediately, but Miss Sykes was realistic enough to know that she couldn't handle them. How could she wash, cook, and clean for the pregnant mother of four children for only fifteen dollars a month? Canada, in its own way, was as foreign as Baluchistan.

She trudged disconsolately through Winnipeg's bustling streets, depressed at her inability to cope. She was accustomed to the leisurely pace of settled England. But here in this raw new country, everything seemed to be moving at the speed of those gigantic CPR locomotives, which roared headlong out of the prairie stations. Even the funeral processions dashed along at an unseemly trot, as if the mourners were in a hurry to fling the coffin into the grave and get back to work. At church, the choirs sang at such a brisk pace she could hardly keep up with the psalms and hymns. She had thought of trying to get a job as a waitress, but she heard again and again that English waitresses were too slow and were swiftly hustled out of their posts by alert Canadians, who seemed to her to do their work at lightning speed. This was a country for the young and the energetic; the streets seemed to be empty of old people. Am I a fool to have started on this absurd adventure? she asked herself.

Back at the Home of Welcome she caught herself starting to criticize the food and the women she shared it with, and felt ashamed. Others at the table were running down Canadians, whom they thought of as merciless taskmasters, even though their wages were at least double those they would have received in England. Miss Sykes understood the problem: in Britain servants were specialists; but they could not understand that in Canada they must be able to turn their hands to anything – to be cook, house-parlourmaid, washerwoman, even baker and dairymaid all rolled into one. It wasn't entirely their fault. No one had bothered to tell them about Canadian conditions – and they hadn't bothered to find out.

Many of these young women, Ella Sykes discovered, did not understand the meaning of hard work and, lacking the strength, self reliance, and money needed in the new land, could not resist the idea of finding a man to fend for them. Some were prepared to hurl themselves into marriage. They crowded into the local matrimonial agency, one or two

158

even going all the way to Vancouver to marry men they had never seen. Others confessed they had deserted an English husband and expected to find a fresh one in Canada. Many, in their innocence, were bitterly disappointed.

"Before I came out to Canada," one girl at the hostel told her, "I read that I should find a number of men on the Winnipeg platform waiting to propose to us girls, but, would you believe it, when I got out of the train not a single man even spoke to me?"

Miss Sykes began to realize that in order to make their way in the new land, English men and women must divest themselves of Old Country prejudices and keep their personal views to themselves. Why, one servant girl had actually objected because her employer sat down at the table in his shirt sleeves! Canadians, she was learning, especially Westerners, were intensely proud; when the English criticized their country, it got their backs up. In this assessment she was not alone. Half a dozen perceptive English journalists were making the same point. Six years before, John Foster Fraser, a British travel writer, had reported that Englishmen were not welcome in Winnipeg because they continually made comparisons to Canada's detriment – "astonished that the conditions of life are not the same as in England, a thing that ruffles the fur of every Canadian."

At last Miss Sykes found a job she thought she could handle, as companion to a farm widow on the Saskatchewan prairie at ten dollars a month. As it turned out, she couldn't. The first night after supper she realized she didn't even know how to wash dishes properly, putting all the crockery into the pan with the cutlery and the greasy plates. Everything, in fact, was strange, including the method of arranging pillows on the bed. In England she had been considered a capable woman; here, at every moment, it was impressed upon her that she was the reverse; she felt humiliated, out of her element, exhausted.

Is this really me? she asked herself, as she cleaned each floor on her hands and knees, scrubbed clothes on the washboard, ironed the hired men's shirts, replenished the "voracious stove" with chunks of wood, made the porridge, and fried the bacon that was the staple meat twice a day. Her headquarters was a fly-infested kitchen, which she thought of as the Black Hole of Calcutta. And yet when she woke one morning to find the spring wind blowing, the snow melting, the birds singing, her depression vanished.

She stayed one week. Her employer, Mrs. Robinson, who was friendly and understanding to the last, gave her notice within a day of her arrival. Like so many Canadian farm women Ella Sykes observed, Mrs. Robinson seemed to have lost the habit of repose. She was unable to stay still for a moment. She would sweep the kitchen and shed and shake out all the carpets after every meal, ply the broom between times when it wasn't necessary, "forever goaded by a malignant dream of unrest." When the time came to leave, Miss Sykes received from Mrs. Robinson a little homily on the subject of her untidiness and then a pat on the back for what she had learned. She accepted it all in humble silence, clutching her wages in her hand. What an immense effort it had been to earn a few dollars!

All together, Ella Sykes took five positions in Canada. Her last job on the prairies was in Alberta. She arrived in Calgary to find the YWCA full but managed to get a room at a women's hostel where once again she was presented with evidence of the jealousy between the English and the Canadians. One of the lodgers, a Miss Bates, told how she had applied for a job in a Calgary home only to be told: "We don't want any English here." To that she retorted: "If I had known you were a Canadian I should never have applied . . ." and flounced out. The remark so struck the fancy of her would-be employer that she called after her, saying she'd like to engage a woman of spirit, but Miss Bates proudly refused to go back.

Some of the inmates of the hostel, in Ella Sykes's opinion, had no right to be in Canada at all. They had been intrigued by overenthusiastic literature, had seen the country through rose-coloured glasses, and were now bitterly disappointed. One frail elderly lady had bought her passage after a single conversation with an enthusiastic Canadian who had spoken vaguely of "crowds of openings for women." She was between jobs, being worn out with work, and when Miss Sykes met her several months later on her return from the West Coast, her health was broken. Another, a former governess who was also an accomplished milliner, refused to work in a shop because asking for such a job, she said, was abhorrent to her. "I want to live in a home and arrange the flowers and help the lady of the house with her correspondence," she announced. Miss Sykes tried to explain, in vain, that no such post existed in the Canadian West.

It was not enough to be able to cook, iron, and sew; one also had to scrub floors and do heavy washing. Another of Miss Sykes's table mates who had been considered highly capable as a governess felt herself stupid and incompetent in Canada. Miss Sykes recognized in her the same feeling of depression and helplessness that she herself had suffered.

160

Nevertheless, Ella Sykes was game to try again. She had attempted to peddle books from door to door in Calgary but found that she too easily took no for an answer. Then a satisfactory reply came to her advertisement, and she went off to work for a fortnight on a large dairy farm, handling the housework and serving the meals to the farmer and his wife – a Mr. and Mrs. Brown – their three children and their three hired men. The fastidious Miss Sykes was taken aback at first to find that meat, potatoes, vegetables, and dessert were all served on the same plate, but relieved later to realize that this meant nine fewer dishes to wash. The three children she found "rough, mannerless and unruly" and ascribed these failings to the fact that, as in many similar cases, their parents were simply too busy, toiling from dawn to dusk, to pay much attention to them. Mrs. Brown was comparatively young, but she looked older than her years, worn out by ceaseless toil. Again Miss Sykes noted that the habit of work was so deeply engrained in her that she was not able to be still. She *couldn't* rest and take things easy.

Mrs. Brown was happy with her husband, but she told Ella Sykes that had she known what she, a young English schoolteacher, was in for she would never have married him. In their early years they had been sodbusters, to use the vernacular, and she had hated it. "I haven't a single good word for the prairie," she said, "and I got to hate the very sight of a man when I was there." Why? "Because a man meant preparing a meal. . . ."

In shearing time, when they kept sheep, she had had to feed fifteen men five meals a day. She had no time to visit her neighbours – the nearest lived four miles away. "I just got into the way of thinking of nothing but how to get through the day's work."

This was a revelation to Ella Sykes.

"Aren't there some women who love the life?" she asked. "In England we hear so much of 'the call of the prairie.'"

"There may be some but I never met them. All my friends hated the loneliness and the lack of amusement and the same dull round day after day. Do you know, if I ever sat down and wrote, or did some sewing, Kitty [her daughter] would come up to me to ask whether it were Sunday, so astonished was she to see me resting, as on weekdays I was on the 'go' all the time."

But surely, Miss Sykes said, she didn't need to work hard any more. The family were well off; she could afford to rest in the afternoons or visit the neighbours.

Mrs. Brown replied sadly that it was too late. She was so wound up she *had* to keep going all day, and she had lost all desire for social intercourse.

When her fortnight's stint was ended, Ella Sykes felt guilty about leaving Mrs. Brown, who had clearly enjoyed her company and felt in her presence a welcome respite from her days of drudgery. But it was time to move on. She ended her trip in Victoria, and here among the rose trellises and rock gardens she experienced for the first time in Canada a leisurely pace reminiscent of home.

But Canada was only an interlude in a crowded career. Back in England she produced a "plain, unvarnished record" of what she had seen during six months in Canada. "I ardently desire that British women shall help to build up the Empire," she wrote, "and the sisters of men who are doing such splendid work in the Dominion are surely fitted for the task."

A few years later, she set off on another adventure to another distant corner of the globe. With her brother, Brigadier General Sir Percy Molesworth Sykes, she travelled to the roof of the world through the oases and deserts of Central Asia into Chinese Turkestan, becoming the first white woman to cross the dangerous passes leading to and from the high Pamirs that lie north of the Afghanistan and Indian frontiers. It was an exhilarating experience, full of high adventure at high altitudes—a far cry from the toil, trouble, and humiliation of Canadian farm life in the Golden West.

5

Don't In spite of the prejudice against them, it is clear that the majority of the
come back, English who came to Canada were, in their own way, as industrious as
Dad the equally despised Galicians and Doukhobors. The story of the Shepherd family of Ramsgate can stand for thousands of similar tales of middle-class English families who, down on their luck in the first decade of the century, sought a new life in the Canadian West.

The family was no stranger to hard work. William John Shepherd was a butcher, but not a successful one. He had operated shops in Canterbury, Deal, and Ramsgate. There, the entire family worked ten to twelve hours a day, six days a week, and barely held their own. American packing houses like Swift's, selling Texas beef, were undercutting English butchers.

What could they do? England seemed barren of possibilities. To young George Shepherd, the second son, the country seemed poky, and when Mrs. Shepherd first broached the idea of emigration it was taken up enthusiastically by the family. Faraway lands seemed glamorous. The Shepherds considered America, Africa, and Australia, but decided at last on Canada. Canada was closest and Canada was British. There was land to be farmed there, and on the map the country looked imposing and Imperial, all tinted red with the words "The Dominion of Canada" spread out across it.

It was a typically English decision: decide first, investigate later. The Shepherds sent off for literature. It came and, as they later realized, was more than a little on the optimistic side. They read it faithfully, called a family council to discuss ways and means, and decided that William Shepherd and young George would go out first to get a toehold on the land. Will, the eldest brother, would help his mother operate the family butcher shop. He, his mother, and the others would follow when the men were settled.

And so, with their goods packed in trunk-sized wicker baskets, father and son set off after enduring the agonizing moment of farewell that every emigrant faced. George Shepherd would never forget that scene: his young brother Charlie, aged sixteen, putting his head through the open carriage window, seizing his father by the hand, and crying out: "Don't come back, Dad, don't come back!" It was those words, more than any other, that kept the elder man from becoming discouraged by his difficulty in adapting to the strange new country.

For it *was* strange. "A welcome awaits you in Canada," the literature had promised. But there was no welcome – only hurry and bustle. The train engines astonished both father and son –great raucous brutes pulling colonist cars that seemed more like moving houses. And the sleeping accommodations! Everyone slept fully clothed, two by two, on wooden slats below or on a wooden tray that pulled down from above. (Young George Shepherd smiled when he was told there would be no charge for sleeping room.) When the engineer turned down the heat at midnight everybody shivered in Manitoba's zero weather. In Winnipeg's immigration hall, where they slept on the floor in their greatcoats and blankets, it was warmer.

Strolling down Main Street, rubbing elbows with a variety of nationalities, they felt very un-Canadian in their English clothes. But they didn't complain; all this discomfort, they realized, was part of the business of emigrating. They had put down their names for work on a farm and a day later found themselves in another immigration hall in Brandon. The following day they signed a contract with a farmer a few miles out of town, and that was the end of the Canadian government's responsibility toward them.

The contract was hard. The two Englishmen must work on Jim Hale's 800-acre farm for the seven summer months at ten dollars a month for both. That, Hale told them, would give them the experience they would need to homestead. But there was a catch: if they didn't work the full seven months they would be paid nothing. For Hale this was good business; he had little to lose and cheap labour to gain. They stuck it out for six weeks, cleaning Jim Hale's barns seven days a week, and then, unable to take it any longer, they quit and went back to Brandon without having earned a nickel. It was the low point of their lives.

They were trudging gloomily down Brandon's main street when they spotted a sign: "READ THE LAND MAN." And: "For Sale, A Half-section of Land in Central Saskatchewan – 320 Acres, No Money Down and Twenty Years to Pay." William Shepherd's face lit up. This looked like the real thing! They'd had six weeks of farm experience; why work for others when they could farm for themselves?

For reasons they could never understand, Read the Land Man took a personal interest in this English butcher and his son. He offered to pay his own way to Girvin, Saskatchewan, to conduct them to the half-section in question. Off the trio went by train to Girvin and by team and democrat six miles to the homestead. But when he saw the property, young George's heart sank. Here was nothing but bare prairie, not a stick or a stone standing, neither building nor well, not even a fence post. How could two inexperienced Englishmen hope to cultivate this endless expanse of turf? He persuaded his father to abandon the idea.

They went to work as farmhands once again. At summer's end William Shepherd opened a small butcher shop in Girvin. It didn't look as if they could last long in Canada.

Suddenly, in September, an astonishing thing happened. The rest of the family turned up in Girvin – Mrs. Shepherd and George's four brothers and his sister, Kit. What had caused this sudden decision? Nobody quite said it, but George was pretty sure his father had written home suggesting it might be better if they both went back. That did it. His mother had no intention of staying put.

Mrs. Shepherd had simply sold the business and loaded her family

164

aboard a ship sailing for Canada, taking with her everything she felt they would need in the wild Canadian West including a Boer War army rifle, two double-barrelled shotguns, another single-barrelled gun, a bowie knife, a naval cutlass, and a pole-axe, all presumably for standing off an attacking band of redskins until the Mounted Police dashed to the rescue.

She also had the presence of mind to bring a keg of five-inch railroad spikes for nailing logs together and a piano, which cost twenty-five dollars in freight charges but which all agreed was worth its weight in gold that winter.

The family worked hard. Mr. and Mrs. Shepherd ran the butcher shop, George toiled as a farmhand, three of his brothers, Will, Harry, and Geoff, laboured at hauling and shovelling grain. Charlie got a job as a well digger. Kit, aged fifteen, worked in the Girvin hotel waiting on tables.

By midwinter none of the Shepherds considered themselves green Englishmen; in fact, they tended to scoff at a fussy little Englishwoman who came in especially to warn Mrs. Shepherd of the blizzards. They had made good and were now trusted hired men. What would the next step be?

It's clear that the family catalyst was Mrs. Shepherd. It was she who had first thought of emigrating, she who had summarily pulled up stakes and come out to Girvin. Now, as George put it, she was bitten by the free-homestead virus. Why wait? Why not act before spring came? Nothing would do but she and her husband must take the train to neighbouring Davidson to visit the land agency, pore through the township books, and return with a handbook of homestead regulations and a good idea of the free land available in the area.

Another family council followed. It was impossible to locate land while the snow was so deep, but it was agreed that everybody would make himself familiar with the Homestead Act and keep in touch with the land office in Davidson to learn what cancellations and changes were being recorded by the government agent there.

This vigilance paid off. At Long Lake, some twenty-odd miles east of Girvin, three quarter-sections suddenly came open, relinquished by a land company that had failed to live up to its agreement with the government. The Shepherds learned of it immediately through their contacts with the agent, who offered to hold on to it for a day.

Will, George, and Charlie went to Davidson at once and "filed blind," that is, without inspecting the land. What was good enough for a land company, they figured, was good enough for them. That done, they went down to the station to return home. The train was nine hours late. They couldn't wait, and so off they trudged down the track – ten miles on foot in the bitter cold. When they reached Girvin it was dark and the thermometer had dropped to forty below. It didn't matter. As they stumbled into the family shack behind the butcher shop and relaxed, they couldn't hide their triumph. Out came the homestead receipts as the entire family gloated. They were land holders at last, with almost five hundred acres to their names, and they felt on top of the world.

They couldn't help but remark on the fortuitous chain of events that had led them to this moment. If they hadn't decided to send father and son to Canada . . . if those two hadn't happened on the office of Read, the Land Man . . . if Mrs. Shepherd hadn't insisted on keeping in touch with the land office in Davidson! It seemed as if some guardian angel was fluttering just above them, leading them through various trials and travails to this moment of jubilation.

That spring they moved their house and their butcher shop by sleigh to the new homestead. It took two days, perhaps the most trying of their lives, for the loads were so heavy they kept veering off the trail of packed snow. But it was a momentous anniversary, for they arrived on the site on March 20, 1909, exactly one year to the day after George and his father had left Liverpool.

They had four oxen, a little equipment, scarcely any cash, but considerable experience. They were healthy, ambitious, and not afraid of work. To hold the land they would have to follow the homestead regulations – put up buildings, break the sod, raise crops. But some of them could also work for others, and they were prepared for long hours, few holidays, and no vacations.

Will and George worked as labourers on a fifteen-thousand-acre farm in the district. Charlie stayed home that first summer and helped break ninety acres of virgin prairie. Mr. Shepherd managed to get a mail contract. When a Canadian Pacific branch line came, two of the boys laboured on the construction gang.

They worked as a family unit: all their wages and profits went into a central fund to improve the farm. There was a closeness here that others, lonely on the prairie, must have found enviable. In George Shepherd's memoirs, written fifty years later, one gets a glimpse of it: Mrs. Shepherd seated at the piano, her bell-like voice joining the others grouped around her singing "Old Black Joe" and "My Old Kentucky Home."

It was a remarkably successful transition. In Kent, the "Garden of England," the family had led a sequestered urban existence. To adjust so swiftly to a raw and foreign rural environment was not easy, especially for the parents. Yet they did not complain. While Canadians were poking fun at "blooming green Englishmen," this family and thousands of others like them were going sturdily about their business enriching the Dominion by the sweat of their brows. In England, the Shepherds could hardly make ends meet; in the Canadian West they thrived. Mrs. Shepherd was the most amazing of all. Within four years of her arrival she was writing articles for the *Grain Growers' Guide* giving advice to farm women on how to raise chickens. She became such an authority on poultry that she took to public speaking. In Moose Jaw, when the Grain Growers held their annual convention, she was chosen as the leading woman speaker. Ramsgate, by that time, must have seemed as distant as the moon.

Chapter Six

The American Invasion

1

Will White thinks big

2

Catching the fever

3

Keeping out the Blacks

4

Loosening Imperial ties

1

It was Clifford Sifton's original belief that "the best settlers are those whose condition in the land from which they come is not too rosy, and who are content in coming here to get along in a humble way at first." It was hopeless, he believed back in February 1896, to expect to fill the country with well-to-do farmers; this was his rationale for bringing in peasants from northern and eastern Europe.

Well before the turn of the century, however, the pragmatic minister had softened his policy. Public opinion was forcing him to restrict Galician immigration. British farmers didn't seem to want to come. But south of the border were tens of thousands of well-to-do Americans who might jump at the chance of selling out at a high price and buying in at a low one. Sifton shifted his sights and concentrated his main thrust on these people. The results were wildly successful.

In the powerful and carefully orchestrated campaign that followed, every technique was used and honed to a fine point. Between 1898 and 1906, the department spent two million dollars – more than a quarter of its budget – to convince Americans that they should come to Canada. They didn't come cheap. It cost an average of $3.22 to bring in an Englishman, but the government spent $5.35 for every American who crossed the border. Sifton obviously thought it was worth the money.

By 1902 he was able to warn an audience of British businessmen in Montreal that "Americans now own the Canadian Northwest." Yet the real invasion had scarcely begun. There were at that time fewer than 40,000 American-born settlers on the prairies. In another ten years the number had jumped to 217,000. Only about 10,000 settled in Manitoba; the majority took up homesteads in Saskatchewan and Alberta.

Sifton turned his propaganda campaign in the United States over to W.J. "Will" White, his old crony from the Brandon *Sun*. White was the perfect choice – a "go-getter," in the phrase of the day, assigned to a nation of go-getters. Back in 1881, chafing at the lack of opportunity in Exeter, Ontario, where he was editor of the weekly *Times*, he encountered a local boy, Tom Greenway, just returned from Manitoba and bursting with enthusiasm for the West. White, the hustler, took Greenway's advice and hustled off to Winnipeg by way of Michigan, Milwaukee, and St. Paul (for the CPR was not completed). So did Greenway, who was destined to become Premier of Manitoba.

In Winnipeg, White learned that there were plans afoot to start a newspaper in the CPR's new divisional point in the Brandon Hills. On he hustled, again as far as the steel would take him, a few miles west of Portage la Prairie. Then, in a driving rainstorm, he trudged the remaining thirty-five miles on foot to Brandon. Two days later he was walking the sawdust-strewn streets of the new community. Shortly afterwards he launched the weekly *Sun*.

It was a one-man operation. White set the type himself, cranked the press, peddled the paper on the streets for a nickel a copy, sold the advertising, wrote every word that appeared, and even swept the floors. As the *Sun* prospered and the West made news, White prospered with it. When Louis Riel touched off the Saskatchewan rebellion in 1885, White began to churn out extras, hiring gangs of boys to turn the press and upping the price to a quarter. Soon he acquired shareholders, Clifford Sifton and James Smart, among others; the *Sun* was always ruggedly Liberal.

White thought big. When Brandon was about to be incorporated as a town, he discovered it cost no more to call itself a city. Why not go for the bargain? Think big, he told the city fathers; vote yourselves a city! They took his advice.

Now, as Sifton's propaganda chief for the United States, White was again required to go on the hustle. He was in his fifties now, at the height of his powers. And, as he set up his network of agents south of the border, he continued to think big.

He had as many as twenty-one immigration offices operating in the most productive U.S. centres, each manned by a salaried manager and a staff. In addition he had twenty-seven travelling agents moving about the country and, by 1901, 276 subagents –farmers and railroad employees, mainly –who received a bonus of three dollars for every man, two dollars for every woman, and a dollar for every child they secured for Canada.

The job of this army of salesmen was to tout Canada as a land of promise where the weather was bracing but never exhausting; where British law, order, and justice prevailed; where the land was rich, cheap, and available; and, above all, where everybody who got in on the ground floor and worked hard could become wealthy and successful.

The agents blanketed the American midwest with lantern-slide lectures and stereopticon views of the Canadian prairies. They devised a chain letter system to get the names of interested farmers and then deluged them with a rain of pamphlets and information. They placed

171

maps and atlases in the schools and persuaded teachers to give geography lessons on the Canadian West. They talked women's clubs, which were eager to study almost anything, into studying the prairies. They buttonholed clergymen and suggested they extol the virtues of the Canadian moral climate. They held street meetings which, for their evangelical fervour, competed easily with the itinerant medicine shows and Saturday-night corner sermons. They squired leading farmers on free junkets to Canada and got them to write up their adventures for the local paper or the department's pamphlets. They turned up at state and county fairs with displays of Canadian wheat.

They were everywhere, it seemed. When a land rush was touched off in Oklahoma by the opening of a Comanche Indian reservation in 1902, the Canadians were on hand in a tent to make sure that those land-hungry settlers who didn't get a homestead would have an alternative. As a result, three hundred families pulled up stakes and left for Alberta.

But the immigration agent was more than a propagandist. He was the farmer's friend, companion, land agent, and travel expert. White's people handed out thousands of "settlers' certificates," each of which allowed the holder to travel on the CPR from the American border to his destination for the ridiculous price of one cent a mile. If many used these certificates for nothing more than a pleasure jaunt, White didn't care. The country *wanted* visitors who would return with glowing reports of the golden land west of Winnipeg. The immigration agent stood ready to help out with advice, to suggest the best land, to arrange for train tickets, and if a farmer set off alone, to make the necessary arrangements for his family to follow.

As a practitioner of hype, Will White deserves to stand with the best of the modern hucksters. Newspapermen were even easier to buy in those days than they were in later decades. A free junket did the trick, especially if there was a prolonged stop at the spas of Banff or Lake Louise. Trainloads of compliant editors, lubricated by good whiskey and warmed by the best CPR cuisine, raced across the prairies at government expense, stopping at wheat fields and handsome farms (carefully selected) or for banquets at the major cities. The Minnesota editors came first, then the Wisconsin editors, and then the National Editorial Association, all six hundred of them, representing a thousand newspapers.

When the editorial junkets began to strain the public purse, White traded free trips in return for free advertising. The press swallowed the bait. The Michigan Press Association was so eager that it offered to give two or three dollars worth of ads for every dollar Canada expended – and all in advance of each junket. To secure the co-operation of the Western American press, White also dangled the carrot of paid advertising. The placing of the most minuscule ad was enough to soften up most newspapers and put them strongly in the Canadian camp, producing glowing accounts of the Western prairies and attacking those interests who were opposed to American emigration. By 1902, Canada was advertising in seven thousand Western American papers – but only in the slack seasons when the farmers had time to read.

White didn't have things all his own way. Midwestern leaders were appalled at the exodus to Canada and took desperate steps to counteract it. At the height of the boom it was estimated the Americans were bringing between $50 million and $60 million a year into Canada in cash and equipment. Peter Muirhead of Oklahoma City, to take one example, arrived in Calgary in 1902 with six carloads of animals, two carloads of equipment, and enough ready cash to buy a three-thousand-acre ranch. That constituted an enormous drain on the small American community he had deserted. No wonder, then, that White found himself in a battle with American land companies, business men, politicians, railways, and real estate interests.

In Wisconsin, the anti-Canadian campaign was so virulent that the Canadian agency was driven right out of the state. The Wisconsin Central Railroad bought off the Canadian sub-agents as quickly as they were appointed. Wealthy Wisconsin lumbermen, who owned millions of acres of cleared land in the state, fought so hard against the resident agent, James MacLachlan, that he asked for a transfer. Business and real estate officials pressured county fairs to reject his exhibits, and he was reduced to operating from rented stores near the fairgrounds. White made no headway with the local paper in Wausau, where the Canadian immigration office was located. It refused all Canadian advertising and published features on disgruntled American farmers returning home from Canada disillusioned. White suspected that Wisconsin land promoters had actually sent fake farmers disguised as settlers into Canada with orders to return with stories of personal hardships and broken government promises.

The last straw came in the summer of 1903, when MacLachlan, arriving one morning at his office in Wausau, found a small package tied to the knob of his door. It contained a condom filled with cotton batting and a card attached with this message: "Suck this, it's good enough for a canuck – why cant [sic] you work in your own country?"

173

That winter, White threw in the towel and transferred his agent to South Dakota.

But White's most formidable opponent was the powerful railroad magnate James Jerome Hill, whose successful completion of the Great Northern from St. Paul to the Pacific was hailed as the greatest feat of railway building on the continent. Hill's was the only transcontinental railroad in the United States built without government subsidy and without financial scandal. A garrulous, one-eyed former Canadian, Hill had also been in on the birth of the Canadian Pacific. But now he had no intention of seeing the hard-won profits of his line diminished by a massive loss of customers to Canada. If he could best E.H. Harriman and keep the Burlington line out of Chicago, why couldn't he just as easily defeat his former countrymen, Sifton and White?

Hill's headquarters, St. Paul, became a hotbed of anti-Canadianism. The St. Paul *Globe*, which Hill controlled, bristled with features purporting to show that Canadian soil conditions were inferior to those below the border. Every effort was made to snatch prospective emigrants away from the Canadians and redirect them to American homesteads. As a result, White's men had to keep them under tight scrutiny as soon as they reached Hill's city. They "should be closely looked after, taken to my office and guarded every moment they spend in this city," the local agent told Ottawa.

Jim Hill was no stranger to the Canadian North West. His closest friend and former partner was Lord Strathcona, who, as plain Donald Smith, had been Member of Parliament for Selkirk, Manitoba, and who was still a major shareholder in Hill's railway. But Hill had no compunction about manipulating the facts to his own advantage; he had done it before when, as a consummate lobbyist, palm-greaser, and propagandist, he had turned a bankrupt railway into a thriving success. Now his efforts were channelled into depicting Canada as an arctic nation whose soil was poor and whose grain yield was pathetic. In a remarkable and widely reported speech in Bismarck, N.D., in 1903, the leonine Hill was at his most pugnacious:

"I am not saying much about the area of their land up there, and I am not so much frightened about their climate or the quality of their soil. They are pretty near where Sir John Franklin met his misfortune, that is somewhere near the North Pole. I have seen fields of their wheat . . . it would not yield a bushel to the acre. It is a handsome growth with nothing in it. I knew these things when I was interested in the Canadian Pacific. Our people who have gone there will, a great many of them, come back."

174

Hill's attempts to depict the Canadian wheat fields as "somewhere near the North Pole" were taken up by friendly American newspapers, one of which went so far as to publish the tale of a Manitoba postmaster pursued by man-hungry wolves to within a mile of Winnipeg and saved only by the fleetness of his team. The story was not short on colourful details: so close was the ravenous pack, the paper announced, that the beasts tore to pieces the buffalo robes hanging over the back of the cutter!

Yet the anti-Canadian campaign failed. Each year, it seemed, the number of Americans flooding into Canada doubled. In both Alberta and Saskatchewan, the American-born soon outnumbered the English by a ratio of two to one. In both provinces they formed the largest single immigrant group, their numbers even exceeding the combined immigration figures from *all* British possessions. Alberta was by far the more Americanized with 80,000 native-born Americans, 67,000 British, and 58,000 Slavs – figures that give a clue to its present-day personality.

In spite of these statistics, Jim Hill didn't abandon his campaign. As late as 1912 he was still vainly battling away. With his blessing and support the northwestern states held a convention in Seattle designed to organize one last-ditch attempt to stop Americans from moving north. Alas, on the very day the convention opened, the delegates were embarrassed to open their Seattle *Times* and discover a large advertisement from Canada showing a Canadian wheat field with a furrow two miles long. "We ought to be ashamed of ourselves to permit such a thing!" cried the president of the Seattle Commercial Club. The convention came to nothing. Jim Hill had by then won his battle with his crafty rival Harriman. But he had not been able to compete with the attractions offered by the Canadian West or nullify the hard sell of Will J. White.

2

In the case of the Americans, Clifford Sifton had no need to defend his *Catching* policies to the Opposition or to the public. Most Canadians, especially *the* Westerners, welcomed American immigration, and with good reason. *fever* The Americans were not paupers; on the contrary, they brought money into the country. More, they were practical farmers with years of experience under conditions very similar to those on the northern

175

plains. They were white, the majority were of Anglo-Saxon extraction, and they all spoke English.

In the eyes of the Westerners, the Americans were everything the English were not. They were go-getters who were willing to work. They did not keep to themselves but mixed easily with their neighbours. They adapted swiftly to Canadian ways. They did not poor-mouth the country but welcomed the Canadian lifestyle with its emphasis on order and security.

Almost every man who crossed the border from Iowa, Nebraska, North Dakota, or Minnesota was a walking success story before he arrived. The Americans had sold their farms for fancy sums, and now they were picking up new land in Canada for a song – 160 acres free, the rest for as little as a dollar an acre. They loved their adopted country, melted easily into the national fabric, and became patriots. More than any other group, they acted as a spark to touch off the prairie land boom.

Small wonder, then, that the press was ecstatic. "Desirable" was the mildest adjective used to describe them. "Absolutely the pick of two continents," was the headline in the *Winnipeg Tribune* in 1906. The Lethbridge *Herald* went into paroxysms of hyperbole over the American invasion: "This class of immigration is of a top-notch order and every true Canadian should be proud to see it and encourage it. Thus shall our vast tracts of God's bountifulness . . . be peopled by an intelligent progressive race of our own kind, who will readily be developed into permanent, patriotic, solid citizens who will adhere to one flag – that protects their homes and their rights – and whose posterity . . . will become . . . a part and parcel of and inseparable from our proud standards of Canadianism."

So let us wait, for a day or two, on the CPR platform in Calgary and watch the Americans pour in.

It is March, 1906. The depot's baggage room, the immigration hall, and the adjacent hotels and restaurants that straggle along the rail line are jammed with newcomers. The wooden platform is crowded with Calgary businessmen, here to welcome "the most extraordinary movement of substantial settlers" ever recorded in the town.

There are no sheepskin coats here, no babushkas, no riding breeches or Stetsons. These are well-turned-out entrepreneurs in expensive suits, with watch chains draped across their vests. Only their faces, weathered by sun and wind, tell us they do not belong in the cities.

A fugue of regional accents ripples across the platform: the flat twang of Iowa, the softer sibilance of Missouri. These people have brought their families; they intend to stay. Small boys in caps and knee breeches dash about. John M. Rowan of Randolph, Nebraska, is heading for Olds with eleven children. Marmaduke O'Malley of Pilot Knob, Missouri – a lean Southerner with a drooping moustache and chin whiskers – has four offspring and doesn't care where he locates as long as the country is as good as advertised. Mary Colwin of Camchester, Oklahoma, a veteran of the Cherokee Strip land rush and a victim of the subsequent drought, has sold out and is starting afresh with her three boys – the eldest barely sixteen – an erect little widow with a face burned brown by the Oklahoma sun.

The trains steam into the depot, section after section, two hours apart, each section containing seven to eleven cars. Captain Jimmy Winn, the immigration agent, has been up since 2:30 a.m., when the first contingent arrived. They say he is the busiest man in Canada this week. One special arrives with six hundred passengers aboard, all wealthy enough to afford sleeping cars. They have come from Indian Territory, Oklahoma, Kansas, Arkansas, Missouri, travelling north through St. Paul to Winnipeg and then west by the CPR. The border crossing is so crowded, they say, that customs agents cannot cope with the crowds, and some settlers have been delayed for days. And this is only the vanguard of the summer rush. As everyone says, the fever is on.

Here is V.D. Hag of Red Oak, Iowa, who has already scouted the land between Edmonton and Cardston and brought scores of neighbours north in twenty-five cars. They will not bother with free land, all being wealthy enough to buy their farms outright. Hag has a fortune on paper, having already refused one hundred dollars an acre for his property at Red Oak. Iowa, he says, is stirred up about Alberta. "You can hear it talked of everywhere. The rush this summer will be something enormous. I don't think you Canadians appreciate the interest of Iowa people in Western Canada. It is as contagious as the fever."

Another Iowan, Charles Cherry, announces that two dozen of his neighbours are on their way from Logan. "We have gone land crazy about Western Canada," he declares. "Where did I catch the fever? Well now, stranger, that would be hard to say but gosh, I've got it all right. For a man of my age – and I just turned fifty-five the day I started for Canada – wouldn't be tramping around in a foreign country looking for a new home among strange people."

177

Sunny Al Welcomes the Horde of Investors and Settlers From the South

But Charles Cherry knows very well how he caught the fever. He caught it because, having learned of free land and cheap land just north of the border, he saw a profit in emigration. No eloquent phrases lured him to Canada. He owned 315 acres of good bottom land in Washington County, has sold 90 acres for $10,000, is hanging onto the rest for the moment and, with the help of the Canadian government's aggressive immigration agents, has arrived in the promised land.

The fever of which Charles Cherry spoke was partly Will White's doing. Yet it's probable that, propaganda or no propaganda, a good many Americans would have come to Canada anyway, enticed by the railways and the land companies or simply by the inexorable pull of westward expansion, which had been a fact of American life since the days of the first colonists. Frederick Jackson Turner's epitaph on the closing of the American frontier, unveiled in 1893, was premature; the Canadian prairies were an extension of that frontier. The Americans flocked there for the same reasons they had flocked to their own West: because it was there, a vacuum waiting to be filled.

Consider the case of Daniel Webster Warner, who scouted the possibilities of the Canadian West in 1898. A forty-year-old dairy farmer with a very American name, a long, rugged face and a patriarchal beard, Warner had been born in Iowa, the son of a farmer and millwright. Neighbouring Nebraska achieved statehood when Warner was nine; two years later the family joined the flood of settlers moving west to the frontier and took up land in Dixon County on the Nebraska-Iowa border. But a decade or so later, as more land opened up and his father retired, Warner himself moved west again and proceeded to build a dairy farm of milking shorthorns. By 1898 he was ready to move once more.

He was no city amateur prepared to grab the first piece of land offered him, nor did he intend to queue up in the land office and put his mark on a quarter-section sight unseen. He set off for Winnipeg and took the CPR as far as Strathcona, near Edmonton, getting off periodically along the way and exploring the prairie country by team until he had logged some six hundred miles. Warner patiently prospected the countryside, then hopped on whatever train was available; one carrying poles for a new telegraph line stopped so often to unload that Warner was able to walk the track in front of the locomotive.

He found what he wanted — a section of land on the south bank of the North Saskatchewan, east of Fort Edmonton. He returned to

Nebraska, sold his farm for eight thousand dollars, and moved with his wife and family to Canada. Before he moved again in the face of advancing civilization, this time to Tofield, he had acquired eight hundred acres and was one of the wealthiest farmers in the district and a pillar of the community. He had also become a politicized Canadian – an executive of the local branch of the Grain Growers' Association and later first vice-president of the powerful United Farmers of Alberta.

With men like Warner, the pull of profit overrode considerations of loyalty and patriotism. About one-third of the American immigrants were newcomers, anyway, from European countries; to them, the United States was no more than a way point on the road to their final destination. And many more were former Canadians. Besides, the American West was seething with agrarian discontent. The Canadians offered better farm legislation, so why stay south of the border when you could get anywhere from $60 to $200 an acre for your farm and pick up in Canada a free homestead for yourself and every son over the age of eighteen?

In the United States there was less and less opportunity for farmers' sons or for farm labourers; land was just too expensive. "Why did I come here?" one Iowa farmer explained. "Because it seemed to be the only place to go. The old homestead was worth $100 an acre. It was too small to divide among the boys and the neighbouring farms were too high priced to buy." He paid seven dollars an acre in Manitoba and by 1905 was making as much as he had in Iowa with the additional satisfaction of having settled his sons on nearby properties.

Every newcomer was eager to get rich quick. Stories flew about the country of the early birds who had paid a dollar an acre, done minimal work on the land, and by mid-decade were selling out at twenty times the price. They talked, for example, of William Wishard, the first American farmer in the Canadian West, who came overland from Missouri in 1875 and settled near Portage la Prairie. Wishard started out with three hundred dollars. By 1905 he had 480 acres of land worth about twenty thousand dollars, a fat bank account, and a completely equipped farm. But the astonishing coda to his success story was that he'd been able to present *each* of his eight children with 320 acres of rich black land. It was Wishard's boast that he hadn't made a dollar he hadn't earned by hard work.

There were similar tales: Thomas Fuqua had sold his Nebraska farm for an average price of $62 an acre, then picked up a better farm near High River, Alberta, for only $3.75 an acre. A.J. Cotton had been staked by his friends to make a new start at Swan River, Manitoba. By 1905 he had three thousand acres; his wheat yield was rarely less than twenty bushels an acre and often as high as twenty-five, a startling contrast with conditions back home where the average yield was only twelve.

There was another attraction: unlike the land companies and the railways, the government was not in the real estate business for profit; its only object was an orderly development of the West. This idea of order was planted in the department's pamphlets; the subliminal message was that there was something more decent about life in the clean, unsullied air of Canada. Divorced from the rabble and the violence of the cities and the gunplay of the American frontier, a man could feel secure north of the border, where British justice prevailed.

One pamphlet, diplomatically avoiding the obvious corollary, declared that "respect for law and maintenance of order are very prominent features of life in Canada, as distinguished from other new countries." As one American immigrant from Ohio told the *Century Magazine*: "You can't monkey with the law here. You can't grease a sheriff's fist."

F.B. Lynch of St. Paul said it all. Speaking to the second annual meeting of the Western Canada Immigration Association in Winnipeg in 1903, he declared: "We are essentially men of peace who have emigrated to your country to find homes and investments in a land that is famous for the home and its purity, for the law in its uprightness and for liberty in its truest sense."

3

There was one class of Americans that Canada didn't want and took firm steps to discourage. It didn't want Blacks.

In spite of the welcoming parties that had greeted the slaves smuggled into southern Ontario in the days of the Underground Railroad, the American stereotype of the Negro was deeply ingrained in the Canadian consciousness. Magazines such as *Grip* caricatured the Black as a shiftless and slightly comic figure who played the banjo, danced all night, and lived on watermelon. In the West, the Negro was feared as a potential rapist who could not control his sexual passions and was a threat to Western womanhood. Even J.S. Woodsworth, in *Strangers within Our Gates*, was prepared to quote an American source describing Blacks as having "an aversion to silence and solitude" and a "love of rhythm, excitability and lack of reserve. All travellers speak of their impulsiveness, strong sexual passion and lack of willpower." Woodsworth's own comment was laconic: "Whether we agree . . . or not," he wrote, "we may be thankful we have no 'Negro problem' in Canada."

The general attitude was that the Blacks could not stand the rigours of the Canadian climate, the very thing that the Immigration Department in its propaganda was trying to play down. That argument was used again and again to discourage Black settlement – the only occasions on which Ottawa admitted that prairie conditions were anything but "bracing" and "invigorating."

White's well-oiled propaganda machine didn't operate for Black Americans. No advertisements were placed in Black publications, no Black agents were hired, no promotional material was sent to Blacks, no settlers' certificates were given them. Agents were told they must discourage inquiries from American Negroes.

When the Kansas City agent, James Crawford, reported that Blacks were visiting his office inquiring about forming a colony in the West, he received a blunt answer from Ottawa: ". . . it is not desired that any Negro immigrants should arrive in Western Canada, under the auspices of our Department, or that such immigration should be promoted by our agents."

Crawford tried to discourage such applicants with tales of terrible cold and racial prejudice. In spite of that, a few slipped through. As a result, the agent received a dressing-down from Sifton's successor, Frank Oliver. Like his colleagues, Crawford was faced with a dilemma: how could he know whether or not a written inquiry came from a Black farmer? The department helped him out. If the request came from a small community where there was no agent, he was to write a letter to the local postmaster asking if the man was Black. The responses were unequivocal. "Black as hell," one man replied. "Nigger!" wrote another.

American Blacks were baffled by the Canadian attitude. Great Britain's early rejection of slavery and Canada's reputation as a country of refuge for escaped slaves did not square with the current policy. To Barney McKay, director of the Afro-American Literary Society in Washington, Canada was "a land free from prejudice, caste and social and political slavery." In actuality it was as racist as the States, as McKay ruefully discovered when the government coldly rejected his suggestion that Canada welcome Black settlers. Letters from Blacks went unanswered, were "filed for future reference," or were answered with the curt reply that Canada wasn't encouraging Black immigration into the North West.

The policy was hypocritical in the extreme. The official line was that Canada welcomed everybody. As late as 1911, when the anti-Black hysteria was at its height in the West, Frank Oliver was telling the House of Commons that Negroes were treated the same as any other immigrant at the border while at the same time reassuring his aroused constituents in Edmonton, *sotto voce*, that, as the Boston *Post* reported, "officials are more strictly interpreting the provision of the act which forbids the admission of persons not likely to make desirable citizens."

The act to which Oliver referred was passed in 1908. By instituting compulsory inspection at the point of entry it effectively ended Sifton's policy of unrestricted immigration, to which Oliver had always been opposed. It was a useful tool to sift the "undesirables" from the desirables. The latter got the most cursory once-over; the former – especially the Blacks – were subjected to intensive medical examinations, which in some cases were fraudulent. In White Rock, B.C., for example, in April 1911, forty Blacks were rejected at the border because the medical officer insisted all were suffering from tuberculosis. In Winnipeg, the Commissioner of Immigration offered a fee to the medical inspector at the port of entry for every Negro he failed to pass.

The anti-Black feeling in the West began to grow in 1910, when it was realized that a number of Negroes from Oklahoma had settled in Canada and that more were preparing to join them. These were the so-called Creek Negroes, descendants of slaves kept by the Creek Indians, with whom many of them had intermarried following emancipation and who thought of themselves more as Indians than as Negroes. Subjected to racial prejudice by southern Blacks as well as by the whites of Oklahoma, denied the franchise by the literacy test, squeezed from the land by the tide of Western settlement, they coveted the free homesteads of the Western provinces. It was difficult to stop them at the border for they fulfilled all the qualifications: they were healthy, wealthy, and good farmers.

The first Blacks from Tulsa and Muskogee reached Saskatchewan in 1909 and settled north of Maidstone, between Battleford and

Lloydminster. They were a tough, determined group of eleven families led by Julius Caesar Lane, a fifty-nine-year-old farmer, and a slender little ex-slave, Mattie Hayes, aged sixty, soon to be known as "Mammy" Hayes, matriarch of the community. Mattie and her husband, Joseph, brought their entire extended family with them to Canada, including ten sons, three daughters, and a host of grandchildren. Mammy Hayes and many of her descendants were still in the same area when she died at the age of 103.

In 1910, Jefferson Davis Edwards, aged twenty-two, despairing of the growing Jim Crow atmosphere in Oklahoma, heard from a friend that there was no prejudice in Edmonton – an assessment that was monumentally untrue. He went up to see for himself, looked about, trudged farther north into the Athabasca country, and decided to homestead at Pine Creek, later to be renamed Amber Valley. Others followed, including his tiny fiancée, another Mattie, just turned eighteen. The grey soil, splotched by muskeg, was so heavily timbered when Edwards arrived that he couldn't see more than a hundred yards, but he and his wife and some three hundred others persevered, cleared it, broke it, and lived in harmony.

It wasn't an easy life. All the land had to be cleared by hand, by axe and grub hoe. It was gruelling work, for the spruce stumps were three feet in diameter. Then, before the land could be cultivated, all the timber had to be piled up and burned. Amber Valley was isolated, the only trails being blazed patches on the trees. It took at least two days to make the return trip to Athabasca, twenty-one miles distant, for groceries. Sometimes when the country was soggy it took Edwards four days, packing the load on his back. During one such absence, his wife bore one of their ten children. But the Edwards family prospered. One son became a doctor, another a Golden Gloves champion, and some of their descendants still live in Amber Valley.

Edwards, on his original trip to Alberta, had taken along a travelling companion, Henry Sneed, a Black Oklahoma preacher. Sneed liked what he saw and began to organize other Oklahoma Blacks to make the journey. In March, 1911, he and more than 160 followers from Weleetka, Oklahoma, arrived in St. Paul to find that the Canadian immigration authorities were making every effort to prevent them from crossing the border. The excuse given was a familiar one. As the St. Paul *Pioneer Press* reported, "the cold of the Northern prairies is said to be disastrous to the health of the negroes."

As the Blacks waited apprehensively aboard their Great Northern coaches in St. Paul's Union Depot and their children scampered about making mud pies in the yard (the waiting room was too small to handle them all), the wires buzzed between Washington, Ottawa, and Winnipeg. The Canadian authorities had made it clear they weren't wanted, but Henry Sneed had no intention of turning back. After he got in touch with the U.S. State Department, the situation began to take on some of the aspects of an international incident. The State Department wired to the American consul general in Ottawa, who had already heard from his colleague in Winnipeg. Could Canada exclude any class from entry on account of colour? No, came the answer, Canada couldn't; nobody had wanted to spell out the specifics of racial discrimination in cold type. Any healthy applicant who had fifty dollars was admissible. Late in the afternoon of March 21, the train moved out of St. Paul toward Emerson, Manitoba, the Canadian border point.

But the Canadian authorities had let it be known that the party would be subjected to a rigorous medical examination and all who failed to pass would be turned back. If, by this warning, Canada had hoped to frighten off the Blacks, they reckoned without Henry Sneed. He had been careful to select only the healthiest and most prosperous families.

The Immigration Department rushed eleven members of its staff from Winnipeg to Emerson, including several doctors. What followed was in marked contrast to the usual cursory examination. Young John Blackburn, from Pennsylvania, who crossed into Canada at Emerson with his family that same month, recalled that "immigration officials at the international boundary were courteous and friendly. There was no examination of luggage, and entry into Canada seemed merely a matter of form." But the Blacks were held up for two days while the doctors examined them from scalp to ankle and other officials questioned them about their finances.

By March 23 they could find no reason to hold them back any longer. Not only were these people in robust health, they were also well off. Most had cash or credit cheques ranging between one thousand and three thousand dollars. Sneed, who was held until the last (the others refusing to proceed without him), was worth $40,000 and was carrying $10,000 of it in cash on his person! Three of his party were turned back; the others went on to Edmonton to settle with the Edwardses in Amber Valley.

By now, however, the department was seriously concerned over

185

what some papers were calling "the invasion of Negroes." Sneed had told the press that he was in the vanguard of five thousand Blacks seeking admission to Canada. Wesley Speers was dispatched post-haste to Oklahoma to warn Black leaders that there was danger north of the border for their people. The department even hired a clergyman – black, of course – to stump the state preaching against Black migration. It sent Will White on a fact-finding mission; he reported, predictably, that in the Black communities, "laziness is abundant and seems to have put its hall-mark everywhere," a conclusion that did not seem to agree with his own observation that the Oklahoma "Negro-Indians" possessed "wealth much greater than that of the white settlers in the State." White advised against any further Black emigration from Oklahoma: "There is so much of the Indian blood in the coloured man of Oklahoma, carrying with it all the evil traits of a life of rapine and murder, that it will not easily assimilate with agrarian life."

In Canada, the objections were nationwide. The Toronto *Mail and Empire*, ignoring Canada's boast that it was a country of law and order, called up the spectre of race riots if more Blacks were allowed into the country. But the protests were most violent in Edmonton, which, rumour whispered, was the main target of the Black invasion. The Board of Trade demanded that all Blacks be banned from Canada. The Imperial Order Daughters of the Empire warned that the Blacks would prey on white women. The city council demanded the immediate segregation of all Negroes.

By May, 1911, the Immigration Department had an order-in-council ready for government approval banning all Black immigration for a year. But Wilfrid Laurier had a problem. An election was coming up, and there was a significant Black vote in Halifax and in southern Ontario. Most of it was Liberal; could the government afford to antagonize these people? The government could not; the order was dropped; Canada continued to pretend publicly that every race was welcome while privately tightening the screws on Black immigration. The CPR co-operated, excluding Negroes from Western tours and refusing them the reduced rates to which every white settler was entitled.

In its efforts to keep the West racially pure, the Department of Immigration was hugely successful. In 1901 there were ninety-eight Blacks on the prairies. In 1911, after the greatest immigration boom in the nation's history, there were only 1,524.

186

By mid-decade it was obvious that the American invasion was chang- *Loosening*
ing the West. The Americans moved confidently and speedily, with *Imperial*
greater assurance than most Canadians, especially Eastern Canadians. *ties*
Ella Sykes was to discover that in Canada life galloped along at a
faster pace than it did in her more leisurely homeland. But Americans
seemed to gallop faster than Canadians, seizing opportunities that
others had missed, stealing a march on cautious Torontonians, pushing ahead as if life were a race with the prize to the swiftest.

One Saturday night in March, 1906, for example, J.H. Roberts, a
South Dakota farmer, arrived in Calgary with his wife and family
and a trainload of fellow Americans. Roberts and seven of his friends
had decided to locate near Mannville on the Canadian Northern east
of Edmonton. They were in such a hurry to reach the site that they
couldn't wait for the Canadian weekend to end. Leaving their families
in the immigration hall (every hotel was full), they pushed on to
Edmonton, found their way into the land office by the back door,
and began rummaging about, looking for maps and information.
Here the agent found them and tried to explain that in Canada
everything closed up tight on the Lord's Day. Roberts and his friends
would have none of that.

"Hurry!" cried Roberts. "Hurry! If you could see them coming
after us you would think there was hurry. We are going out to Mannville on tonight's train and we want a map." They got what they
wanted.

The Americans brought a more aggressive style to the West. American entrepreneurs were prepared to take greater risks than Eastern
Canadians. They poured into Winnipeg in the early days of the
century, as strange in their own way as the Doukhobors, with their
broad-brimmed felt hats, their fierce moustaches and goatees, their
strange cuts of chin whiskers and their midwestern drawls – buyers,
speculators, land company men, intent on buying up large blocks of
the prairies to sell at a handsome profit to their fellow countrymen.

As a result, the American land companies made the largest profits.
They were often prepared to buy marginal land that others would
not take a chance on and, by high pressure methods, make it popular
and saleable. Their willingness to spend large sums of speculative
money, to organize every detail, and to advertise freely astonished the

more conservative real estate interests in Canada. "These companies work on different lines altogether from any of the real estate agents here with whom we have hitherto done business," F.T. Griffin, the CPR's land commissioner, wrote to a Canadian developer. "They go after their purchaser, pay railway fares, accompany them to the land, personally conduct them over it and stay with them, eat, sleep and drink with them if necessary until a sale is made or they fail in the attempt."

The Americans were even more aggressive than this comment suggests. B.L. Grant, president of the Grant-Armstrong Land Company of St. Paul, described the technique in detail in 1903: "We do more than sell the lands; we colonize them. We organize excursions from different parts of Wisconsin and Illinois, giving a special rate of $18 for the trip. We bring the people to Winnipeg where we have our rooms and treat them as guests. We show them over your city, take them out to our lands where we have our carriages waiting to drive over the entire district, and we take them back, all for $18, which is refunded if they purchase the land. Why those people talk of . . . the wonders of the west continuously and that is the best advertisement we could want."

The biggest and most controversial of the American land speculations was that of the Saskatchewan Valley Land Corporation, which in 1902 purchased a vast block of more than a million acres of railway and government land between Regina and Prince Albert. The larger portion of this block — some 839,000 acres — was part of the land grant awarded to the Qu'Appelle, Long Lake and Saskatchewan Railway and Steamship Company, as "fairly fit for settlement." The railway, whose front man was E.B. Osler, M.P., a well-known Toronto banker, had rejected much of it, however, as sub-marginal, and the matter was being disputed in the courts when the newly organized Saskatchewan Valley company of Minnesota businessmen jumped in and offered to take it over. The land company, made up largely of former Canadians who had immigrated to the United States and had acquired broad experience in previous land speculations there, paid $1.53 an acre for the railway lands and $1.00 an acre for 250,000 adjoining acres of government land.

The deal was made in secret between Clifford Sifton and the principals of the company. Once the details were revealed they touched off a raging controversy in the House of Commons. The land company made a staggering profit because it sold the lands quickly for prices ranging between six and ten dollars an acre. The presence, as directors and incorporators, of two prominent Liberals, D.H. McDonald of Qu'Appelle and A.J. Adamson of Rosthern, heightened the Conservatives' suspicions. The latter was a candidate in the 1904 election and, more significant, a brother-in-law of J.G. Turriff, Sifton's Chief Commissioner of Dominion Lands. The Americans were wise in the ways of politics: Adamson and McDonald were obviously in on the original deal to grease the political skids. Once the contract was approved the company was reorganized to include others, almost certainly including Turriff, who did not deny under oath that he was involved.

Nevertheless the Conservatives found it difficult to make political capital out of the enterprise. For one thing, the land had stood empty for years; even the railway didn't want it. One man who did have faith in it was Wesley Speers, who visited St. Paul and convinced the Americans (including several executives and stockholders of the Quaker Oats Company) that the land was suitable for flax growing. Secondly, the government had driven a hard bargain; the new company had to place a minimum of twenty settlers per township on the adjacent public lands within a five-year period. And finally, the scheme was wildly successful: a vast strip of Saskatchewan country was rapidly filled with colonists, thanks to the Americans' bold tactics. They at once set about building hotels, boarding houses, and livery facilities for the newcomers. They brought in a trainload of two hundred American businessmen, merchants, bankers, and reporters to look over the property and publicize it. They spent forty thousand dollars the first year in advertising. They set up twenty-two hundred sales agencies in twelve states. All this investment paid off handsomely; no other land company had, to this point, been so successful. Land that no Canadian wanted had been bought for a song—the Americans used discounted half-breed land scrip rather than cash, which meant that their original investment was as low as fifty thousand dollars—and sold for ten times its original cost. It was, as Cy Warman, a U.S. writer declared, "one of the first guns in the 'American invasion' of Canada."

The American invasion caused considerable soul searching on both sides of the Atlantic. What would be the result of all this influx? It was certainly changing the West; would it change Canada? Would the nation become "Americanized," or, worse still, would it become part of the United States? Many Americans thought so. Would the Amer-

189

ican presence mean a loosening of Imperial bonds? Many Britons believed it would. Or would the West become a separate nation, neither British nor American? The American frontier novelist James Oliver Curwood was convinced of that. "A new nation," he declared, "will be born in the West, formed of the very flesh and blood of the United States." As Curwood noted in Alberta, "every town is hustling with American spirit" and former Americans were entering politics, becoming reeves and councillors in Alberta communities.

The general attitude south of the border was that the West would soon be part of the United States. The *Saturday Evening Post* referred to Alberta as "the Yankee province." Such Eastern papers as the Brooklyn *Eagle*, the New York *Post*, and the Detroit *Journal* were convinced that annexation was inevitable. Western American politicians echoed these sentiments. Senator Moses E. Clapp of Minnesota thought the union would come as the result of assimilation. Marsh Murdock, the powerful Republican congressman from Kansas, was for outright capture. The Governor of North Carolina predicted a struggle that would result in "one great republic under the government of what is now the United States."

Such a possibility failed to raise the hackles of Canadians, giddy from the prosperity the Americans were bringing. John Dafoe said he saw no sign that Westerners viewed the invasion with any feeling of dread. Frederick Haultain, the Premier of the North West Territories, agreed that there was no political danger in the influx. The Toronto *Globe* was worried at first: five out of eight Alberta newspapers were edited by former Americans. It sent a reporter out west only to be told that the editorial ideas expressed were no different from those of other Canadian newspapers.

The Americans in the West, in fact, turned out to be among the most enthusiastic Canadians. "It is the Americans rather than the Canadians who show jealousy at the flocking in of people of other nationalities and raise the cry of 'Canada for the Canadians,'" the national president of the British Brotherhood Movement discovered during a trip to Canada. Those Americans who were not European-born or ex-Canadians were, in the words of Dr. Peter Bryce, chief medical inspector for the Immigration Department, "accidental" rather than "essential" Americans. This type of American, Bryce explained, "came to the [American] West for bread, and not for liberty; he will come north into Canada for bread, regardless of national flag or tradition."

It was the British in Canada and the British press in the mother country who worried about the effects of the American invasion. British periodicals and newspapers were concerned about the dilution of British blood in Western Canada, the "loosening of ties," as a writer in the *Fortnightly Review* called it. The Americans might make good Canadians, he wrote, but would they become loyal subjects of the Empire?

Another British writer warned of a Canadian policy "seemingly not pro-British" and wrote darkly of future political complications. And the correspondent of the London *Daily Mail* asked: "Is Canada going to absorb these people or are they going to absorb the Northwest?" He was not worried about Eastern Canada with its Loyalist strengths, but English settlers in the West might easily "be lost in the multitude."

The English came to Canada with a strongly developed national personality, honed over the centuries. Unlike the Americans, they had not developed an individuality by breaking the soil or hewing down the forests. The Englishman was far more conservative than the American, who had learned to mould himself rapidly to new conditions during his westward trek. It's significant that while the English in Canada invested cautiously in real estate and bonds, the Americans put their money at risk into industrial firms and branch plants. By 1909, one hundred branches of American companies were operating in Winnipeg.

The Americans were adaptable. They gave their allegiance swiftly to the new country that nurtured them so well. "Four years ago," one American farmer told a Canadian journalist, "I lived in Iowa with a $2000 mortgage hanging over me. Taxes and interest were eating me up. I came up here, got 160 acres of land as a gift from the Canadian government, and for two years I lived in that shack. Now I own that house and every board in it is paid for. Eighty acres of my land are under cultivation. My wife and my children are well fed and well clothed for the first time in years. Do we want to be annexed? I guess not!"

The British were right to worry about the loosening of Imperial ties. F.E. Kenaston, an American businessman, correctly predicted in 1903 that within a few years the Americans in the West would be more ardently Canadian than the Canadians themselves. But *not* more ardently British. The result of the American invasion was to produce exactly what the British feared.

With the coming of the Americans, the population shift was accelerated. Soon, almost one-third of the settlers in the West would have no sentimental attachment to the Empire. But they did have a strong feeling for the land that nurtured them, and some began to question the Imperial connection. Why was another nation still in control of Canada's foreign policy? And what was a titled Englishman doing in Rideau Hall? The idea of a British peer dictating to Canadians even in the mildest way did not sit easily in a region where, in principle at least, every man was considered the equal of every other if he was willing to work. Like the young aristocrats in their breeches and puttees leaning on the bar of the Alberta Hotel, the governor general lived on a *remittance* from the Old Country; to some, the difference was only one of degree.

No Eastern Canadian newspaper, indeed, could have supported the attitude that two wildly different Western papers, the *Free Press* in Winnipeg and the *Herald* in Calgary, adopted toward the King's representative. As early as 1901, John Dafoe, whose burgeoning nationalism was to be reflected more and more in *Free Press* editorials, was sharply critical of Lord Minto's attempts to act as viceroy rather than governor general. His Excellency, Dafoe declared, had a radical misconception of his position, an extraordinary belief that Canada wasn't in total control of its own army. Dafoe was more judicious than his Alberta contemporary, couching his thoughts with ifs and buts; but there was no mistaking the veiled warning in his editorial:

"If . . . there is to be built up at Rideau Hall, a military, political and social power with roots beyond the sea, which is to regard itself as privileged and exempt from the obligations of Canadian law, it is well to know the fact, in order that proper steps may be taken at once to prevent any such condition of things becoming established here."

The *Herald* tossed diplomacy out the window when Lord Minto's successor, Lord Grey, came to town in 1906. It was an embarrassing visit. When a reception was planned in His Excellency's honour, scarcely anybody turned up, to the dismay of his staff. There were extenuating circumstances: a Masonic excursion to Banff, a bad storm, a civic holiday. But when the Governor General's entourage let it be known that they considered Calgary ungrateful and disloyal, the *Herald* responded with a broadside entitled "The Sentiment of the West":

"Vice-royalty is a mere accident. High position has a mere cash interest but a dollar's a dollar, and Western men are after it.

192

"The West usually takes a man at his face value. The graduate drops his degree . . . the nobleman loses his title. . . . In the face of this levelling process . . . can Lord Grey or any other nobleman expect a great demonstration?

"The West, moreover, is becoming more democratic through its American immigration. Thousands from the United States have come into Canada, and with them have brought their conception of the sovereign people. All that is formal and symbolic in our institutions and our government must give way before the democratic leaven which has been coming into Canada during the past five years. . . ."

Both editorials brought howls of protest from Eastern Canada, but it was sentiments such as these, both circumspect and crude, that paved the way for the Balfour Declaration of 1924 and the Statute of Westminster, which, in 1931, created the Commonwealth, loosened Imperial ties, and was more in keeping with the new spirit of democracy bubbling up on the Canadian plains.

Chapter Seven

The Passing of the Old Order

1

Nineteen hundred and five, like most other years, was one of beginnings, endings, and turning points, in Canada as in the rest of the world. Jules Verne died; Greta Garbo was born. Einstein published his Special Theory of Relativity, Freud his "Three Contributions to the Theory of Sex." Russia crushed a revolution; Norway and Sweden parted company. Ty Cobb began his baseball career and Isadora Duncan opened her dancing school. The Rotary Club was born; so were the Wobblies. Picasso began his "pink period"; Debussy wrote "Clair de Lune"; Upton Sinclair published *The Jungle*. The world was introduced to Ovaltine, Vicks VapoRub, Palmolive Soap, and the first neon sign. The New York censor closed Bernard Shaw's play *Mrs. Warren's Profession* after a single performance. And in Pittsburgh, David Belasco had a new hit, *The Girl of the Golden West*.

The Golden West! In Canada that phrase had a romantic ring, for the West had reached the half-way point of what can be called its Golden Age. Nine years had passed since Clifford Sifton and the Laurier Liberals took office and launched the settlement wave. Another nine lay ahead before the opening thunder of the Great War would cut off the flow of immigrants. In the West, too, 1905 was a year of beginnings and endings. It was the year in which two new provinces, Saskatchewan and Alberta, were carved out of the old North West Territories. Provincial autonomy, for which Westerners had fought so long and often so bitterly, was a *fait accompli* at last. And 1905 was also the year in which Clifford Sifton suddenly resigned as Minister of the Interior in the Liberal government, signalling the end of one era and the beginning of another. The two events were not unconnected.

Sifton's resignation followed the federal election in the late fall of 1904, a particularly hard-fought contest, bitter and acrimonious in the Minister's case. Sifton's nerves were badly shattered. As soon as he had cleaned up the backlog of work in his office after the Liberal victory, he left Ottawa at the end of the year for treatment in the mud and sulpho lithia water baths of the Indiana Springs Company at Mudlavia. His staff expected him back within two or three weeks, but Sifton stayed out of the country for two months. His nerves, he wrote to Laurier, were much worse, "more shaken than I thought." He did not return until after Parliament opened near the end of February, 1905.

It is difficult to picture the imperturbable Sifton, the platform battler who sprang joyously into the lists each time an election was called, emerging with nerves shaken so badly he was forced to immerse himself in mud for the best part of two months. But then the fight in his own constituency had been particularly nasty. Vicious rumours flew about regarding Sifton's private life: stories that he had been caught in an affair with a married woman, that he would be named co-respondent in a messy divorce suit.

The rumours were so persistent that Sifton's own paper felt the need to try to scotch them, charging that they were planted by campaign workers for his old nemesis, R.L. Richardson of the *Winnipeg Tribune*, who, the paper said, was planning "a sensational roorbach" on the Brandon electorate. Richardson vigorously denied the charge while making it clear that the rumours regarding Sifton's private life did exist. "They originated in Ottawa and have been in circulation over all the eastern provinces for some weeks," the *Tribune* reported, adding piously that even if there were grounds for the rumours, the paper would never use them in any campaign against the Minister.

Sifton's resignation was precipitate. Parliament opened on February 21. Sifton returned on the twenty-fifth and officially resigned two days later, touching off a bitter political and religious controversy that saw the West pitted against the East. Sifton gave as his reasons his objection to the educational clauses in the government's bill to create the two new provinces, although there is no hint of that in the curt, one-paragraph letter of resignation he submitted to the Prime Minister.

In hindsight, the affair looks like a tempest in a teapot. Hairs were split, constitutional phrases subjected to legal quibbles. But it is necessary to understand the temper of the period, the depth of feeling in Ontario and the West, to comprehend the bitterness of the issues involved.

The North West Territories were demanding total autonomy, which meant the right to control their own educational system. Laurier had no intention of giving them that, nor was he legally required to do so. He insisted on safeguarding minority rights in education but was prepared to maintain the status quo in both new provinces. Territorial law had allowed minority groups to establish separate schools (in practice, Roman Catholic) and to be "liable only to assessments of such rates as they may impose upon themselves." In practice these schools weren't all that separate. A series of federal acts, consolidated in 1901, had made education, textbooks, curriculum, and teachers' qualifications uniform throughout the Territories. Instruction was in

English, but a half-hour was set aside for religious instruction (in French if desired) for any minority group that wanted it. That was the status quo; the Territories were happy with it.

Laurier turned the job of drafting the educational section of the bill over to his Minister of Justice, the prickly Irish Catholic Charles Fitzpatrick, a Quebecker and former Laval professor. There was no love lost between Fitzpatrick, the one-time chief counsel for Louis Riel, and Sifton, the former Methodist lay preacher. Sifton had wanted the Justice portfolio for himself; he didn't get it. Fitzpatrick is said to have declared that "as long as Sifton is in the cabinet we are sitting on a powder keg." No doubt that attitude helped to frustrate Sifton's ambitions. When the remark was relayed, Sifton, it was reported, announced that "Fitzpatrick carries a knife in his boot for me."

Fitzpatrick boasted that he had drafted the new bill entirely by himself, "with my own hand clause by clause, line by line, word by word." He relied, however, on the loose phrasing of the original federal legislation of 1875, which did not make it clear whether the Catholic Church or the government controlled the minority schools. It hadn't mattered then, with only a handful of settlers in the West, and for a time the church had run its own schools but the later federal acts had changed all that, and the West was satisfied. Nobody considered turning back the clock.

What was in question wasn't much more than a matter of wording, of tightening up an ambiguous piece of legislation. But Sifton clearly had other views. Was the cunning Fitzpatrick, whose piety sometimes seemed to exceed that of the Pope, trying to bring back Catholic-run schools in the West? That was Sifton's publicly expressed opinion, and it was enough to arouse Orange Ontario. And there was more: when school lands were sold by the new provinces, where was the money to go? Laurier wanted the educational funds to be shared by the schools on a proportional basis. To Sifton that was "a most colossal endowment of sectarian education from public property." Why, there'd be a Catholic university next, paid for out of public funds! By the time Sifton returned from Mudlavia his resignation was being hinted at. He met with Laurier on the night of February 27 and quit immediately.

This was an odd business. In Sifton's correspondence with Laurier during his stay in Indiana, the educational provisions in the new bill were barely discussed. The two colleagues went into some detail in their letters about grazing leases, irrigation policies, and public lands, but on the highly sensitive schools question there was scarcely anything. "You do not say anything about the school question and I assume that you have not as yet discerned any serious difficulty in dealing with it," Sifton wrote to Laurier on January 22. Four days later, in a letter that crossed the Minister's, Laurier remarked casually that "there also remains the school question which I am slowly working out. I am satisfied with the progress which we have made on it, though everybody dreads it." That was all. Sifton, who had originally joined the Laurier cabinet only after the Prime Minister came to an agreement with him on similar terms in Manitoba, showed no further curiosity. Laurier made no effort to enlighten him on the details of a bill the effect of which he admitted he dreaded.

This is remarkable. Clifford Sifton was the Liberals' strong man in the West; it was his personal fiefdom. Very little went on of which he was not fully aware and which he did not control. Why did Laurier not consult him on the details of the new educational clauses? Why didn't he wait for Sifton's return before placing them before the House? Sifton asked for a brief delay of Parliament, but Laurier declined. It was almost as if the Prime Minister considered that Sifton was irrelevant, expendable.

And why did Sifton choose the moment he did to leave Ottawa – the most significant period, surely, in the entire history of the North West Territories? Ever since the Liberal government had come into power, the Territories had been demanding autonomy; Sifton was their champion. He had fought hard in his provincial role during the Manitoba School Crisis. Why had he absented himself in the very month in which the educational policies of the new West were being drawn up? It is true that he had his leader's assurance that the status quo would be maintained. But Sifton was a man who liked to dot every *i* and cross every *t*. Was his health so imperilled that he could not postpone his trip to the mud baths? He'd put off rest cures before, simply on the argument that he couldn't afford to leave his work. Now he not only left town but he also delayed his return. The correspondence shows his staff expected him back much earlier. He didn't come. Why?

Dafoe, who checked everything with Sifton and thought he knew his mind, was stunned by his resignation. It came to him, he said, like a bolt from the blue. His *Free Press* editorials had been supporting the 1875 legislation without any dissent from his employer. Now he had to find a way to make a right-about-face. It put him, as he told Sifton, "in a very difficult position." But the ex-Minister helped him find a way

199

out by pointing to the hated new clause that would allow both public and separate schools to share proportionately in funds derived from the sale of public lands. Lawyers for both parties argued over the implications of this clause, which Sifton, in a later speech, claimed would put "a constitutional, irrevocable earmark on the public funds of the Northwest." That gave Dafoe something to attack.

Sifton's resignation made him a hero of the moment, "worshipped as a martyr from one end of the country to the other" in the sardonic words of a political opponent, William Northrup. Did he, then, resign purely on a point of principle? It's more likely that he used his dispute with Laurier to effect an honourable retirement, which had for some time been rumoured in Ottawa. "Many rumours have drifted down to us in the past ten years," Northrup said guardedly, "but I venture to say that none of them will be received with less credulity by the country than the statement he [Sifton] . . . made as to the causes of his resignation."

Certainly Sifton's deafness was a contributing factor. His own newspaper went so far as to say that his resignation was "not unconnected with the state of his health." By this time Sifton was almost stone deaf. He could not engage in the cut and thrust of Parliamentary debate but was forced to wait for the Hansard reports to be published before he could respond to Opposition attacks. And, for the past year, as Dafoe noted, Sifton had seemed bored with his ministry – "there was an evident slackening of energy and interest in departmental detail." One might have guessed, Dafoe wrote, that "Sifton had very little desire to continue much longer in the position he occupied."

And then there were the rumours that Northrup had mentioned. Early in March, a few days after Sifton's resignation, tantalizing references to dark manoeuvrings began to appear in the anti-Sifton papers. On March 1, Richardson's *Tribune* revealed that "for several weeks reports have been current that Mr. Sifton was about to retire. Various reasons have been assigned from time to time. . . . It is suggested in some quarters that, if he was being forced out of the cabinet, or had any intention of retiring on other grounds, the present situation would give him an opportunity to withdraw on what he and his friends might easily say was a question of principle."

On the same day the Calgary *Herald*'s Ottawa correspondent went a step further: "While it is declared that Mr. Sifton has resigned in order that he may have a free hand to discuss the school question, it is commonly understood here that other considerations of a very personal character are the chief factors in his retirement.

"This subject has been the talk of the capital for many days, and it is no secret that the difficulty was likely to make his resignation imperative, aside from any political questions."

Clearly, all of political Ottawa was abuzz over *something*. What was it? On March 5 the irrepressible Bob Edwards published in the Calgary *Eye Opener* his own account of why Sifton had resigned:

"Clifford Sifton has resigned, ostensibly over the school question. This implies a conscience on the part of Clifford. The idea of Clifford resigning on the grounds of conscientious scruples is laughable in the extreme. What has really made him resign is the trouble he has gotten himself into over a married woman in Ottawa. . . .

"The story of Sifton's escapade, wherein he seems to have been ministering to the interior in great shape, reads like some of the spicier cantos of Don Juan. The outraged husband is Walter Mackay, son of the late millionaire, William Mackay, the old lumber king of Ottawa. It appears that Mackay started for Montreal one night but for some reason turned back and spent the evening at the club instead. Returning to his residence about two o'clock in the morning, he tried to open the front door with his latchkey, but the latch was fixed on the inside so that he could not get in. So away he went round to the back door of the house to see if he could get in that way.

"Approaching his back door, what was his surprise to see it cautiously opened from the inside and a big, tall man issuing therefrom. 'Burglar,' thought Mackay. . . . It was pretty dark at the time and the two of them tussled and rolled all over the backyard. Finally, to Mackay's astonishment, a ray from the moon revealed the sinister features of the Minister of the Interior.

"'Hello, Sifton! What are you doing here this time of night?'

"'Oh,' quoth Clifford, panting, 'your wife was in trouble over some legal matters and sent for me to discuss them.'

"'Well, that's strange,' said the husband scratching his neck dubiously. 'I suppose it's all right, though.'

"Next day, however, Mackay put on his thinking cap, and rather foolishly aired the story down town, telling all his friends about it. Their ill-concealed amusement showed him too plainly that they had for some time been alive to what he, husband like, had been blind. Then the row began.

"A private conference was held at the Mackay home, among those present as conciliators being Father Whalen, Archbishop Duhamel and Sir Wilfrid Laurier. Father Whalen next day took the lady to her former home in Quebec. Sifton just about this juncture left for the

201

west, this stirring incident having taken place shortly before the elections. Ye Gods, and we didn't know about it!

"By the time he returned, the scandal had become the property of the politicians and the inner circles of society, though no newspaper dared breathe a word.

"What between the uproar in his own family and the demands for reparation on the part of the husband, Clifford thought it was up to him to duck out. . . . He left for parts unknown, and remained away from his seat in parliament, neglecting his duties and pretending that he was in a sanitarium somewhere for his health. His health must have been all right about this juncture if we know anything about this line of business.

"Sifton returned to Ottawa a discredited man and handed in his resignation. For the benefit of the public, it was arranged that he should retire with dignity under the benign wing of the school question. . . .

"In the meantime, we understand, hubby has filed for divorce. The Governor General, we presume, could not stand for his most important minister being co-respondent in a divorce case, though certain other cabinet ministers are not a whit more virtuous than Clifford. We are ruled over by a fine gang at Ottawa. . . ."

Edwards's article was clearly libellous, particularly if untrue – dangerously so. Sifton, however, took no notice of it. That, of course, was part of his philosophy. "Ignore all whispering campaigns," he advised a young man entering politics. "If you once show yourself affected by it, you are lost. The more you try to stamp it out, the more it spreads." He did not believe in suing newspapers for libel, he said in 1899, because if you sued once and won and then didn't sue again, every slanderous statement made by the same paper would be believed simply because you didn't take action.

Yet this was no ordinary political attack. Copies of the *Eye Opener* were rushed to Ottawa and eventually became collectors' items selling for upwards of twenty-five dollars. The New York *Telegraph* reprinted the article word for word. And Edwards's report was particularly damaging. It was not just that Sifton was charged with being the principal in a seamy sex scandal (to the considerable embarrassment of his wife and children) but also that he had used the excuse of principle to cloak his retirement from the cabinet. Edwards had impugned his honour, his political integrity.

If the *Eye Opener* story had been a fabrication, Sifton could easily

202

have destroyed Edwards, politically and financially, by putting a single witness – Walter Mackey (the name had been misspelled) – on the stand to refute the allegations, not to mention the two ecclesiastics and the Prime Minister himself. He did not do so.

In spite of the *Eye Opener*'s reputation in some quarters as a scandal sheet, Edwards himself was remarkably careful about what he published. It is true that he poked fun at the pompous and that he invented so-called news stories that were strictly satirical. This one did not fall into that category. Edwards checked his copy with his friend Paddy Nolan, Calgary's best-known lawyer; he was caught out only once in twenty years. He must have been convinced the story was true and he must have had good sources, for he was dealing here with something more than defamation. If the story were false, Edwards could have been charged with criminal libel; the statute had been part of the Criminal Code since 1892. Arthur Sifton, Chief Justice of Alberta, was a power in the provincial Liberal government. He could have leaped to his brother's defence and helped send Edwards to jail. He did not choose to do so.

Nor did the Siftons respond when, in April, the issue was raised again with screaming headlines on the front page of the Conservative Toronto *World*. The paper reported that Sifton's cabinet rival, Charles Fitzpatrick, was the man behind the resignation. According to the *World*, Fitzpatrick had been conspiring against Sifton for some time, feeding the Tories ammunition regarding Western land scandals. When the Tories refused to bite, the *World* said, "Mr. Sifton's enemies . . . laid another trap, one of a very delicate nature, and Mr. Sifton appears to have been an easy victim.

"Mr. Sifton became involved in a scandal. The incident was canvassed all over Ottawa. It spread westward where it was cultivated by the conspirators and embarrassed Mr. Sifton considerably in the Brandon election.

"When the scandal became general public property in Ottawa, Mr. Sifton's colleagues interested themselves in it. They said a settlement of some kind must be arranged. Mr. Sifton was forced to make himself party to a formal settlement. . . . It was arranged that immediately after the elections Mr. Sifton would retire immediately from the cabinet on the plea of ill health. But Mr. Sifton did not retire. He went south for his health, and while he was away the autonomy bill was introduced in parliament.

"Mr. Sifton saw a more plausible excuse for getting out of politics, an excuse right in line with his convictions. He hastened northward, and after a brief conference with Sir Wilfrid Laurier, in which the latter treated him very cavalierly, he handed in his resignation. . . ."

According to the *World*, the *Eye Opener* story and its reproduction in a New York daily were the first guns in a campaign to force Sifton to compromise on the educational clauses and support them in the House, which, as he told the Commons, he did "reluctantly and with no great enthusiasm."

"The compromise, as a matter of fact, is worse than the bill in its original form," the paper declared. "When Mr. Sifton says it is not, he speaks not as a public man but as a husband and father terrorized by unscrupulous conspirators who have his reputation at their mercy."

It must be remembered that all these personal attacks on Sifton (including the *World*'s crocodile tears) were made by opposition papers. Scandal or no scandal, it was hardly in character for Clifford Sifton to bow to blackmail, especially from men like Fitzpatrick. The charge of dalliance by itself was scarcely enough to drive him from office; other cabinet ministers had weathered worse blows. One can only surmise that the constant gossip that had dogged him since the previous fall was the final straw. He had served his leader faithfully for almost a decade, yet he had been passed over for the promotion he surely deserved. Worse, the hated Fitzpatrick had been given the plum! His deafness was now almost total; his health had been undermined; the attacks on him, both personal and political, showed no signs of abating; and Laurier had treated him shamefully.

He went out with trumpets blowing and all flags flying. His differences with Laurier were easily patched up in the month following his resignation. They were, as his own newspaper said, "a matter of degree rather than a direct conflict of opinion." Why could they not have been resolved in private? By forcing the issue publicly, Sifton made himself a hero in the West but at the expense of his own party and of his own leader, whose reputation was weakened by the perception that he had been pressured into a compromise by the Young Napoleon. And the shrill public argument had exacerbated the religious and regional tensions between Central and Western Canada.

The Sifton-Mackey scandal died down and was forgotten. There was no divorce – that would have required a special act of Parliament – and the Mackeys remained in Ottawa until 1910. The press never again referred to the story nor did the historians of the period, except in the most guarded and subtle way. Though Sifton may have been a loss to the cabinet, his task was really finished. Through his drive, his stubbornness, and his imagination he had solved for his country and his party the problem of the empty West. In the face of mounting opposition, he had bulled through his policies, ignoring the cries of mongrelization, secure in his own conviction that the best prairie immigrants were practical farmers, whether they came from Krakow or Bukovina, Kronoberg or Saxony, Ayrshire or Idaho. The times were in his favour, but it is doubtful if anybody else in the Laurier cabinet could have done the job with the dispatch and the efficiency that Sifton brought to it.

He was not the most popular minister in the Government. James A. Macdonald went so far as to say, in 1911, that during his ten years as editor of the *Globe*, Sifton "was absolutely the heaviest and most irksome burden we had to carry." Once the compromise with Laurier was effected, it was widely believed that Sifton would return to the cabinet. He did not. "There are a variety of reasons for this which I am hardly at liberty to explain," he told a Winnipeg friend. Whatever these reasons were – and it would require exceptional naïveté to believe that the autonomy question was the only one, or even the most important one – Sifton was wise to leave office when he did. The Conservatives had wind of a series of major scandals within his own department involving grazing leases and timber rights, which they intended to exploit to the fullest. These involved most of the senior members of the Sifton organization, up to and including his own deputy. It was clear that an era was over, another beginning. The great movement that Clifford Sifton had launched was accelerating under its own steam. Sifton had been the catalyst that helped transform the West; now his usefulness was at an end.

2

The extent of Laurier's disenchantment with his former minister may be gauged by the selection of his successor. Sifton had recommended Walter Scott for the post. The former editor of the Regina *Leader*, dispenser of patronage for the region, and the man who defeated the redoubtable Nicholas Flood Davin as Member for West Assiniboia, Scott was the best Westerner, in Sifton's view, to carry out his policies. Scott was not chosen and went on to lead the Liberal party in

*The
new era*

Saskatchewan to victory and to become the province's first premier. Instead of Scott, Laurier gave the ministry to the one man who was diametrically opposed to the Siftonian concept of open immigration – to Frank Oliver who, in 1901, had cried out in the House that "we resent the idea of having the millstone of this Slav population hung around our necks." The appointment was unexpected in Edmonton where it was widely believed that Oliver would become the first premier of Alberta.

It was inevitable that Oliver would drastically modify the open door policy in favour of a more selective approach to immigration that would, in his words, build up "a kindred and higher and better civilization in the country." Anything else, Oliver believed, was simply "railway traffic."

Both Sifton and Oliver were powerful politicians who knew how to use the devices of patronage, gerrymander, and, when necessary, out-and-out bribery to gain electoral victory. Ten years before, Sifton had seconded Oliver's nomination as Liberal candidate for Alberta, declaring that he was "Liberal enough to suit him and independent enough and honest enough to be a North West man first, last and all the time." Both men were also ardent prohibitionists as well as committed Westerners, but there the similarities ended. In almost every other sense the two were opposites. Sifton, with his cold eyes and plump cheeks, posing for his portrait in his riding pinks, was every inch the Ottawa sophisticate. Oliver, with his cadaverous Irish features, his deep-set eyes, rugged cheekbones, and vast handlebar moustache, was still the rough-hewn prairie pioneer. Sifton was a pillar of the Ottawa Hunt; Oliver was president of the Edmonton bicycle club. Sifton kept as tight a rein on his emotions as he did on his geldings; Oliver was passionate in his oratory and explosive in his editorials. Sifton hired an editor to speak for him in print; Oliver was his own editor, the *Bulletin* his personal organ.

"His is the temperament of the pioneer," Sifton's own newspaper wrote in April, 1905, in a eulogy of the new minister. Certainly no other member of the House had seen so much of the pioneer West. An itinerant journeyman, Francis Robert Oliver Bowsfield (he shucked off his father's name when he left the Brampton farm after his mother's second marriage) was helping to print the *Free Press* in 1873, long before it became a Sifton paper. Three years later he joined a bull train, following the ruts of the famous Carlton Trail to Fort Edmonton. He bought the first lot in town, opened a store in a log cabin – the first emporium to be independent of the Hudson's Bay Company – and in December 1880 started the *Bulletin*. He printed it himself on a second-hand press in an abandoned smokehouse not far from the Edmonton Hotel. Potential subscribers were exhorted to "read the *Bulletin* and the Bible." It was the first newspaper in Alberta.

Oliver called himself an Independent Liberal, with emphasis on the adjective. As an editor and a politician – he was elected to the North West Council in 1883 – he fought the establishment. He wanted the Crow's Nest Pass railway to be publicly owned, and he opposed the twenty-year tax exemptions on real estate granted to the CPR in the original contract. His public speeches and his editorials made up in vehemence what they lacked in grammar. He and his paper made enemies, especially in Tory Calgary. The shrill *Herald* called the *Bulletin* "the meanest paper published by the meanest man in Canada."

He was no paragon. Shortly after he entered the cabinet, he allowed the Grand Trunk Pacific to pump fifteen thousand dollars into his paper secretly through a nominee. It was a serious conflict of interest; the railway at the time was dealing with the new minister on land acquisitions involving rights of way, townsites, and terminals. No other paper received such largess. On another occasion he leased out the mineral rights on his Alberta ranch and during a six-year period enjoyed the royalty on eighteen thousand tons of coal mined on his property. He didn't own the mineral rights, and he knew it; the government owned them. But Oliver pocketed the money. He also parcelled out fake squatters rights to political friends in the Riding Mountain forest reserve so that they could take up free homesteads when the acreage was withdrawn from public settlement. These were Liberal hacks who got valuable land they had never seen, much less squatted on.

The most blatant case of personal profiteering by Oliver was his handling of Christopher Fahrni, who had bought twenty-three sections of the Michel Indian Reserve west of Edmonton for $25,000. When Fahrni couldn't keep up his payments, Oliver's department cancelled the sale. But Oliver's lawyer, John J. Anderson, who was also his son-in-law, moved in and grabbed the property from the luckless Fahrni for $5,000, the amount of the original down payment. With that the sale was miraculously uncancelled. Anderson transferred the property to Oliver, who got a mortgage at once by swearing the land was now worth $71,460.

After the Liberal win in 1896, Oliver became the most powerful politician in the West after Sifton. Now, with Sifton out, he was calling the tune. Although Calgary was the larger city, Edmonton became the pro tem provincial capital, thanks to Oliver's influence. Calgary still had hopes of claiming the prize when an elected provincial government was formed, but these hopes were dashed by Oliver's backstage manoeuvres. He managed to gerrymander the electoral boundaries of the new province to give the northern (Liberal) half of Alberta a numerical advantage in the legislature not warranted by population. That ended Calgary's aspirations and renewed the fierce traditional rivalry between the two cities.

He was not, as we have seen, one of Sifton's admirers. Oliver favoured British immigration above all others and, after that, to a lesser degree, immigrants from Scandinavia, Holland and Belgium, France, and the United States. Like Clifford Sifton, the men in sheepskin coats had had their day. By the time the two new provinces celebrated their status with drumroll and rocket, Frank Oliver was truly in charge.

We are standing on South Railway Street, Regina, the Queen City of the Plains, on this, the most important day in her history – September 4, 1905. The old capital of the North West Territories is about to become the new capital of the Province of Saskatchewan, and everybody from the smallest Indian tot to the Governor General himself is here to preside at the ritual.

The weather has co-operated. A brilliant sun bathes an ocean of ochre-coloured wheat fields in a morning glow. A cloudless sky rolls on, seemingly without end, to the distant line of the horizon. Along the muddy little Wascana, the poplars show a touch of yellow, but this is still summer, with the harvest yet to come.

Excursion trains loaded with thousands of celebrators have already steamed into town from the outlying communities. The city is awash with flags, pennants, decorations – a kaleidoscope of bunting. Four triumphal arches have been raised, two constructed of cereal grains, two of evergreens. Mottoes abound: "God Bless Our Provinces," they read, for Saskatchewan is also including Alberta in today's festivities. Over Mickleborough's store a huge horseshoe proclaims: "Peace, Prosperity and Progress." These, after all, are the three benefits that most people have come west to enjoy.

It is 9 a.m. and a thousand children are on the march, the girls in white and the boys in caps and sashes, each carrying a flag and heading for Victoria Park to be greeted by Governor General Earl Grey and his lady, Sir Wilfrid Laurier, and a host of other dignitaries including Sir Gilbert Parker, poet, journalist, and cleric, the doyen of Canadian literature and the closest thing to a media celebrity the country can muster.

The children sing of Wolfe, the Conquering Hero, and all the little flags flutter – a sea of vibrating scarlet. The Governor General speaks. Children of the King, he says, you must be ready to die if ever the occasion should arise that you are called upon for your service. More cheers, more flag waving follow these words at the prospect of sacrifice in the service of the Empire. Then the Prime Minister speaks. He would rather be down there among them singing "God Save the King," Laurier tells the children, than occupying the high position he holds.

But the official party must hurry away because another parade is forming. Eight bands, thousands of marchers pass the reviewing stand on South Railway Street. Here comes the 90th Rifle Regiment, resplendent in dark uniforms and white helmets, South African campaign medals glittering on chests; then the Indians, feathered and painted and led by their wrinkled chief, the famous Piapot; more than twenty years before, he and his braves had tried to halt the westward drive of the CPR, but all that is forgotten today. Without the CPR there would be no Regina, no Province of Saskatchewan. Then why, everybody asks, is the CPR station undecorated when every other building in town is festooned? But the CPR is a law unto itself.

More bands blare past us, more marchers. The old-timers stumble along to the music of fife and drum – as wrinkled and as brown as the Indians. A gigantic float, bearing the flower of Regina's womanhood, drawn by four richly caparisoned horses and titled "Our Fair Dominion," comes into view. Each Canadian province is represented by a young woman, the two newest, appropriately, by little girls. The entire fire brigade is here complete with steam engines, reels, and ladders, followed by a body of Germans representing the largest foreign language group in the area (loudly cheered) and a stream of carriages carrying politicians and ex-politicians including the former premier of the North West Territories, Frederick Haultain, who, being a Conservative, has been deposed in favour of a Liberal. Then finally – an incongruous spectacle in this land of antelope and gopher – the camels and elephants of the Floto Circus.

The great procession winds its way through Regina's dusty streets and finally back to the reviewing stand. Now the crowd in its thousands *breaks away and dashes for the CPR depot. The railway is part of the celebration after all. Its trains depart every fifteen minutes for the Exhibition Grounds, where there will be more speeches, more ritual, games of lacrosse and pushball, the musical ride of the Mounted Police, and, of course, the reason for all this day-long, night-long extravaganza: the official swearing in of Amédée Emmanuel Forget as first lieutenant-governor of the new province.*

3

The The two groups who received the loudest cheers in Regina's great
Indian parade were also the most colourful and the most romantic, the
dilemma reminders of an era past: the Indians and the Mounted Police. Each
had dressed for the occasion in unaccustomed finery, the Indians
discarding their dark and shabby suits for feathers, necklaces, and war
paint, the Police doffing their working fatigues for scarlet serge.

The cheers rang out not only for the men on horseback – the Indians
on mottled cow ponies, the Police on jet black steeds – but also for
what these gaudy riders represented: the romantic version of the West,
the Old West of nostalgia; a West that had never quite lived up to its
billing and that was now officially ended. Many of those who watched
on the sidelines as the riders cantered past had been seduced by that
image: feathered and painted natives, fearless red-coated horsemen
brandishing guns, hordes of savage animals. An extraordinary number
had invested much of their capital in buffalo knives and firearms. The
Barr colonists arrived armed to the teeth and, as we have seen, the
Shepherd family of Ramsgate were to bring a veritable arsenal to the
West, even including a naval cutlass. As young George Shepherd put
it, "Thus armed, the family felt confident of their ability to stand off
attacking bands of redskins, long enough at least for the Mounted
Police to hear the firing and dash to the rescue."

That West had never existed. But there had been a time, more than
thirty years before, when the Indians had ridden free across the empty
grasslands, chasing the buffalo, and the Police had patrolled the plains
as a quasi-military force, driving the Montana whiskey traders out of
their armed forts and back across the border. Now the Indians were
hived in reserves, trying to learn the fundamentals of agriculture, and
the Police had become glorified civil servants. Since firearms were
taboo, gunplay was almost unknown. In 1905, there were only nine

210

murders in the territories that had become provinces. The statistics remained stable. As the commissioner reported some years later, the causes were always the same: "jealousy, drunkenness, desire of gain, quarrels and revenge. They are in no sense the result of lawlessness."

The most serious crime among the Indians and also among the Police (and for which constables were instantly dismissed) was drunkenness. The Indians drank because they had no future and their past was destroyed; the white man had taken away their religion, their language, their dress, and their culture. The Police drank because they felt isolated and frustrated; like the Indians, they belonged to another era, and their needs were made subordinate to the government's policy of filling up the West with farmers. Between these two pioneer groups, so different in background and culture, a bond sprang up. "The first thing I learned on the force," one veteran wrote, "was that the Mounties felt a lot more sympathy for the Indians than they did for most of the white men there."

Both were victims of departmental penny pinching. As in most elections, the Liberal party in 1896 had attacked what it called lavish spending by the Tory government. When Sifton took over, he slashed away with a will. Personnel were dropped, agencies reorganized, salaries reduced. The Indian Department had had its own deputy minister, but Sifton made two jobs into one, giving both the Indian Department and Immigration to James Smart, who, knowing nothing about Indians, paid very little attention to them. When in 1902 the Indians again got a deputy minister in the person of Frank Pedley, the section was still the poor relation of Sifton's organization. Sifton's overall budget was quintupled during his tenure; that of the Indian Department went up by a slim 30 per cent.

Rations were slashed. One civil servant expressed the general philosophy when he declared that the natives would never be self-sufficient "if officers continue the system of handling Indians through bribing them with food." By 1905, the various tribes were making do on three-quarters of a pound of food less per head a day than they had received in 1897. One Indian agent went so far as to suggest that this belt tightening was to the natives' benefit because "not only have these supplies been saved to the government, but it has tended to make the Indians more self-reliant and industrious and consequently more easily handled. Besides, the Indian is more healthy as no doubt he has suffered from over-feeding and lying around in his camp – now they get more exercise and have something to live for."

In reducing medical assistance to the tribes, Sifton used the same arguments that would be marshalled against universal medicare half a century and more later. "The more medical attendance that is provided, the more they want," he claimed. That was the philosophy of most of his agents. As one put it, "the more the government assists them the more they will ask for."

Penny pinching all but destroyed the educational system on the reserves. The Indians required superior teachers, but it was almost impossible to get teachers with third-class certificates when the three-hundred-dollar annual salary paid on the reserves was only half that paid in the cities. As Joseph Armstrong told the House of Commons, the only qualification a teacher needed was that he have the right politics. The general Western attitude was that it was hopeless to try to educate the Indians. But the experiment was never really attempted because the government wasn't prepared to pay for it.

The traditional Indian way of life collided with the Western work ethic. All the tenets of the agrarian philosophy – thrift, ambition, Christian morality, the mystique of the soil – had little meaning to the tribes. Ottawa's policy was to keep the Indians quiet on the reserves, out of the political limelight, and with the help of the churches to prepare them for a different culture and prevent their exploitation. Some aspects of this policy did not differ greatly from the policy for the Galicians, the Doukhobors, or the British. The Indians were to be assimilated, turned into Christian Canadians, speaking English, wearing "civilized clothing," and working the soil.

Mike Mountain Horse of the Blood tribe would always remember his first hours at the residential school to which he was sent. His blanket, breech cloth, leggings, shirt, and moccasins were taken from him, and he was plunged into a fibre tub of steaming water and well scrubbed. Then his long braids were snipped off, his hair shorn and trimmed, and he was presented with a white child's suit of clothes: knee pants, blouse, lace collar, a tiny cap with an emblem sewn on it, and shoes. None of this fazed him; in fact, he strutted about like a young peacock. It was only in later years that Indians like Mike Mountain Horse began to ask themselves why it was necessary to remove these visible signs of an ancient culture in the interests of a studied conformity.

The Western tribes had hunted the buffalo. This extraordinary animal, roaming the plains in the tens of thousands, had supplied them with hide, bones, and flesh – everything they needed for clothing, shelter, fuel, food, and culture. The transformation of hunters into farmers is, historically, a process that requires centuries. But such was

212

the optimism of the times that the government expected to achieve it in a few years.

Since it was universally agreed that the Indian culture was inferior, no one disputed the benefits this policy would bring to the Indians, least of all the agents of the Indian Department, whose annual reports tended to be patronizing. One praised the sacrifice of the missionaries "whose duty it is to lead these sheep of the wilderness to higher moral values"; another wrote that "to uplift the Indian, his whole character has to be reformed." The answer lay in working the soil, the reserve being "a forcing ground where the lesson of work may be imparted." But, since the Indian's idea of work was quite different from that of the Western farmer, "he must be kept at work by a ceaseless vigilance." In a 1902 editorial titled "Civilizing the Indians," the Calgary *Herald* bluntly advocated that all Indians be forced to work.

With such assessments the Westerners had no quarrel. Thousands had been subtly lured to Canada with the philosophy that agriculture was a noble occupation that equipped the farmer and his sons for future success. James Smart's 1898 report to Parliament on Indian Affairs gave voice to the concept that would have its echoes in the department's most successful pamphlet, *The Last Best West*.

". . . the initial step toward the civilization of our Indians," Smart wrote, "should be their adoption of agricultural pursuits. . . . Cultivation of the soil necessitates remaining in one spot and then exerts an educational influence of a general character. It keeps prominently before the mind the relation of cause and effect, together with the dependence upon a higher power. It teaches, moreover, the necessity for systematic work at the proper season, for giving attention to detail, and patience in waiting for results.

"It inculcates furthermore the idea of individual proprietorship, habits of thrift, a due sense of the value of money and the importance of its investment in useful directions."

But it was hard to convince the Indians of these high-flown advantages. They didn't give a hoot about the future. As one agent noted, "a net put in at nightfall gives at dawn a full day's eating. A crop put in during early April must be watched and tended for three months and a half before the time of harvest." The concept of thrift was foreign to them. Hoarding, in Indian eyes, was a sin. Agents railed against "the giving away evil," to use David Laird's phrase. The Indian "would almost burst with indignation if not allowed . . . to show how big his heart was and give away a good deal of his wealth."

What was seen as philanthropy on the part of a generous white man was thought of as foolishness when indulged in by a native. "As soon as an Indian . . . acquires a little money over and above his present needs he just itches all over to give a dance and feast to show the other fellows . . . what a big hearted chap he is, and probably impress the other sex. . . ." So wrote the agent at Portage la Prairie in 1902, oblivious to the fact that he was also describing the accepted mores of his own society. To solve the problem it was generally agreed that all children must be taken from their parents and sent to boarding schools to remove them from "home influences, and consequently the more speedy and thorough inculcation of the habits, customs and modes of thought of the white man."

"Indolent" was the word used over and over again to describe the Indian's reluctance to work the soil. This trait, together with his apparent lack of ambition, his improvidence, his so-called immorality, his refusal to espouse Christianity – in short, his inability and disinclination to conform to white standards – baffled and frustrated the department in Ottawa. This frustration was expressed in the government's attempt to stamp out the Sun Dance, the one rite above all others that had an enormous religious and sociological significance for all the Western tribes. The Sun Dance, with its days of feasting, ceremony, giving, and ritual, can be described as roughly equivalent to the white man's Christmas in importance. To forbid it was akin to forbidding all Yuletide festivities in a Christian society.

It is the last day of the Sun Dance of the Sarcees, near a copse of tall timber on the north side of the Elbow River at the time when the chokecherries and saskatoon berries ripen. The sweat lodge has been built by the young men out of one hundred poplar poles with one hundred stones set in hollows inside. The privileged have already taken part in the sweat-bath ceremonies, accompanied by twenty prayers of invocation.

The Sun Dance lodge itself has also been constructed of sweet-smelling balm of Gilead poplar, with a smaller lodge within, the tepees of the tribe surrounding it in an irregular circle, that of the hostess and her husband at the centre. The woman has arranged the ceremony in gratitude for answered prayers: a sick relative has recovered, and so she is honouring the pledge she made – to be absolutely faithful to her husband and to mount this ceremony in return. The pair are painted dark red – not just their skin but also their hair, their clothes, and their moccasins. They have fasted for several days. From this ritual they will derive great honour.

214

The young men have brought in a great tree which has become the central pole in the Sun Dance lodge. A nest of small willows has been lashed in place at its crotch. Offerings of clothing, drygoods, and moccasins are attached to it. There have been days of dancing, chanting, and drum beating. Chiefs and warriors have come to the lodge to recite and act out their exploits. One hundred buffalo tongues, secured in the hunt long before the ceremony, have been distributed, all according to ritual and custom.

It is time. Two young men who have taken vows to undergo torture enter the enclosure prepared for them, disrobing except for belt and breech cloth. Fillets of sage are placed about their heads, ankles, and wrists; a whistle is suspended about the neck; their bodies are rubbed with white clay. So adorned they enter the main lodge and lie down on their backs on buffalo robes.

Others who have previously endured the ordeal knead their breasts and attach the thongs, asking whether the cuts should be made deep or shallow. The reply is interpreted in the opposite fashion so that if a young man says "shallow" it means he wishes a deep cut. The flesh and skin are drawn up, a cut made, a stick thrust through the opening. Two ropes hang from the centre pole. These are secured to the stick with a loop. The Sun Dance is about to begin.

The young men approach the pole, embrace it, pray silently. Now they come into dancing position, cross their arms four times on their breasts, jerking at the ropes to elongate the folds of pierced flesh. They dance to the east as the singing begins, then to the west, going through a semicircle on the north side of the pole so that they always face the sun. They blow on their whistles, lean back to stretch the thongs taut until the flesh is torn loose and they are free. The longer the dance continues before their breasts are torn, the longer, it is said, they will live on this earth.

When the dance ends and there are no more young men to be honoured, the camp circle is broken and the ritual is over.

The official reason for the ban on the Sun Dance was that torture was involved. This was a pretext, because only certain tribes practised self-torture, yet all Sun Dances came under some form of interdict. The real reason, expressed in dozens of agency reports, was that the celebration of the Sun Dance disturbed the normal work pattern of the Indians.

"A vigorous effort was made during the year to suppress illegal dancing on most of the reserves," David Laird, the Indian Commissioner of the North West Territories, reported in 1902. "On the Blood reserve, however, I am sorry to say, a sun dance was held. . . . These large gatherings are of a very injurious character; much valuable time is wasted when they ought to be occupied with their hay-making . . . it can scarcely be doubted that besides the loss of time, immorality, gambling and other such evils were practised. . . .

"In a few years it may be hoped that these foolish practices will die out; but measures must be taken to hasten their end. They are vestiges of savage life, and while they continue . . . the work of civilizing must be comparatively at a standstill. The farming instructor, the teacher, and the missionary cannot accomplish much among people who give themselves for weeks together to the excesses of a heathen celebration."

It was not just the Sun Dance that was proscribed. The more severe and committed Protestant sects on the frontier were opposed to *all* dancing. As Magnus Begg, the agent on the Crooked Lake Reserve near Broadview, Assiniboia, reported triumphantly in 1902: "The Indians, although mostly pagans, are thrifty and good workers; but they are also inclined to dancing. They built a nice dance house for the purpose of holding regular dances. It was necessary for me to have it destroyed, which put a stop to it all. . . ."

Yet when it came to white festivals, parades, and celebrations, the Western attitude toward the Indians underwent a transformation. The same people who wanted them to abandon their rituals for hard work and to dress and act like white men suddenly wanted them to take time off, don feathered bonnets and buckskin, perform tribal dances, and lead the parade. When, in these instances, the natives threw off the thin veneer of civilization to become noble savages once again, the white men cheered. These attempts "to perpetuate the old order" did not sit well with Commissioner Laird, who in 1908 urged that Indians "cease to be used as painted and bedecked things for the amusement of others."

Laird's hope went unfulfilled. The Indians looked back nostalgically on the older order as the Mounties looked back nostalgically on their own golden age. The natives preferred their own religion, which fitted in with their philosophy of living for the day. In the Blackfoot faith, for example, there were no rewards or punishments beyond the grave. These were earned or suffered in everyday life. The Indians did not have what one agent called "the sacred appreciation of virtue." The white attitude baffled them just as theirs baffled their white protectors. The Inspector of Indian Agencies in Manitoba referred to the Long

Plain Band as "an all round hard lot" because "they cannot understand why the government interferes in what they call their religious worship." Few became bona fide Christians, although a great many saw the advantages in pretending. One Indian woman at Stony Plain, Alberta, became a Methodist, Roman Catholic, and Presbyterian, and "works the three successfully to the tune of numerous blankets, quilts, clothing and other presents."

The wonder is that, given the prevailing attitudes, some natives actually did become successful farmers and ranchers – this in spite of strong attempts to persuade them to sell off portions of their reserves under the pressure of advancing white settlement. As the *Edmonton Bulletin* declared: "The Indians make no practical use of the reserves which they hold. Where the land is good and well situated for market, white men can turn it to much better account. . . . It is a loss to the country to have such lands lying idle in the hands of the Indians when white men want to use them and are willing to pay for them."

Canada respected the wording of the treaties it made with the Indians, if not the spirit. The government did not actually force any tribe off its reserve, but it offered every inducement to make them give up their lands. The main argument was that the price paid would provide a handsome annuity for the band in question. But the price paid was often scandalously low while the pressures were hard to resist, as we shall see later.

In 1909, to take one example, the Piegans sold a chunk of their land for seventy-one cents an acre after the government forced a vote, which the chief, in an affidavit that was conveniently ignored, insisted was fraudulent. The Sarcees, on the other hand, with a reserve on the very outskirts of Calgary, resisted all pressure from the city to sell. They still occupy the land. Nonetheless, a quarter of a million acres of Indian reserves have in the intervening years reverted to the white man, usually to the detriment of the native people.

By 1909, Frank Oliver was ready to admit that the "Indian problem" had not been satisfactorily solved. Given the lack of money and understanding, it would have been remarkable if it had been. Yet, if it was asking too much of the Indian to comprehend white ways, it was also asking a great deal of the government agents and the new settlers to sympathize with the natives. One such was John Semmens, Inspector of Indian Agencies for the Lake Winnipeg area, who in 1907 in his annual report to Ottawa wrote this defence of his charges:

"The red man must not be judged by standards designed to measure a white man. He is quite another being. . . . Our strong points may be his weak ones and we may flatter ourselves and despise him; but this will not prove that he is without virtues or that he cannot rise to the attainment of higher things. Canadians are not likely to forget that the extinguishment of the Indian title in the great Northwest has never cost a drop of blood; or that in every rebellion which has marked our later history, the Indian has been our loyal ally and friend. All that he asks in return is our strong true friendship and wise persistent assistance; and out of conditions which we despise he will yet rise to fuller knowledge and nobler conduct. . . ."

But even the perceptive and sympathetic Semmens wasn't prepared to concede that the Indian lifestyle was anything but inferior to that of white Canadians.

4

The Imperial Force There were many in the West who believed that the Mounted Police were all that stood between the peaceful farmers and an armed Indian uprising. If autonomy were granted to the Territories, what would happen? To the Calgary *Herald* it was inconceivable that the government would "leave us in the unprotected state which would be occasioned by the disbandment or removal of the North West Mounted Police." One of the chief jobs of the Force, the paper insisted, was to keep a close watch on the natives. "The Indians are pacific now, but no one can tell how long they would remain so if the police were withdrawn."

The Police, of course, were not disbanded; the Force entered into contracts with both the new provinces, but scarcely to protect the farmers from the Indians. Of all the polyglot people on the prairies at that time the natives were the most docile. Nor was there the slightest hint of future trouble, police or no police. In report after report, NWMP officers made the point that the Indians were easier to handle than the white man. Lawrence Herchmer, the chief commissioner, reported in 1898 that "infinitely more cattle are killed by whites than by Indians." Inspector Burton Deane reported from Fort Macleod the following year that the Indians deserved all possible praise for their behaviour and "give less trouble than the white man." A.B. Perry, the new commissioner, in 1900 said the Indians of the plains "maintain their reputation for good behaviour." G.E. Sanders, writing from Calgary in 1902, praised the Blackfoot, Sarcee, and Stoney tribes, adding that "had we to deal with white people under the same conditions, I am afraid they would compare very unfavourably with the Indians."

It was forgotten by many that the Force had been originally established in 1873 to protect the Plains Indians from the twin ravages of smallpox and Montana whiskey. Those days were long gone. Having succeeded in maintaining peace in the West, the Police had all but done themselves out of a job. Like the Indians, they were victims of the government's penny pinching, which, in the view of Commissioner Herchmer, left them worse off than the natives, at least in one instance. "While the Indians at the Industrial school have iron beds, this, the finest body of men in the country, still sleeps on boards and trestles," Herchmer exclaimed.

Gone were the great days when the Force captured the imagination of the nation and the government scrambled to maintain it in dignity and power. In 1885, the year of the driving of the Last Spike and the Saskatchewan rebellion, the Force had numbered one thousand scarlet riders. In 1896, the new Liberal administration reduced it to 750; the following year it was cut again to 500 and the annual budget cut from $530 million to $385 million. The government was intent on investing in the new West, not the old.

Until 1905, the NWMP had been considered a temporary force, to be abolished when the West was tamed; as a result, its members received no pensions. Equipment was allowed to run down: Winchester rifles were wearing out; Enfield revolvers had long been obsolete; and the famous buffalo coats were so worn that in 1898 Burton Deane at Fort Macleod claimed they wouldn't last another year.

Buildings were old and ramshackle. At Fort Saskatchewan, the inspectors' quarters were in an old ice house, "a wretched hovel quite unfit for habitation"; the kitchen in the officers' quarters at Calgary leaked like a sieve; the south block in Regina was falling down and by 1904 was described as "uninhabitable," although it was still in use.

Salaries had not risen in twenty years. Pinkerton detectives were being paid eight dollars a day in 1904; NWMP constables got seventy-five cents for the same work. As a result, the turnover was heavy: the veterans refused to re-enlist, and others bought their way out, attracted by better offers. The Force was so overworked that there was little time for drill, and target practice suffered.

In 1897, when the news of the Klondike gold strike reached the outside world, the strongest and best men were sent to Yukon service. On the prairies new recruits were so green that each one needed a guide. The Force was spread desperately thin—an average of one constable to every five hundred square miles. Some immigrants, in fact, had never seen a Mounted Policeman, and as late as 1911, one constable whose district covered two thousand square miles reported that a farmer's wife thought he was a sewing machine salesman.

By 1905, when Saskatchewan and Alberta entered into five-year contracts with the Police, some of these problems abated. Pay was raised to a dollar a day, but only after eight years' service. Meagre pensions were established. The decision was made to re-arm the Force, and its numbers were increased by one hundred.

One problem, however, did not go away—that of political patronage. Like the Indians and the settlers, the police were its victims. Herchmer, the blunt, red-bearded commissioner appointed under the Tories, soon made way for Perry, an ambitious closet Liberal during the old regime whose promotion under the new was swift. The redoubtable Sam Steele, a strong Conservative, was personally removed from his Yukon post by Sifton for refusing to go along with a political appointment: Sifton's former campaign manager, J.D. McGregor, wanted the lucrative patronage job of liquor licensing commissioner. Steele left for South Africa and never rejoined the Force.

New recruits were selected not on the basis of ability but from a list of politically acceptable candidates. Some arrived in Regina deaf, one-eyed, or, more usually, several inches below the regulation height of five feet eight. As Fred White, the comptroller in Ottawa, said, "the most generally undesirable candidate has the strongest influence." White, himself a staunch Conservative, did not care for Perry and even less for Sifton.

Behind the stern façade of the officer class, petty jealousies simmered. Deane and Herchmer were such bitter enemies that when the commissioner visited Fort Macleod, Deane made it a point to be away; they communicated only by written note. Deane insisted he was transferred to a less attractive post as the result of the capture of 596 cattle smuggled into Canada by friends of Clifford Sifton. When Sanders, a veteran officer, was promoted to superintendent at Calgary, it was expected he would lead the Mounted Police contingent to Queen Victoria's jubilee. At the last moment, however, the job was given to a young inspector who just happened to be the son of Sir Richard Cartwright, one of the oldest and most prominent front-bench Liberals.

Again like the Indians, the Police were viewed in the context of Western settlement. Their tasks became more mundane: they acted as land agents, welfare officials, immigration officers, agricultural experts, customs collectors, game, timber, and fire wardens, magistrates, and seed distributors. They continued to patrol the North West from the American border to the Arctic's rim, from the shores of Hudson Bay to Alaska, but they were rarely called upon to perform any feat more glamorous than hoisting a naked Doukhobor woman aboard a train. It was a far cry from the image that the new Hollywood films were beginning to invent.

They were an Imperial force, implicitly charged with maintaining a British-Canadian West (as opposed to a European or American West). Their numbers were largely élitist. Eighty per cent of the officers came from upper-rank Eastern Canadian families, members of the governing class. Half the rankers and NCOs were born in Britain. They understood their role: to mould the West to their own ideals. "Our mission, I take it," Superintendent Sanders wrote from Regina in 1907, "is to firmly established the fundamental principles of British law and order amongst the different nationalities. . . ."

The Canadian West was as much an outpost of Empire in 1905 as the South African veld or the tea plantations of Ceylon. The emphasis was on "British order." "It is claimed," Perry wrote proudly in 1904, urging the government to maintain the Force, ". . . that no country was ever settled up with such an entire absence of lawlessness. . . . The North West Mounted Police were the pioneers of settlement. They carried into the Territories the world-wide maxim that where the British flag flies, peace and order prevail."

Without the Police, the inference was, the West would be a lawless region because it was peopled by socially inferior classes. The Mounted Police subscribed to the commonly held belief that criminality was a phenomenon largely confined to inferior people at the lowest stratum of the social order. This isn't surprising. Even J.S. Woodsworth, the leading social reformer in the West, held similar views. The officers were treated as members of the upper class in the so-called classless West; their quasi-military balls were the social events of the season. In Calgary they tended to identify with the ranchers, who were seen as several rungs above the new Canadians grubbing in the dirt with hoe and mattock. Thus, Commissioner Herchmer felt that the Galicians were "a very undesirable class . . . [who] generally arrive here with very little money and are very ignorant," while the settlers at Red Deer, Innisfail, and along the Calgary-Strathcona railway line, who came largely from Ontario and England, "were a good class." Actually, the Galicians and other Europeans were remarkably law abiding, but Herchmer explained that away by insisting that only "constant patrols . . . convince these foreigners that law and order must be respected in this country. . . ."

Law and order, of course, was something the American immigrants did not understand – at least in the Force's view. The Mounted Police tended to despise the grassroots democracy that had produced elected peace officers south of the border. After all, John J. Healy, the most implacable of the Montana whiskey traders whom the police had driven out of southern Alberta, had also been sheriff of Chouteau County! "I suppose," Commissioner Perry wrote to Ottawa in 1903, "that the peace of the Territories may seem assured to those who are in the East. . . . They know little of the reckless class of American outlaws to the south of us."

But the Americans who came to Canada were mainly well-to-do farmers, the most peaceable of all classes. American badmen were so unusual in Canada that when the occasional one crossed the border he made headlines – such as Ernest Cashel of the Butch Cassidy gang, who was hanged in Calgary, or Cowboy Jack Monaghan who tried to terrorize Estevan, Saskatchewan, and was jailed for six months, or the infamous Idaho Kid, who tried to shoot up Weyburn, Assiniboia, in 1903.

The Idaho Kid sits on the verandah of Beach's Hotel in Weyburn, shooting holes in the ceiling. It is late afternoon of a warm June day, and the townspeople have taken cover because the Idaho Kid is shooting up the street. When one curious citizen pokes his head out of his hotel window, the Idaho Kid, whose name is Brandenburger and who hails from Montana, not Idaho, shoots his hat off and tells him to stick his head back inside or he will turn him into a sieve. The citizen obeys and the Idaho Kid takes another drink.

Another citizen, bolder than the rest, makes his way down the street. The Idaho Kid brandishes his revolver and orders him to hold out his hat. When the citizen complies, the Idaho Kid fills it full of holes. This angers the citizen, who tells the Kid he'd better stop or the Mounted Police will run him in. But there are no Mounted Police in town, and the Kid alleges that no one has ever run him in – no Montana sheriff has ever dared tackle him.

The Idaho Kid says he will die with his boots on if necessary, but that

222

is unlikely because if any Mounted Policeman butts into his game, he will eat his liver cold. He is too hard and too wild for any Canadian constable, the Idaho Kid declares, and offers to bet twenty-five dollars that no one can take him alive. At that, three other citizens who have taken cover become emboldened by avarice, swallow their timidity, and come out into the street to cover the bet.

The local justice of the peace is urged to send for a Mounted Policeman to settle the wager. Off goes a brief wire to the nearest detachment at Halbrite: "Come up next train party running amok with revolver."

Enter Constable H. "Larry" Lett, burly and bullet-headed, five feet nine, 170 pounds, father of two, veteran of eight years in the Dragoon Guards and six on the Force. Having flagged down a freight train, he arrives in town to deal with the party running amok. The constable attempts to swear in a citizen or two to help him tackle the Idaho Kid, but no volunteer comes forward.

The Idaho Kid is now holed up in his hotel room with his wife and a bottle. Constable Lett persuades the J.P. to stand within calling distance, then proceeds to bash down the door of the Idaho Kid's room. The Idaho Kid reaches for his gun. The constable jumps him. The Idaho Kid's wife jumps the constable. A rough-and-tumble follows.

The citizens wait outside the hotel, listening to the sounds of the struggle, wondering if their money is safe. They need not worry. When the pair emerges, the constable is carrying the Idaho Kid's gun and the Idaho Kid is wearing the constable's handcuffs. For this demonstration of British coolness and pluck in the face of American anarchy, the Force is duly grateful. Constable Lett is swiftly promoted to corporal for proving that British Canada wants no truck or trade with the wild and woolly West to the south.

Chapter Eight

The Sifton Scandals

1

Historians have dealt gently with Clifford Sifton, relying until recently on the gospel according to John Dafoe: *Clifford Sifton in Relation to His Times*, which Dafoe himself, not surprisingly, called "a labour of love and an obligation of friendship." The Sifton that emerges from Dafoe's laudatory biography is the Sifton of history: the man who changed the face of the prairies, a highly intelligent, strong-willed, ambitious politician with a capacity for leadership and organization, and the energy to go with it – a man who did not suffer fools, who hated incompetence, who could be agreeable in private life if chilly publicly, staunch and unswerving in his friendships, and indifferent to praise and contumely alike.

This is a reasonable assessment, but it fails to come to grips with one question that hangs over the Sifton years. To what extent did this minister whose job it was to protect the settlers and the native peoples from exploitation conspire in that exploitation? To what extent did he use his position improperly to benefit his friends and colleagues? To what degree did his well-known loyalty to political comrades collide with the public interest? And why did he condone flagrant wrongdoing among the senior members of his department?

In the period between Sifton's resignation and the federal election of 1908, three major scandals in the department under his ministry came to light. These dealt with the farming out of European immigration propaganda to a mysterious group known as the North Atlantic Trading Company; the granting, under dubious circumstances, of a vast acreage of timber leases to Sifton's lumberman brother-in-law, Theodore Burrows; and the granting, in equally dubious circumstances, of closed grazing leases in southern Alberta to Sifton's political cronies. Dafoe in his biography glosses over all three, and historians have taken his word for it that nothing untoward took place. A careful study of the evidence suggests the opposite. Sifton's response in the House to his accusers may indeed have been a *tour de force*, as Dafoe called it, but it evaded much of the sworn testimony heard by a series of parliamentary committees. And Dafoe entirely ignored the fourth and worst scandal – the profiteering on Indian lands by James Smart and two colleagues – which was not publicly exposed until the middle of the Great War.

It has been said that Sifton's opponents held back until after he

226

resigned, afraid of facing the Minister in the House because of his powerful debating skills. This is not true. The Opposition suspected malfeasance, but the principals in the Sifton scandals had been adept at covering their tracks. They hid behind the names of nominees, concealed their affairs by using legal firms as fronts, and escaped being found out by inventing bogus "companics" whose only address was a post office box. In one case the real principals behind a dubious transaction were revealed only because they eventually issued a stock prospectus in Great Britain, where the laws were tighter than in Canada.

The Liberal government was equally adept at resisting demands for public inquiries. The Moose Mountain Indian Reserve scandal – there is no other name for it – was not revealed until after the Conservatives took office and in 1913 appointed a royal commission of inquiry under T.R. Ferguson. The Ferguson report has vanished; no copy can be found. Fortunately, it was quoted at length in the press and in Parliament and should have served to destroy the reputations of three of Sifton's closest allies – Smart, Pedley, and White. But by then the war was at its height and such exposés weren't much more than a three-day sensation. The Canadian electorate has rarely shown much concern over political scandals. The Liberals in 1908 easily survived the Conservative onslaught just as later administrations under Mackenzie King survived even worse revelations. Any party that rides the crest of an economic boom, as the Liberals did in Canada's first decade, need not worry too much about revelations of wrongdoing. Sifton is remembered as the man who brought people and prosperity to the West, not as the minister who presided over a corrupt department.

2

Shortly after Sifton's resignation, the Conservatives began to ask *The* questions about the mysterious organization known as the North *mysterious* Atlantic Trading Company. "Mysterious" is the right word, for the *company* company wasn't a company at all, and it didn't do any trading in the North Atlantic. Its job, for which it was paid handsomely by the Canadian government, was to persuade European farmers to migrate to the Canadian West. But to this day nobody knows exactly what the company was, who its principals were, who formed its board of

227

directors, or, indeed, how many immigrants it actually persuaded to come to Canada.

The company was organized – "invented" would be a better word – at the instigation of W.T.R. Preston, the Canadian Inspector of Immigration in London. For most of its existence, Preston acted as if it were his corporate child. And so, to understand the political row over this particular immigration scheme, it's necessary to look into Preston's background and reputation.

They were, to put it mildly, unsavoury. "Malodorous" is the adjective most commonly used. No one laboured more diligently in the Liberal vineyards than Preston – or more awkwardly. For twenty years he had been an organizer for the Ontario Grits, rewarded twice with a political job in the legislative library. He was a wiry man with a sharp, terrier's face and a clipped military moustache, skilled in the art of electoral manipulation. Nobody cared that Preston cut corners; after all, bribery, corruption, and ballot-box stuffing were all standard techniques in the elections of the day. The trouble was that Preston kept getting caught; his efforts in support of the party were herculean but clumsy. When, for example, he offered a former Liberal M.P., Hermon Henry Cook, a Senate seat for ten thousand dollars, the matter became public as the result of a court case.

Worse was to come. As chief Liberal organizer for the province of Ontario, Preston masterminded the West Elgin provincial by-election of January 1899, an election the Toronto *World* called "the most scandalous in the history of Canada." Preston imported carloads of ward heelers from Toronto, hid them in the homes of the West Elgin faithful, and filled their pockets with cash to bribe voters, the average price being five dollars a vote. He went further. He arranged a masquerade in which strangers were brought into town to impersonate bona fide voters. The sheriff was persuaded to accept as returning officers strangers disguised as prominent citizens of the riding, who collaborated in stuffing the ballot boxes and vanished the next day without claiming their fee. One fake returning officer was discovered with a drawerful of blank ballots and a piece of pencil lead concealed under his fingernail with which to mark them. Some boxes were spirited away to be returned the following morning by men who hadn't any official connection with the election.

Preston's techniques in West Elgin were so blatant that the defeated Tory candidate prepared a list of two hundred charges of corruption against his Liberal opponent, Donald Macnish. Macnish knew when he was licked. He resigned his seat immediately and, to prevent the worst sort of dirty linen being laundered in court, admitted everything.

The ex-candidate tied Preston neatly to the West Elgin chicanery by quoting a telegram Preston had sent him the day after the election. "Hug the machine for me," Preston had wired. From that moment on, Preston was known in the Conservative press as "Hug the Machine Preston." Much hilarity also stemmed from the revelation that Preston, a prominent Methodist and temperance leader, had led his Sunday School class in singing "There Is Sunshine in My Soul" the day following the Liberal's fraudulent victory.

But Preston was soon out of reach. Immediately after the by-election, the federal government spirited him out of the country, creating for him the new post of immigration inspector in London.

The North Atlantic Trading Company has had a clean bill of health from historians, many of whom, following Dafoe's lead, have tried to suggest it played a key role in bringing European immigrants to Canada. But any investigative reporter poring over the sworn evidence taken before two parliamentary committees must come to the conclusion that it was very largely a boondoggle created by Preston for his own personal profit with the connivance of Sifton's deputy, James Smart.

Smart, who quit his job shortly before Sifton left office, turned up a few weeks later as Canadian manager of the mysterious company. His testimony and Preston's before the Public Accounts Committee is slippery in the extreme. Both men suffered convenient lapses of memory, were caught in contradictions and circumventions, and, on occasion, uttered explanations so patently evasive as to be fraudulent.

Preston's reputation as a prevaricator was in no way redeemed during these hearings. His disgruntled colleague Alfred Jury testified that he wouldn't believe anything Preston said, even under oath. Similar testimony about Preston's disregard for the truth had been given some time before in another court case, when Preston's uncle brought a series of witnesses to the stand, all of whom swore they would never believe Preston. As for Smart, he was, as we shall see, perfectly capable of using his position as an immigration official to line his own pockets.

Preston's argument for farming out all immigration propaganda in continental Europe to a private firm seemed to make sense. Because most European countries discouraged the open solicitation of prospective settlers, the government wanted to be at arm's length from any scheme that might be viewed as illegal. The law varied from country to country, being toughest in Germany, which specifically banned any inducement designed to lure away its population.

According to Preston, the N.A.T. Company – or Syndicate – would "have in its number some of the most experienced Booking and Emigration Agents in Germany – men of responsibility, who thoroughly understand all the various phases of Continental Emigration Laws and who intend to start with a capital of $200,000 to prosecute this work." At no time, however, was it made known to anyone in the Immigration Department who these men were; nor did anybody ask. Preston himself, at one point in later testimony, indicated that even *he* didn't know, although he clearly did.

The scheme was obviously designed to circumvent the law, especially in Germany, yet the loose agreement arranged through an exchange of letters with the department in the fall of 1900 specifically stated that "the company is to do nothing in contravention of the laws of the country named."

In 1906, when the details of the various agreements with the mysterious company caused a public sensation, Sifton's successor, Frank Oliver, tried to blame Lord Strathcona. The High Commissioner shot back a firm telegram of denial. On the contrary: his lawyers had warned him of possible diplomatic complications. He'd gone along reluctantly because Preston seemed to want it. The two men had no use for each other.

From the N.A.T.'s point of view, it was a profitable arrangement. The company was to get a five-dollar bonus for every man, woman, and child over twelve who arrived in Canada from Europe. Later the deal was sweetened: even babes in arms would be worth a pound sterling. The bonus was supposed to be paid only for bona fide farmers and their families carrying with them at least one hundred dollars in cash – two hundred dollars in the case of the Galicians. But even though only 12 per cent of the Galicians who arrived in Canada had the required cash, the company was paid for them all. Hundreds moved directly on to the United States, but the company got paid anyway. In 1901, a group of 275 Jews arrived; the N.A.T. Company had nothing to do with bringing them out, but under the contract the bonus had to be paid.

In fact, there was no way whatsoever for Ottawa to check up on the mysterious company. It claimed to be distributing maps and pamphlets in sixteen languages, to be planting articles in newspapers, to have agents secretly moving through European villages touting Canada, but there was little firm evidence to back up these statements. Sample pamphlets arrived in Ottawa, but there was no way of finding out whether they had been distributed. Vouchers arrived for work done; but *was* it done? Nobody knew. Did the immigrants pouring into Canada arrive as the result of the N.A.T.'s work? Again, no one had any idea. There is no evidence that either Preston or Smart ever spoke to a single emigrant to discover why he had decided to leave his birthplace. The most curious aspect of the N.A.T. story is that nobody *was* curious – not Preston, not Smart, not Sifton himself. Nobody asked any questions.

For some time the very existence of the company was shrouded in secrecy. James Mavor first heard of it during a trip to Vienna. In London he asked Preston about it. Preston claimed he'd never heard of it. None of the agreements, letters, or contracts were submitted to the scrutiny of Parliament; all had been arranged through orders-in-council. The first brief public reference to the company occurred about 1903, but most M.P.s were in the dark as to the details as late as 1905. There's little doubt that Preston *was* the company. He paid one N.A.T. agent with his personal cheque. He went off to Scandinavia, not on government business, but for the explicit purpose of hiring agents for the company. More often than not he spoke for the company: the correspondence, from the company's Amsterdam office, was signed with a stamp or an indecipherable initial. Nobody seemed to think that odd.

February, 1904. James Smart, Deputy Minister of the Interior, arrives in Amsterdam – a bulky man with a balding head and a black smear of a moustache. For more than three years he has been in correspondence with the North Atlantic Trading Company, a corporation believed to be licensed under Dutch law and, if vouchers mean anything, to be operating a bustling head office at 73 Damrack in the heart of the city's business district.

The department's auditor has already called attention to the company's claim for office expenses, which he considers suspiciously high. Eight thousand dollars a year for rent, postage, and clerks! In Toronto you can rent a seven-room house for $15.00 a month, buy a wool serge suit for $6.95, and enjoy a three-course roast beef dinner at McConkey's for a quarter. Eight thousand dollars is an enormous sum! The place must be humming.

But Jim Smart discerns no sound of humming at 73 Damrack. There is nothing at street level to indicate that the North Atlantic Trading Company exists. Smart negotiates the steep flight of stairs to the first landing, looks about, discovers a door bearing the company's name, knocks, waits. Nothing. The door is locked, the one-room office empty.

Smart searches about, finds some neighbours, asks about the locked, empty office. Ah yes, they tell him; there is a man who drops in periodically to pick up letters – nothing more. The office, in short, is nothing but a mail drop.

Does this not pique James A. Smart's curiosity? Not a bit. He seems perfectly satisfied, makes no further inquiries, does not discuss the matter with anyone, does not even raise it with Preston when the two meet in London. No doubt the eight thousand dollars went mainly for postage, Smart tells himself – or so he will testify when, two years later, he is asked about this unproductive visit.

All this time, the government had operated without a formal contract with the mysterious company, only a loose exchange of letters. Not until the summer of 1904 did it think to tighten its agreement with a legal document designed to weed out the sick, the mentally ill, the non-farmers, and the transients for whom it had been paying five dollars a head. As for those impoverished Galician immigrants, the company now would receive a flat annual bonus of five thousand dollars, no more.

Nobody seemed to be aware that this contract was being made with a non-company, whose letters were still being signed with a stamp or an illegible signature that seldom carried a title. Nobody seemed suspicious that some letters were typed by an amateur. As for the identity of the principals – their financial status, their business background, their immigration experience – this was known only to Preston and perhaps to Smart; the later testimony of both was vague, evasive, and contradictory.

In the summer of 1905, the Opposition grew suspicious. Who were these people who were being paid out of public funds without any reference to Parliament? Preston moved swiftly to create a real company. The N.A.T. was suddenly incorporated, not in the Netherlands, but on the Isle of Guernsey, which allowed corporate directors to hide behind the names of nominees. The job was done by Preston's son-in-law, A.E. Alexander, two of whose relatives became bogus directors.

According to Preston, the bulk of the shares were held by one Albert Pfeifel, said to be an officer of the company in Amsterdam and as mysterious as the company itself. When an English paper, the London *Tribune*, tried to find Pfeifel, it couldn't uncover any trace or memory of him.

What was the reason for all this secrecy? Historians have accepted the explanation of both Smart and Preston that it was necessary to protect the anonymous directors from legal action by European governments. Yet nowhere in all of the correspondence or in the contractual agreements between the N.A.T. Company and the Canadian government was a pledge of secrecy asked for or given. Preston insisted he'd made a verbal commitment to the directors and that the government's honour was at stake to protect that commitment. Smart backed him up. In the face of the most persistent questioning both men stuck to their insistence that the principals behind the company would be in great danger if their names were revealed, and refused to identify them.

These excuses seem as thin as parchment. When Lord Strathcona's lawyers pointed out possible future problems, especially in Germany, where it was illegal to promote emigration, the N.A.T. negotiators had treated the presumed difficulty with contempt and scoffed at the prospect of arrest. Or at least that was Preston's original report to Smart in 1900. Later on he changed his tune.

In the original agreement, the company had promised not to break the law. Then what was it afraid of? It couldn't legally advertise in Germany and, according to its own reports, it didn't. If some of its operations were clandestine, there wasn't any documentary evidence that would stand up in a court.

It is true that it collected names and mailed literature to German addresses, but it did so from England under another front name – the Farmers' Auxiliary. Indeed, there is no evidence that the mysterious company operated in a manner different from such countries as Brazil, Australia, or the United States, which were also competing for European immigrants. Nonetheless, it was broadly hinted that certain people might go so far as to commit suicide if the names were released; and they never were.

The Opposition's suspicions were increased when it was disclosed that, at Smart's suggestion, Preston had given, without public tender, $58,000 worth of government printing work in London to the Arundel Printing Company. Preston and Smart were almost certainly silent partners in this firm, whose front man was the son of a former Liberal M.P., Roy Somerville. Somerville farmed the work out. The Immigration Department was his only client, and when the government work was done the company went out of business. When Preston's deputy, C.F. Just, complained that the prices were exorbitant, that one fifteen-thousand-dollar job could have been done by the department's regular printer for less than four thousand, Preston suspended him. Later Preston denied any connection with the company. But if Somerville was the only principal in the firm, why was one account paid with four cheques — three issued on the same day?

In the words of Alfred Jury, Preston had two "gold mines," the N.A.T. Company and the Canadian Labour Bureau. The front man for the bureau was a German named Louis Leopold, who had been an N.A.T. agent and who was remarkably cosy with Preston. The two had adjoining offices; they shared a telephone; they both used the legal services of Preston's son-in-law. Preston set up Leopold as a ticket agent for several steamship lines and channelled all non-agricultural business his way, using a stock form he'd devised for that purpose.

In fact, the Canadian Labour Bureau was a fraud. To the unwary, it was an official arm of the government: its stationery bore the Canadian coat of arms and the address of the Immigration Department. Actually, it operated in direct contravention to Sifton's policy, which was that only farmers and female domestics were wanted in the West. With Preston's connivance, the bureau was used to attract mechanics and artisans in order to provide Canadian employers with strikebreakers. It also guaranteed work that didn't exist and caused hundreds of disgruntled English immigrants to walk the streets of Winnipeg, inveigled into Canada with false advertising, which claimed that twenty thousand jobs awaited them. The immigrants' loss was Leopold's gain, and also, presumably, Preston's.

The Labour Bureau was supposedly a one-man operation, but Preston was clearly in charge. If Leopold was sole owner, why was he sneaking around, booking passengers on his own, and pocketing the money without reference to the bureau? When the bureau was hired to break a coal miners' strike at Fernie, B.C., the money was banked in Preston's name. But Preston denied everything. When a parliamentary committee examined him on his blatant disregard of department regulations, he blandly replied that he hadn't studied them carefully and had no knowledge of a public policy that had been shouted from the housetops since 1896. He was skilled in the art of stonewalling; but

234

only the Liberal majority in the Commons saved him from dismissal.

In the face of bitter protests from the Canadian labour movement, Leopold's bureau vanished from the scene. So, in time, did the mysterious company. In 1907, Frank Oliver found a loophole in the contract and cancelled it. A government auditor was able, at last, to go through the company's books. It had, in its final three years (the only ones for which there were adequate accounts), spent $84,000 and received $239,000, a profit of $155,000, or more than $1,250,000 in 1984 terms.

Was it worth it to Canada? Nobody knows, since nobody bothered to look for a cause and effect between the company's advertising and those Europeans who arrived in Canada. And Canada was the only country that farmed out its continental immigration and the only one that paid a bonus of five dollars a head. The United States paid no bonuses; on the contrary, it charged between two and five dollars for the privilege of landing on its shores. None of its agents hid behind a syndicate or corporation; none got into trouble with the law. In 1905, some 828,000 emigrants left Europe for the United States. But then, as Preston and Smart kept saying, the United States was much better known in Europe than was Canada.

Preston was enraged at the cancellation of the N.A.T. contract and so was Sifton, who told Laurier that it "represents unquestionably the best plan of immigration of the best class." Preston, in his memoirs, said the cancellation of the contract was a "flagrant breach of faith and lack of common honesty." In his view "there was never a more honest contract or one more honestly carried out." But Preston was not in Europe when the contract was cancelled. His Liberal friends defeated a motion in Parliament to fire him, but he was obviously too hot to handle in his old job. The time had come to get Mr. Preston as far away from Canada as possible. Even Europe was not far enough. And so, on August 31, 1906, he was given a new post on the opposite side of the Pacific Ocean as trade commissioner to Korea, China, and Japan.

3

It was Clifford Sifton's boast that he "never recommended a relative *A* for an office much less appointed one." That was certainly true. On *favoured* one occasion he was asked to authorize the appointment of a *relative*

J.D. Sifton as a digger of artesian wells. The Minister refused: "He is a distant relative of mine and that is sufficient reason why he should not have any business connection with the Department."

The dictum, however, did not apply to favours granted. The most flagrant example is that of Theodore Burrows, a prominent lumberman and Liberal politician who was Sifton's wife's brother. Between 1902 and 1905, Burrows and his lawyer-associate, A.W. Fraser, former head of the Ottawa Liberal Association, tendered for Western timber limits on twenty occasions, often concealing their interest by the use of nominees. In an astounding nineteen cases out of twenty, they were successful. And in every case they won out by a suspiciously narrow margin, the average difference between their bid and the next closest being no greater than 6 per cent. No one came close to this remarkable record. Burrows's nearest rivals, the MacDonald brothers, tendered thirty times during the same period and failed in sixteen cases. They paid three and a half times as much for their limits, on an average, as was offered by the next highest bidders.

During this period, half of all the timber holdings under lease in the West – three thousand square miles of selected timber – fell into the hands of speculators. Half of that amount was acquired by the Burrows-Fraser combination and held for speculation. It could not have happened without Sifton's help. In 1903, Sifton made two changes in the timber regulations that helped enrich his relative at the expense of the settlers who were pouring into the wooded areas of the West. Until that point, a licence to cut timber had to be renewed annually; if the land was required for settlement, the licence could be cancelled. That encouraged early logging operations, discouraged speculation, and ensured that vast areas could be made available for newcomers. In addition, the homesteaders in the area were given a special privilege: they were allowed to enter the timber reserves to cut logs for their own use – for building materials, fence posts, firewood.

Sifton changed all that. Timber licences could now be held until all the timber was cut, which meant the lands could be tied up indefinitely by speculators and closed to settlement. In addition, homesteaders were barred from using any of the timber. Most of Burrows's leases were acquired immediately before or soon after these changes were made. The new regulations increased the value of his holdings and gave him greater security. He didn't have to worry about his leases not being renewed, and so he didn't have to plunge into a logging operation immediately; he could wait until the price went up. And he wouldn't be bothered by homesteaders cutting his trees.

He had plenty of clout with the department. His requests sounded more like orders, and even when he broke the rules an exception was made for him. "I want this permit," he wrote to James Smart on one such occasion. "Kindly have permit sent to me. I intend cutting on it this spring." In this instance, all other flawed applications had been rejected, but Burrows's wasn't. Even though at the time he was cutting on a forbidden area, it didn't seem to matter. The disputed tract was simply added to his lease.

Burrows was a master of tricky tendering. The accepted method of bidding on timber leases was straightforward. You used the department's forms, stipulating the number of the timber berth, the amount of the enclosed marked cheque, and the name of the bank on which the cheque was drawn. When the advertised deadline was reached, two officers of the department opened the tenders and awarded the lease to the highest bidder.

Under this system nobody possessed of inside information could slip an extra cheque into the envelope at the last minute. But Burrows and his nominees didn't use the departmental forms. In case after case he declined to stipulate the amount of the cheque enclosed. His bids came in at the last moment, and he often enclosed two and sometimes three cheques; at times he paid in cash.

Nor were these tenders opened in the presence of two witnesses as before. In the winter of 1902-3, James Smart turned the job over to one man, the Dominion Lands Commissioner, John Gillanders Turriff (a secretary was usually present but was not required to see the bids). Turriff was a Liberal stalwart, a former member of the North West Council and Legislative Assembly, a defeated candidate for federal office (he was eventually elected in 1904), and a close and long-time friend of Burrows and of Fraser.

Burrows was careful to conceal his own part in this suspicious method of tendering. No one would have known, for instance, that he was behind the successful bid for a valuable limit on the north slope of the Porcupine Hills. The bids were made in his stenographer's name, and the envelope referred only to an unnamed amount. It wasn't until the Public Accounts Committee subpoenaed the original documents instead of copies that it learned from the marginal notes in ink that three cheques were enclosed, each one just managing to outstrip the other bids by a fractional amount.

In January, 1903, an American syndicate applied to enter a 7,000-square-mile forest north of Prince Albert and select 500 square miles of the best timber. It was an unprecedented idea of a magnitude never before contemplated, for whoever gained that limit would have a monopoly of the timber in the area. In the end, it turned out, the American syndicate didn't have a chance. But Burrows did, in spite of a violent protest from the mayor, the board of trade, and the leading businessmen of Prince Albert.

The department put the area up for tender but made sure that nobody – including the Americans – would have time to examine it. Interested parties had only a month to cruise the 7,000 square miles and decide what to pay for 500 square miles spread out over the whole region. There was no competition. Burrows and Fraser, hiding behind nominees in the name of the Big River Lumber Company, got the timber rights on a billion feet of spruce for less than two cents an acre. The profits were enormous. Burrows had paid five thousand dollars. He sold half his interest for eighty thousand dollars before the land was even explored or blocked.

Another of Burrows's façades was the Imperial Pulp Company, a firm as mysterious as the North Atlantic Trading Company. Sifton's political opponents tried for years to find out who was behind this shadow firm, which apparently lived in a Winnipeg post office box, owned no sawmills or equipment, and had no officers. Its letters were signed with a stamp; it was not listed in any business directory; it had never applied on its own for a timber limit, but bid on other applications. This company did not use the department's printed form; though more than one cheque was enclosed, that fact was not stipulated on the envelope; and the total amount bid was scribbled in ink.

Between December 1902 and February 1904 this firm, under various names, tendered for nine timber leases in the Territories and was successful in every case. The total amount of its bid was $54,975, a sum suspiciously close to the total amount bid by the nine closest bidders: $51,771. It took the Opposition Conservatives five years to discover whose company this was. In 1908, it finally came out. The president was Sir Daniel McMillan, Lieutenant-Governor of Manitoba and a prominent Liberal; the managing director was Theodore Burrows. The leases had been obtained entirely for speculation, the land tied up from settlement. In all the intervening years the company hadn't built a single sawmill or cut a stick of timber, and hundreds of homesteaders had been prohibited from cutting firewood or building materials in the area. For its investment of fifty-five thousand dollars, the "company" had obtained timber limits worth, in 1908, in the neighbourhood of one million dollars.

Again, in some of these cases the department left so little time for exploration after advertising the timber limits that Imperial Pulp had the bidding all to itself. In one such case, Burrows's lawyer, Fraser, attempted to preserve the appearance of competition by preparing two bids, one in Burrows's name, one in the name of W.H. Nolan, a political crony. Nolan got the two limits for eleven hundred dollars and turned them over within a few hours to the Imperial Pulp Company. But the fiction that Nolan owned the leases remained on the books for years, frustrating the attempts of investigators to tie them to Sifton's brother-in-law. Like Burrows, Nolan was an old friend of Turriff's — a school chum he had known for forty years. Imperial's nine successes all took place when Turriff was opening the tenders. Burrows's successes all took place during the time Sifton headed the department.

Very little of this was known, however, during Sifton's term of office. The full details did not appear until 1908 when Herbert Ames, the Conservative member for Montreal—St.-Antoine, with terrier-like tenacity forced an investigation by the Public Accounts Committee. Ames, who travelled the country before the 1908 election lecturing on this and other scandals, summed up his own argument in Parliament on May 19:

"I feel a great opportunity has been lost; it has been lost in order that certain gentlemen, close to the Government, might become millionaires. And to this end our three provinces have been despoiled. The day will come when there will be handed over to these provinces the remnants of the lands that should have been theirs long ago. But before that is done, practically all the timber of value will have been given away. These are the assets the provinces should have in order to develop themselves and carry on their internal affairs. . . . Yet you propose to shear Alberta and Saskatchewan of practically all their assets to give them into the hands of speculators.

"Mr. Speaker, the circumstances connected with the tenders we have examined . . . lead, to my mind, to one inevitable conclusion, and that is that there has been either fraud or imposition practised in obtaining some of these limits. If it is well founded, what is the logical conclusion of the matter? It is that the country has been robbed and that certain persons today are in possession of stolen goods, that should be restored to the people of Canada."

The goods were not restored, but after Sifton left office his successor abolished the system of tendering for timber leases, substituting public auctions, with the government placing a reserve bid on each lease.

Ames's exhortations fell largely on deaf ears; in those heady days of the Western boom, the public was happy to return the Liberal government to office. But Sifton's margin was reduced in Brandon and Burrows went down to defeat largely because of the publicity surrounding the revelations. It did no permanent damage. He survived the disgrace, pocketed his profits, and in 1926 was appointed Lieutenant-Governor of Manitoba.

4

Big Jim's During his term as Minister of the Interior, Clifford Sifton moved to
political gather all the reins of power into his own hands. This was particularly
clout true when it came to granting valuable grazing leases to ranchers in the dry cattle country of southern Alberta. By 1902, the Minister had taken unto himself the absolute right to grant or deny such leases and to do it without the names of specific individuals being placed before the Privy Council. In this way he was able to reward friends and political associates without arousing public suspicion. Under this system, leases were granted to men who did not at the time live in Canada, who owned no cattle but held the leases for speculation, while the bona fide cattlemen and ranchers in the area who tried to obtain similar privileges found themselves shut out.

One such friend was J.D. McGregor, the one-time livery stable keeper and cattle man in Brandon who had, since 1888, been one of Sifton's strongest political supporters and also his campaign manager. McGregor was a mountain of a man, smooth-faced and double-chinned, a pioneer whose family had arrived in Manitoba in 1877, when he was only seventeen. In the smoky back rooms of Brandon politics he was known by his initials, as J.D., and sometimes as Big Jim. As we have seen, Sifton made sure McGregor was given CPR meat contracts on the Crow's Nest Pass line. In the Yukon, as a paid employee of Sifton's department, McGregor received other benefits, all of them potentially lucrative. He was named Inspector of Mines and given the job of collecting royalties in cash from Klondike prospectors, a task hitherto performed impeccably by the Mounted Police.

In that job there was room for considerable graft. There was even more in the disposal of liquor licences. Thus, when Sifton named McGregor liquor licensing commissioner for the Yukon, Superintendent Sam Steele of the Mounted Police, who sat on the liquor board, balked. The job, he said, was an open invitation to illicit wealth. The veteran policeman lost the round. In a brutal telegram dated September 8, 1899, Sifton pulled him out of the Yukon and effectively ended his career. When McGregor returned to Brandon, the plum jobs in the Yukon were transferred to his brother, Colin.

In 1901, in the cattle country of southern Alberta between the Bow and the Belly rivers, Big Jim McGregor and a banker partner, A.E. Hitchcock, a prominent Medicine Hat Liberal, managed to tie up some ninety-one thousand acres of land for grazing cattle. As in the case of the timber lands, these twenty-one-year leases were temporary; they could be cancelled on two years' notice if homesteaders wanted to move in on the land. But in December 1904, with Sifton's former law partner, A.E. Philp of Brandon, McGregor went to Ottawa to see his friend the Minister and changed all that. As a result, he and six other prominent Liberals were given special privileges: their leases were granted irrevocably for twenty-one years. Shortly after Sifton resigned that law was rescinded.

Big Jim and his partner had another privilege: they were allowed to select 10 per cent of the leased land for outright purchase. Again the law was bent. That land was supposed to be in the vicinity of the ranch buildings only, but McGregor chose the finest ninety-one hundred acres he could find; the two men paid one dollar an acre in a private deal with the department. A year later the same land was valued at twelve times that amount.

But McGregor had made more than a profit. By tying up the land for twenty-one years he had made it impossible for anyone in the adjacent area to tap the Bow for irrigation without first settling with him. And that is exactly what Big Jim had in mind. In southern Alberta, land was of little use to immigrants unless it was irrigated.

Like Theodore Burrows, McGregor was adept at hiding his tracks. A mysterious Englishman named Guy Tracy Robins now entered the picture and with a partner managed to get a vast irrigation concession – 380,000 acres – in the same area. Robins was a wealthy tennis-playing Englishman who knew nothing about irrigation and was simply a front for an unregistered syndicate consisting of McGregor and his partner Hitchcock. Once again, the Department of the Interior had made a contract with a company that had no corporate existence, that could not be sued, and whose ownership was secret. The company was required to make a down payment of only five cents an acre and was allowed to have the land for a dollar an acre on condition that it spend three-quarters of a million dollars irrigating part of it over a ten-year period. But it didn't have to pay up until 1914 if it did the work. Thus it tied up the land for a mere $19,000. Now the way was clear to form a limited stock company and raise the needed money from British investors.

By January 1907, McGregor and his friends had merged everything – grazing lands and irrigation lands – and, through a promoter, sold the package to the newly formed company in Britain: the South Alberta Cattle Company. The so-called cattle company's main interest was in selling land to settlers at a profit, once the irrigation scheme was complete. It paid off McGregor and the others in cash and stock. The Robins property went for $485,000, the grazing lease for considerably more at $654,000, an inflated price because McGregor controlled the water supply and also because the principals wanted to evade the tough British corporation laws and conceal the promotional costs of the venture. Only at this point was the Opposition able to learn from the company's printed prospectus exactly what was going on. The managing director of the new company was J.D. McGregor.

The profit to the favoured few was enormous. And nobody in the government, apparently, gave a hoot about the settlers. In 1893, one of the main planks in the Liberal platform had been that "no middlemen in land transactions should be allowed to come between the government and the settler." But in this case, a whole platoon of middlemen were scrambling for their share of the boodle. The price of land soared to twelve dollars an acre, and there was nothing the government could do about it.

In an earlier and similar transaction involving irrigation lands, Sifton's department had been careful to insert a protective clause putting a maximum sale price of five dollars an acre on the land. But in the case of Robins's irrigation company, this clause was not included, even though the head of the Irrigation Branch had recommended it. Once again, McGregor and his friends had been granted a special privilege.

Sifton was out of the ministry by this time, but he was the main catalyst in McGregor's land scheme. For it was he who broke trail for his old campaign manager; had the path not been so smooth, it couldn't have happened. McGregor had no trouble grabbing the land without rent even before the original leases were granted. He had no trouble getting the leases extended irrevocably for twenty-one years.

He had no trouble selecting the finest acreage for a pittance. Sifton had more than a thousand applications on his desk for similar leases in the year before he left office. Only a handful were granted before the door was slammed, and these all went to the Minister's closest supporters: a Liberal senator for one; several prominent liquor wholesalers; and, of course, Big Jim McGregor.

McGregor had his finger in more than one southern Alberta land scheme. He was also the man behind another mysterious figure, one Hugh P. Brown of Great Falls, Montana, who had somehow got one of the valuable twenty-one-year leases: almost one hundred square miles of grazing land directly across the river from the McGregor property. This was a murky business. Brown applied for the lease on May 26, 1902. The airplane hadn't yet been invented and the mail was even slower then than now, but Brown's letter must have had wings, for it was stamped "Received" in Sifton's department the day after it was mailed. But Brown didn't sign the letter. His signature was marked "Per J.D.M." The indefatigable Tory M.P. Herbert Ames, poring over the departmental correspondence, decided to match those scrawled initials with one on a similar document signed "James D. McGregor." They were, as he suspected, identical.

McGregor, then, had initiated the Brown lease, and everybody in the department must have known it. Brown was actually a bookkeeper for a Great Falls butcher, but the department kept up the charade of dealing with him in Montana – or trying to.

Suddenly, the mails, which had carried Brown's original application to Ottawa with telegraphic speed, slowed to a crawl. Letter after letter went off to Brown, telling him he had the lease, asking him to pay rent. No answer. But the department didn't cancel the lease: in some magical fashion Brown's holdings were increased from 32,000 to 60,000 acres.

A year elapsed. Letter No. 6 went off to Brown. Again, no reply. Eleven settlers in the area had petitioned the government, protesting the lease and urging its cancellation. But the unreachable Mr. Brown had the inside track; the settlers were told the land wasn't available.

In fact, by this time Brown had nothing whatever to do with the matter. He'd never been more than a convenience for an interlocking group of Liberals, all closely tied to Sifton, who wanted to get control of Alberta land without the public or the Opposition catching on. McGregor peddled the lease to the Galway Horse and Cattle Company, which wasn't a company at all but another name for A.J. Adamson, a prominent Western Liberal. Adamson's brother-in-law was one of

Sifton's key employees, the Dominion Lands Commissioner, J.G. Turriff, the same man who had opened the curiously worded timber bids of another brother-in-law, Theodore Burrows.

Adamson we have also met before. He was the key political figure in another deal – the sale of a quarter of a million acres of Saskatchewan land to an American syndicate, the only time the government sold homestead land outright rather than parcelling it out into free blocks for settlers. The sale was kept secret and did not become public knowledge until questions were asked in the House a year after it was consummated.

Adamson, thanks to his pal McGregor, now had something that was, on the face of it, worth nothing: a non-existent lease, unsigned and never paid for, on behalf of a firm that had no corporate existence. Even Frank Oliver, when he succeeded Sifton, knew nothing about it: *he* was still trying to get Brown to answer his mail! But on July 17, 1905, Adamson, now a Member of Parliament, popped into Oliver's office to reveal he'd been carrying the Brown lease around in his pocket for twenty-two months and hadn't even bothered to pay a nickel of rent. Oliver told him to pay up or the twenty-one-year lease would revert to an ordinary two-year lease.

Adamson agreed and vainly tried to peddle the lease. But now Turriff entered the picture. He, too, had become a Liberal Member of Parliament and, as such, put pressure on Oliver, who wilted and agreed the lease would be irrevocably closed for twenty-one years. With that assurance Adamson had no trouble selling it. The purchaser was a bona fide cattleman, John Cowdry, who had been in Ottawa trying to get a grazing lease for himself. The price was said to be $22,500, which in 1984 dollars would be more than $200,000.

It was a nice profit for Adamson and also, of course, for Big Jim McGregor, who had made the whole deal possible. Adamson did not bother to run for Parliament in the election of 1908, but his brother-in-law, John Gillanders Turriff, the man who helped grease so many wheels within the department, continued his successful career in politics, being named to the Senate in 1918. As for J.D. McGregor, further honours awaited him. When Theodore Burrows died in office in 1929, Big Jim replaced him as Lieutenant-Governor of Manitoba. It was, after all, an obvious choice.

Canada's Century had scarcely dawned when the three key civil ser- *Cheating*
vants in Clifford Sifton's Department of the Interior entered into a *the*
successful conspiracy to defraud the two bands of Assiniboine Indians *Indians*
in the Moose Mountain agency of the Assiniboia District of forty-five
thousand acres of prime farm land. The three covered their tracks so
well that no whisper of scandal leaked out until a royal commission
under Thomas Robert Ferguson, established by the Conservative
government, brought down its report in 1915. By then it was past
history.

The three men in question were James Allan Smart, Deputy Minister of the Interior as well as Deputy Superintendent General of Indian
Affairs; Frank Pedley, Superintendent of Indian Affairs; and William J.
White, inspecting officer of the Immigration Department. We have
met them all: Smart, the former mayor of Brandon and Sifton's
right-hand man; Pedley, the Toronto lawyer and Liberal organizer
whom we last saw facing Nicholas Zibarov in the first of the Doukhobor demonstrations; and White, the former editor of the Brandon
Sun, who masterminded the department's propaganda in the United
States.

As early as 1898, Smart had cast a speculative eye on the Moose
Mountain country near Moosomin, Assiniboia, and described it as
"magnificent." It was, he intimated, far too good for the Indians. "If it
is at all like a portion of the country under cultivation near it, it cannot
be excelled, possibly, in the territories," Smart told Sifton, adding that
there were only about 220 Assiniboines on the reserves "and it seems
ridiculous to lock up such a splendid piece of land for so very few
people."

Everybody seemed to agree that it would be more convenient for the
agency if the Assiniboines of the Pheasant's Rump and Ocean Man
reserves were moved off their land and settled among the Crees on the
White Bear Reserve on the other side of the mountain. It would also
bring considerable savings in agency salaries and rations if the three
reserves were amalgamated into one.

No one worried about the effect on the Indians, who had by the end
of the century become agriculturally self-sufficient – the primary objective of the department's policy toward the native peoples. They were of
Assiniboine and Sioux descent. The Indians of the White Bear Band,

however, were of Cree and Salteaux descent, spoke a different tongue, and were continuing their traditional activities of hunting, fishing, and trapping. They were not agriculturally inclined and were not self-sufficient. The removal of the two farming bands could only reduce their self-sufficiency, decrease their standard of living, and make them a disadvantaged minority on the White Bear Reserve. Why move them? Their yield of grain per acre had been increasing year by year, and in the words of the government instructor "they appear perfectly contented . . . are manly in their dealings and give no trouble."

In December 1898, however, James Smart, who was charged with the welfare of all Western Indians, moved to get the Assiniboines off their land. H.R. Halpin, the Moose Mountain farm instructor, was told to sound out the Indians. Halpin reported that three of the four chiefs opposed the move but added that, should they want too much money for the land, they could easily be brought to heel by packing a future meeting with young Indians from across the mountain.

What was the land worth? Smart in 1898 had thought it the finest in the Territories, but in 1899 wrote: "I am inclined to think that $1.00 per acre is all the land would be valued at as it stands." Now Frank Pedley and Will White got into the act. Up to Ottawa to talk with them came White's Chicago agent, Wilbur Bennett. Shortly thereafter an offer came in from an American syndicate to buy the land, and after some wrangling the price was set at Smart's estimate of a dollar an acre. The membership of this syndicate was never made clear to the department, which exhibited a total lack of curiosity regarding the principals. The president was supposed to be Joseph C. Armstrong, an Omaha banker, but it's doubtful if he'd ever heard of the company as Bennett had apparently forged his signature. The other principal was Bennett's brother-in-law, F.G. West, a subagent from Omaha.

Whatever the makeup of the so-called syndicate, its offer gave Smart the excuse he needed to force the Indians off the land. He wrote to Sifton on March 5, 1901, urging that the American offer be accepted and, directly contradicting his earlier assessment, added: "I am inclined to think [his favourite phrase] from my observation that there is not a great deal of first class land on the reserve." Smart explained that the department's assessment valued the land at seventy-five cents an acre but magnanimously suggested the Indians get at least a dollar. By contrast, adjacent CPR land had sold for three dollars. As for the Indians, Smart declared that they were "anxious that this arrangement be carried out."

Events moved swiftly. Sifton agreed to the final terms on March 8. A fortnight later a meeting with the Indians took place on the White Bear Reserve with David Laird, the Indian Commissioner of the North West Territories, representing the government. According to the Assiniboine interpreter, Xavier James McArthur, there were many objections from the band until Laird, in a fury, stamped out of the room, warning them that if they didn't agree to the terms the police would evict them forcibly. In the end, the Indians gave in and almost immediately vacated the land.

Laird had promised that as soon as the land was sold the Assiniboines would receive a five-thousand-dollar bonus from the Americans to cover the cost of putting up houses and barns in their new home. But the land wasn't sold. A group of prominent Liberals protested that they wanted to buy the land themselves. Sifton gave in. The government announced it wasn't prepared to complete the sale. But the Indians weren't allowed to go back to their homes, nor were they given funds to build new houses.

The government's announcement led the public to believe that nobody — least of all Americans — could make a profit from speculating in Indian lands. The plan now was to put up the acreage for auction, parcel by parcel, as soon as it was surveyed. With autumn fast approaching, the Assiniboines continued to ask for money to build shelters. There was none.

Now Smart changed the rules. Instead of selling the lands by public auction, the government would sell them by private tender. Thus the matter passed out of David Laird's hands; the sale would be controlled entirely by the department. Posters were prepared in early October, 1901, for distribution to post offices within one hundred miles of the reserve, outlining the form of tendering and payment and giving a deadline of November 15. But then Smart ordered changes in the posters that considerably cut down the time available to inspect the property and mail in the bids.

One change had to do with the value of the land. The department's own man, William Underhill, a homestead inspector, had valued it at about $1.10 an acre. A later valuation by John B. Lash, Laird's secretary, gave a more glowing assessment, with $2.12 as the average value. Smart ordered that the last appraisal not be advertised and that the various bidders be responsible for examining the land themselves. Thirteen years later, Smart perjured himself before the Ferguson Commission, saying he knew nothing of such a report.

Because the amended notice didn't make its appearance until October 25, 1901, prospective purchasers had only about twenty days to scramble over the property, find the most suitable land clear of swamp or coulée, and get their bids to Ottawa. Smart, Pedley, and White had the field practically to themselves. The sale by tender was advertised in only three newspapers — two in Winnipeg, one in Moosomin — and some advertisements actually didn't appear until *after* the November 15 deadline.

On November 8, 1901, after working hours, the three men, operating from Frank Pedley's Ottawa office, typed up 313 tender forms for the Moose Mountain Reserve. On November 12, these tenders were delivered to the Toronto office of Pedley's former law partner, A.C. Bedford-Jones. Here, Bedford-Jones filled out the forms with the names and signatures of three other Toronto lawyers and land speculators and shipped them back to Ottawa.

The tenders were opened on November 15. Predictably, Smart and his colleagues, hidden behind the three nominees, had managed to secure 298 of 308 quarter-sections, a total of more than forty-five thousand acres, for which they paid an average of $1.23 an acre. According to regulations, they were required to enclose with each tender a cheque for 25 per cent of their bid. They didn't. That money wasn't paid until April, 1902, two months after the trio had sold the lands for $112,500, or roughly $2.50 an acre — twice the price the Indians had received. The speculators who bought them out did even better. By 1904, the land was selling for $4.50 an acre, by 1906 for at least $6.75.

This was not the only profit that Smart and his friends made out of Indian lands. On the same day, November 15, 1901, the former Chacastapasis Reserve was put up for sale. Smart, at the last moment, had extended the deadline by one week, allowing himself and his two colleagues to bid through nominees. As a result of inside knowledge, they got the land and sold it at a profit of $8,155. On the sale of a third Indian reserve, they made a profit of $18,000.

So successful were these three civil servants that they incorporated themselves for the purpose of handling land deals. One of their circulars contained a telling phrase: "We also have exceptional facilities for dealing with Government lands and acting as Parliamentary agents for same."

Pedley and White were still with the department when these revelations became public in 1915. No sooner did the evidence appear in the press than Pedley was forced to resign. White survived. Pedley, however, had no difficulty in finding a new post. The Liberal party, which always took care of its own, made him its organizer in northern Ontario.

6

To what extent was Clifford Sifton involved in these various scandals? *Every-* Was he aware of them? And if he was aware, did he profit from them or *body's* merely condone them? *doing it*

It strains common credulity to believe that Sifton did not know what was going on in his own department and also among his friends and in-laws. The Minister of the Interior liked to have a finger in every pie; he even made specific suggestions about details of the subject matter in the immigration pamphlets. Was he totally blind, then, to Preston's manoeuvrings of the North Atlantic Trading Company? Was he so incurious that he didn't ask for a shred of background detail on the mysterious company's principals? Did he ask no questions, not raise an eyebrow, when he learned that his people had made a contract for tens of thousands of dollars with a group that had no corporate existence?

It could scarcely have escaped the Minister's notice that his wife's brother was getting every timber contract he bid for at suspicious prices, or that he was hiding behind the names of nominees to get them. Sifton himself had changed the regulations that increased the value of these limits. Was he so obtuse that he didn't know the Imperial Pulp Company was just another name for Burrows? When Smart gave the job of opening tenders to Turriff, did Sifton not realize what was happening? Again, it beggars the imagination to believe that all these civil servants were acting without the Minister's knowledge or direction. To believe otherwise is to believe that Sifton was an incompetent, but that is a charge that cannot be fairly levelled at him.

Did Sifton not know that his pal Big Jim McGregor of Brandon and his political allies were getting extraordinary favours from the department? Sifton's law partner and dispenser of patronage, Philp, and his client, McGregor, were constantly meeting with the Minister in Ottawa. Philp and McGregor, in fact, formed a limited company to exploit grazing lands. Was Philp acting as Sifton's nominee in this company? A remarkable handwritten letter, dated January 21, 1905, suggests it. In it, Philp reported to Sifton: "I found everything at the ranch okay," referred to an earlier trip the two friends had made to the same property, reported on the work that needed to be done, and explained that the bank had been paid off and an application made to grant a new lease to replace an old one. It is a remarkably cosy document; with it, Philp enclosed his application for incorporation, naming himself and McGregor but leaving the name of the company and its address blank. This is the same letter in which Philp asked Sifton to lift the two-year cancellation clause in grazing leases in southern Alberta, a suggestion that was immediately accepted, but only for a handful of Liberal friends.

Did Sifton not know that his three senior civil servants were using inside knowledge and manoeuvring to profit from the sale of Indian lands? The Minister may have been deaf, but he was not blind. After all, in 1903 the trio publicly boasted in their brochure of their influence with the department. The question is not whether Clifford Sifton knew of the unwarrantable actions of his staff. The question is, why did he wink at them? Was it because so many others in the government and the Liberal party were up to their armpits in graft? Possibly. The Conservatives during their term of office had been no better, as many a Liberal pointed out in the House when these charges were aired. Standards were still loose at the turn of the century. The phrase "conflict of interest" had not entered the political lexicon. It was accepted that men entered politics not for the pittance that was paid but for the profit that could be gleaned from patronage or simply from being on the inside. The public, of course, was kept in the dark because the public's standards were far stricter than those of the politicians it put into office. Otherwise men like Burrows and McGregor would not have felt it necessary to conceal their manoeuvres.

But Sifton was human, too. All the old-time Liberals whom he had brought into the department – Smart, White, Pedley, Turriff, Preston – were making a good thing out of their positions. His closest friends and Liberal allies, including his own brother-in-law, were enriching themselves because of his political power. Everybody was doing it, including several of his fellow cabinet ministers. Was Sifton alone immune? He had started with nothing, yet he lived far beyond his salary in a style more splendid than did any of his colleagues. When he died, he left a fortune worth close to $20 million in 1984 dollars. Did he come by it honestly, through clever investments and perspicacious real estate transactions? There is nothing on the record to say that he didn't, but, in the Duke of Wellington's memorable phrase, anybody who would believe that would believe anything.

250

Chapter Nine

The Spirit of the West

1

West When Alberta and Saskatchewan were finally given provincial status
versus in 1905, the long, bitter campaign that the West had fought to attain
East autonomy was ended. The prairie country was no longer a colony of
Canada. Or was it?

In making a new constitutional arrangement with the fledgling
provinces of Alberta and Saskatchewan, Ottawa denied them the
same kind of autonomy enjoyed by the older provinces. Instead, the
federal government kept control of the forests, public lands, water
power, and educational policy as it had in the case of Manitoba. In
short, the three prairie provinces found themselves in an inferior
position relative to the rest of Canada, a status *The Times* of London,
in a prescient editorial, predicted would sow "the seeds of future
mischief."

The average immigrant didn't care. In 1906, in Saskatchewan and
Alberta, he voted with the government, which was bringing prosperity
to the West through its immigration and railway policies. In both
provinces, the Liberals were swept into power with healthy majorities.
But the politicians cared, and these included a good many Western
Liberals. Sifton had been applauded for resigning over the school
question. Behind that question lay an older and more serious controversy over federal rule versus the principle of provincial rights.

Ottawa, in many Western eyes, was Laurier and his French-Canadian colleagues. If Ottawa controlled the prairies' natural resources,
then Ottawa controlled the patronage. And patronage could be used
as a lever to prevent any of the prairie administrations from trying to
evade those clauses in the new constitution that conferred certain
educational privileges on religious minorities.

This suspicion of "Eastern" motives (for the East, in Western terms,
meant Ottawa, Ontario, and Quebec) was one of the ingredients in the
cement that was binding the West into a distinctive and, in many ways,
a separate nation within a nation. Patrick Burns, the successful Calgary meat packer, put it into words in March, 1905: "I think the general
feeling is that we should largely be left alone to manage our own
affairs. There is a feeling of resentment against eastern interference in
any shape more than is actually necessary. Western men fancy they
understand the situation far better than it is possible for eastern people
to do, and they would prefer having all matters in their own hands."

252

The constant hammering by the press on Eastern perfidy became almost an article of faith in the West. The government's immigration policy had been based on the concept of the West as a rural community feeding the East and enriching Eastern manufacturers by giving them a new domestic market. This "theoretical folly," as the New York *Tribune* called it in 1904, did not sit well with the moulders of prairie opinion. More than one Westerner wondered why condensed milk had to be shipped three thousand miles from Nova Scotia to stores in Calgary!

The patronizing and sneering attacks in some Ontario papers before the turn of the century hadn't helped. The Toronto papers were especially vitriolic. The *Star* attacked Manitoba as a "foot pad province" intent on having "its grasping desires gratified no matter how the rest of the Dominion feels about it" and in spite of the fact that the East had borne the burden of the railway and supplied the population that made Manitoba prosperous. As for the *News*, it claimed it would be cheaper for the East to give everybody in the North West a generous pension rather than to continue to subsidize the prairies. The Bobcaygeon *Independent* leaped at that suggestion:

"Let us do as The News suggests – buy them and have done with them. . . . Buy them . . . and hand them over to the Americans or the Phillipines [*sic*] or the Cubans . . . and get rid of the whole content. . . . What does the possession of the Northwest add to the comfort, pleasure, happiness or enjoyment of the people of Ontario? Nothing. Absolutely nothing. Then toss it overboard for we have no use for it. . . ."

That item was widely publicized in the West as an example of the Eastern attitude. It was, the *Winnipeg Tribune* declared, "quite representative of what many eastern Canadians really believe."

The most extreme utterances against the East came from Alberta and are to be found in the editorials of the Conservative Calgary *Herald*. The paper harped on three themes: total political autonomy for the Western provinces in general and Alberta in particular; freedom from exploitation by Eastern manufacturers; and the developing image of the Westerner as a distinct personality, implicitly superior to the more effete Easterner.

With a circulation of thirty-six hundred in 1904, the *Herald* was the largest daily newspaper in Alberta and certainly the most rambunctious. It was the kind of paper that kept a large vat of cold water in its press room into which printers were periodically dunked to sober them up enough to run the linotypes. Its owner was John Jackson Young, who bought the paper in 1894 and, in the words of Bob Edwards, took hold of "a moribund fragment and nursed it into a thing of life." Young had had a long and colourful career as a prairie newspaperman, beginning in Regina on Nicholas Flood Davin's *Leader*, where he made his reputation through a long series of exclusive interviews with Louis Riel in the prisoner's cell before his execution. A staunch Conservative and a member of the North West legislature, Young was also a consummate musician who could play any instrument. He acted as choirmaster and organist at the Central Methodist Church, was first president of the Calgary Operatic Society, and was also a good amateur artist and actor.

His paper was nothing if not theatrical. Its editor in 1904 was the colourful Garnett Clay Porter, a Kentucky colonel who boasted that he had once been forced to flee across the Mexican border as the result of a hill feud that had seen one man hanged. Porter, who had also taken part in the Klondike gold rush, was news editor of the *World* in Toronto when Young hired him. A hard-drinking poker-playing journalist, he fitted the Calgary image and caught the foothill spirit from some of the other tenants of the Hull Building in which the paper was published. These included Bob Edwards of the *Eye Opener*, P. J. "Paddy" Nolan, the most eloquent criminal lawyer in the province (who had on occasion written editorials for the paper), and J.E. Brownlee, a future premier of Alberta.

No modern journalist can pore over the *Herald*'s yellowing pages without mixed feelings: unease at the virulence of its regionalism and racism, dismay at the bullying extremism of its opinions, but admiration for its trenchant style, which makes present day editorial writing seem pallid.

Here is the *Herald* in 1902, roaring away in one of a score of editorials demanding provincial autonomy for the Territories: "We are not dogs nor serfs to be placated with a niggardly dole barely sufficient to sustain life. We are freeborn Canadian citizens who stand for our unalienable heritage, and shame on the traitor who will abate one jot or tittle of our just demands."

The *Herald* had guts; it was quite prepared to put its money where its editorial mouth was. In 1901 it had pointed out that there was no excuse for Calgarians to send orders back east since most Eastern concerns were "cheap john places of business," and Calgary products were just as good. Four years later when Alberta achieved autonomy

254

the paper responded by refusing all advertising from Eastern department stores.

Ottawa's centralist treatment of the new province that year – "the country's shame" as the *Herald* called it – drove the paper to a series of apoplectic editorials. "Can Albertans be forced to eat dirt and say they like it?" the paper cried. Alberta was "a political Cinderella . . . robbed of freedom . . . deprived of the sacred right of home rule." Alberta, screamed the *Herald* headline, "has been cut up to suit the purposes of the Ottawa conspirators."

In these machinations the *Herald* thought it saw a sinister Roman Catholic plot. Catholic Edmonton, which the paper called the "centre of French-Galician power," had been named the capital in spite of its much smaller population because of the political influence of Frank Oliver. The paper went so far as to suggest that Laurier, guided by the Pope's representative in Ottawa, was planning to establish a French-Canadian province in the North West.

In refusing full autonomy, the paper declared, the government was fastening upon the new provinces "a system marked by the worst form of coercion and intrigue." From that day on the *Herald* rarely mentioned the word "Liberal." It referred instead to the "coercionists" or the "coercion machine." When the Liberals won Alberta's first provincial election in November, 1905, its news columns reported that "by the worst exhibition of Ottawa interference ever displayed at a provincial election, the coercion plot has been forced upon the electors of Alberta."

The *Herald* saw the West as a distinctive entity, its very newness an asset, unshackling the people from the hidebound East. More than any daily paper of its day – more than Frank Oliver's *Bulletin* or Dafoe's *Free Press* – it managed, in its ebullient, free-swinging fashion, to capture the spirit of the West. That was, in fact, the title it placed on one of its more memorable editorials, written on May 16, 1905, at the end of the Sifton era, when the long fight for provincial autonomy had been realized:

"Undoubtedly there is something about the West and western life that gives it distinctiveness and creates a certain peculiar temperament; and for lack of a definite term they call that something 'the spirit of the west.' The western spirit is a composite quality. National conditions of geography and climate are at the bottom of it and beget, in the first place, enthusiasm; energy and optimism are the outcome of enthusiasm; and these three are balanced with a healthy sincerity. . . . The West

255

is strong and free, it has no vain traditions; it is rich in possibilities and even richer in hopefulness. The ozone of the wide expanses has got into the ways and methods of business, and pioneer courage has developed courageous enterprise. Therein consists, as nearly as one can express it, the spirit of the West, which brings even the unenterprising under its sway and promises to change the whole complex of our modern conditions."

In a later editorial, the *Herald* returned to this theme and defined its own concept of the Westerner as a man who had cut his ties permanently with the East: ". . . he must be true to the West before the West will be good to him. It will not do, for instance, to have his body in Vancouver while his heart is rooted in Toronto. The jealous West soon smells that out and gives him the cold shoulder. . . . He throws in his lot altogether or the West throws him out."

Those words were written in 1910. It would surprise few Westerners if they appeared in the Calgary *Herald* of 1984.

2

The *common* *experience* Westerners, of course, *were* different, no matter where they came from. Most shared some form of common experience, the very stuff of nationalism. They were bound together because, in so many instances, they had come through the fire and survived; and they were proud of it. The settlement period was for the three Western provinces what the Voortrek had been for the Boers or the Long March would be for the Chinese. The *Herald* could look down on the "vain tradition" of the East; but in the act of settlement and survival, the West was developing a tradition of its own.

Thousands remembered, and not without a pang, the goodbyes on the docks of Liverpool or at the railway depots of Austria-Hungary: the sudden realization that they were saying farewell to these grandmothers, cousins, and close friends as surely as if death had claimed them ("Inexpressible grief seized my young heart. . . . The parting and the mournful keening were heartbreaking. Old and Young wept as they bade us farewell, perhaps forever . . ."). Thousands remembered the cursory medical examinations as they boarded the immigrant ships ("What's your name? Are you well? Hold out your tongue . . ."); the dreadful storms on the Atlantic ("We all felt trapped. Some of us

256

thought we were doomed. . . . We lost all count of time . . ."); the first unprepossessing view of Canada ("It smelled of fish, of wood, of pine trees. It was unkempt and ragged and slapdash . . ."); the slatted seats on the colonist cars, imprinted forever, some would claim, on parts of the body; the hasty meals snatched at divisional points ("All you can eat for a quarter"); and the homesickness, the shock of anticlimax in the pit of the stomach at the first view of the stubbled prairie, the long wait at the land office, the bone-rattling ride across the open plains to the new homestead, the despair, the toil, the loneliness. These experiences, remembered, exchanged, sometimes exaggerated, contributed to the folk memory of the prairie people.

It is the spring of 1905, and we have arrived at last at the Dominion Land Office in Saskatoon, housed above an agricultural implement shop and reached by a rough wooden ladder. We grip the handrail, climb the breakneck stairway, and find ourselves in an office crowded with applicants for homesteads and presided over by a single youth.

We struggle for a place at the counter, but it is some while before we reach it. Here we are referred to a large wall map, marked out in townships, sections, and quarter-sections. This is the grid that has been imposed upon the West from the Red to the Rockies, disdainful of natural borders and barriers, criss-crossing coulée and river, lake and marsh – a surveyor's dream, a homesteader's nightmare.

Some of the sections are already marked off with pencilled crosses, chosen by early arrivals. We note with dismay that all the little crosses radiate out from Saskatoon for thirty miles before any vacant land is available. Have we come too late? Where should we locate? The youth in charge cannot advise us; that is not his responsibility. We must put a cross on our chosen homestead on the map, find our own way to the land, look it over, and if we like what we see, make our weary way back to Saskatoon, wait in line again, and file our homestead entry, hoping that no one else has beaten us to it.

We ask for a map of the Saskatchewan Valley, but there are none; the rush has been so great that all the maps have been snapped up, and the new ones have not yet arrived. The best thing we can do is to hire a rig at eight dollars a day, drive out across the open prairie, and find a man who can "locate" us – that is, show us what land is still available.

The next day we head out along Saskatoon's main street, clinging to the high cliff above the bend in the river. Soon the river is behind us and we are out on the lonely prairie. The trail takes us past a tiny settlement: a few farmhouses and a school on one side of the road, a few new gravestones on the other, but neither church nor post office as yet. We travel another twenty-five miles before we reach the next school, another wooden shack with a single teacher, stark on the prairie.

Our objective is the Eagle Hills, but we cannot reach them in one day. At last we find lodging – a kind of half-way house consisting of a one-room shack with a sod stable run by a bespectacled Englishman from Surrey, who puts us up on a mattress on the floor while he and his wife retire behind a curtained partition. The following day at noon we come in sight of the Eagle Hills, a long, low range rising sharply from the plain. Here in a big two-storey farmhouse a goateed farmer from Oregon offers to locate us for ten dollars a head and five dollars a day for driving the team.

Off we go for three hours across the wild prairie seamed by old buffalo tracks and pockmarked by gopher holes, following the wisp of a trail until we reached the area marked on the land office map. Back and forth we rattle, searching for good land, rejecting section after section. The land here is too rolling; there the soil is too light. It is too high; it is too low; there are too many sloughs; there are not enough sloughs. At last, after much zig-zagging, we make our decision, scribbling down the section numbers on the iron corner stakes, looking for the holes in the ground that mark the quarter-sections, and selecting alternative homesteads in case our first choices have already been reserved.

By the time we return to the farmhouse, just before dusk, the saffron sun of late evening is gilding the feathery grass, the tones changing as the sky reddens. Here and there we can see the green shoots of spring poking through the dead stubble. We have travelled close to sixty miles this day and our task is not yet ended.

We rise early in order to make the long trek back to Saskatoon in a single day. The hotels are full when we arrive late at night, but we find a spot to sleep on the floor of a Chinese restaurant. The next morning in the land office, we swear an oath on a greasy Bible that the land we have located is unoccupied and unimproved, pay our ten dollars, pocket our receipt. Now we own a piece of the West – or we will own it someday. For we are gambling with the Canadian government, betting our ten dollars that we can hang on to our 160 acres for three years and make a go of it in the promised land.

The darker themes interwoven into the symphony of prairie settlement were universal. Whether he came from the Caucasus or the Black Hills, from Petworth in Sussex or Coboconk in Ontario, almost every settler experienced in some form the drudgery, the monotony, the loneliness, and the terror of homestead life. They never forgot it. In later years, when life was sweeter, when the frame farmhouse had replaced the log shack that had replaced the sod hovel, they looked back on it all with wonder, pride, and not a little affection. The dreadful food, the fearful prairie fires, the terrifying white-outs became part of a prairie tradition. People talked nostalgically of fat bacon, soggy flapjacks, rabbit stew, and tea as soldiers talk of bully beef and Spam. Who did not remember the day when a ring of flames surrounded the farm buildings and men dropped exhausted from beating out the embers with wet sacks? They were members of an élite, these prairie pioneers; they had come through experiences that no other Canadians would ever understand.

John Diefenbaker, for instance, would never forget the night when, as a boy, he was lost in a Saskatchewan blizzard, unable to see ten feet before him, forced to cower all night in a snowbank, his home only two and a half miles away, kept alive by an uncle who wouldn't allow him to go to sleep. *March 11, 1908:* that date was engraved on his memory; it was something he couldn't forget, and it became something to boast about. It set the Prime Minister apart from the effete Easterners who had no conception of pioneer prairie life. It made him one with his constituents in Prince Albert, veterans all, who knew from their own experience what he, the quintessential Western maverick, had gone through.

And who but a real Westerner could know or comprehend the haunting loneliness of the prairie? Maria Adamowska knew. When her husband was forced to go away to work and she was left alone on the farm, "my heart broke with loneliness. I almost died of boredom. I wept, my children wept, and my despair almost drove me crazy." Evan Davies, the Welsh immigrant, encountered one settler whose wife had actually gone insane from loneliness.

The checkerboard pattern of the prairies accentuated the solitary life. People couldn't hive together. As one woman, Mrs. Carl Tellenius, remembered, "you couldn't even see the light of a neighbour's house." But the pattern of settlement, awkward as it was, put a special stamp on the West, giving this one Canadian region a geographical individuality shared by no other. The West was one vast checkerboard of townships, sections, and quarter-sections. Each six-mile-square township contained thirty-six sections of land; each section was divided

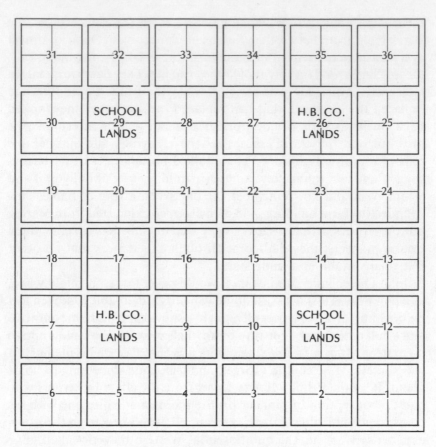

A Prairie Township

into quarter-sections, each one 160 acres in size. Two sections were set aside for the Hudson's Bay Company and two more for schools. The odd-numbered sections belonged to the Crown or to the railways as part of the original land grants given to encourage development. The even-numbered sections were available to homesteaders. Every home-steader was required to build a habitable house, prepare twenty-five acres for seeding, and live on his land for at least three years. At the end of that time it was his. And if he prospered and if the odd-numbered section next door was still available, he could buy that, too – as much as he could afford. Unlike the older regions, the West was developed in a single, disciplined fashion. And that, too, was part of the common experience.

3

Westerners were proud and Westerners were cocky. Their lives were *The* modest success stories, for they had made it when others faltered and *Western* went home. And so they were like war veterans who, having survived *ethic* the battlefield, display their medals and boast about the hard times.

Hard times meant hard work, and that was the key to success. If a man was seen to have worked hard he was admired, as Pat Burns the meat packer was admired. Patrick Byrne, to give him his proper name, so it was said, had made his first million before he could read or write, never stopped working, never understood what leisure was, never for an instant considered sitting back and taking life easy. Like the farmer whom Ella Sykes encountered aboard ship who was not content unless he was buying more and more land, ploughing longer and deeper furrows, Pat Burns was never at ease unless he was expanding. His life was his work; he had no hobbies, read little, wrote few letters, and skipped social functions pleading pressure of business. Bob Edwards claimed Pat Burns's idea of a good time was "attending the funerals of rival butchers."

Burns was held up as an example of what hard work could do. As a boy on an Oshawa farm, he was forced to pick his way through a tangle of forest, following three miles of blazed trees to reach the schoolhouse. As a result, he was the least-educated businessman in Western Canada, but also the richest. In Calgary, where he made his fortune, only one prominent businessman in seven had been to business school or college. The majority hadn't finished high school. Burns didn't even finish public school.

He had started west with nothing, so poor he was forced to leave the train at Rat Portage and walk the rest of the way to Winnipeg to keep enough money to eat. Later, he thought nothing of walking another 160 miles to locate a homestead at Minnedosa. Then he went farther west. To earn money to buy livestock, he worked blasting rock for the CPR. After that he never worked for anybody but himself.

He started as a cattle drover and freighter in the foothills under contract to the railway and raised himself bootstrap by bootstrap – a beef contract here, a hog contract there. An old friend from Kirkfield, Ontario, William Mackenzie, the railway contractor, gave him another boost; by 1890 he was supplying beef to the Mackenzie and Mann railway system, soon to become the Canadian Northern. He never looked back, never stopped working, set no finite goals for himself, seeing instead a future that had no limit to progress. In that sense he typified the West.

Since he had no end point in sight, he simply arranged for his empire to grow with the country. In him was distilled all the optimism of the new frontier. Warm and genial, he had supreme confidence in himself and in the West. There wasn't a neurotic bone in his body. An early riser, he could catnap any place, any time; a good listener with a good memory, he was never brusque or impatient. He preferred to conduct his business in person and was shrewd enough to seize what the West was offering. As early as 1885, with the CPR scarcely completed, he grasped the opportunity it offered and so became the first man to move hogs by rail. When news of the Klondike strike hit the world in 1897, he lost not a moment in shipping cattle to Skagway and rafting them down the Yukon to the goldfields.

With his Klondike profits, he moved in 1902 into real estate: a ranch, a slaughterhouse, a business block, several butcher shops. Now he was producer, manufacturer, and sales department all rolled into one. Soon he added dairy products, vegetables, and fruits to his list of merchandise. By 1906, he had markets in sixty Western towns and headed the largest corporation on the prairies dealing with livestock and meat. He was not a Calvinist but an Irish Catholic, but, as one Chicago cattleman said of him, "he resembled the proverbial Scotsman who keeps the Sabbath Day and everything else he can lay his hands on."

He stood five feet seven in his socks – a swarthy man with piercing, deep-set eyes, broad shoulders, and a long torso that made him seem taller than he was. He walked with a rolling gait but despite his short legs could beat anybody in a foot race. He loved to race, for he was incurably restless, incurably competitive. He found it impossible to sit still, physically or financially. He was forever getting up and pacing about his vast eighteen-room mansion of oak and sandstone, designed by Francis Mawson Rattenbury who later built Victoria's famous Empress Hotel. He was never idle, a man on the move who believed that money, too, should never be left idle. He had no sooner completed one project than he invested the profits in the next. When his first slaughterhouse burned down, he built a larger one. Years later, fire took another slaughterhouse. Before the flames had died, it was said, he was planning a bigger replacement.

In a province where businessmen liked to think of themselves as rugged individualists, few were as rugged as Pat Burns. Listen to him in 1907, defending his credo before an Alberta commission looking into possible monopolies in the meat business: "I am running my own show, standing on my own bottom, having nothing to do with any person else, and don't want to. I never squeezed a man and for that reason have all the business I want and I pay the highest prices. Certainly I like opposition. I like it because it makes business better, and the more the merrier." With that spirited response, Burns emerged from the hearing unscathed.

No one else had such an influence on the livestock industry in the West. Burns opened up new avenues of Canadian trade to Australia and Japan, shared the export trade to Britain, found new markets in the East, and built large packing houses in Calgary, Edmonton, and Vancouver. His company was one of the largest of its kind in the world, with branches in Liverpool and Yokohama. Like Robert Chambers Edwards of the *Eye Opener*, he became a Western icon, the symbol of a nation within a nation where, it was devoutly believed, any man could rise to the top from the humblest beginnings if he had faith in the country and was prepared for hard work.

Like Burns, Westerners thought of themselves as a special breed. One former Scot, who had grown wealthy farming near the Qu'Appelle Valley, went so far as to boast to an English reporter that Westerners were the physical, moral, and intellectual superiors of any in the Old Country. It was that kind of remark that caused the *Scotsman* of Edinburgh to comment on the "savage arrogance" of the Western Canadian farmer. Yet the settlers had reason to be smug. In the Old Country they had been the prisoners of class. Here they were as good as any man. The first thing that struck the English who came west was (to quote one) "that every Jack seems to be as good as his master – or to think he is." J.B. Bickersteth, a Church of England missionary, noted that everybody seemed to be in a conspiracy to make the greenhorn understand that he had reached a classless society where each man or woman was the social equal of his neighbour.

"I call upon people who would not have taken any notice of me in England," one woman told Ella Sykes. Westerners learned early the virtue of co-operation. Social custom required that any stranger caught by darkness or weather several miles from a settlement was to be fed and his horse stabled by the nearest farmer. It was this attitude that helped set the mood for the co-operative movement on the prairies.

Almost every immigrant had seen the West as the Promised Land, a phrase used more than once in the pamphlets of the Immigration Department. The Americans came for profit, the Slavs to escape penury and authority, the British to flee the smoky cities and return to the agrarian past. But the West was not the sylvan paradise for which so many had hoped; nor was it a get-rich-quick gold mine of a country. The farmer was not necessarily the noblest of God's creatures, and the "garden city" of the nineteenth century was a long cry from the dusty, manure-befouled streets of Calgary and Edmonton or the wretched slums of Winnipeg.

Those who sought Utopia on the Canadian plains were doomed, like the Doukhobors, to disappointment. The Trochu colony of Alberta, an idealistic French community of bachelor aristocrats founded near Three Hills by Count Paul Beaudrap, lost its homogeneity with the coming of the railway. The model socialist community founded by striking French coal miners at Sylvan Lake, near Red Deer, succumbed to "an insane desire to get rich quick." The small band of a dozen Adamites, disciples of James Sharpe, who claimed to be Jesus Christ himself, were quickly shoved back across the border for bringing firearms into the country. And that charismatic and occult sect known as the Dreamers, who settled near Medicine Hat in 1907, quickly broke up in the wake of a sensational murder trial, which disclosed that these apostles believed they were entitled to kill any enemy revealed to them in their sleep. Only the Mormons, who fled religious persecution in the States, and the Mennonites persevered because, like other successful immigrants, they discarded visions of Utopia, irrigated the land or worked the black prairie soil, and tended to their own affairs. For these hard workers the Westerners cast aside their prejudices. That was part of the Western ethic.

The personal pride that Westerners felt in themselves was translated into a local and regional pride. Newcomers, visitors, and old hands talked of the West as if it were a separate state. Certainly the clear demarcation of the Cordilleran spine on the West and the Precambrian schists and muskegs on the East gave it a clear outline. But it was more than a geographical entity; it was also a state of mind and an attitude. To the Westerner, anything was possible; there was no problem that could not be surmounted; the future was rosy and never ending. Had he not proved it?

There has never been such a period of optimism in Canada as there was in the years before the Great War. It was, of course, part of the worldwide innocence that was shattered forever by the cannon of 1914. But in the Canadian West it reached heights unattained elsewhere. We have not again known that giddy buoyancy, that boundless enthusiasm that rippled across the plains in ever-widening circles touching, eventually, both the Atlantic and Pacific coasts. The West did not suffer, in those heady days, from the so-called Canadian inferiority complex.

Visitors to the West were caught up in the enthusiasm and remarked on it. John Foster Fraser reported in 1905 that "there are not half a dozen wooden shacks on the prairie, called a 'town', where the inhabitants do not believe that in a very few years that town will be one of the most famous and prosperous cities in the entire Dominion." The following year another traveller reported: "Every Winnipegger is afire with zeal and confidence." And a reporter for the Saint John *Telegraph* exclaimed in 1910: "We have not met one individual who is not full of the most absolute faith in the country."

It was generally accepted that the West would outstrip the East and that Winnipeg would one day become the capital of Canada. By 1906, the Calgary *Herald* predicted, the majority of Canadians would probably be living west of Lake Superior. The *Canadian* magazine, a Toronto publication, was predictably more cautious. It estimated that the balance wouldn't shift until 1931.

By 1905, the Toronto papers had ceased to grumble about Western "kickers." The West was bringing prosperity to the whole country, and the eyes of the world were fastened on Canada. For decades the world had ignored the new nation. Now a stream of books and newspaper articles focused not only on the West but also on the entire Dominion. The regional pride that Westerners felt was being transformed into a new nationalism. Since 1867, Canada had been an awkward entity, its Pacific province cut off from the East by two thousand miles of empty prairie. Now Canadians saw their Dominion with new eyes. The vacuum was filled; a new heartland had emerged, vibrant, confident, prosperous.

One longs in vain for the same yeastiness, the same bubbling enthusiasm, the same rock-like confidence in the Canada of today.

4

No other Westerner managed to capture the buoyant, restless, iconoclastic spirit of the West in the way that Bob Edwards did. The country has never known –probably never will know –a publication as outrageous, as irreverent, or as ebullient as his personal creation, the Calgary *Eye Opener*. Among the so-called legitimate dailies, the

Bob Edwards and the Eye Opener

Calgary *Herald* had no rival for flamboyance. But there were times when the weekly *Eye Opener* made the *Herald* seem like a Sunday School tract.

The essence of the paper's appeal was that in an era when journalists could be bribed for a pittance, when newspapers shamelessly distorted the truth, when publishers were caught in political scandals, when editors kowtowed to politicians, stuffed shirts, property interests, and advertisers, Robert Chambers Edwards was ruthlessly honest, ruggedly independent, and totally fearless. More than that, he was very funny.

He pricked balloons, jeered at the newly rich, attacked the blue-stockings, poked fun at boosterism, jibed at humbug and bombast. His paper struck a chord with those settlers who had fled the bureaucracy of Europe, the snobbery of England, or the hypocrisy of the Eastern Canadian establishment. It tickled them when Edwards attacked Harry Corby's elevation to the Senate because he made bad whiskey or wrote that "the CPR, Clifford Sifton and the Almighty comprise the Trinity of Canada, ranking in importance in the order named."

In an era when a circulation of seventy-five hundred was considered hugely profitable, the *Eye Opener* reached a peak of thirty-five thousand. It could make and unmake politicians. R.B. Bennett ascribed his federal defeat in 1904 to Edwards. The mayor of Calgary refused to run for re-election when the *Eye Opener* opposed him. No wonder Edwards made enemies. At one point the *Eye Opener* was denied the mails. The CPR banned it from its trains. The ministerial association attacked it. Edwards was even challenged to a duel. But he prevailed, even though his paper often missed several issues in a row and rejected advertising for any product Edwards felt he couldn't support. He was more than a humorist; he was a genuine prairie reformer, "a Robin Hood of the pen" in the words of the Winnipeg jurist Roy St. George Stubbs. He opposed restrictive divorce laws and Sunday blue laws, was sympathetic to prostitutes, suffragettes, and trade unions, and regularly exposed shady and fraudulent deals, some of them the work of community pillars.

His was a one-man operation, run from a cluttered one-room office by an editor who kept no accounts, no subscription lists, no receipts, and who refused to solicit business. Edwards wrote almost every word in his paper, with painstaking care and impeccable grammar, for he had been a university gold medallist in Scotland before emigrating. His literary antecedents were impressive, his grandfather having been that same Chambers whose name appears to this day on one of the best of the international encyclopaedias.

In Canada, after his arrival in 1894, Edwards had pursued the career of an itinerant journalist; but except for a brief, unhappy period as an employee in Winnipeg, he controlled his own destiny and ran his own individualistic and irreverent journals – the Wetaskiwin *Free Lance*, the Leduc *Strathcoholic*, the High River *Eye Opener* – before he settled permanently in Calgary in 1904.

His greatest appeal was his refusal to take himself or his newspaper seriously, although he was deadly serious in his attacks on grafting politicians and rapacious real estate interests. He once wrote that the three biggest liars in Alberta were "Robert Chambers – Gentleman; Honourable A.L. Sifton – Premier; and Bob Edwards – Editor." Arthur Sifton tried to sue him for that, whereupon Edwards offered to collaborate in a joint suit since Edwards, the Editor, had also slandered Chambers, the Gentleman. The Premier quickly retreated.

Another public figure who threatened suit but thought better of it was the austere High Commissioner to Great Britain, Lord Strathcona, the former Donald Smith, who in 1885 had driven the last spike of the newly completed CPR. The *Eye Opener* was always a curious pastiche of fact and fancy, hard news and invention. But everybody (or *almost* everybody, as it turned out) knew at once when Edwards was being serious and telling it straight and when he was indulging in satire. Characters real and imaginary romped through his news columns, the most imaginative being Peter J. McGonigle, the hard-drinking editor of the Midnapore *Gazette*, from whose non-existent columns Edwards claimed to be printing items.

In October 1906, Edwards decided to satirize the succession of public banquets being tendered to various dignitaries by announcing that the Calgary Board of Trade had given one in honour of McGonigle to mark his release from penitentiary after a conviction for horse theft. At this imaginary affair letters, purportedly from various dignitaries, were read aloud, one allegedly from Strathcona:

"... The name of Peter McGonigle will ever stand high in the role of eminent confiscators. Once, long ago, I myself came near achieving distinction in this direction when I performed some dexterous financing with the Bank of Montreal's funds. In consequence, however, of C.P.R. stocks going up instead of down, I wound up in the House of Lords instead of Stony Mountain."

To John Willison, the sober editor of the equally sober Toronto

News, this was sensational stuff. Willison may have been the dean of Canadian journalists, but in this instance he was remarkably gullible. The idea of the Canadian High Commissioner in London paying tribute to and admitting kinship with a horse thief struck him as big news. Like many a journalist before and since, he did not stop to ask himself if the story might be a hoax; he was, after all, the Canadian correspondent of the equally gullible *Times* of London and this was good copy. Not long afterwards, the humourless Strathcona was jolted from his breakfast kippers by a full account in the British Thunderer of the spurious banquet and his equally spurious telegram.

Strathcona was purple with fury, not only at the effrontery of the quoted cable but also, one suspects, because there was more than a grain of truth in the fiction. He *had* after all, performed some dexterous and quite illegal financing with Bank of Montreal funds in his early railway ventures. Off went a peremptory telegram to James Lougheed, the establishment lawyer in Calgary, ordering him to sue Edwards for libel. It took all of Senator Lougheed's considerable diplomatic talents to persuade the outraged peer to withdraw the action and save himself from becoming the laughingstock of Western Canada.

Those who knew Bob Edwards from the *Eye Opener* alone might be pardoned for conjuring up an image of him as spurious as that of McGonigle. There were those who thought of him, no doubt, as a wild-eyed roisterer, slapping backs in local saloons, as fiery and as loud as his paper, always at the centre of the crowd. He was anything but that – the direct antithesis, in fact, of the image he projected in print. He was a plump, bright-eyed, rumpled man with a sparse, sandy moustache, who dressed in sombre suits and sported a wing collar. He was diffident, uneasy in a crowd, and taciturn with any but a small circle of friends. Nobody could persuade him to make a public speech. Like an actor who exists through his stage roles, he came to life only in the columns of his paper.

He had more culture in his big toe than most of Calgary's upstart establishment exhibited in their entire bodies. He was a lover of the theatre, of music, and, above all, of good literature. Before he was thirty he had seen most of Europe and had even edited a small journal on the Riviera. He had experienced the watering places of the gentry and wanted no part of them; instead, he chose Calgary and the long bar of the Alberta Hotel.

He was a solitary creature. All his life he had been a loner, marching to his own music, never part of the band. His parents had died before he was five, and he was raised in Scotland by two maiden aunts. A bachelor, he knew something about loneliness, for he lived by himself in a hotel room and worked alone in his office. Thus, he could sympathize with the thousands of others who, like him, had come to a strange land, friendless and womanless. Much has been written about the loneliness of farm wives during the period of Western settlement, much less about the plight of the thousands of single men, roaming the streets of the burgeoning cities. But Edwards knew.

"You who have your own firesides do not know what you possess," he wrote at Christmas, 1905. "You do not know what it is to go without having anyone say to you: 'Goodbye, will you be gone long?' Or to come back without anyone to welcome you and say, 'Oh, how late you are!' Think at this time of the year of the many young men far from their own homes back east, living in Calgary with no place to go of an evening, moping in their $8 a month rooms reading Frenzied Finance or hanging round hotels hitting up the booze. Give them a thought."

Edwards himself hit up the booze, hard and often, and made no secret of it. "Every man has his favorite bird," he wrote. "Mine is the bat." He was not a steady drinker, but when he fell off the wagon – "leaped" would be a better word – he landed hard. During those sprees the *Eye Opener* failed to publish and the whole town knew that Edwards was drunk. There were others in Calgary who drank as much, but they did not proclaim it to the world.

"Most of our tragedies," he once wrote, "look like comedies to our neighbours." Edwards was under no illusion about his own tragedy; he knew that "gallons of trouble can come out of a pint flask." Though he could not control his alcoholism, he could and did advocate the closing of Calgary's saloons and campaign strongly for prohibition.

Why, then, did he drink? To blot out, one suspects, consideration of the What-Might-Have-Been.

Stubbs, who knew Edwards, wrote that he drank because only in alcohol could he find a temporary solution to problems he could not solve when sober; that just as he kept no books of account for his newspaper, he kept none for himself, "so that he could find out where he stood as he went along."

It is said of Edwards that if he had not gone to drink he might have been a Canadian Mark Twain or, had he stayed in Europe, he would almost certainly have become a major literary figure. Perhaps in those rare moments of self-examination that led to the inevitable spree and the inevitable drying out at Holy Cross Hospital, Edwards himself contemplated those possibilities. If he did, he missed the point. Although his work has escaped the dubious immortality of the school text, he *was* the Canadian Mark Twain; he became and remains a major literary figure. He is constantly being rediscovered, anthologized, eulogized. His aphorisms have stood the test of time:

Don't meet trouble half way. It is quite capable of making the entire journey.

Too many people salt away their money in the brine of other people's tears.

The good don't die young; they simply outgrow it.

No man does as much today as he is going to do tomorrow.

It's as easy to recall an unkind word as it is to draw back the bullet after firing the gun.

In Calgary an annual luncheon is held in his honour and an annual Bob Edwards Award marks his memory. No other figure from the West of that era, literary or otherwise, merits such an accolade.

Although Edwards's journalism might seem reckless to his readers, he was far more cautious than he appeared. His friend and drinking companion, Paddy Nolan, the best-liked lawyer in town, checked every line he wrote. The only time Edwards was forced into a legal retraction was by another lawyer, E. P. Davis, who, Edwards suggested, was seeing snakes as a result of being stranded on an island with a dozen bottles of Scotch. Edwards hated Davis, who had been his opponent in the famous McGillicuddy trial, the most spectacular event of his career.

The incident, which drove Edwards temporarily out of Calgary, almost certainly had its origins in the *Eye Opener*'s report on Clifford Sifton's Ottawa dalliance at the time of his resignation in 1905. Sifton did not sue Edwards; he merely bided his time. In 1907 an Eastern journalist, Daniel McGillicuddy, launched a new newspaper, the Calgary *News*, with the announced intention of putting the *Eye Opener* out of business. It was McGillicuddy's boast that he had Sifton's backing and encouragement.

On October 6, 1908, three weeks before the federal election, the *News* launched a personal attack on Edwards that for virulence and savagery has never been equalled in Canada. The attack took the form of a two-column letter on the front page, written by McGillicuddy but signed "Nemesis." It referred to the *Eye Opener* as "a disreputable sheet, the mission of which has been blackmail and the contents of which [are] . . . slander and smut." It called Edwards a "ruffian," a "moral leper," and a "skunk . . . whose literary fulminations cannot but create the impression that he was born in a brothel and bred on a dungpile." That was only the beginning. Edwards was "a four flusher," "a tin horn," and "a welcher on poker debts." Nemesis promised more in future issues: "I intend to show that he is a libeller, a character thief, a coward, a liar, a drunkard, a dope-fiend, and a degenerate." Nemesis promised to prove all these charges, but before the next issue appeared a shaken Edwards had, with the help of Paddy Nolan, sued McGillicuddy for libel.

The trial made national headlines. The defence went to Vancouver for Davis, the top lawyer in the West. McGillicuddy could not prove his charges, and after five hours of deliberation, the jury found for Edwards. Alas, it was a pyrrhic victory. McGillicuddy was fined a nominal one hundred dollars without having to pay costs. The jury expressed disapproval of the *Eye Opener*'s stories, and the judge rebuked Edwards, describing the paper's articles with such words as "debasing and demoralizing." None of this had any effect on the *Eye Opener*'s fortunes. The paper's circulation increased while the *News* foundered; a few months later McGillicuddy sold the paper and vanished from the scene.

But Edwards was disenchanted with Calgary. In April 1909, shortly after the trial, he left for the East, first to Toronto, then to Montreal, finally to Port Arthur, where the *Eye Opener* resumed publication. It didn't work; he needed the Western environment. In December he moved to Winnipeg and for the next year published the *Eye Opener* there. Many of his faithful readers in Calgary and even his advertisers supported him, but Winnipeg wasn't really *Eye Opener* territory. In 1911 he was back in Calgary. In two months the *Eye Opener*'s circulation zoomed to 26,000.

In 1917, Bob Edwards the lifelong bachelor married Kate Penman, a twenty-four-year-old girl from Glasgow, who worked in the office of his old rival, R.B. Bennett. By all accounts it was not a successful marriage; Edwards was too set in his ways, nor would he modify his drinking. But drunk or sober he had become a Calgary fixture, a member of the establishment, a vibrant symbol of the West's adolescent years, and, by 1921, a successful provincial politician. McGillicuddy was dead, but Edwards was unforgiving. "Is it not remarkable," he wrote to a friend, "here I am in the Legislature and McGillicuddy is in Hell." Shortly after that, on November 14, 1922, he died of influenza, and his paper, which more than any other had captured the Western spirit, died with him.

271

5

Radicalism Apart from those Canadians who arrived from the older provinces,
and the people who settled the West had no traditional party loyalties. To
populism the Americans and Europeans, the titles "Liberal" and "Conservative"
had no sentimental association and little meaning, especially as the
Tories, unable (then as now) to come to grips with their political
philosophy, insisted in defiance of all logic on calling themselves
"Liberal Conservatives." If the new arrivals voted for the Liberals, it
was because the Liberal government had brought them to Canada and
helped them prosper. But these ties were ephemeral. By 1905, they
began to equate the government with Central Canada, and therefore
with villainy. Even the Canadian-born found traditional loyalties
beginning to loosen.

The Eastern Canadian was born into a political party. The sons of
Grits were themselves Grits; the sons of Tories remained Tories and
passed their Toryism on to *their* sons. But the newcomers were perfectly
prepared to toss aside old ideas and accept fresh and even radical ones
if they felt they were to their benefit. After all, they had renounced
their homelands, in itself an act of radicalism. Now they were caught
up in the political restlessness that affected Western attitudes in the
early years of the century.

These attitudes can be defined as generally anti-establishment – the
secret of Bob Edwards's appeal. The European peasants had defected
from a society in which they were literally required to bow and touch
their forelocks when encountering a bureaucrat or landowner. The
English had left behind a rigid class system that conspired against
upward mobility. The Americans brought to Canada the ferment of
agrarian dissent. The Upper Canadians, after a few years in the West,
found themselves railing against the railways, the elevator monopoly,
and the high price of agricultural equipment.

American periodicals spilled across the border as easily as American
farmers. This was the era of the trustbusters and muckrakers. Magazines such as *McClure's* and *Collier's* carried sensational articles
attacking the great mercantile monopolies, which were also the enemies
of the American farmers. Ida M. Tarbell went after Standard Oil;
Lincoln Steffens exposed political corruption in the cities; in *The
Jungle*, Upton Sinclair hit hard at the meat-packing industry in
Chicago.

272

More than one American farmer remarked that he had come to Canada to escape the establishment. An Iowa farmer was quoted in *The World's Work* in 1905 as declaring: "I didn't much mind leaving the States. The trusts were getting so bad there that it didn't seem to be the same country to me anymore." Agrarian radicals, influenced by the Farmers' Alliance, the populist crusade, the Grange movement, and the Society of Equity were moving into Alberta – men like Henry Wise Wood, the lanky, soft-spoken Missouri farmer who took up two sections of land at Carstairs in 1905 and was to become president of the politically powerful United Farmers of Alberta.

Wood was the most important of the American immigrants who influenced Western politics in general and Alberta politics in particular. The day would come when the American-born would outnumber all other national groups, including the Canadians, on the executive of the United Farmers. Wood even *looked* like an American. With his long, loose limbs, his craggy face, and his dark, flashing eyes, he was often compared to Lincoln, in spite of an almost totally bald head. This brooding and methodical ex-cowboy, who peppered his speech with Biblical quotations and steeped himself in lyric poetry, philosophy, and nineteenth-century classics, was drawn to Canada like most of his countrymen because he wanted land for himself and his four sons and could not afford it in his native Missouri. In 1910 he became a Canadian citizen.

He would become a political force, yet he had no political ambitions. In the United States he had worked for William Jennings Bryan, the populist Democrat, but had turned down a congressional nomination from Bryan's party as he would one day turn down a cabinet post in Robert Borden's wartime Union government. In Alberta, he joined the Society of Equity, a Canadian offshoot of an American agrarian movement. When, in 1909, it merged with the Territorial Grain Growers' Association to form the UFA, he became part of the new movement. He had as little interest in power as he had in money, but his integrity was such that power sought him out. He always thought of himself as a spokesman for the farmers, not a leader, for he had a sense of fundamental democracy that was rooted in his faith. He was a member of the Campbellite Church, Disciples of Christ, which eschewed hierarchy, allowing both laymen and laywomen to conduct services. He had little use for political parties, believing that officeholders should be elected by occupational groups – farmers representing farmers – yet in the end he found himself at the head of the most successful party in Alberta;

273

when it finally took office, he shrugged off the premiership, turning it over to his vice-president. There was nothing extreme or radical about him, and yet, in the end, this cautious, God-fearing former American would, more than any other single person, touch off a revolution in his adopted province and help to radicalize the West.

By the time Henry Wise Wood arrived in Alberta, the West was ready to be radicalized. The catalyst in that process, and also the chief villain to Westerners, was the Canadian Pacific Railway. Controlled by Eastern interests, it was seen as the enemy of the farmer. It was blamed for holding on selfishly to its free, untaxed lands, waiting for real estate prices to rise. It was blamed for not providing loading platforms and, at harvest time, for a shortage of freight cars. Western farmers were convinced this perennial car shortage was part of a deliberate conspiracy to force them to bow to the equally villainous elevator monopoly. Most would agree with the resolution passed by one angry meeting in Elva, Manitoba, in 1902, which had accused the CPR of plundering the farmers of $25 million through excessive freight rates and which railed against "the extortion practised by its favorite partner in spoil, the grain elevator system."

The hatred of the railway at the turn of the century was pathological. Newspapers controlled by the CPR – and there were several – tried to deny any connection with it. Politicians subsidized by the CPR – and there were many – pretended they had nothing to do with it. As Clifford Sifton wrote to a Winnipeg supporter: "Just fancy yourself in the middle of an election campaign having the charge made on the platform that your candidate was an employee of the Canadian Pacific Railway. The probability is that he would lose his deposit."

The antipathy toward the CPR monopoly brought about demands for competing lines. That, in turn, brought about the astonishing and costly railway expansion that touched off the great Western land boom of 1911-13 and led to the subsequent financial collapse. It also helped to radicalize the West. Such newspapers as the *Herald* in Calgary and the *Tribune* in Winnipeg repeatedly called for public ownership. Thomas Greenway, Premier of Manitoba, said bluntly in 1899: ". . . if we cannot get the railway companies to be reasonable, we will build the railroads ourselves and the benefit will come to the people. . . ." His successor, Rodmond Roblin, took up the cry.

But the CPR was also the symbol of the West's quasi-colonial status. The Pacific railway and the protective tariff had been the foundations of John A. Macdonald's National Policy. Was there any real difference,

274

Westerners asked, between the prairie region and any other half-developed country ripe for exploitation? Imperial forces from the East had bartered away prime prairie land to get the railway built. And the railway had been built to enrich the East: to bring out settlers who would work the land cheaply, thus keeping costs down, to open up a new field for Eastern investors, and to create another domestic market for Eastern manufacturers who, propped up by the tariff, could charge what they wanted.

In this atmosphere, farmers' organizations flourished like spring wheat. The British brought to the West the traditions of the trade unions, the co-operative movement, and the Labour party; the Americans brought the experience of agrarian populism that had launched the Progressive Movement. By 1909, the two Grain Growers' Associations in Saskatchewan and Alberta and the recently formed United Farmers of Alberta were speaking with a single voice through the pages of the *Grain Growers' Guide*, the most radical publication in the West and the only one the farmers trusted.

The *Guide* demanded the end of Eastern protectionism; government control of grain elevators, transportation, and meat packing; and the construction of a railway that would carry grain to a saltwater port on Hudson Bay. It could be inflammatory. Here is one of its leading contributors, J.E. Stevenson, attacking the structure of Canadian economic life: "It corrupts our political system, our political system corrupts and degrades the public administration, and the corroding influence extends to the social system and business life until the disease permeates the whole community." In a later era such sentiments would be considered dangerously socialistic or even communistic, but on the prairies in 1910 they reflected the view of the farming class to which the *Guide* catered.

Side by side with this movement for agrarian reform – a movement that was in many of its aspects continent-wide – marched the Social Gospel of such unorthodox Protestant churchmen as J.S. Woodsworth and Dr. Salem Bland in Winnipeg. Both believed in the "applied Christianity" of the trade unions, the grain growers, and the co-operative movement. Bland looked like an Old Testament prophet, but his views were in advance of his time. It was, he declared, the Christian duty of all farmers to get behind these movements in the "real and bitter war between capital and labour." As for Woodsworth, he wrote a regular weekly column for the *Guide* entitled "Sermons for the Unsatisfied."

Revolution, albeit a peaceful one, so the *Guide* believed, was the key to the future stability of Canada, revolution that would "shake Canada to its very foundations." The Laurier government – indeed all government – was seen to be riddled with graft, bribery, and corruption. Even John Dafoe, no stranger to back-room Liberal politics, was dismayed at the way votes were bought and sold in Manitoba. He told Clifford Sifton as early as 1903 that the loosening of party ties on the prairies was contributing to the corruption. Since the voters were now convinced there was no difference between the two parties and that all politicians were on the make, they thought they might as well make something too. "Therefore they sell themselves."

Western farm leaders, like the Christian progressives, were sickened by the political opportunism of both parties, but for many years they shied away from launching a new political movement. The experience of the populists south of the border wasn't encouraging; they hadn't made much political headway in a two-party system. Actually, the West didn't really want a two-party system, certainly not at the provincial level. It was like an emerging nation that has shaken off the Imperial yoke and is determined to rally under one united political force. The real enemy was Ottawa; then why should Westerners divide among themselves when their interests were identical? The West was too young to organize parties along class lines; there wasn't a privileged class or an exploited class. The old North West Council had operated more like a municipal council without traditional parties; Frederick Haultain, the Territorial premier, had been strongly against that kind of division. And the day was coming when Alberta, the most restless and extreme of the three provinces, would, in effect, reject it too. After 1921, the province would be governed successively by three powerful political movements, each with a majority so overwhelming as to make the province a one-party state. It was no coincidence that Alberta, the prairie province farthest from Ottawa, also had the lowest proportion of Eastern Canadian settlers in its heavily British and American mix.

At the federal level, however, the two-party system could not be shaken. The *Grain Growers' Guide* was convinced the farmers would have to become politicized. It took the Reciprocity election of 1911 to achieve that.

The farmers wanted free trade, or something close to it. For one thing, if the Eastern manufacturers were forced to compete with the Americans on an equal basis, prices of farm equipment would drop. But the Liberals, in spite of their traditional free trade philosophy, had not dared to tamper with the National Policy; too many powerful

Eastern commercial interests supported it. Now, with his party growing tired in office and racked by scandals, Laurier needed an issue. The Americans, in a startling right-about-face, were offering virtual free access to their markets for Canadian primary products in exchange for tariff reduction. In his tour across the prairies in 1910, the Prime Minister had been impressed by the grain growers' arguments. The so-called "siege of Ottawa" followed in December, with eight hundred farmers massed on Parliament Hill. Laurier decided to go to the country on the issue of reciprocal free trade.

Clifford Sifton bolted the party on the issue, taking eighteen other Liberals with him. Some said he had been seeking a chance for revenge against those who had helped oust him in 1905. J.A. Macdonald, the former editor of the *Globe*, using a common phrase of the day, said it was an "infinite relief" when Sifton joined the enemy, "knowing for years, as we did, that he had carried a knife in his boot for members of the government." However that may be, the former minister became the chief tactician behind the Tory campaign, speaking forcefully and without let up from Windsor to Halifax against reciprocity. In this he certainly had the support of his friends in the Eastern financial establishment, but not of his editor, Dafoe, who for the first time broke with his chief. Dafoe really had little choice. His editorials had always been pro-free trade; the phrase, in fact, was emblazoned on the masthead of the *Free Press*; to have switched sides at that moment would have been journalistic suicide. He could scarcely afford to be seen to be in the same bed with such Eastern financiers as Sir Edmund Walker, president of the Canadian Bank of Commerce, who felt that the attitude of Western agricultural leaders regarding free trade and freight rates was "both selfish and ignorant."

The emotional campaign that followed was enlivened and muddied by American expansionists such as J.B. "Champ" Clark, the Speaker-designate of the House of Representatives, who welcomed the day "when the American flag will float over every square foot of the British–North American possessions to the North Pole," and by Ontario patriots who wrapped themselves in the Union Jack and warned that reciprocity would water down British preference and loosen Imperial ties.

The West didn't care. A good many of the most prominent farmers were Americans – men, as we have seen, such as Henry Wise Wood and Daniel Webster Warner. These people did not fear American expansion. Even the British in the West, with their traditional belief in free trade, could not be convinced of the evils of tariff reduction.

Laurier was trounced in 1911, reciprocity was dead, and the traditional split between East and West was widened. In the rueful view of the *Grain Growers' Guide* "the rest of Canada must bow to Ontario, the most powerful province, politically, in Canada." And the farmers began to consider direct political action. "What is needed in Canada is a radical party with the courage of its convictions," George Chipman, the *Guide*'s editor, wrote shortly after the election.

It took the best part of a decade to achieve that, but by 1921 the traditional two-party system on the prairies was dead. The Conservatives, having rejected free trade, were a spent force; the provincial Liberal parties were badly shattered. Faced with a minority government in Manitoba, they were forced by the farmers into a Liberal-Progressive coalition that in various forms would govern the province for more than three decades. In Saskatchewan they just managed to survive by chameleon-like tactics, becoming in effect a farmers' government at arm's length from Ottawa. In Alberta, in 1921, Henry Wise Wood's United Farmers finished them off, sweeping into power to remain until 1935, when another populist movement calling itself Social Credit took over.

In 1921 the psychological and economic split between East and West was confirmed politically in a federal election. The Progressive party, sparked by farmers' movements in every province, took sixty-five federal seats, leaving Laurier's successor, Mackenzie King, to head a minority government. The continental West turned to the Progressives. On the prairies the Liberals managed to elect three members, no more. The Conservatives elected ten, but eight of these came from Manitoba. The settlers' discontent had changed the political face of Canada. That discontent too was part of the Western spirit.

6

The In the first decade of the century, Western Canadians developed a
un-Western strong image of themselves. It didn't fit everyone; in fact, it might be
Westerner argued that it really didn't fit *most* Westerners, but it persisted. Rituals such as the Calgary Stampede, lauched in 1912 and emulated in various forms throughout the West, helped to intensify the stereotype and plant it in the minds of all Canadians. Westerners *were* different, like Texans. There was a swagger here, a looseness, a gambling spirit, the kind of devil-may-care style that was the attraction of the chuck wagon races.

Nowhere was the Western spirit more in evidence than in Calgary, that most American of all prairie cities. This was ranching country, and ranchers tended to take chances; they had to, because they knew a bad winter could wipe them out. Since mixed farming provided a hedge against acts of nature, northern Albertans didn't need that same recklessness; if the crops failed, one could fall back on the hogs.

It is passing strange, then, that the West's most illustrious citizen should have been nurtured in the high, wide, and handsome atmosphere of the foothills, for Richard Bedford Bennett simply didn't fit the image. There was little of the West about him – except for naked ambition – even though he served it for the best part of four decades. And his ambition was not of the Western kind: it was dogged and unswerving; there was no fun in it.

See him now in January of 1897, a gangling, freckled-faced, twenty-six-year-old from the Bay of Fundy, arriving in Calgary in his dark suit and bowler hat having already announced that he intended to become (a) a millionaire and (b) Prime Minister of Canada. R.B. Bennett – nobody ever called him Richard or Dick – would achieve both goals. In the first half of the century he was the only Westerner to lead the country.

It's hard to think of him as a Westerner, much less a Calgarian, even though Calgary was his constituency, in and out of office, for forty years. Bennett the politician was from the West but not *of* the West. He didn't even own a home in Calgary, preferring to occupy a suite in the Alberta Hotel and later in the Palliser. One thinks of him as an Ottawa man, and that is the way the cartoonists portrayed him, in silk topper and morning coat. He was, in fact, the first and perhaps the only man to stroll down Stephen Avenue in that attire, an incongruous spectacle among the crowd in Stetsons, checked vests, and buckskin jackets. His clothes, at least in the early days, weren't even made in the West but fashioned to his specific instructions by a Maritime tailor.

But R.B. Bennett didn't need a silk hat to stand out like a nun in a brothel in that liveliest of cities. A dedicated Methodist and Sunday School teacher, he took his religion as he took his life, with deadly seriousness. He did not drink. He did not smoke. He deplored dancing, hated cards, eschewed all games of chance, wouldn't even enter a bowling alley. In his early days he carried a Bible with him – a tall, austere, forbidding figure, "conscious of coming greatness," who devoured vast breakfasts in the accurate belief that it would eventually give him the commanding figure, the ample girth that was in those days the hallmark of the successful man.

"Fun" is not a word one associates with R.B. Bennett. He clearly believed he was brought into the world not to have fun but to make his mark. "R.B. Bennett's idea of happiness," Bob Edwards wrote, "is a seat in heaven with the privilege of addressing angels from the throne."

What brought this shy, introspective law graduate and one-time high school principal to the West? Partly the determination to make his fortune, something he couldn't achieve on those harsh Atlantic shores, but also, one suspects, the need to escape. In this, at least, Bennett was a typical Westerner. Thousands had arrived on the prairies for the same reason. The difference was that Bennett did not choose the West; he could have gone anywhere. The West chose him.

Money was always important to him; he had little enough as a boy in New Brunswick or as a law student at Dalhousie. His mother had to watch every penny, for the Bennetts were victims of the Maritime ship-building depression, and of the elder Bennett's lack of foresight. When Richard's parents were married, the Bennett shipyard was a thriving operation, but it fell into decay in the age of steam, and Henry Bennett made little attempt to adapt to changed circumstances. He was a genial, easy-going man who enjoyed a drink, didn't take religion seriously, and was perfectly willing to let his wife take charge. She was everything her husband was not – a dedicated teetotaller, a fervent Methodist, a fiercely ambitious and firm-minded woman determined that everything her husband had failed to be her eldest son would become.

Young Richard was shaped by his mother. All his furious energy, his resentment of competition, his shyness and introspection, his moods of despair, his outbursts of temper, his apparent arrogance and insensitivity, his courage and tenacity – all this mixed bag of strengths and flaws were surely the product of his mother's strength of character and implacable will, and of the tensions that must have existed in the household of that strangely assorted pair. All his life R.B. Bennett worshipped his mother. It was a rare Christmas that he did not spend with her. Yet he left her when he was twenty-six, and in all his long, spectacular, but lonely career he never sent for her; she remained in Hopewell Cape, N.B., he in Calgary and Ottawa.

He might as easily have gone off to Montreal or Toronto. But the West sought him out in the person of one of its favourite sons, Senator James Alexander Lougheed. Lougheed was Calgary's first citizen in more ways than one. He had followed the CPR to the end of steel and put up his lawyer's shingle when Calgary was still a tent town. He had married into one of the pioneer fur-trading families of Alberta; his wife was a Hardisty, the niece of Lord Strathcona. Lougheed was wealthy, with more work on his hands than he cared to do. He needed an assistant, and the dean of Dalhousie, trying to come up with somebody who would meet Lougheed's exacting standards, finally remembered a young student who had been so wrapped up in his studies that he had no life apart from law school – a poor mixer but totally dedicated. Bennett, who was already establishing a reputation as a lawyer in Chatham, got the job.

He was everything that Lougheed was not. The elder lawyer was one of the few members of the Western establishment who could also be called a member of the leisure class. For him the hard grind was no longer necessary; a natural gambler, he preferred the adventure of the unpredictable. But Bennett could never be inveigled into Lougheed's various speculations. A financial as well as a political conservative, he preferred the solidity of corporate bonds. Even after he grew wealthy he persisted in salvaging unused stamps from unposted envelopes and retrieving spare pieces of writing paper from letters he had received.

It is instructive to compare the Bennett style and temperament with that of another Calgary lawyer, the famous Paddy Nolan. Nolan was, and in legend remains, a Calgary institution; Bennett never was. Nolan was a big, handsome Limerick Irishman with such a gift for blarney that it was said he could talk about a barber's pole and make an absorbing tale of it. A man of electric personality and flashing wit, he could charm a jury, confuse a witness, and bemuse a judge. Bob Edwards, his closest friend, wrote: ". . . every man in these parts who gets found out and is conscious of being in the wrong, instinctively turns for aid to P.J. Nolan." Nolan, who never took himself seriously, would certainly have agreed.

Nolan stories abound in the West. There is, for example, his famous cross-examination of a Moose Jaw girl who had charged his client with indecent assault and told a convincing tale of how she had been sent to fetch a pail of milk when, en route home, the accused had attacked her. Nolan winkled out the admission that the gallon pail had no lid on it and was filled to the brim. "Gentlemen," he told the jury, "this young woman says she lost her virtue, but saved her milk. What do you think about it?" He won the case.

Nolan once prevailed upon a Calgary judge to purchase, out of sympathy, two tickets on the gold watch of a dead man that the poverty-stricken widow was forced to raffle off. What the judge didn't know was that he was shortly to preside over the trial of the same woman charged with conducting a lottery. She was guilty, of course, but Nolan got her off with a suspended sentence by directing his argument to the judge: "Your honour knows full well the danger of these lotteries and how even the best intentioned people in the community fall victim to them and out of sheer sympathy for their object commit offenses by buying tickets in them, as no doubt Your Honour has done on occasion himself."

There are a score of such stories about Nolan, few about Bennett. "It is almost impossible to get any human interest stories about you," a reporter once complained to him. "There are none," Bennett replied shortly.

Nolan had no enemies; Bennett had many. In court, every opponent was to him an enemy, and his vituperative form of attack, his compulsion to win got him into trouble. One lawyer called him "a God damned liar" in court; another rushed at him and slapped his face. On the other hand, Bennett himself had an ungovernable temper.

He plunged into politics almost from the moment of his arrival in Calgary, turning up at one of Frank Oliver's meetings and heckling him so unmercifully that the audience, intrigued by the brash newcomer, insisted he speak. Bennett made his reputation as a loyal Tory and an effective platform orator that night. Less than two years later he was elected to the Territorial assembly.

Bennett treated the Liberals as he did his legal adversaries: as enemies. One day when he was visiting J.J. Young at the *Herald*, the publisher remarked that his brother, David, who was lounging in the rear of the main office, was a Liberal. Bennett stormed over to David Young. "Is it true you're a Grit?" he asked. Young allowed that he was. Bennett turned on his heel, left the office, and didn't speak to David Young again for years.

He was a traditional Conservative by upbringing, an emotional Conservative by temperament. Disraeli, Rhodes, and Kipling were his heroes, the Empire the object of his veneration. The ripple of nationalism that grew out of pride in Western expansion did not, in the end, tie him to his native land. The Imperial bond was stronger; and when, in 1938, he finally quit politics, he did not return to Calgary but opted instead for the life of an English peer in the Mother of Parliaments.

Bennett brought party politics to the Territorial legislature. That was an Eastern idea, and Frederick Haultain, the Fort Macleod lawyer who was premier, denounced it. The last thing Haultain wanted was the kind of bitter party split that would break up the common front against the East. But Bennett wanted to introduce Eastern factionalism and finally succeeded. Haultain had never cared for him, even though they were fellow Conservatives.

Bennett quit his Territorial seat in 1900 to run in Calgary for the federal Conservatives. When he lost, he bounced back into Territorial politics, running in a by-election in 1901 but without Haultain's support. The Premier backed C.A. Stuart, the secretary of the local Liberal party, used every tactic to prevent Bennett from re-entering North West politics, and at one memorable and riotous meeting in Calgary effectively muzzled his pugnacious opponent.

It is 11:30 on the evening of March 29, 1901, and we are rising to our feet with the shouting, gesticulating crowd in the cavernous Hull Opera House in Calgary, where the air is blue with cigar smoke and alive with the taunts and catcalls of embattled Liberals and Conservatives.

Frederick Haultain stands on the thrust stage before the vast proscenium arch trying vainly to make himself heard. He has been speaking for the best part of two hours, attacking R.B. Bennett's legislative program. Bennett keeps rising, attempting to seize the floor, but Haultain is adamant: it is his meeting and Stuart's; they are determined to have the last word.

But so is Bennett. He has refused to speak in the slot assigned him by Haultain – sandwiched in between his two opponents. He has insisted on speaking after the Premier so he can answer the attack. Now it begins to look as if he will not get the chance to speak at all. Haultain struggles to continue; groans, cheers, and hisses drown him out. Bennett is on his feet again; Haultain says he needs another fifteen minutes. The crowd won't let him have it.

The entire theatre is in a turmoil. Even the ladies in the dress circle join the pandemonium. We are all stamping our feet in unison, hissing, shouting, booing, whistling. Small boys rush up and down the aisles, contributing to the babel. One man tries to leap up on the platform and is forcibly ejected. Half the audience wants Haultain to continue; the other half wants to hear Bennett.

Haultain announces he will hold the platform if necessary to "the grey hours of the morning." More pandemonium! Unable to utter a word, the handsome premier takes his seat, coolly consults his notes, makes a pencilled addition here, strikes out a redundancy there, takes the occasional sip of water, refuses to relinquish the stage. The noise, echoing down from the vaulted ceiling, is cacophonic, but Haultain

still holds onto the platform, conversing with his chosen candidate,
Stuart, and receiving deputations and delegations from the Dominion
Land Surveyors, from chiefs of police, from ex-trustees of the irrigation
districts.

For more than an hour the bedlam continues. At one o'clock, with
the crowd still in full cry, the Premier rises, puts on his overcoat, picks
up his carpetbag, salutes the audience like a courtier, retires at last
from the stage, and, accompanied by cheers and catcalls, vanishes into
the night.

Stuart leaps to his feet and tries to launch into a political speech. In
the front row Bennett's supporters begin to bawl, "We won't go home
until morning." But it is clear that their champion will not be able to
speak this night. Finally, Bennett himself stands up and saves the
situation by calling on us all to sing "God Save the King." At last, in
the early hours of the morning, the meeting breaks up.

Bennett won the seat in spite of Haultain's opposition, or perhaps
because of it. When the North West achieved self-government in 1905,
he ran in the first Alberta election and found himself beaten by
twenty-nine votes. It was clear to him why he had lost; Bob Edwards
was his nemesis.

Edwards poked fun at Bennett because the firm of Lougheed and
Bennett had the CPR's retainer and, like most Westerners, Edwards
hated the CPR. The *Eye Opener* campaigned strenuously for the
elimination of level crossings, playing up accounts of collisions at
these junctions and running photographs of the wreckage. In his most
famous barb, Edwards pretended to have mixed up the captions under
pictures of various CPR calamities, so that a pen-and-ink drawing of
Bennett appeared with the caption "Another CPR Wreck." But, CPR or
no CPR, the mischievous Edwards must have seen in the fastidiously
dressed and straight-laced Eastern lawyer an irresistible target:

"What," thundered R.B. Bennett during the temperance address
at Red Deer, "would be more terrible than to feel the wild desire
for strong drink surging through every vein?" (The knowledge
that you haven't got the price.)

Bennett's response to Edwards was heavy-handed and ineffective.
He managed to have the sale of the *Eye Opener* banned on the CPR
trains and refused Edwards the customary pass that every other
newspaperman received. When that didn't work, however, he aban-

doned the frontal attack and settled on a more subtle approach from the flank.

He wanted to drag Edwards to lunch at his famous table in the Alberta Hotel, where half a dozen of Bennett's legal and business associates regularly gathered. To this end he persuaded one of the company, Paddy Nolan, to reassure his old friend that such an invitation wouldn't hurt him and might even help him. Bennett delivered the invitation in person, going so far as to abandon for one Sunday his own attendance at the Methodist church and insinuate himself onto Edwards's bench at the Salvation Army citadel. In the face of this obvious effort, Edwards accepted the invitation.

Bennett, expansive, cordial, and clearly out to capture Edwards's friendship and the *Eye Opener*'s support, asked the editor to say grace. A dreadful silence followed. At last Edwards spoke up in his quiet Scottish voice: "If you don't mind, Mr. Chairman, I'd prefer the Good Lord didn't know I was here."

Bennett could turn on the charm when he wanted to, and he succeeded in slowly charming Edwards in the only effective way, by indulging in banter and telling stories, even at the expense of himself and of the CPR. Edwards, a maverick but also a Conservative, became a regular member of the Bennett table. In the 1911 federal election, he threw his support behind him. Bennett was elected to the House of Commons for Calgary and began his long march toward the prime ministership. Calgary remained his constituency throughout his long career.

Why, then, has Calgary rejected him? Calgary's main street, Stephen Avenue, is named for a St. James Street Scot who rarely set foot in the city. There is a Burns block and a Bob Edwards luncheon. James Lougheed's name is almost as well known as that of his grandson, Alberta's premier. But there is no carefully restored Bennett home, since he had no home in Calgary and there is no Bennett building nor even a Bennett salon in the Palliser. Nor is there a Bennett Boulevard, only a tiny one-block crescent in a recent subdivision that may or may not commemorate the name of the West's first prime minister. Why? The answer must be that in the eyes of most Calgarians, Richard Bedford Bennett, with his striped pants, his carefully nurtured paunch, and his tightfisted outlook on life did not fit the freewheeling, rough-riding image that Westerners had created for themselves. Bennett got the votes, certainly; but he never seemed to catch what the *Herald* called the Spirit of the West.

Chapter Ten

The Dark Side of Boosterism

1

In the summer of 1913, the gifted young English poet Rupert Brooke travelled to Calgary from Edmonton in the company of two Westerners, one from each city. Hour after hour, to Brooke's astonishment, the two men disputed the merits of their rival communities, not on the basis of culture or achievement, but on size and wealth. Land, the Calgarian boasted, had risen in value in his city from five dollars a front foot to three hundred dollars a front foot. But in Edmonton, his companion retorted, land had risen from three dollars to five hundred dollars; and Edmonton had gone from a population of thirty to forty thousand in just twenty years! To which the Calgarian responded that *his* city had gone from thirty to thirty thousand in just twelve years.

Finally, the two were prompted to ask the poet where he hailed from.

"I had to tell them," Brooke recalled, "not without shame, that my town of Granchester, having numbered three hundred at the time of Julius Caesar's landing, had risen rapidly to nearly four hundred by Doomsday Book but was now declined to three-fifty. They seemed perplexed and angry."

By that time, the lusty optimism of the West had deteriorated into something more flamboyant but less admirable. Brooke found that Westerners were proud of their cities but having put down no roots didn't have the same quiet affection for them that one found in the Old Country. Instead they loudly flaunted their love, displaying both the passion and the jealousy of adolescents.

"They boost. To boost is to commend outrageously. And each cries up his own city, both from pride, it would appear, and for profit.... It is imperative to praise Edmonton in Edmonton. But it is sudden death to praise it in Calgary."

By 1910, with the price of land rising swiftly, prairie boosterism had become a religion to which all were required to submit. "Boosting Edson is like making love to a widow – you can't overdo it," was the slogan on one local weekly. Quiet pride didn't count. Evangelism was the order of the day. The virtues of each community must be shouted from the housetops:

THE EYES OF THE WORLD ARE UPON REGINA,
THE CAPITAL AND WONDER CITY OF THIS MIGHTY PROVINCE

The basic tenets of boosterism were that size meant progress and expansion brought wealth. The *Manitoba Free Press* gave expression to this philosophy as early as 1904 when it wrote that "the essential and paramount need of the West is population." In 1904 that was "an article of faith with every man possessed of the most elementary knowledge of the conditions and needs of the west. It permits of no argument. It is an axiomatic truth."

But whether it was an axiomatic truth by 1910, with every city ballooning in size, spilling out onto the bare plains, its municipal services straining to keep up with expansion and its immigrant population hived in slums, was a different matter.

The West was slogan mad. Every community gave itself a title, several making comparisons with larger American cities as if the very act of shouting the comparison aloud would make the dream come true. Thus, Winnipeg was always known as the Chicago of Canada. Calgary was the Banner City of the Last Great West. Tiny Prince Albert saw itself as the White Coal City of the West – the Gateway to Europe. (To the initiated, white coal meant energy, but by what magic was Prince Albert a gateway to anywhere?)

But Saskatoon outdid all others. It was the Minneapolis and St. Paul of the West, "the fastest growing city in the world," "one of the most astounding modern miracles," "the eight-year-old wonder of the British Empire," "the Largest City in the World for its Age," "the greatest example of town and city building in the world's history." The little community, founded by temperance zealots, had come a long way since the days of the Barr colonists but perhaps not quite as far as it boasted.

Saskatoon's boosting techniques sprang from the fertile mind of Harold M. Weir, organizer of the Industrial League for the promotion of local enterprises. Weir was a cosmopolitan, born in Australia, reared in California, educated in England. He had studied art in France, circled the globe for English investors, and had a variety of business interests in the United States. His father, Colonel John Weir, president of the Nevada and Utah Mining and Smelting Company, went down with the *Titanic* in 1912. The following year, Harold Weir talked the citizens of Saskatoon into subscribing one million dollars for his Industrial League to promote the city and bring in new business.

Weir was magically persuasive: the sum was raised in just four and a half days, on paper at least.

To boosters like Weir, size was everything. "The more people, the more trade," was the way the Winnipeg Board of Trade put it in 1906, and in 1906 that was certainly true. In a curious form of wishful thinking each city claimed it had a larger population than the statistics suggested.

The federal census figures were ever in dispute. As early as 1896, the city of Winnipeg insisted the official figures were wrong and demanded that the census be retaken. Calgary was never happy with the census takers. In 1907, after the census finally revealed that Edmonton and Calgary each had only about eleven thousand people, the *Herald* hinted darkly at Eastern skullduggery and suggested the count was out by at least eight thousand. "Shall a haphazard government census rob us of our own right?" the paper asked. So great was the pressure that the census was hastily revised to give Calgary fourteen thousand people and reduce Edmonton's count by several hundred. Then, in 1909, Calgary boosters were driven to a new fury by government pamphlets that gave the city's population as 1,700. This was clearly a misprint for 17,000, but Calgary was not mollified. The same pamphlets had given Edmonton 25,000, a statistic achieved by lumping in the people of Strathcona across the river. Calgarians insisted that *their* population was 30,000. Even in 1911 when the census showed Calgary with a population of 43,376, the civic boosters insisted that an accurate count would have given a still higher figure.

Saskatoon was just as angry. The federal census in 1911 put its population at 12,002 but gave its rival, Regina, 30,210. That, cried the mayor, was "absolutely unreasonable, unbelievable and absurd." Nothing would do but that the board of trade and the leading real estate men should organize their own census. By counting "every living being" in town, including transients, they managed to come up with a figure of 18,000. Even that wasn't good enough; somehow Saskatoon had to get closer to Regina's size. The following year, the city claimed a population of 27,000, arguing that many of its Chinese and other foreign citizens avoided the census takers for fear of having to pay the poll tax.

Like Pat Burns, the prairie cities saw no limit to their expansion. Most Westerners believed Winnipeg would soon be the largest city in Canada, outstripping both Toronto and Montreal. In November, 1906, Calgary's boosters, determined that the city should reach a

290

population of 50,000, organized themselves into a Fifty Thousand Club for that purpose. The boosters boosted so valiantly – with a monstrous parade, a display of fireworks, and an automobile show – that, dazzled by their own enthusiasm, they voted immediately to change the name to the One Hundred Thousand Club. That didn't last long. Six years later the city's population had yet to reach 50,000, but the boosters insisted on changing the name again. In 1912 it became the Quarter Million Club. Perhaps they thought that wishing would make it so; it didn't. Half a century would pass before the city reached that figure. Other prairie communities were even more optimistic. Medicine Hat predicted in 1913 that it would have a population of *half a million* by the time its young men reached middle age.

Again, for sheer, goofy optimism, Saskatoon was far ahead of its sister cities. In 1910, its mayor predicted a population of 100,000 within a few years. That was considered far too low by a group of real estate promoters who forecast a population of between 400,000 and 600,000 by 1940. Yet that seemed too low: in 1912, a full-page newspaper advertisement predicted a future population of one million. Even the academics were caught up in these statistical absurdities. The president of the University of Saskatchewan firmly believed that by 1931 his institution would be as big as the University of Toronto.

Boosterism was quantitative. Each city boasted of the number of miles of street paving, water mains, and sewers it had installed, carefully qualifying the statistics to give the most favourable impression. In 1913, for instance, Calgary was able to boast that it had laid "more miles of street paving than all other cities in the middle west excluding Edmonton" and in miles of sewers built that year "had surpassed the total of all cities in the middle west excluding Saskatoon." Its building growth eclipsed "any city of comparable size in the history of the world."

Size – that was the goal: size in population and also size in acreage. City fathers were obsessed by acreage. Villages wanted to be called towns and towns struggled to become cities, partly to increase their tax bases and partly because they were pushed into it by the real estate interests. In order to become incorporated as a town in 1903, Saskatoon needed a population of 450. It achieved this by counting all the hotel guests during the spring immigration rush. Two years later, by using similar tactics it achieved city status.

And it *still* wasn't enough. In 1911 Saskatoon arbitrarily doubled its acreage. That same year Regina quadrupled in size. Calgary, with only sixteen hundred acres in 1884, kept annexing surrounding land not once but six times, until it had reached almost twenty-six thousand acres by 1912. Edmonton went one better by undergoing *seven* expansions between 1896 and 1914. As a result, the population was thinly distributed; in fact, in some outlying areas it was non-existent. Of Canada's twenty largest cities, these four – Saskatoon, Regina, Calgary, and Edmonton – had the lowest population ratios per acre. Forty years were to pass before they again extended their boundaries.

The taxpayers subsidized the boosters. The business and real estate interests who controlled the local councils used public money to hustle their message. The Winnipeg-dominated Western Canada Immigration Association spent fifty thousand dollars, almost half obtained through government grants, pushing prairie cities. The *Free Press* praised the operation as "of invaluable benefit to the country," but immigration officials disagreed. As Will White pointed out, the message wasn't directed to settlers but to speculators interested only in booming land values. To Obed Smith it was "nothing less than a big real estate concern" using tax money for private profit. Nonetheless, the boosters marched ahead unhindered, drums beating, trumpets blasting. In March 1912, the Calgary Board of Trade announced an Advertise Calgary Day, in which every soul in the city – man, woman and child – was expected to write a letter to a friend or relative somewhere else in the world boosting Calgary as a place to live and own property. We have no record of how many loyal Calgarians actually took up the challenge.

2

Slums The boosters weren't concerned with social conditions; it was the
and image of their community that obsessed them, and woe to those who
brothels persisted in revealing the reality behind that image. These people were derided as heretics, or, in the vernacular, "knockers," who were bringing bad publicity to the community. The sins of the flesh were tolerated in the West. The real sin was to expose them.

The boosters' image of the expanding prairie cities didn't always mirror reality. Behind the handsome new buildings springing up along the main streets were some of the worst slums in Canada. Saloons and brothels, tawdry hotels, wretched overcrowded shacks were concomitants of the boom era.

The cities stank of horse manure. Calgary was the worst, "the horse smellingest town I ever remember," in the words of an old-timer. In 1910 the down town area had fifteen livery stables and twelve blacksmith shops. One gigantic barn on 11th Street housed sixty teams of dray horses that produced a mountain of ordure, which, after a rain, assailed the nostrils of passengers boarding the train at the CPR station across the tracks.

There was little attempt at street sanitation. Clouds of dust rose from the new excavations and from the vast mounds of coal heaped in the railway yards. When the rain fell, the dust and horse droppings formed a liquid gruel six inches deep on Calgary's narrow streets. A passing dray could throw several gallons of this filth a distance of ten feet, showering the unfortunate pedestrians.

On Tenth Avenue West, near First, the Chinese launderers dumped the contents of their tubs into the street and lanes. "They have not the slightest idea of cleanliness and sanitation," one alderman said of the Chinese, but in fact the North Americans weren't any better. In the open shops along Eighth Avenue layers of dust caked the fruit and vegetables while fish and fowl were covered with flies. The sidewalks were slippery with spittle and tobacco juice. Outside the Royal Hotel, where loafers congregated day and night, men leaning against the side of the building sent streams of tobacco juice in the paths of women trying to reach the CPR station from the streetcars. The police were finally goaded into taking action, with little result: the first man arrested got off when he explained to the court he had merely been combing his moustache.

All the prairie cities were hideously overcrowded, a direct result of the city fathers' hunger for more and more people. In Calgary in 1905, in spite of soaring rents, the demand for space exceeded the supply by ten to one; thousands lived in tents, barns, and shacks. In Edmonton in 1907, 1,550 homeless newcomers were living under canvas. Calgary's booster pamphlets showing James Lougheed's resplendent Beaulieu, with its landscaped terraces, its ornate fountains, its Italian marble and Spanish mahogany, or Pat Burns's sandstone castle with its ten bedrooms and four bathrooms, its oak panelling and stuffed trophy heads, didn't portray the immigrant shantytown near the Langevin Bridge.

To those newcomers who had not found their dream homestead and were confined to the cities, looking for work or taking any job they could get, the traditional Western boast about a classless society must have sounded hollow. In Winnipeg in 1909, thirty-two men were discovered crammed into a boarding house licensed to hold seven. A few doors away, in a similar house, twenty-five men and women were crowded together without distinction as to sex. The situation in Regina was appalling: 60 per cent of all its houses were overcrowded. Again and again, five-room houses were found to contain ten double beds. In spite of this, scores had no shelter. One March night in 1910, a newspaper reporter counted four hundred homeless men walking the streets.

Each city had its immigrant section across the tracks, usually named "Germantown" after the largest of the urban ethnic groups. In Regina's Germantown, in the city's East End, members of twenty-two separate nationalities were crowded into an area six blocks square. Here were more than six hundred dwellings, many little better than shacks, jammed together on twenty-five-foot lots. Only forty-eight had plumbing; only fifteen had baths. When it rained, the area became a quagmire. J.S. Woodsworth, who studied it in 1913 at the request of the Methodist Church, found one house where a man was forced to sleep in a clothes closet, another in which three families were crammed into four small rooms, a third in which one couple and six boarders shared four rooms with a flock of chickens.

Under such conditions, babies sickened and died. In July of 1913, a Winnipeg woman reporter, Genevieve Lippett-Skinner, appalled at the high rate of infant mortality in the city, paid a visit to the tenements on Barber Street in Winnipeg's North End – "fearfully and wonderfully made death traps," as she called them.

"Yes, I know a lot about children," one German immigrant mother told her. "I had ten. They are all dead but three."

In one rabbit warren of a tenement, when a baby died, the parents kept the corpse for three days before a neighbour phoned the city's health department. In another room, Miss Lippett-Skinner found a young woman whose five-month-old infant was covered with flies; the odour was overpowering. Downstairs she encountered a tear-stained Greek woman living with her family in a single room. Insects had bitten her baby so badly that the child had been hospitalized. The mother's arm was a mass of poisoned bites. For this unfurnished room the family paid seven dollars a month.

In the backyard of this same building, a deserted mother and two children shared a woodshed with rats and other vermin. The father had been gone for more than four months, but the wife refused to move for fear he might return and not be able to find his family.

In Calgary that winter, while the boosters were still inflating the census figures and urging their fellow citizens to write letters to bring in more people, the superintendent of the associated charities uttered a plaintive appeal for private aid to the city's poor: "There are lonely widows in Calgary who sit shivering in poorly heated rooms. There are bed ridden invalids who draw insufficient bed clothing around their chilly forms. There are scores of underfed and poorly clad children who watch with anxious glances their rapidly diminishing coal heap and wonder what will happen when that is all done, for mother said she hadn't any more money. For over a fortnight, the thermometer has been ranging between 15 and 20 degrees below zero. Will you try to imagine what that means to the poor of the city?"

But the local authorities were less concerned about the poor than they were about the get-rich-quick opportunities the Western boom was providing. There was little public charity, let alone money for parks or recreational facilities. The loneliness of the sod house was paralleled by life in the urban Germantowns. After a ten-hour working day, some men found their only relief in the saloon, the brothel, or the dance hall. In Regina's Germantown there were five hotels with saloons, seven pool halls, but only three dance halls. These were crowded and noisy, frequented by prostitutes, and plagued by drunken brawlers, but for many a lonely immigrant they provided the only respite from a harsh existence.

"I like this better than to lie on my dirty bed all the time," one young man in Regina explained. "The room where I am staying drives me mad. I am not satisfied with these people with whom I live and my job is hard in the day time. So I am very willing to spend my 50 cents twice a week because I have here an hour of life."

"For the poor," wrote Woodsworth, "there is no substitute for the barroom." On six blocks of Winnipeg's Main Street were twenty hotels, all serving liquor; twenty-four more stood shoulder to shoulder on the side streets. Convictions for drunkenness in Manitoba were double those for Ontario, triple those for Quebec.

In spite of an active temperance movement and considerable lip service paid by politicians at every level, from the mayor of Winnipeg to Clifford Sifton, those in power shied away from direct prohibition. Woodsworth noted that in Regina, which had a Liberal administration, the president of the Liberal organization kept a liquor store and the chairman of the East End Liberal committee ran one of the licensed hotels. "It would appear," he wrote, "that the liquor men hold a strong grip on the political situation."

For there was money in drink and even in drunkenness. In 1910, a group of live wire Calgary businessmen took advantage of the situation and opened an Institute for Drunkenness, proclaiming, in full-page advertisements, that there was HOPE FOR BROKEN HEARTED WIVES AND BALM FOR THE MOTHER'S TEARS. For a fee, the institute offered to cure anyone of chronic alcoholism in just three days.

The overwhelming presence of saloons in the West is no more surprising than the overwhelming presence of brothels. The nature of Western settlement made large-scale prostitution inevitable. With 100,000 bachelors on the prairies, most of them young and virile, the bawdy houses did not lack for customers. Every city had its red-light district, winked at by the authorities, such as Calgary's Nose Creek Flats and Moose Jaw's notorious River Street. According to one madam, Edmonton alone had by 1914 between four hundred and five hundred prostitutes; Winnipeg probably had more.

The authorities were generally lackadaisical in enforcing the law. In 1906, the Calgary chief of police, Thomas English, insisted there was less gambling and prostitution in his city than in any community of comparable size on the continent. "There may be houses of prostitution in Calgary but I do not know of them," he declared. Two days later the *Morning Albertan* identified nine brothels within the city known to everyone "except the chief of police."

Even during the periodic vice cleanups, prosecutions were difficult to achieve. When the Mounted Police raided one Nose Creek brothel and found a customer in bed with one of the girls, they were sure they would get a conviction. The accused got off, even though he admitted he was in a house of prostitution, by swearing that the woman was ill and he was simply nursing her.

In Winnipeg, in 1909, there was a concerted effort on the part of churchmen and reformers to expose the brothels. As a result the city fathers tacitly gave the chief of police the right to find a district where prostitutes could be segregated, away from the eyes of respectable citizens. The chief, John C. McRae, went to the fount of all knowledge, Minnie Woods, "The Queen of the Harlots," the best-known madam in town. With her help he selected the MacFarlane–Rachel–Annabella streets area north of the CPR tracks, suitably enclosed by a gas plant, a lumberyard, and a power station and within easy walking distance of the CPR depot and the major hotels. Here, in a space of two city blocks, some two hundred prostitutes began to ply their trade.

There was, of course, a profit to be made from the kind of mass segregation undertaken by the city of Winnipeg. Into town one day before the decision was made crept a mysterious figure, one J. Beaman, a so-called real estate operator with no real estate experience and no affiliation with any local firm. Beaman stayed in Winnipeg for one year only – the year the city moved the brothels. And it was to Beaman that Chief McRae went for help in the switch of location. Beaman bought twenty-two buildings and resold them to the madams at sky-high prices, making a total profit of seventy thousand dollars before he vanished. He was almost certainly a front man for the chief, or the chief's friends, or the local politicians, or perhaps all three.

Nobody paid any heed to the fifty-odd immigrant families living in the area, who complained, vainly, that intoxicated men were stumbling into their homes looking for girls, that residents were being propositioned going to and from work, that drunks, bounced from the brothels, lay on the sidewalks or in the gutter, and that on occasion bare-breasted women could be seen dashing through the neighbourhood and even riding horseback up Annabella Street.

An April evening in 1910. Three men knock on the door of the Bradley home at 70 Higgins Avenue, at the corner of Annabella. Mrs. Bradley hears the knock and thinks it's a little early for the Tribune *carrier. As she goes through the kitchen toward the front door, she hears a man cough. Then, just as she enters her front parlour, a stranger catches hold of her dress.*

"Don't be scared," he says and calls to two friends on the doorstep. "I say, come in, it's all right."

Before she can remonstrate, all three sit down on the sofa and throw their hats on the floor.

"I'll lie down," one says, and proceeds to do so.

The man holding Mrs. Bradley's dress rises and tears it from waist to shoulder, then pulls off her skirt. All three lay some crumpled bills on the table and ask for drinks. Mrs. Bradley tries to explain that this is neither a bawdy house nor a tavern. There are no girls here, she says, but the men search the bedroom for women and the cellar for drinks. They find nothing.

One loosens his pants, pulls them off, and starts to remove his underclothes. Mrs. Bradley runs out into the yard, finds a neighbour, a teamster, and asks him to run for her husband. As Mr. Bradley appears, the three strangers can be seen leaving hastily.

Mr. Bradley calls a policeman. The policeman produces a notebook and pencil and begins to take down the details. Mr. Bradley becomes impatient.

"Why aren't you going after the men?" he asks.

"I have to report it," says the policeman.

But there is no report filed, and when, some weeks later, Mrs. Bradley finally sees an inspector and asks for police protection, he is not helpful.

"You can't expect the police at your door all the time," he tells her.

The city fathers may have been complacent about their red-light district, but they certainly didn't want it publicized, especially in the East, as the Reverend Dr. J.G. Shearer discovered in 1910. Shearer told the Toronto *Globe* that "they have the rottenest condition of things in Winnipeg in connection with the question of social vice to be found in any city in Canada." The Toronto papers were delighted with this intelligence. "WINNIPEG WALLOWS IN VICE" was the *Star*'s headline.

Shearer was no fly-by-night cleric. He was secretary of the powerful Moral and Social Reform League and was a key figure among those who, in 1907, had forced the Lord's Day Act through the federal parliament. But he was reviled in his home town by the city fathers and the business community. The church considered Winnipeg's red-light district a disgrace. But Mayor W.S. Evans, who was up for re-election, cleverly muddied the argument by switching it away from the evils of white slavery to the question of the city's image. "As citizens of our community, we should be, if possible, even more jealous of the good name of our city than of our homes," he declared. ". . . It is patent that those who have the welfare of the city at heart would not advertise it abroad as the rottenest city on the continent. I stand for the best and cleanest and purest city in the world – for Winnipeg and the reputation of such." After all, real estate values had to be maintained.

Evans's opponent, E.D. Martin, backed by church and reform groups, didn't stand a chance. Even the *Free Press* tacitly supported Evans, though his opponent was a Liberal. In December 1910, the Mayor took fifty-seven out of seventy-two polls. Every incumbent was returned. A hurriedly organized royal commission of inquiry reassured the world that Winnipeg was definitely *not* the "rottenest" city in Canada. The city's image was restored, and the brothels on Rachel, Annabella, and MacFarlane streets were allowed to operate openly for the next three decades with no obstruction apart from the quarterly payment of a fine.

3

The immigrants had little say in the policies and destinies of the *The* Western cities; the power lay in the hands of the white Anglo-Saxon *Social* businessmen who controlled the municipal governments. In Winnipeg, *Gospel* for instance, every mayor and every controller from 1896 to 1914 was a WASP. Of 515 councillors elected in the city between 1874 and 1915, only three represented labour. Financial success was the key to both social status and political power. Since there was no established élite of old families, the business entrepreneurs had the control of the city to themselves.

The drain on public funds to support boosterism left little for social welfare programs. In Regina in 1908, the local council turned down as too costly a by-law that would have required all milk to be delivered in sealed bottles to prevent disease. One alderman, Dr. W.A. Thomson, led a battle to improve the city's health. He wanted a new incinerator for the immigrant district, but his opponents called that "a monument across the track." They even went so far as to hide blocks of ice in the garbage so that the incinerator would fail an official test. When Thomson ran for mayor in 1908 he lost.

Woodsworth, in his report on Regina, pointed out that seven of the ten aldermen were in the real estate business. In his mild way, he argued that "it is not wise to entrust the government of the city so largely to a group of men representing one particular class." The greatest danger, however, was "the indifference of the majority of the citizens to public affairs." Those who might care – the immigrants, the poor, and the working people – had no vote because they rarely owned property. Only landowners had the franchise, and, since they could vote in any ward in which they owned real estate, some entrepreneurs had several votes. Thus, again in Woodsworth's words, "public welfare has been sacrificed to private gain."

In spite of the prairie dogma that every man was as good as the next, some were, in Orwell's classic phrase, more equal than others. The Calgary *Herald* might sneer at the English nobility, but it devoted more columns to the city's small power élite than it did to exposing immigrant conditions on the wrong side of the tracks. Most of Calgary's leaders were Anglo-Saxon Protestants from Ontario or the Maritimes (Pat Burns, the Irish Catholic, being a notable exception). They may have rejected Eastern domination, but they aped Eastern high society, sending their offspring to private schools, such as the exclusive Bishop Pinkham's, where the students wore Eton jackets and collars and played cricket and football to "build character." They played polo, rode with the hunt (chasing coyotes, not foxes), had their own exclusive copy of Montreal's St. James's Club – the Ranchmen's Club – and their own exclusive subdivision, significantly labelled Mount Royal. Yet, as one student of the period, Paul Voisey, has shrewdly pointed out, this pseudo-nobility could scarcely label themselves members of the leisure class because, in spite of their cavernous sandstone mansions, they were unable to break the work habit and so enjoyed little leisure.

Nor did the workingman, earning as little as fifteen dollars for a grinding sixty-hour week. His newly rich employer, convinced that hard work was its own reward, secure in the belief that every Westerner was capable of rising in the world (*he* had made it, hadn't he?), kept wages as low as possible and fought the labour unions as ruthlessly as he fought his competitors. In 1910 in Regina, where the cost of living was the highest in the West, wages were the lowest because, so the Trades and Labour Congress claimed, contractors were flooding the market with workers to keep wages down. Here unskilled men were paid only twenty cents an hour. They got little help from the established churches. As one Regina clergyman put it, "workingmen have no right to organize to force their masters to pay higher wages. . . . Servants, obey your masters, for it is right."

Given these attitudes and conditions, it's not surprising that a radical reformist movement should spring up in Western Canada. Its epicentre was Winnipeg, the oldest and largest city on the prairies, the community with the greatest immigrant population, the worst slums, and, since it was the major manufacturing centre in the West, the most extensive factories and the most appalling factory conditions.

In Winnipeg, five skeins of social protest were, by 1910, woven together into a concerted radical fabric. These were the temperance movement, the trade union movement, the women's suffrage movement, the agrarian reform movement, and the "Social Gospel" of the evangelical Protestant churches. All had a common purpose: to change the established order; and, though each had separate goals, these goals often overlapped as the individual movements raised their sights and evolved from narrow objectives to broader ones.

Thus the leadership and rank and file of the Woman's Christian Temperance movement, one of the most powerful and acceptable of the activist groups in the West, found themselves also adopting the cause of female suffrage. This came about because the WCTU set up reading rooms and sponsored debates on topical subjects, thus providing a central focus for concerned women. Fighting discrimination against women and recognizing women's rights became an obvious cause. The WCTU, therefore, launched an investigation into conditions under which female factory workers laboured. That led to a common front in Winnipeg with the radical Methodists, themselves temperance advocates – men like James Shaver Woodsworth, who had left the established wing of the church to minister to the poor through the All Peoples' Mission in the city's North End.

The cross-fertilization continued. In 1910, the Ministerial Association appointed Woodsworth delegate to the Winnipeg Trades and Labour Council, forging a link between the radical churchmen and the union movement. Meanwhile the Grain Growers' Association, with its widely read *Guide*, was also supporting the burgeoning female suffrage movement. The Western farmers considered women equal partners in building the homestead; why shouldn't the politicians also treat them equally? And Woodsworth himself had strong links with agrarian reform; he wrote articles for the *Guide* and the book *Studies in Rural Citizenship*, which carried an introduction by the president of the Manitoba Grain Growers.

Thus it could be said that this slight, ascetic figure was the hub of the radical wheel in Western Canada. Ruthlessly honest, totally dedicated, utterly without interest in personal gain or fame, Woodsworth came to the All Peoples' Mission in 1907 with a social conscience already nurtured in the Methodist Church and honed in the slums of London. Six years later, when he left to pursue broader interests, the experience had thoroughly politicized him.

He was a child of the West, brought from the Toronto suburb of Etobicoke by his father, a Methodist minister, to Portage la Prairie in 1882 when he, the oldest of six children, was only eight. Like Clifford Sifton, another Methodist, he was raised from the age of ten in Brandon, but Woodsworth's idealism – implacable, unswerving – was the antithesis of Sifton's pragmatism. Woodsworth never ducked an issue. One can imagine the consternation of the Winnipeg establishment, sitting in their comfortable Grace Church pews, when Woodsworth first arrived in the city and began to preach his radical sermons from the pulpit. These were some of the wealthiest and most powerful leaders in the community; but that had no influence on him:

"I fear that in our city we have not yet learned the vulgarity of a lavish expenditure of newly acquired wealth. Costly dresses, magnificent houses, expensive entertainments – those are the things we seek after. And the snobbishness that goes with such vulgarity! The pride of wealth. . . ."

No wonder he was unhappy at Grace Church! No wonder the congregation was uneasy with him! One leading member urged him to give "less ill-digested sociology and more simple gospel preaching," but Woodsworth was having none of that. He could no more smother his opinions than he could smother one of his own children. Besides, he was having trouble with the literal truth of the Bible. Instead, he left Winnipeg, and after a spell in British Columbia he tried to leave the church. He was urged to stay and was offered the little mission on the wrong side of the tracks.

It's typical of Woodsworth that he wasn't content to operate a mission that catered to the immigrant poor near the North End's rim. Nothing would do but that he plunge into the heart of that foreign world; and so within two years he moved the mission and his own family deeper in, where the unpaved streets were cluttered with pigs and chickens and the infant mortality in those overcrowded shacks was among the highest in Canada. It could not have been an easy move for a man who had known London and Paris and had taken courses at Oxford, but Woodsworth had as little interest in the comfortable life as he had in comfortable ideas. This was the man who one day, as head of the CCF, would sit up all night on the train from Ottawa to Winnipeg rather than charge the party with the expense of so much as an upper berth. This was the man who would rise in the Commons in the autumn of 1939, a solitary figure, utterly alone yet somehow ennobled, to announce that his conscience could not allow him to vote for a declaration of war. That act would spell the end of his public career, and Woodsworth knew it; but he had never been one to compromise.

His forthright character had bewildered his own parents. His children were in awe of him and so were his siblings, even when they were "grown men and women with no reason in this world to fear his poor opinion," in the words of his son, Charles. They would, he recalled, "quail before his frown of irritation in some altogether trifling matter." Even when they disagreed with his strongly held opinions, they found it simpler to hold their tongues rather than risk his active disapproval.

With his slight figure and pale eyes, he looked mild enough, but at second glance those eyes took on a sterner look – resolute, unfaltering. He was a neat man with a neatly trimmed black beard, which resembled that of the reigning monarch. "King George! King George!" a swarm of small immigrant boys cried out mischievously as he chased them from his vegetable garden.

With his family he could be strict; rules were not to be broken. With the immigrants, struggling to learn a strange tongue, he was unfailingly patient. His daughter, Grace, remembers him trying to teach them basic English by carrying out familiar routines with words and gestures: "I wake up in the morning. I put on my shirt. I put on my pants. I put on my socks. . . ." In spite of what he had written in his book *Strangers within Our Gates* about the problems of assimilability, they were all instant citizens to Woodsworth. He stubbornly refused to list his father's racial origin for the census taker, insisting that he was a Canadian. Once he corrected a newcomer who had identified himself as a European. "Canadian!" cried Woodsworth. The puzzled immigrant shook his head. "Not many of *dem* around," he said.

To Woodsworth, whose fundamentalist beliefs were already shaken, personal salvation was no longer enough. He had seen the dreadful condition of the urban poor at first hand, and he knew that the missionary field was too narrow; it must be broadened. The activist doctrine of the "Social Gospel" was then sweeping the continent, especially among the lower echelons of the non-conformist Protestant churches. Its adherents included, besides Woodsworth, such luminaries as Salem Bland, the radical theologian from Wesley College, whose Old Testament features would soon be immortalized by Lawren Harris, and the Reverend Charles William Gordon, who, under the pseudonym of Ralph Connor, had become the nation's best-selling author with an eventual three million copies of his books in print. These men were the conscience of the West.

Woodsworth expressed their credo in his sermon "The Sin of Indifference," in which he attacked the social apathy of the booming prairies: "A curse still hangs over inactivity. A severe condemnation still rests upon indifference . . . Christianity stands for social righteousness as well as personal righteousness. . . . It is quite right for me to be anxious to save my never dying soul; but it is of greater importance to try to serve the present age. . . . If it is right to help the sick, it is right to do away with filth and overcrowding. . . . We have tried to provide for the poor. Yet, have we tried to alter the social conditions that lead to poverty. . . ?"

It was largely through Woodsworth's efforts that Winnipeg got its first juvenile court in 1908 and its first public playground in 1912. In the Great West Saddlery strike of 1910, with Bland and Gordon he took the side of the workers in their struggle against a union-busting corporation. It was inevitable that he would move into a wider field. In 1913, he left the mission and became the general secretary of the newly formed Canadian Welfare League. Like the Grain Growers and the suffragettes, this implacable clergyman was becoming politicized by the bubbling ferment in the West. His career had only begun: ahead lay the agony of the Winnipeg General Strike and after that the Regina Manifesto and the heady intoxication of a new political movement.

4

Our If the dedicated Woodsworth provided the flint for the radical move-
Nellie ment exploding in Winnipeg, Nellie Letitia McClung provided the spark. Like Ralph Connor, she was a best-selling author at a time when Canadian novels, and especially Western Canadian novels, achieved six-figure sales records. Her widely popular *Sowing Seeds in Danny*, based on her pioneer childhood in Manitoba, sold 100,000 copies; her later novel, *The Second Chance*, exceeded that. In those days the world wanted to read about Canada; no author needed to conceal his origins or hedge her locale; a Canadian setting was an asset, not a hindrance. Nellie was a celebrity before she became an activist.

She was also the kind of woman who inspires epithets. To her enemies, led by the arch-Tory Winnipeg *Telegram*, she was Calamity Nell. To her friends she was Our Nellie. To the Eastern journals she was Mrs. Western Canada. Breezily flamboyant, she provided a strong contrast to the serious, quiet-spoken Woodsworth and the sombre Salem Bland. She was the very antithesis of the mannish stereotype that the anti-suffrage journalists and politicians invented to caricature the women activists. She had an hour-glass figure, a rosy complexion, and handsome features. She piled her soft brown hair in the fashion of the day and surmounted it with one of a series of vast flowered hats. She had a passion for brightly coloured gowns and a talent for equally bright oratory. She radiated joyousness: she was never bitter, but she was also as tough as nails. Her credo was distilled into a single sentence: "Never retract, never explain, get things done and let them howl."

She had her Irish father's turn of phrase, her Scottish mother's sense of dedication. "You say that 'women are angels' and you plead that politics are 'corrupting,'" she told an audience of males who believed that women should not sully themselves by a public career. "Well, in that case you can't get women into public life too soon as there is a big shortage of angels in politics just now."

She was a product of the prairies, as Western as Red Fife. Her parents had brought her west from Chatsworth, near Georgian Bay, when she was seven. The family of nine (Nellie was the youngest) travelled from Winnipeg to a homestead in the Souris Valley by ox cart. Her strict temperance views came partly from her mother, who felt that liquor was "one of the devil's devices for confounding mankind" and partly from her own memories of drunken neighbours spoiling a peaceful picnic. Always theatrical, she had, at the age of thirteen, successfully staged a performance of *Ten Nights in a Barroom.*

In adulthood she became a leading member of the Woman's Christian Temperance Union at a time when the anti-liquor movement had radical rather than moralistic overtones. No woman could enter a saloon. It was the men who squandered in the barrooms the money that should have gone into the family coffers. Liquor was a genuine social evil, and many who opposed it did so on humanitarian rather than moral grounds. The WCTU was a powerful force in the West, and it was not surprising that its leaders should move from this indirect exploitation of women to the broader political and economic discrimination against their sex in general.

Nellie McClung made her first public speech at a WCTU convention in Manitou in 1907, thrilled, if a little nervous, to be asked to give an address of welcome on behalf of the local chapter. Typically, she bought a new dress for the occasion, of navy blue and white striped voile trimmed with narrow white Valencienne lace and, of course, a white leghorn hat resplendent with red velvet flowers.

Sensibly, she decided to avoid all the boring statistics about drink and especially any reference to prohibition – "a hard sounding word worthless as a rallying cry." She understood why Westerners drank: "It answered something in the blood, some craving for excitement and change." She herself had known a similar feeling on the homestead when, as a young girl, she had swirled about enjoying a brief moment of dizziness, blotting out the familiar landscape. It was not enough to banish the demon rum; something better must take its place. And so Nellie McClung, at the age of thirty-four, in her crisp new dress and her big, bright hat, talked of the need for parks and games, handicrafts, orchestras, folk dances, better housing – civilized substitutes for liquor that might help make life more bearable on the harsh prairies, but which the boosters had neglected. Whatever effect she had on her listeners, the effect on herself was electric. She saw the faces of her audience light up, and their eyes glisten. She felt the atmosphere crackle. From that moment on she was a political animal.

She arrived in Winnipeg in 1911, at the height of the Western boom. Her husband had sold his drugstore in Manitou and taken a post as district manager of Manufacturers Life. She was disgusted to learn that insurance companies, too, had a double standard. Men could be insured against various disabilities but women only against death. *Why?* Because, she was told, women were more sensitive than men; they could be more easily hurt in accidents; they were often the victims of pure nerves and "would like nothing better than to lie in bed for a week or two." They would think they were hurt when they were not and "there would be no end of trouble."

Winnipeg completed the political awakening of Nellie McClung. When Emmeline Pankhurst, one of the most fiery members of the British suffragette movement, came to town, the seeds of the Western women's movement began to sprout. Conditions among women workers in the Winnipeg factories were appalling. The Local Council of Women decided that a woman factory inspector was needed. The council deputed Mrs. McClung and Mrs. Claude Nash, a friend of the Premier's, to urge him to accompany them to see these conditions for himself. Reluctantly, he agreed.

Sir Rodmond Roblin, Premier of Manitoba, sits nervously in the rear seat of his limousine, his plump hands gripping the gold handle of his cane. He is a big, florid man in his sixties, more than a little pompous, and flanked now by two determined women: Mrs. Nash, in her grey lamb coat and crimson velvet hat, on one side and the splendidly attired Mrs. McClung on the other.

Sir Rodmond is engaged in a monologue about working women. It is good for them to work, he says; there is far too much idleness these days. He himself worked a full day as a boy, and loved every minute of it! Are the ladies not being too sentimental about factory conditions? These young girls in the factories: are they really underpaid? No doubt they live at home and work for pin money. At any rate, work won't hurt them; it will keep them off the streets. Anyway, most workers are foreigners from countries where life is strenuous. They are used to hard work. Let them understand how money is made. Extravagant women are the curse of the age. And so forth. The monologue drones on. Mrs. Nash and Mrs. McClung grit their teeth and say nothing.

They reach a grubby factory, lead their man down a set of dark, slippery stairs and into an airless basement where naked light bulbs hang from smoky ceilings. The floor is ankle-deep in apple peelings and discarded cloth. There is no ventilation, no heat. A long line of untidy women crouch over sewing machines. Roblin takes one look, tries to leave; but his companions urge him to speak to the workers. Finally a question occurs to him: doesn't anyone sweep the floors? He has to shout to make himself heard over the sound of the machines. No one answers. One woman shakes her head and keeps on working. Mrs. McClung reminds the Premier that all are on piecework; they cannot afford the time for conversation.

Again he tries to leave, but they will not let him go. They push him through a side door into a foul passage to show him a queue forming before a door marked "Toilet." There are no separate facilities for women, and the plumbing isn't working.

"For God's sake, let me out of here," cries Rodmond Roblin. "I'm choking. I never knew such hell holes existed!"

But they are implacable. "These people work from 8:30 to 6:00, Sir Rodmond. Six days a week," Mrs. Nash tells him sweetly. "But no doubt they get used to it." Her sarcasm is lost on the Premier.

Back on the street, he suddenly remembers an important interview and tries to break away, but they coax him into a shirt factory to witness young girls who are being "kept off the streets." Here is a young woman whose hand, bound up with a dirty bandage, has been injured in a machine. Here is another who coughs continually with bronchitis but who cannot afford to stop work because she must support her family; if she takes time off somebody will be hired at once in her place. The manager arrives to tell the Premier that he doesn't need any factory inspectors because "all the girls are glad of the work. I have no trouble with them."

"How about the girl who coughs so much?" asks Nellie McClung. "Couldn't she be given a few days off with pay to get built up a bit?"

"The company is not a charitable institution," the manager tells her. ". . . If the girl is sick she can always quit!"

307

Roblin edges toward the door and escapes into the protection of his limousine.

"I still can't see why two women like you should ferret out such utterly disgusting things," he says.

Once again they urge upon him the need to appoint a trained social worker as a woman factory inspector.

The Premier grows impatient at the harangue. "I tell you it's no job for a woman," he says. "I have too much respect for women to give any of them a job like this." He admits he's greatly disturbed. He didn't know such places existed in the highly publicized Chicago of the North. He'll speak to his people about the problem. But he promises nothing.

Out of this encounter was born the Political Equality League to fight for women's rights. The provincial Liberals, more sensitive to the winds of change than Roblin's Tories, jumped on the bandwagon and included a female suffrage plank in their platform. The Premier sneered at that, declaring it was supported only by "short haired women and long haired men." When a delegation appeared before the provincial legislature on January 27, 1914, asking for the vote for women, Roblin was at his pompous best.

"Any civilization which has produced the noble women I see before me is good enough for me," the Premier intoned. "Gentle woman, queen of the home . . . set apart by her great function of motherhood . . . and you say women are the equal of men." *Dramatic pause*. "I tell you you are wrong. You do your sex an injustice, which I shall not allow to pass unchallenged. Women are superior to men, now and always!"

Roblin did not realize that he had fallen into a trap. Mrs. McClung, watching every gesture, memorizing every phrase, was about to take the role of the premier in a satirical presentation and to throw his words back at him.

The next night, in the Walker Theatre, the league produced its drama *The Women's Parliament*, set in an all-female legislative assembly in a mythical province where only women held office and no man had the vote. The climax of the evening would come when a delegation of men appeared before the lady premier, abjectly appealing for the franchise, asking for joint guardianship of their children and a right to their own earnings. Nellie McClung, of course, took the Roblin role.

The play was presented twice in Winnipeg and again in Brandon and was an enormous success, thanks to Mrs. McClung's parody of

308

the Roblin style. Almost every sentence produced a roar of laughter:

". . . man is made for something higher and better than voting. Men were made to support families. What is home without a bank account? . . . In this agricultural province, the man's place is the farm. Shall I call man away from the useful plough and harrow to talk loud on street corners about things which do not concern him? Politics unsettle men and unsettled men means unsettled bills – broken furniture and broken vows – and divorce. . . When you ask for the vote you are asking me to break up peaceful, happy homes – to wreck innocent lives. . . ."

In the provincial election that followed both Mrs. McClung and J.S. Woodsworth campaigned for the Liberals. She stumped the province, addressed one hundred meetings, was even burned in effigy in Brandon, and loved every minute of it. Years later she recalled that "every day felt like the day before Christmas" during that tempestuous campaign, a campaign of which it was said that "never again will any politician in this province have the temerity to scorn women's power." Roblin won, but by a slim margin. The following year he was driven from office after Dafoe in the *Free Press* published revelations of political corruption. With the Liberals in power in 1916, Manitoba granted its women the vote, the first province in Canada to do so. This free wind, blowing out of the West, was soon to have its effect on the entire nation. That was something the boosters might have proudly proclaimed in their expensive real estate pamphlets, but by then the boosters were muted. For the boom had collapsed and sanity had returned to the Canadian West.

Chapter Eleven

Boom and Bust

1

Railway By the time the prairie land boom reached its peak, the West had gone
madness railway mad. Two new transcontinental lines were snaking across the
prairies and piercing the wall of the Rockies to do battle with the CPR.
Branch lines wriggled over the West, crossing and criss-crossing the
plains, turning the land into a vast spider's web of steel. Every community, no matter how small, felt itself entitled to at least one railway.
Almost every community got one, and some got several.

Nobody seemed to care if rail services were duplicated. For seventy
miles out of Saskatoon, two transcontinental lines paralleled each
other, a mere gunshot apart. In one forty-mile strip east of Brandon,
there were no fewer than eight east-west lines. Fourteen separate
ribbons of steel crossed the Manitoba border into Saskatchewan.
Who worried? The railway boom was the product of boosterism, and
boosterism, in turn, thrived on the sound of clanging metal.

The railways created instant towns, "built while you wait," in the
words of a Chicago journalist, W.J. Shunks, who visited the West in
1911 and was astonished by what he saw: "Half way between Lake
Superior and the Manitoba prairies, in the heart of the virgin forest,
the Grand Trunk Pacific town builders put their pencils on the map
and give orders. Presto! The new town of Graham, with its divisional
railway shops, its roundhouses, its stores and banks, springs into
being. At the edge of the prairie section they decree another larger
railway city with immense repair shops, car works and foundries.
Transcona is born! As the rails are flung Pacificward across the
prairies, there springs into being a string of communities with important divisional centres of the Melville, Watrous, Wainwright and
Edson type at regular intervals."

One such town was Mirror, Alberta, named for the London *Daily
Mirror* and located half way between Edmonton and Calgary, a
divisional point on the GTP's line from Winnipeg. The Mirror town-
site was placed on the market on July 11, 1911. In just eleven hours,
577 town lots were sold, a rate of almost one a minute. The total purchase price was a quarter of a million dollars. Before the town was
a month old, it had two banks, five stores, three lumberyards, a hotel,
three restaurants, two pool rooms, a sash and door factory, and a
newspaper.

To everyone in the West, railways spelled profit and progress.

Merchants saw their businesses skyrocket. Real estate men saw land prices zoom. Politicians gained power by promising a railway and stayed in power by getting one. Back in 1900, the veteran Prince Albert politician T.O. Davis had ensured his re-election when, with Clifford Sifton's help, he got the Canadian Northern to announce the start of grading in the Melfort area. The previous year, Theodore Burrows had saved his political bacon with a similar ploy: when a construction train laden with rails puffed into his constituency, Burrows won his provincial seat easily even though his party was badly shattered elsewhere.

The railway boom was the product of prairie optimism, political opportunism, local boosterism, and the traditional hatred of the CPR. In the depression of the nineties, the Canadian Pacific managed to pay its dividends by keeping freight rates high and refusing to spend a dollar on branch lines; between 1893 and 1896, it didn't build a mile of track. One can scarcely blame it for this policy – by contrast, the CPR's American counterpart, the Northern Pacific, went into receivership in 1893 – but the West did blame it. Every town considered itself the victim of the CPR monopoly; thus the climate was ripe for the arrival on the scene of those two remarkable entrepreneurs, William Mackenzie and Donald Mann, whose Canadian Northern Railway grew piecemeal, in a Topsy-like fashion, bit by bit, here and there, thriving on the railway hunger and financed by bonds guaranteed by two levels of government.

The two partners, both knighted in 1911 for their achievements (not long before those same achievements began to pale in the taxpayers' eyes), were a remarkable if dissimilar pair. Mackenzie, a wiry, sharp-featured financial wizard with a neat imperial beard and an agile mind, was the physical antithesis of his massive, slow-moving partner, a bluff and rough-hewn ex-blacksmith with a black spade beard. Mackenzie was a Conservative, Mann a Liberal. Mackenzie was a swift thinker, Mann slower to make up his mind. Yet the two complemented one another, Mackenzie working on his Tory friends while Mann handled the Grits. Like police interrogators who operate in pairs, the two entrepreneurs played alternate Good Guy–Bad Guy roles in their dealings. One would use the other's obstinacy as an excuse to drive a harder bargain, explaining that any other position would cause the breakup of the partnership.

Railways were their real politics and their only passion. Mann's three brothers were railway men, and Mann himself had brought the first locomotive into Winnipeg in 1876. Mackenzie, when asked why he refused to sell out to the rival Grand Trunk, replied, "Because I like building railroads." It was true. The acquisition of money for money's sake was of less interest to both men than the actual financing and construction of lines of steel. It was just as well, since both were destined to end up with very little.

Both were workaholics in the best Calvinist tradition and both were intensely religious. Mackenzie was a Methodist, Mann a Presbyterian. In his early days as a CPR contractor in the mountains, Mann used to spend his Sunday evenings hammering out Sankey hymns, accompanying his own clear tenor on a piano he had brought with him. Behind that rough, cigar-chewing façade was hidden a sensitive, even mystical character. Donald Mann was more at home on the frontier than in the boardroom. He preferred solitary walks in the wilderness to the clamour of the city. Like Mackenzie, he believed implicitly in the power of prayer, and when his partner died in 1923, Mann publicly urged the country to pray for him.

The two first met in the summer of 1884 when both were working as contractors for the CPR. Mackenzie was forty, Mann thirty-six. Mackenzie, the humourless ex-schoolteacher from Kirkfield, Ontario, had attempted several vocations with varying success. He had opened a lumber business near his home, which failed to prosper. He had worked cutting ties for a railway north of Toronto and then, with that experience, had eased himself into contracting. Faced with the need to raise a five-thousand-dollar performance bond on a small contract between Lindsay and Haliburton, Mackenzie, who was broke, managed to borrow the money from the mother superior of a Montreal convent, which his wife, a Roman Catholic, had attended. That technique – to build railroads on borrowed funds – was to be used again and again in the years to come. To build the Canadian Northern, Mackenzie and Mann would eventually borrow more than three hundred million.

Mackenzie's reputation for getting the job done on time eventually brought him a contract on the CPR's mountain section. Mann was already in the West. He'd risen from blacksmith to lumberman to railway contractor, a great, brawny figure of a man with an unconventional reputation. There is a story that Mann was once challenged to a duel by a pompous German army officer. Invited to choose the weapons, Mann opted for broadaxes. That mordant decision ended all talk of duelling.

The two men teamed up in 1886 to help build the CPR's branch line through Maine, but conditions in the West were such that nothing could be accomplished on the prairies until 1895, when Mann convinced Mackenzie to help him buy the charter and finish building the Lake Manitoba Railway and Canal Company line. Mackenzie by then had established a double reputation as a result of his successful amalgamation and electrification of the Toronto tramway system. On the one hand he was known for his financial acumen and for always completing his contracts on time. On the other, thanks to some shady dealings in Toronto, including the bribing of public officials, he was also known as a sharp and unethical operator. But the Bank of Commerce cared less about ethics than it did about results. With Mackenzie's name linked to Mann's company, it advanced the money to finish the railway. The two partners repaid the bank with more borrowed money — the proceeds from the sale of bonds, which, being guaranteed by an eager Manitoba government, were almost as good as cash.

That was to be the pattern followed by the partners for the next two decades. Mackenzie handled the money, Mann the construction. At first they had no other plan than to build or buy up small rail lines. Then, in 1899, they formed the Canadian Northern "from a series of disconnected and apparently unconnectable projections of steel hanging in suspense," to quote David Blythe Hanna, their new superintendent and future vice-president. It was an astonishing performance. Hanna likened it to the main title of a motion picture in which a handful of sticks, tossed into the air, miraculously form themselves into words.

In 1901, the two men got their jerrybuilt enterprise under way by using Manitoba's anti-CPR sentiment to outbid the older railway for the unfinished Northern Pacific lines projected from Duluth to Winnipeg. In this they had the support of the press and the politicians of both parties who had been working for two decades to get freight rates reduced. By guaranteeing a rate reduction, and promising never to amalgamate with the CPR, the partners struck a fantastic bargain with the Manitoba government, which agreed to lease the Northern Pacific line with an option to purchase and turn it over to Mackenzie and Mann. More, it also agreed to guarantee the partners' bonds on a line to the lakehead, which would compete with the CPR, as well as on the unfinished extension south of the border to Duluth. In short, a Canadian province was backing bonds on railway construction in another province and also in another country.

The following year, Mackenzie and Mann got further guarantees by

315

making themselves the heroes in another battle with the Canadian Pacific.

It is the afternoon of November 8, 1902, in Edmonton, and we have joined a wagonload of vigilantes heading for Strathcona to do battle with the CPR. Strathcona is a CPR town, a divisional point on the branch line from Calgary. Edmonton is not. It sits across the river without any rail transportation to connect it to the outside world. But Mackenzie and Mann's Edmonton, Yukon and Pacific Railway will provide that link if it can only connect with the CPR line at Strathcona.

The CPR is determined that will never happen. It has sent a switch engine, loaded with a CPR crew, to puff back and forth over the spot where the upstart railway plans to make the connection. It has a court order refusing any connection and a uniformed policeman to back the order up. That is why we are rumbling down McDougall Hill and across the Low Level bridge, where the new tracks are already in place, and up the incline of Scone Hill, past the CPR roundhouse to the spot where the hated engine is blocking all chances of a link-up.

A crowd has gathered on the scene, but we vigilantes are helpless because nobody has turned up from the new railway to force the issue. The hours tick by. Dusk gathers. A chill wind whistles up the valley of the North Saskatchewan. What has happened? Where is W.J. Pace, the E.Y. & P. construction chief? Has he given up without a struggle?

Not quite. At 5:15 Mr. Pace appears, ambling cheerfully up the line from Mill Creek. Has he got something up his sleeve? His countenance does not suggest it. He whistles to himself under his breath, looks about casually, talks to friends in the crowd, acts as if he hadn't a care in the world.

We check our watches. It's 5:25; the through train from the south is due at any moment. Down from the CPR roundhouse comes a messenger with orders to release the engine from its sentry duty long enough to make way for the oncoming locomotive. Off it chugs; a moment later the big train roars into view, flashes past, and rumbles away.

A sharp whistle splits the air — a signal from Pace. Out from a nearby copse of bushes leaps a concealed crew of construction men. They rip up the tracks as we fight back an attempt at interference from the CPR's employees. Before the guard train can return the switch is in its place. The CPR has been beaten. The Strathconians are in retreat. Edmonton has its connection, and a court decision will allow it to remain.

316

As Mackenzie and Mann well known, railways, real estate, and politics were inextricably mixed in the West. In 1905, the partners decided to ask for federal bond guarantees to build a line between Saskatoon and Calgary. The Conservatives failed to oppose the scheme in Parliament probably because Tory insiders were shown the route of the proposed line, a piece of information that allowed a favoured few to buy up land close to the right of way. They got the land cheap by pressuring the CPR, which owned it, to reduce the price from $5.00 to $3.50 an acre. The money for the purchase came from George Foster, a former Tory Minister of Finance who was then general manager of the Union Trust Company. Foster simply appropriated cash from the funds of the Independent Order of Foresters, which the trust company was administering, and then sold the lands back to the Union Trust at a profit of two dollars an acre. Foster and his political friends, who included such Tory stalwarts as Rodmond Roblin, made a $200,000 profit on the deal, with Foster keeping ten thousand acres of the best land for himself.

In this way, Mackenzie and Mann pulled the Opposition's teeth and got the guarantees needed to build the railway without spending a penny, while the Tory insiders, using other people's money held in trust, turned a handsome profit. The real loser, however, was the Conservative party, which had hoped to make use of the Liberal political scandals to fight the election of 1908. When a royal commission issued its report in 1907, it became difficult for the pot to call the kettle black.

The Canadian Northern grew in such a haphazard fashion that it was not until after the turn of the century that the country woke up to the fact that the two partners were planning to stitch the pieces together into a new transcontinental railway. Meanwhile, Sir Wilfrid Laurier was dreaming dreams of his own.

Laurier was haunted by the ghost of John A. Macdonald, whose Pacific railway policy, bitterly attacked by the Liberals at the time, had turned out to be a political asset, keeping the Conservatives in power for almost two decades. If one transcontinental railway had done that for Macdonald, why couldn't another do the same thing for Laurier? The Prime Minister saw himself in the history books of the future, a man of vision tying the country together, the saviour of the West.

This was the genesis of the Grand Trunk Pacific, a child of the ailing Grand Trunk, the company that had missed its big chance in the 1880s when it turned down the Pacific franchise. Now $400 million in debt, saddled by inefficiency, red tape, lack of initiative, and above all, absentee control vested in an English board of directors, the pioneer railway began to consider missed opportunities. It looked to the West for succour, or at least its hard-driving general manager, Charles Hays, did. An American entrepreneur who had pulled the moribund Wabash railroad out of a morass of debt, Hays had been hired by men who remembered what another Yankee, Van Horne, had done for the CPR.

Van Horne had been brought to Canada for a princely fifteen thousand dollars a year. Hays's salary was twenty-five thousand dollars. He defected briefly when the Southern Pacific offered him four times as much but bounced back north again after a frustrating year with the American line. By 1902, he was ready to span the awesome desert of the Canadian Shield and spread the tentacles of his road into the lucrative prairies. The time seemed right. As the *Manitoba Free Press* reminded its readers that year, "the vital importance to this part of the Dominion of having all the transportation facilities that can possibly be secured is . . . ever foremost in the public mind."

Hays, who was well aware of the Western clamour for more railways, wanted as many concessions from the government as he could squeeze out of Laurier. He wanted a land grant, a cash subsidy, and tax exemptions in return for his pledge to build from North Bay, Ontario, to the Pacific Coast. Laurier balked. The government wanted no more land grants: the 25 million acres ceded to the CPR were causing enough problems. But Laurier was desperate for an election issue: what better than the bright promise of a new transcontinental railway stretching from Moncton, N.B., to Port Simpson, B.C., on the northern Pacific coast? He made a counter-offer: the Grand Trunk's subsidiary, the Grand Trunk Pacific, would build the western half of the new line, starting at North Bay, rounding the Great Lakes, crossing the prairies, and driving through the Yellowhead Pass of the Rockies. The money would be raised partially by government bond guarantees and partially by the parent company itself. At the same time, the government would build the eastern half of the line, from North Bay to Moncton, to be known as the National Transcontinental, and lease it back to the Grand Trunk.

This plan was scarcely on paper before it met with resistance. Hays's London boss, Sir Charles Rivers-Wilson, was terrified of the country north of Lake Superior, an uninhabited, agriculturally unproductive thousand-mile expanse of granite, schist, and muskeg. There was no profit in it; indeed, it had almost destroyed the CPR. Laurier, still

318

hypnotized by the memorable railway debates of 1881 that had helped sink the Liberal party, gave in. The government would build *all* the line from Winnipeg to Moncton; the Grand Trunk could stop worrying about the empty desert of the Shield. And when the job was done, the Grand Trunk could lease the whole thing.

It was a sweetheart deal: the government was going to build the difficult half of the railway and, in effect, underwrite half the cost of the rest. It required all of Laurier's eloquence that summer and fall of 1903 to get the measure through the House. "I am well aware that this plan may scare the timid and frighten the irresolute, but, sir, I may claim that every man who has in his bosom a stout Canadian heart will welcome it as worthy of this young nation, for whom a heavy task has no terrors, which has the strength to face grave duties and grave responsibilities."

There it was, an echo of Macdonald, to whom Laurier, as an up-and-coming young parliamentarian, had listened in 1881. Now he was about to see his own national dream come true.

There was bitter opposition, as there had been in Macdonald's day, but now it was the Conservatives who cried giveaway. Every opposition paper in the country sided with A.G. Blair, the Minister of Railways, who thought the plan disastrous, quit the cabinet, and crossed the floor on the issue. A stout defender of the government-owned Intercolonial that had united the Maritimes in 1876, he saw no reason for a second transcontinental line. It was, he declared, "one of the most indefensible railway transactions which has ever taken place in this country."

All this time, the team of Mackenzie and Mann, supported by provincial bond guarantees, had been gluing their various Western lines together into a pastiche that was beginning to resemble a national network. Why didn't Laurier turn to them to build a railway to the Pacific? They were clearly prepared to build one anyway. Or, alternatively, why didn't he suggest an amalgamation of the Canadian Northern and the Grand Trunk?

Actually, he had tried to do that the previous winter, but not very hard. There were overtures, conferences, discussions, proposals between the two factions. These came to nothing. The Easterners looked upon the Western partners as brash upstarts; the ambitious Hays wanted to drive them out of business and swallow them. Mackenzie and Mann saw the Eastern railwaymen as fogies, taking their orders from London. It was *their* plan to gobble up the Grand Trunk.

Laurier, who could have waved a big stick and forced amalgamation, declined to do so. Mackenzie and Mann were a little too slick, a little too sharp for his taste; seasoned political manipulators, they seemed to have Blair in their camp. Nor did he believe that they had the finances to do the job. And yet the pair had those very qualities he would praise in the House – men for whom a heavy task held no terrors. Again it was a case of the East-West schism, the West suspicious of the East, the East underestimating the West.

Clifford Sifton wanted to divide the country between the two forces, with the Grand Trunk building the line east from the lakehead, the Canadian Northern building west to the Pacific. In that way the Eastern company would get all the Western business, the Western company would enjoy the traffic from the East. Sifton tended to lean toward Mackenzie and Mann, which perhaps explains why he wanted to give them the easier half of the project. Hays he dismissed as a "cold blooded raider of the treasury." Sifton's plan made some sense, more sense certainly than Laurier's, but it never came to fruition.

But why should the government turn the rich prairie territory over to a private firm? Why should the government not own the railroad its bonds were helping to underwrite, especially when it had assumed total responsibility for building the most difficult part of the line? Several Western papers wanted nationalization; Sifton, too, was leaning that way. But Laurier had bleak memories of the ill-fated attempts of Alexander Mackenzie, his former leader, to build the CPR as a government venture. And the case of the Intercolonial was just as bad – an invitation to graft and inefficiency.

The Prime Minister felt he could not wait. Grain was piling up along the main line of the CPR, and the railway did not have enough freight cars to move it east. Beyond the main line, new settlers sat idle, unable to produce at capacity because their farms were too far from the nearest railhead.

"We cannot wait because in these days of wonderful development time lost is doubly lost," a weary Laurier told the House. "We cannot wait because at this moment there is a transformation going on in the conditions of our national life, which it would be a folly to ignore and a crime to overlook . . . our duty . . . is not of tomorrow but of this day, of this hour and of this minute . . . Heaven grant that while we tarry and dispute . . . an ever-vigilant competitor does not take to himself the trade that properly belongs to Canada."

Laurier got his way. Now, at last, he had his election issue. Unhappily, it turned out that the Grand Trunk could not borrow enough money to finance its part of the bargain. The election was put off, a new session of Parliament called, and the deal with the railway watered down once more. Among other things, the government now agreed, in effect, to guarantee, if necessary, *all* the funds needed to build the mountain section of the line.

Thus the way was cleared for two new Pacific railways, both supported largely with public money. Laurier's original plan, to run the GTP far north of the CPR, was abandoned. The two railways would often parallel one another across the plains and through the mountains. In retrospect it seems idiotic, but in those euphoric days nobody bothered to look into the future. The West was railway-crazy, and the East was basking in the West's prosperity. The cost of building the new transcontinental Grand Trunk line would nearly equal the cost of digging the Panama Canal, but when the Liberals went to the country in the late fall of 1904 with their railway policy in place, the country gave them an overwhelming mandate.

Few in the East, least of all Sir Wilfrid, had believed that Mackenzie and Mann could transform the jerrybuilt sections of their line into *another* transcontinental road. They reckoned without the Western hunger for railways. Not only were the prairie provinces eager to shore up the Canadian Northern's credit by guaranteeing its bonds, but the federal government also found, in the end, that it too must support the upstarts. Between 1903 and 1911, Mackenzie and Mann got $56 million in bond guarantees from the Laurier administration. By 1914, Robert Borden's Conservatives had poured in another $49 million. But who cared? The Canadian Northern was stitching the country together with ten thousand miles of steel. The West had what it wanted. Only the insiders realized the hollowness of the victory.

2

Winnipeg throve and grew fat on the railway boom. By 1911 no fewer *The* than twenty-four separate lines of steel radiated out from the miracle *land* city of the prairies. Its balloon-like expansion could not keep pace with *frenzy* the demand. More wheat poured into Winnipeg in a year than into any other market on the continent. The Canadian Northern's new yards at St. Boniface could handle twenty-five hundred cars, the new CPR yard at Transcona thirteen thousand. And it still wasn't enough.

The world's eyes were focused on Winnipeg. A Chicago paper announced that no city in the United States had "such an absolute and complete command over the wholesale trade of so vast an area." The New York *Commercial* predicted its population would reach three-quarters of a million by 1920. The *Canadian Annual Review* predicted a million.

The city buzzed with the clamour of construction. By 1910, Eaton's had completed an eight-storey building and was planning to go to twelve storeys. Fourteen banks moved their regional head offices to the city. By 1912 the Empire's largest stockyards were completed to handle the flow of cattle to Europe. Seventy-one apartment buildings, sixty-eight industrial buildings, thirty-seven warehouses, and fifteen movie theatres were under construction that year. Contractors couldn't handle all the business; there wasn't enough cement.

Winnipeg merchants enriched themselves by opening branches in the new towns along the extended lines of steel. Some communities sprang up even before the railway reached them. Elbert Hubbard, the American businessman turned writer – his best-known work was the popular *A Message to Garcia* – visited Winnipeg in 1913 and was astonished at what he saw: "Business booms and bustles. . . . Sky-scrapers go up overnight. You remain away from Winnipeg six months and when you come back you have to hire somebody to conduct you around the town."

Winnipeg, then, provided the spark that ignited the prairie land boom. Winnipeg's real estate men invaded the cities of the Far West, buying up blocks of property, sub-dividing the bald prairie, pushing development, inflating prices. One Winnipeg syndicate owned 250,000 acres of land in Edmonton. Another bought $800,000 worth in Moose Jaw for subdivision. The entire townsite of Dunsmore, Alberta, at the eastern terminus of the Crow's Nest Pass, was owned and promoted by Winnipeggers.

The specifics of the land boom boggle the mind. Everybody – clergymen, actresses, academics, farmers, politicians, blacksmiths – went insane over real estate. As Bob Edwards put it, everybody had a lot on his mind. The boom began in 1906 following the creation of the two new provinces. In February of that year the Calgary *Herald* nervously reported "some of the earmarks of a genuine boom," and said that the more conservative citizens were worried about it reaching the frenzied stage. The danger ended with the recession of 1907-8, but the frenzy was not long in coming after the recovery of 1909. By the

322

following year everybody was affected, including Calgary's "more conservative citizens." By midsummer, 1911, it was moving ahead at full steam. By November it was out of control.

Clerks, barbers, motormen, storekeepers all became instant realtors. In 1908, Saskatoon had eight real estate brokers; by 1912 it had 257. In the same period, with both the Grand Trunk Pacific and Canadian Northern moving in, the number of real estate brokers in Calgary jumped from 54 to 443. They employed some two thousand salesmen, which meant that 10 per cent of the adult males in that city were involved in selling land. So great was the demand that Calgary's forty-eight architects couldn't keep up with it. Some contractors had to go as far as Australia to get their buildings designed.

To be a realtor one needed no more than a hole-in-the-wall office, a counter, a table and a few chairs, a typewriter, and some correspondence paper. This was all that D.E. MacIntyre and his partner had when they opened a real estate office in Moose Jaw in 1910. MacIntyre had been a storekeeper; now, with an investment of one hundred dollars and no experience, he meant to cash in on the boom; and he did. In their first month the partners cleared eight hundred dollars. "Better than storekeeping," said MacIntyre, "and no butter to handle!"

In Edmonton, a conductor and a motorman actually opened a real estate office in a streetcar, displaying maps of a subdivision in the motorman's compartment so that any passenger could take a fling while riding to his destination. This was small stuff compared to success stories such as that of Bert A. Stringer, a former cattle buyer who turned himself into a realtor and made so much money out of real estate in Calgary and its environs that by 1912 he was planning a modern building on Eighth Avenue, complete with a glass-enclosed roof garden, "a luxurious catering establishment which will rival the cafe in the clouds of the Call Building, San Francisco, and excel anything of which Canada now boasts." Stringer, whose brother Arthur was one of the country's leading writers, was listed in Bradstreet's as "one of Calgary's busiest, brainiest boosters." And he was only thirty-two years old.

Edmonton was also in the grip of the land frenzy. Some four hundred real estate offices lined Jasper Avenue to First Street and ran all the way to 97th. Each office employed runners – as many as ten – who pushed subdivisions on commission. Unlicensed curbside brokers operating near the railway station grabbed strangers off the trains and foisted lots on them. Their profit was enormous, for they had no

323

overhead and they could option a lot for as little as a dollar and peddle it for as much as one hundred dollars. Some sold non-existent lots and pocketed all the cash. One smart young man from Saskatoon, Seth Isaac Cook, invented a title for himself – "Cook and Bruce" (there was, of course, no Bruce) – sold an unfortunate newcomer named J.W. Caldwell two lots for a down payment of two thousand dollars, and then decamped with one of the city's prettiest girls. When Caldwell tried to claim his property he found it was already owned by a man in Ontario.

The frenzy fuelled itself. People scrambled to buy property, terrified that the best real estate would be gone before they got their chance. In Moose Jaw in 1913, a British visitor was astonished at the spectacle of a drunk, staggering about the streets and crying jubilantly, "I've got some lots! I've got some lots!" Drunks didn't count, but when some famous and extraordinary figures were also caught up in the euphoria of the moment, they lent credence to the mania.

Sarah Bernhardt stimulated sales in Calgary when, on one of her farewell tours in January, 1913, she announced through her manager that she intended to purchase lots in that city. Jan Kubelik, the great violinist, made a similar announcement in Winnipeg. The tallest man in Canada, Joseph Lawrence, was photographed buying the first lot in the instant community of Maharg, which advertised itself as "The Debtless City."

At the Saskatoon Methodist Conference in 1912, Dr. A.J. Sparling felt the need to rap the knuckles of certain men of the cloth who, he said, were spending more time in the real estate offices than in visiting the homes of their congregations. His chief target, the Reverend M.M. Bennett, was unmoved. "I have bought real estate and still hold it and thank God I have it," he declared.

Real estate and local politics became hopelessly entangled. City councils tended to be influenced and often dominated by realtors who used their political power and inside knowledge to make paper fortunes. In Edmonton in 1911, one streetcar line was diverted to serve the subdivision of Inglewood, in which several councillors had an interest. In 1909 the real estate lobby on the Calgary council pushed construction of a streetcar line, which increased property values. The following year, certain Calgary councillors leaked valuable details of the Grand Trunk Pacific's route into the city to their real estate friends; by 1912, the value of property along the route had risen to one thousand dollars a front foot. The presence of a new rail line always meant astronomical profits for property owners along the right of way. One single lot along the Canadian Northern's route into Calgary, close to the new terminal, sold in 1911 for a staggering thirty-seven thousand dollars.

At the same time the Canadian Pacific announced it would build car shops at Ogden, four miles from Calgary. The project would cover six acres and eventually employ more than five thousand men. F.C. "Freddy" Lowes, the founder of the largest real estate business in the West, was the first to grasp the profit potential of this move. In what was described as the biggest real estate transaction in the city's history, he paid $775,000 for a subdivision directly to the south of the new locomotive sheds. In gratitude, no doubt, he called it "Ceepeear."

No single Westerner symbolized the real estate boom as handsomely as did Freddy Lowes. He flung money about like a gambler, which, of course, he was. In 1912, the same year in which he launched Ceepeear, he laid out another $650,000 for residential property in Edmonton. He controlled five million acres of farm land in the province, had offices in all the Alberta settlements, and was planning to open more, not only in Vancouver, Toronto, and Montreal but also in New York and London, for it did not enter Freddy Lowes's handsome head that Western progress was finite, that booms do not go on forever, that fevers burn themselves out, and that much insanity is temporary.

The English were charmed by Lowes and caught up in the magic of his success. The papers wrote romantic pieces about him, all exclamatory. The *Sphere*, which carried an article under his by-line extolling Western Canadian real estate ("The Romance of City Building"), called him "the master builder of the Canadian West." Well it might; he had induced English investors to sink half a million dollars in Alberta properties. *Master builder*: that had a nice, substantial ring.

Lowes fitted the Calgary entrepreneurial image. A one-time amateur boxer and lacrosse player from Brampton, Ontario, he had arrived in the city at the start of the first boom in 1906 – a good-looking, square-jawed insurance agent, clean shaven, hair parted neatly in the middle, a pearl stickpin in his tie, smooth as silk and a born salesman. By 1911 he had his first million, and he acted the part. He lived expansively, breeding carriage horses and winning first prizes for his entries in the Calgary horse show. Cars were his passion as well as horses; and it was impossible not to notice his passing, for he drove a five-thousand-dollar Pierce Arrow sedan. That wasn't enough for Lowes: he owned two Pierce Arrows. In fact, at one point, he had *four* cars. Once, while visiting California, he turned up at the Santa Monica auto races and was so taken with one entry that he bought the car on the spot. That was Lowes's style: act on impulse. He encouraged his customers to do the same.

Calgary warmed to Freddy Lowes. He refereed boxing matches, turned up at hockey games to cheer the local team, thought nothing of bringing in an American landscape architect to beautify one of his subdivisions. Once, on an impulse, he wrote out a cheque for ten thousand dollars for the YMCA, the biggest single donation in the association's history.

For Lowes was another who thought big. To create his best-known subdivision, Roxborough Place, he tore down a hillside with hydraulic nozzles and raised a valley to form a plain, on which he installed sidewalks, curbs, and streetlights. The investment cost him $7.5 million, but that did not faze him. "Here, where the great railway companies meet and the farmers . . . come in ever-increasing numbers . . . the pace of progress is astonishing and shows no sign of slackening," he declared in 1913. But the signs were there for the prudent to see, and the pace was already slackening as he would soon learn to his dismay. Three years after he penned those words, Freddy Lowes was broke.

3

Get your feet wet Something fundamental was happening to the West. Hundreds of thousands had come for land. Land was something to hold on to, to grow with. Land was productive; it required hard work; but it was, in the long run, like the principal in a bank account, something that provided a regular income and therefore should not be dissipated.

But now land was merely a chip in a game of chance in which every man saw himself as dealer. People were buying land not to cultivate but to turn over as quickly as possible for the highest possible profit. When J. Burgon Bickersteth, the young theological student, arrived in Edmonton from England, he was struck by the fact that all the people talked about was real estate profits – not crops or production or new farming methods. How serious they were, he thought, so single-minded! They never seemed to relax. The Westerner, he concluded, "gives one the impression of being engaged in a great dollar-making campaign – a campaign which is lifelong, knowing no peace, not even a truce. Real estate and business matters are his one topic of conversation."

326

Of course, it was a distorted view. Not all Westerners were like that; on the farms men still tilled the soil, and women toiled with them. But when Bickersteth arrived in Alberta at the height of the property craze the only topic in the cities *was* real estate profit. The boom mentality was a disease that people caught from each other. Like young men who rush off to war, not for reasons of patriotism but because everybody is doing it, so thousands followed their peer groups in the mad scramble to purchase property; it was the thing to do. Not much more than a decade before, the Klondike strike had touched off a similar mania. Now the West was caught up in a different kind of gold rush, and the newspapers were again full of stories of those who had struck it rich.

Elbert Hubbard came back from Saskatoon with his notebook crammed full of stories of fabulous overnight wealth: O.M. Helgerson was so broke in 1908 he almost had to pawn his watch; but in seventeen months he had made $238,403.87. (How impressive that decimal figure sounded: Helgerson's fortune could be counted to the last penny!) And look at J.F. Cairns: in 1902 he opened a bakeshop; in 1912 he owned a department store. Charlie Wentz subdivided his lumberyard when the boom struck. *Presto!* He made a profit of a quarter of a million. Charlie would never have to work again (although he did keep on working, piling up more and more property). Nor would N.G. Boggs, the former button clerk from Donegal who made a million, buying and selling town lots one at a time, or Frank Cahill, M.P., who had gone broke in Sault Ste. Marie and started out once more with a one-eared mule and a cow, and would now again be worth at least two million if he liquidated. But, of course, Frank Cahill had no intention of liquidating; like everybody else he was certain the boom would roar on.

No wonder people were dazzled: there were lots in Calgary that jumped in price from $2,000 in 1905 to $300,000 in 1912. Some lots changed hands three times in three hours. D.E. MacIntyre, the prairie storekeeper turned realtor, sold the same house twice in one day. The Mayor of Edmonton said it was a slow day when he didn't make a profit of fifty dollars over lunch. In 1912, a quarter-section homestead on the edge of Edmonton doubled in price so that the new owner who had paid $35,000 in thirty days was asking $73,000.

But that kind of profit was illusory. Nobody paid cash in full. "Low down payment" was the clarion cry. You could get a lot in Pleasant Park, Saskatoon, for a dollar down. You could buy lots in Calgary's Belfast and Fairview districts for payments of a dollar a week for five years. By then, it was said, the property would be at the city's heart

"with big skyscrapers going up all around." Property was turned over again and again on the down payment principle. Profits looked big – on paper.

The real estate promoters in each city fanned the flames of hysteria with screaming full-page advertisements that flattered, seduced, cajoled, and even bullied the customers but which were as spurious as those for cancer cures that ran in the same papers. One Calgary entrepreneur, C.T. Lewis, invariably referred to himself in his full-page advertisements as "Millionaire C.T. Lewis," a title that fitted the Western get-rich-quick image as surely as "Baron" or "Duke" fitted a European peer. "The first installment of my millions has arrived," Lewis declared in one of his paid pronouncements. "I will now start giving them away."

The real estate hucksters, in urging prospective customers to "come on in and get your feet wet," used various standard come-ons:

1. *Flattery*: The really smart, go-ahead individual who has brains and foresight will get in on the ground floor before prices rocket.

2. *Greed*: We're here to make you rich: don't delay. Let us help you NOW to become a millionaire.

3. *Shame*: You fool – are you going to let opportunity pass you by, with your stick-in-the-mud attitude? Repent! Buy now or you'll regret it.

4. *Security*: These are "snaps," sure-things; there's absolutely NO risk; profit is virtually guaranteed IF you act NOW!

WHY STICK IN A RUT?

Show the world you are going to
do something more than merely exist . . .

* * *

DON'T DIE POOR . . .

Take a pointer from your neighbour
who has become a millionaire . . .
Do as he did . . .

* * *

THE CERTAINTY NOT THE POSSIBILITY OF PROFITS

A Little Buys a Lot in Hampstead . . .

* * *

MR. MAN – IT IS YOUR MOVE

Do You Want the Profit?

"Get It While You Can"

Do Not Be Stampeded Into Unbelief, But,
Instead, Be Influenced by Investigation . . .

* * *

THE LATCH STRING OF OPPORTUNITY

Is Albert Park. We invite you to
lift this latch; it is to your
advantage to do so . . .

* * *

There was something tantalizing about the text of these gigantic advertisements with their flaring headlines and their vast but inviting expanses of breathless prose. They belonged to the same literary tradition as the earlier pamphlets of the Immigration Department, for they offered hope, opportunity, security, and success. But they were far more florid, far more extreme. Yet it is possible to believe that many who read them had been softened up by the earlier pitchmen and made susceptible to this new assault on their imaginations. By 1912, many who had made good in the West were ready to believe that the printed literature that brought them to the new land wasn't too extreme. It might have been harder going than they had expected, but the promise had been fulfilled. They had prospered, hadn't they? Now they were being invited to prosper again.

Reading, say, the big advertisement by the McCutcheon brothers for Connaught Park, a projected subdivision in Regina six blocks from the nearest streetcar line, a settler might easily have been persuaded to invest some of his savings. "Big Money Is Going to Be Made by the Man Who Buys in CONNAUGHT PARK NOW" the headline shouted. "IT IS BETTER THAN A GOLD MINE:

MR. MAN:—"IT IS YOUR MOVE"

"Get It While You Can"

Do You Want the Profit?

Do Not Be Stampeded Into Unbelief, But, Instead, Be Influenced Into Investigation.

Buy To-Day In

ALBERT PARK

LOTS ARE SELLING FAST

MERE advertising claims do not make a property. Solid facts backed up by the possibilities of increase in value of a property, regards location, etc., are the only consistent means whereby a conservative investor makes his decision. Scores of long-headed conservative buyers have analyzed the situation in East Calgary and invested their money for a purpose and the expectation of a great increase in value at an early date. Fortunes are made by the men who get in on the ground floor, just ahead of the locomotive whistle---when the railroad comes, their turnover at a big profit, is realised. The new railroads will be into Calgary before 1911 ; and there is going to be the biggest turnover in all kinds of realty ever known to the west. According to the estimates of the Dominion Immigration Department, there will be an influx of between 400,000 and 500,000 people from England alone this year. From the States there will be an immigration of at least 100,000. What does this mean? It means that hundreds of thousands of dollars are to be brought into Alberta for investment. Calgary will get its share of both the percentage of settlement and the investment of money. These buyers will want property---they may want yours. The market for quick turnover this fall is undoubtedly doubly assured. The best possible investment of any description for the amount of outlay, is Albert Park, the Subdivision to East Calgary---understand it plainly--- it is NOT a Subdivision to Calgary on the east, but a Subdivision to the town of East Calgary, which today, the supply for cheap adjacent building lots is big. The first payment on a lot in Albert Park is only $41.25---think of it---an investment of less than fifty dollars and six months to turn it in without another cent invested. The liability is small, the asset is big and the possibilities for profit are without question, the best that can possibly be offered the man with little money who wants to make it more.

Up to date, the sale of Albert Park lots has been going at a record rate and the number of wholesale purchases have been practically as large as the retail sales. Real estate agents have taken advantage of the proposition and have picked up entire blocks of the property with the view of reaping the big profit when the tide starts. If it is good enough for them in blocks of thirty and forty, is it good enough for you? The best are being selected first. The advice of the slogan, "Get It While You Can!" was never more imperative. Step in tomorrow, or even tonight, and select your lots. Automobiles at your service.

| Prices : $25 Extra for corners | $125 | Terms : 1-3 down, bal. 6 and 12 months. | Open Nights 9 o'clock | JOE | Limited Under Royal Bank of Canada | Phone 385 Phone |

East
Calgary

The
Choice
of the
Railroads

ALBERT
JOE

PARK
LIMITED
PHONE 385

East
Calgary

The
Choice
of the
Railroads

Follow That Impulse

A certain wise man with a long head once remarked that "The best way to get a chance is to take one." This philosophy is founded on a fact that is true to nature. When you strike a certainty, you generally strike limitations. The making of big profit always means the taking of risk. ¶ At one time it was considered that any profit to be made out of western real estate, was purchased at a risk. The percentage of risk has been reduced within the past few years to a very low figure; in fact, the element of speculation, if any at all, has been practically eliminated. ¶ Within the past thirty days the investing public have directed their attention to the possibilities of East Calgary, and have subsequently followed it up and evidenced their faith in the future by placing their money in property of every description in such a manner that it is now conceded by all to be the best possible investment offered the public. ¶ ALBERT PARK lies some ten blocks directly east of the industrial centre of East Calgary, and is at the present time the only consistent property available at such a low price to be found in or near the hotbed of realty activity. The property was placed on the market a week ago, and over one-fourth of it has been picked up by big and little buyers, for both speculative and investment purposes. ¶ If possible drop into our office today or tonight and look over the proposition, investigate it, get some information and then get some lots. Read price and terms below, and "Get It While You Can."

| Price $125 $25 Extra for Corners | Buy Today in ALBERT PARK "Get It While You Can" Open Nights 9 p.m. JOE Limited Under Royal Bank of Canada Phone 385 Phone | Terms One-Third down, balance six and twelve months; five per cent. discount for cash. |

... Any man or woman who has a hundred
dollars to invest should not hesitate to
secure one or more lots. They will be worth
double the money in a few months.

We advise you to buy just as quickly as
you possibly can. In doing this we are advising
you as we would a friend. You cannot lose:
it is safer than a gold mine; it is sure. You
can see it growing in value.

The people who achieve success, are the men
who enjoy the good things of life that money
buys, are the men who think quickly and act
unhesitatingly. If you put this matter off
until some other time the chances are you
won't get in at all. . . .

Since nobody intended to live on any of this land but only to turn it over for the fastest possible profit, large numbers of investors didn't even bother to inspect their property. Out-of-towners bought Calgary lots below the high-water mark of the Bow River. Thousands owned lots so far out on the empty prairie that it would be half a century before the land was actually developed. By 1911 all land within three to five miles of the Calgary post office was in the hands of speculators and selling for between fifty and three hundred dollars a lot. One section five and a half miles from the city sold for a million dollars. And there were at least ten subdivisions more than ten miles from the town centre. In Saskatoon, even after its boundaries were extended, there was enough subdivided land beyond the city limits to accommodate houses for half a million people.

"I'm subdividing my farm," an Edmonton lawyer told a friend in 1911. "It's half way between Edmonton and St. Albert. I haven't decided yet whether to make it a subdivision of Edmonton or St. Albert."

Western optimism, that admirable quality that sprang out of the painful but ultimately rewarding experience of settlement, was running out of control. The Calgary *Herald* of 1911 gloated over "a future of marvellous and ever-increasing prosperity reaching out ten years hence." It was only reflecting the giddy conceits of the city fathers who were planning electric trams to run to Banff, Lethbridge, and Medicine Hat and even talking of diverting the course of the Elbow River to accommodate the Canadian Northern. Nothing was considered too grandiose, too impossible in those heady days.

Even a devastating tornado in July, 1912, failed to dampen the spirits of Regina. The twister wrecked thirty-six blocks in the city's heart, destroying five hundred buildings and causing three hundred injuries and thirty-one deaths at a cost of $5 million. The Regina *Leader* brushed it all away as a man brushes an insect from his shoulder: "Nothing – mark the word – nothing – can check Regina's progress. . . . There is no fear of discouragement, no fear of the future. Trouble, difficulty, they are but spurring on our people. Disaster cannot check the advancement of a city with Regina's opportunities and with the spirit of her people."

Disaster of a different kind was already looming on the financial horizon, but few saw it coming. The most intelligent and, arguably, the most perceptive men in the West were blinded by the get-rich-quick frenzy. The president of the University of Alberta and an academic colleague owned a double corner lot at Whyte and 103rd in Edmonton, which they had purchased before the land boom. In 1912 they were offered thirty-three thousand dollars cash for the property. But like almost everybody, they had stars in their eyes and so turned it down. A few years later, unable to afford to keep up the tax payments, they lost it all.

4

The As the land boom roared to its climax, Westerners thought nothing of
lottery standing in queue for hours to pay inflated prices for property they had never seen. In Calgary, on a chilly April day in 1912, men stood in the pouring rain right through the night for a chance to buy a maximum of two lots, each priced at eleven hundred dollars, in a CPR subdivision optimistically named Sunalta. In Lethbridge, hundreds came prepared to camp for days in front of the land office to file for title to farm land until the authorities solved the problem by chalking a square on the pavement to mark each man's place and photographing him standing on it.

But the most astonishing queue of all formed up in Edmonton on the night of May 12, 1912, when some fifteen hundred people waited as long as sixteen hours, not to buy a lot, but simply to take part in a lottery that *might* allow them to buy a lot.

The land was part of the reserve deeded to the Hudson's Bay Company as part of the agreement made in 1870 when the firm ceded its territorial rights in the North West Territories to the new confederation of Canada. It was seen as prime property, six thousand acres surrounding the old trading post near the heart of the city. With the land boom at its height, the company decided to put up thirteen hundred lots for sale and agreed to spend half a million dollars on Portage Avenue, which ran through the heart of the new subdivision. In its turn, the city promised to add a double-track streetcar line. In the eyes not only of Edmontonians but also in those of real estate developers everywhere in the West, this property was truly a gold mine. How could it miss? With prices leaping up from day to day, each of these lots was the equal of a handsome bank account.

It was obvious that unless the sale was carefully managed a riot would ensue. To forestall it, the company decided to hold a lottery to determine which lucky persons would have a chance to buy up to four lots in the new subdivision. Tickets, numbered consecutively from 1 to 1,500 (more than there were lots available), would be placed in a drum at an undisclosed address. That address would not be announced until the first edition of the *Edmonton Bulletin* appeared on Monday morning, May 13. At two that afternoon the draw would commence.

The tickets were to be drawn, one at a time, until all fifteen hundred were dispensed. On the following day, May 14, the man holding ticket No. 1 would be given first choice of lots at the company's office. The other ticket holders would follow in numerical order, selecting their lots until all were sold. The company expected it would take five days to complete all the sales. Thus it was not enough simply to hold a lottery ticket because, if every ticket holder bought to his maximum, the lots would all be gone after ticket holder No. 325 made his selection.

That possibility deterred nobody. By Sunday, May 12, the city was taut with excitement. Everyone was asking: where will the draw be held? The company had taken extraordinary precautions to keep the address secret. The advertisement announcing the location would not reach the offices of the *Bulletin* before midnight, and all the employees of the paper were sworn to secrecy. The first copies were scheduled to roll off the presses at 5:30 a.m. Every important real estate man in town had runners with fast automobiles waiting at the door to seize a copy and speed away to the secret site. But long before this happened that secret was out.

At five the previous afternoon, a local grocer, F.T. Aitken, was

335

strolling down 103rd Street on his way to a Sunday band concert. His course took him past the Gospel Hall, between Athabasca and Peace. There he spied a group of men carting a typewriter and a safe into the building. Aitken guessed, correctly, that the lottery would be held there. He went to the Empire Theatre, enjoyed the band concert, then returned to the Gospel Hall and squatted on the front doorstep. He was soon joined by six real estate employees who had been nosing about the city searching for clues to the secret.

It took several hours for the news to filter through town. Few noticed the small group standing or sitting in front of the Gospel Hall. But by nine that evening the word was out, and for the next six hours a steady stream of humanity flowed toward the site.

It is 10 p.m., May 12, 1912, and we are waiting patiently in the human crocodile winding down the street from the Gospel Hall. The line has already turned the corner onto Athabasca, and now as more join it – women, children, men in their seventies, even – it moves down another block, turns the corner onto Second, and begins to snake its way down Second to the Castle Hotel. As the hours lengthen, so does the queue. By one in the morning it has circled the block. By 4 a.m. there are close to fifteen hundred people waiting with us for a chance to pull a low ticket from the drum when the lottery begins at two this afternoon.

The people sit on upended boxes, nail kegs, inverted buckets, lawn and kitchen chairs. Youngsters run up and down the line, hawking old boxes at a dollar and broken chairs at two dollars. Others offer to go a block for coffee and sandwiches, a fifteen-cent value now inflated to a dollar. The people are orderly except for one man who tries to break into the queue and clings to a fence, refusing to relinquish his spot, until four men begin to pummel him, and a policeman saves him from a worse beating.

A foursome plays bridge in the light from an automobile. Others, keeping a sharp lookout for their places in the line, throw quoits at a mark. Real estate men walk up and down offering large sums for a spot. Thousands of dollars are offered to the first ten men in line, but the price drops as the hucksters work their way farther back. One man offers $3,000 for three places in the 200s; he gets no takers. But place No. 341 goes for $140, and place No. 734 for $50. At the end of the line people hold up signs offering to sell their places, but those closer to the front refuse all offers.

336

Dawn breaks. One group lights a bonfire and starts cooking a breakfast of toast and coffee. The people are cold, tired, and a little nervous. Who can be sure if this is the right spot? Maybe it was all a ruse by the company to throw the hunters off the scent! Some real estate men have covered their bets by posting runners at the Bulletin *office as well as in the queue. One firm has a hundred men in the lineup.*

At last the news arrives: the paper is out; the Gospel Hall it is! A sigh of relief passes down the waiting hundreds and circles the block. It is Monday morning. The jobs of many standing here all night are threatened. But no one budges. Teachers who should be preparing for the classroom cling to their places, chancing reprimand or even dismissal. Who cares about tomorrow if Lady Luck will smile on him today?

The big real estate men arrive with coffee and sandwiches for their weary employees. Now the crowd grows restless. With more people standing in line than there are lots available, why wait until the afternoon to start the draw? A petition makes its way down the line urging immediate action. We all sign. Off to the Queen's Hotel trots a young law student to present the document to the Hudson's Bay land commissioner, who is eating a quiet breakfast and refuses to be disturbed. An hour later a Bulletin *reporter returns with the news. The company will not budge. The sale has also been advertised in the out-of-town papers. Hundreds will be arriving this morning by buggy, train, and automobile. If they were to find the sale has been held without them there would be a dreadful protest, even though none has a chance of getting a ticket.*

We all groan at this intelligence. It is nine o'clock. We have been waiting all night. But the man at the head of the line won't get his ticket for another five hours. And it could be another four before the entire queue is accommodated. And even then, if every early ticket holder selects four lots, almost three-quarters of us will be out of luck. We can only wait and hope.

Two o'clock came at last. A company employee, Jessie Kinnaird, churned the big drum containing all the tickets. Up stepped Aitken, the grocer, who had waited all night at the head of the line and turned down fifteen hundred dollars for his place. Miss Kinnaird put her hand into the drum and pulled out a ticket. Aitken had drawn No. 910, which meant that 909 others in the queue would have a chance to buy lots before his chance came. If even half chose to purchase their maximum of four lots each, he would be out of luck, his long vigil wasted.

The drawing continued at the rate of seven tickets a minute. More than two hours later, James Walsh, a retired farmer living in the Richelieu Hotel, stepped into the hall and waited for Miss Kinnaird to pull his ticket. She looked at it, looked at Walsh, looked at it again in surprise, and handed it to him. He gazed at it several times and then allowed a deep sigh to escape him. He had drawn the coveted ticket No. 1. When the crowd grasped the fact, three cheers went up. Walsh stepped out of the building to a second ovation. Somebody immediately offered him twenty-five thousand dollars for his ticket. He turned it down.

Others sold their tickets. Arthur Davies, the former mayor of Strathcona, who had paid forty-five dollars for a place in line at 1:30 a.m., drew ticket No. 87 and sold it for a thousand dollars. Ed Alexander, a young visitor to the city, drew ticket No. 5 and sold it for five thousand dollars; his friends had rousted him out of bed to take part in the all-night vigil. Real estate men bid briskly for low numbered tickets. Those in the twenties brought up to three thousand dollars; anything lower than 200 was good for five hundred dollars.

At last the lottery ended, the excitement died down, and suddenly the heart seemed to go out of the city. The entire community had been intoxicated by the land boom; the spree had reached its climax on this one demented night; and now Edmontonians were suffering a hangover. As they sobered up they began to ask themselves, as topers often do: did we really do all those crazy things? Did someone actually offer one man twenty-five thousand dollars for a chance to select four city lots, even before he *bought* those lots? By what logic was a place at the head of the queue worth any more than a place at the rear, when all had an equal chance at any ticket? Were all those sleepless, hungry hours worth it? Was the property itself worth it? Was it sensible to expect the boom to go on forever?

When an auction sale of the tickets was held in Edmonton's Separate School, the place was packed with the curious. Oddly, few tickets were sold. Those who had refused large sums for low-numbered tickets now tried to peddle them in barber shops, pool halls, and drugstores, only to discover that there were few takers. The fever had broken. In the end, the Hudson's Bay Company found that it could not sell all its lots. For Edmonton, and shortly for the West, the boom was at an end. Disillusionment, too, was catching.

5

In 1912, at the height of the boom, an itinerant evangelist, haranguing *Shattered*
passersby on Calgary's Eighth Avenue, cried out: "Woe unto you, real *dreams*
estate men; your folly is like that of Sodom. Repent before you reap
destruction." Few listened. Repentance did not come until 1913, and
by then it was too late.

It's easy to look back on this period and wonder why thousands of
otherwise sensible people went crazy over real estate. It seems obvious
that given the inflated prices based on paper profits, the bubble would
burst. But it wasn't so simple when the fever was at its height. When
you learned that a Boston grain merchant had stopped off in Edmonton en route to California and made six hundred dollars in four hours,
it was difficult not to plunge in. With low down payments, it didn't cost
much, and it didn't matter if your lot was on a cliffside or in a swamp.
All your neighbours, friends, and colleagues were dabbling in real
estate. If you didn't join the crowd you became an object of contempt
or pity. "*Get out of your rut!*" the real estate ads screamed. Had you
really come west, endured all the toil of homesteading, saved and
scraped to move out of that sod house, only to be left behind? Most
settlers had taken a chance, gambled with their future, seized an
opportunity to better themselves. Now, with opportunity hammering
away at the door, they were ready to gamble again.

They hadn't learned from history, and that is strange because
history was repeating itself with blinding speed. There were thousands
in Winnipeg and Edmonton who could not help but remember the
great boom of 1881, when the golden highway of the CPR inflated land
prices and touched off an almost identical craze; when lots in Portage
sold for fifteen hundred dollars and property on Winnipeg's Main
Street went for as high as two thousand dollars a front foot; when
Coolican the Real Estate King peddled property in the paper community of Cartwright at the rate of twenty thousand dollars' worth a
night; when there was one realtor in Winnipeg for every fifty people;
when names like Dobbyn City, Clearwater, Rapid City, and Minnedosa
were on everybody's lips; when Edmonton was a fool's paradise, with
lots worth twenty-five dollars going for four hundred; when little girls
gambled in lots for dolls' houses and everybody from the Lieutenant-
Governor of the Territories to new brides answered the pleas of the
speculators to come in and get their feet wet. When that bubble burst

339

in 1883, 75 per cent of the businesses in Manitoba were broke; but nobody apparently remembered.

The euphoria of 1910-12 was virtually identical. It seemed almost supernatural, this instant growth. As one returning Saskatoon citizen put it: ". . . you wonder if you are in a dream city or can this really be the little village of yesterday? Saskatoon has risen like a magic city. . . ." There was indeed a dreamlike quality to the boom. In the magic city of Saskatoon there was a subdivision actually called Utopia, one of fifty-two being touted at that time. The name was chosen in a public contest, won by a Miss Constance Cameron, who received a prize of fifty dollars from the developers – in gold, naturally. Another Saskatoon subdivision, to be known as Factoria, was to have "large factories and big shops with their noisy whirr of machinery, their huge stacks sending up great volumes of smoke and their shrieking whistles summoning hundreds of wage-earners to their daily labour." Factoria, it was said, would attract a million dollars' worth of industries and would have a population of two hundred in its first year. "When a man stops dreaming, he stops PROGRESS," one advertisement read. "A short time ago 'FACTORIA' was a dream – but the dream has come true. . . ." But the dream didn't come true; the project was dead by 1913. As for Utopia – a quarter-section of scrub brush – it wasn't developed until the late 1950s.

There were warnings, but few listened. In June, 1913, Sir Max Aitken, the future Lord Beaverbrook, no stranger to Western Canada, reported that the English money markets were drying up because the West was overborrowing. "The west . . . has been going too fast in a great many ways . . . Alberta financially has been anything but wise. The western municipalities generally have also been going it at a pace a great deal too rapid. . . ."

The same year, Henry Howard of the *Investor's Guardian* in London revealed that Saskatoon had nearly reached the limit of its credit. Most Western cities found themselves in the same predicament. The loan companies were out of money. Too many people had borrowed to buy land, too many businesses, riding the wave of boosterism, had overextended themselves. Interest rates leaped from 3 per cent to 9. "Tight money" became the phrase of the day.

Yet it was considered close to treason to hint at disaster. The newspapers continued to act as if the boom were in full swing. As late as July, 1913, the *Herald* was enthusing that "never before in the history of Calgary was there a more prosperous outlook for the city."

340

The Mayor dismissed gloomy reports about the city's finances; these were merely being spread by the city's enemies, he charged. That was the general line. When several American papers began to report the collapse of the boom, the *Herald* blamed it all on "knockers." But the knockers were right. A month later Calgary withdrew all its debentures from the bond market; they weren't selling. By this time the recession was in full swing.

The West was suffering from too much success. Like a celebrity who cannot cope with instant fame, it was done in by the pace of its development. It grew too quickly. Businessmen who had once been lauded for their "faith in the future" (a common expression in those days) now found the future had caught up with them. Few had paused to consider that the miraculous expansion of the first decade was not limitless. In the words of F. McClure Sclanders, Saskatoon's hard-headed trade commissioner, "the lily of the field never exhibited greater indifference for the morrow." Anybody felt they could do anything, Sclanders said, because credit was granted promiscuously and with almost prodigal generosity.

Land booms always collapse when prices become inflated, but there was more than that behind the slump of 1913. Though few faced up to it, this was the end of an era – an era of free land, wide-open settlement, easy money. The period of swift expansion was over because most of the free land was gone. The West was no longer empty of farmers. By 1913, 65 per cent of all prairie immigrants weren't going to the farms at all but to the burgeoning cities. In 1912, a special report had warned the government that its immigration policy must change: money should now be moved into the scientific development of the land.

With the European powers at each other's throats and the threat of war increasing, the international market for wheat was contracting. And, in spite of all the railway expansion, freight rates remained high because the railways were in trouble. They had helped produce the boom; now they contributed to its death. British investors could no longer be expected to carry the enormous burden of government and railway debt that was crushing the country. Building the federally owned National Transcontinental was costing twice as much as contemplated. The Grand Trunk Pacific was foundering on the cost of the mountain section. The Canadian Northern was in worse shape.

Mackenzie and Mann had got millions in provincial guarantees by promising to cover the West with a network of branch lines. Now, in order to pay for the mountain and eastern sections, they were forced to abandon construction of further feeders. Once again, the West saw itself sacrificed for outside interests.

The provinces were in no position to meet their guarantees. Saskatchewan had made an enormous commitment to the Canadian Northern. If the railway could·not meet its interest payments, the province would have to. But that sum was equal to half its annual budget. Mackenzie, looking haggard, worn out and twenty years older in the description of Laurier's Conservative successor, struggled to keep the tottering railway alive. The Prime Minister drove a hard bargain. The two partners were forced to forgive a $20-million debt owed them personally by the company and, in return for a new federal guarantee, to give up to the government another $40 million in stock. The final blow came when war was declared in Europe. Guarantees or no guarantees, Canadian Northern bonds were no longer marketable in London. The Canadian government still flinched from nationalizing the railway, but that, too, was inevitable. Apart from Russia, Germany, and the United States, Canada now had more miles of steel than any country in the world. It could not afford three transcontinental roads. Like the dream cities, the dream lines collapsed. The Canadian Northern became a government railway, like the National Transcontinental. The Grand Trunk Pacific slipped into bankruptcy and, with its parent, was eventually taken over. Thus was formed the Canadian National Railways System, which for the next half century would be saddled with a burden of debt produced by the boosterism of that first turbulent decade.

As the boom wound down, the prairie cities were left with vacant lots, scattered clusters of houses, half-finished buildings, empty subdivisions. By 1913, all business in Saskatoon had come to a stop. The much-touted Fairhaven subdivision, which went on the market in 1910 and was virtually sold out by 1911, was not opened for development until 1976. In Edmonton, seventy-five thousand lots went back to the city in lieu of tax payments. The Hudson's Bay Reserve, which had caused such excitement in 1912, stood empty for more than a quarter of a century, a desolate acreage of brushland, cut diagonally by Portage Avenue, renamed Kingsway in honour of the 1939 Royal Visit – an imposing boulevard, eight lanes wide, with scarcely a building on it. The reserve was not fully built up until the 1960s. In Calgary the story was the same: ten subdivisions stood empty until the 1960s. Who today has heard of Balaclava, Pasadena, Sarceedale, or Hiawatha?

Real estate operators such as Freddy Lowes, who continued to

342

borrow when others pulled back, went magnificently broke. Lowes's half finished mansion stood for years in southwest Calgary, a monument to overoptimism. Bert A. Stringer followed Lowes into oblivion, his roof garden cafe a dream turned into a nightmare. As Bob Edwards, the sanest voice in town, wrote in 1912: "Calgary never hears the truth about herself. Even though she did she wouldn't listen. The great trouble with the West is that it is never told the truth, men are afraid to open their mouths. . . ."

Edwards had it right. Even as the boom collapsed several Western cities were still contemplating grandiose schemes designed to enhance their prestige. Edmonton in 1913 was laying plans for a magnificent city centre surrounded by park land, gardens, fountains, and tree-shaded boulevards. Plans were still being drawn up as late as 1915, but the project never got past the drawing board.

Saskatoon brought in C.J. Yorath, a noted English planner, as city commissioner to redesign the community. Caught up in the traditional Western enthusiasm, Yorath failed to notice what was going on. "I believe the high optimism of Saskatoon is justified," he declared in 1913. "We are on the threshold of greatness." He had some difficulty superimposing the baroque features of a European circular plan on the narrow grid system of the Dream City, but his final drawings were impressive, showing broad avenues, boulevards, and parks. Unfortunately, the drawings are all that survive.

The real estate interests that controlled city planning had thought in terms of the largest number of lots on the smallest amount of acreage. The grid system of the prairie cities was by far the most profitable but by no means the most inviting. Tragically, by the time the city fathers in the West began to realize the need for city planning, the collapse of the boom made it financially impossible. Calgary, Regina, and Winnipeg brought out one of the best-known landscape architects and city planners in the world, Thomas Mawson. Regina managed to complete his scheme for Wascana Park, but Winnipeg didn't even bother to pay his bill. As for Calgary, his ambitious drawings for a new city ended up lining the walls of a garage. Mawson's plan might easily have turned Calgary into the Paris of the prairies, for he envisaged a circular system of roads with wide boulevards and arcaded sidewalks fronting on a civic square and leading to the CPR station, classically designed with pillars and statuary. But the plans for Calgary, like the plans for Utopia, remained a dream.

The dreams of the West were shattered finally by the nightmare of

343

the Great War. The dreamers themselves went off to the battlefields and were themselves shattered. Thousands who had crossed the ocean in search of the dream now re-crossed the water to defend it. Thus ended the golden years of the Canadian West, not with a whimper but with a bang.

In a single generation, the land between the Red River and the Rockies had been transformed. In that brief period, the West, a nation within a nation, had experienced infancy, childhood, adolescence, and now maturity. As a result, Canada itself was a different country, its character and outlook altered by the prairie miracle. After just eighteen years of settlement and boom, it could never again be the same.

Epilogue: On the Winnipeg Platform

It is a little before six on the afternoon of Saturday, August 15, 1914, and we are standing on the platform at the CPR station in Winnipeg, looking back at the packed depot, watching the new recruits of the Princess Patricia's Canadian Light Infantry bidding their friends and families goodbye.

It is a not unfamiliar scene. The tear-stained faces, the sea of fluttering handkerchiefs, the last-minute embraces are reminiscent of other farewells on other platforms and docksides in the years since 1896.

We have been here many times before. We stood on the Winnipeg platform at the beginning, when Josef Oleskow came through in 1895 on his way to the empty West, seeking a haven for his people. We were here two years later when the Humeniuk family and their Galician neighbours leaped through the train windows, refusing to go farther. We were here again that fall of 1897 to watch Prince Kropotkin board the westbound train after his trolley tour of Winnipeg; and we were here when the first of the Doukhobors arrived to be greeted by a harried Bill McCreary and pots of soup made by the women of the city. At Christmastime, in 1902, we stood on this same platform to watch the commanding figure of Peter Verigin step from his coach, and on a cold March midnight in 1908 we saw William Shepherd and his son George shiver their way from the colonist cars to the warmth of the immigration hall.

And we have stood on other platforms: at Brandon in 1896, to see the triumphant homecoming of Clifford Sifton; at Saskatoon in 1903, to watch the Barr colonists tumbling off the cars; at Calgary in 1906, to witness the American invasion; at Edmonton in 1911, to observe the crowd of curbside brokers mulcting the would-be fortune hunters as they, too, stepped from the train.

The railway platform, like the sod hut and the grain elevator, is a genuine Western artifact, a springboard to settlement; and the railway itself, more than the beaver or the maple leaf, is our true national emblem. For if the symbol of American expansion is the covered wagon, then the symbol of Canadian expansion has been the colonist car, with its slatted seats and its single glowing stove.

We stand now, as the bugles sound and the flags flutter, at the neck of the funnel through which almost every homesteader has been squeezed on his journey to the promised land. This worn platform at Winnipeg bears the marks of hundreds of thousands of feet – boots and oxfords, brogues and moccasins, shoe packs and slippers.

But now we are witnessing a reversal of the familiar process, a departure, not an arrival. Five hundred and fifty young men recruited for the new regiment are saying their last goodbyes and lining up to leave the West, some of them forever. They come from all across the prairies: 74 from Winnipeg, 64 from Saskatoon, 14 from Prince Albert, 260 from Calgary and Edmonton, and now, as another train puffs in, 123 from Moose Jaw, these last in full uniform, purchased with their own money.

The others are still in mufti – labourers in soiled overalls, farmers in field clothes, office workers in ready-made suits and starched collars. As they are herded from the depot to line up in fours on the platform, the tears begin to flow. A woman rushes forward and pushes a baby into one man's arms; he carries it as far as the gate, covering its face with kisses. Then he hands it back and is gone with the others.

They pull in their stomachs and chins, thrust out their chests as the Veterans' Band strikes up the National Anthem. The farewell words of the district officer commanding, Colonel Sam Steele, Big Jim McGregor's old adversary, ring in their ears as they board the eighteen-car special: "This land has been your home for some time and I hope you will return in good health and spirits. . . . Shoot well and be men all the time."

Tens of thousands will follow, and if we were to stay here on the platform watching the troop trains pull out, month after month, year after year, we would recognize some familiar faces: Rattlesnake Pete, the remittance man from Edmonton, one of the first to rush to the colours; Mike Mountain Horse from the Blood Indian reserve, who discarded his Indian dress at the residential school; the Shepherds' young son, Harry, who will have a close call at Amiens; D.E. MacIntyre, the Moose Jaw storekeeper turned real estate salesman, who will rise to be a lieutenant-colonel and win a D.S.O. at Vimy; and others whom we recognize only in the mass – all the anonymous Dutchmen and Scots, Icelanders and Danes, Barr colonists and displaced Ontario farmers, together with so many of their sons, grown to manhood on the harsh prairie and destined for a grave in Flanders, including some of those same children who, on a bright September day

346

in 1905, stood in Victoria Park in the Queen City of the Plains, waving their flags, singing of Wolfe the Conquering Hero, and listening to their governor general tell them that some day they must be prepared to sacrifice themselves for the sake of their country, for the sake of the Promised Land.

Author's Note

The Promised Land is the final volume in a tetralogy dealing with the opening of the Canadian North West in the half-century following Confederation. It begins with *The National Dream*, which describes the beginning of the vision of a nation extending from sea to sea. *The Last Spike* details the culmination of that vision: the building of a railway to the Pacific Coast. *Klondike* is the tale of the gold rush that focused the eyes of Canadians on their own northland. The present volume completes the story.

The book has had a long gestation period. My intention was to complete it immediately following the publication of the revised and expanded edition of *Klondike* in 1973. I did a year of preliminary research with the assistance of Glen Wright but in the end decided the task was too formidable and put it aside. In the years that followed, I published nine other books, but this one was always in my thoughts. Finally, in 1981, I decided to tackle it again with the help of Barbara Sears, who has been my research assistant on six other books.

The result is not meant to be definitive. No single volume could be. I have not gone into detail, for example, about every ethnic group that came to this country before the First World War; their experiences, after all, did not differ greatly from those I have described here.

Although much of my research comes from primary sources, a study of this complexity must necessarily lean on the spadework of others. All are listed in the accompanying bibliography, but I should like to single out some for special mention.

I found *The Doukhobors* by George Woodcock and Ivan Avaku-movic to be the best work on that subject. Unfortunately, the authors did not have access to the James Mavor papers in the Thomas Fisher Rare Book Library at the University of Toronto. I was able to examine these through the kindness of the late Dora Mavor Moore; I am also grateful to her son Francis Mavor Moore for allowing me to read and make use of his two monographs on the Doukhobor emigration based on his grandfather's records. Helen Evans Reid's story of the Barr phenomenon, *All Silent, All Damned*, was extremely useful, especially in the background material she so diligently unearthed about Barr's background and subsequent history. She is more charitable towards Isaac Barr than myself, but that does not detract from her research.

Readers who would like to know more about Ella Sykes are directed to her own book, *A Home Help in Canada*. The Shepherd family story is told in George Shepherd's *West of Yesterday*, and the saga of the Humeniuk family from Galicia is related by Peter Humeniuk in *Hardships & Progress of Ukrainian Pioneers*.

Other secondary sources that I found especially useful include the initial volume of D.J. Hall's *Clifford Sifton*, the first new biography of the Minister since Dafoe's flawed work; James B. Hedges's *Building the Canadian West*; Harold M. Troper's *Only Farmers Need Apply*; Karel Denis Bicha's *The American Farmer and the Canadian West*; Grant MacEwan's *Eye Opener Bob*; James Gray's *Red Lights on the Prairies* and *Booze*; Paul F. Sharp's *The Agrarian Revolt in Western Canada*; Alan F.J. Artibise's collection, *Town and City*; Ruben Bellan's *Winnipeg First Century*; A.W. Rasporich and H. Klassen's collection, *Frontier Calgary*; and J.G. MacGregor's *Vilni Zemli*.

The book would not have been possible without the help of a number of people. The indispensable Barbara Sears again proved to be invaluable in searching out hard-to-find sources and poring through the various archives and libraries to supply me with raw material. Ennis Armstrong helped to organize the research with the assistance of Diane Jermyn. Caryle Jakobsen typed and re-typed the various drafts of the manuscript, always at top speed. Without the critical assistance of Janice Tyrwhitt Patton, who forced me to rewrite most of an entire draft, this would be a lesser work. Janet Craig, who has one of the sharpest eyes in publishing, again saved me from inconsistencies and imbecilities. Elsa Franklin's help and advice were invaluable. My wife, Janet, who is, in my opinion, the best proofreader in Canada, kept the finished typescript clear of errors.

Miss Sears and I would also like to thank the following people and institutions for their assistance: Lindsay Moir and Hugh Dempsey at the Glenbow Museum; Gordon Dodds at the Provincial Archives of Manitoba; Norma Dainard and her staff at the Metropolitan Toronto Central Library Newspaper section; the staff of the Canadian History department, Metropolitan Toronto Central Library; Fred McGuinness at the Brandon *Sun*; Andrea Clarke at the Oklahoma Historical Society; Stan Horrall, RCMP historian; Jean Dryden at the Provincial Archives of Alberta; the Saskatchewan Archives Board; the staff of the Public Archives of Canada; the Minnesota Historical Society; the Athabasca Public Library; the University of Manitoba Archives; the Cameron Library, University of Alberta; the Ontario Archives; Roy St. George Stubbs; Charlie Thompson; Charles Woodsworth; Grace MacInnis; and Mrs. Alice Dexter.

Select Bibliography

Unpublished Manuscript Material

Public Archives of Canada:

MG 27 II D15	*Clifford Sifton Papers*
MG 27 II B1	*Minto Papers*
MG 29 C16	*Mavor Papers*
RG 76/65101	*Immigration Records: the Doukhobors*
RG 15	*Department of the Interior Records*
RG 18	*RCMP Records*
RG 2	*Privy Council Office Records*
RG 10	*Department of Indian Affairs Records*
RG 76/194804	*Immigration Records: the Barr Colonists*
MG 26 G	*Laurier Papers*

RCMP Archives:
Transcript, interview with Christian Junget

Saskatchewan Archives Board:
Oral history tapes: interview with Paul Sylvester Hordern by D.H. Bocking
E.J. Ashton reminiscences
Robert Holtby diary
Alice Rendell letters
J.A. Donaghy reminiscences
Stanley Rackham diary

Thomas Fisher Rare Book Library, University of Toronto:
James Mavor Papers

Legislative Library, Manitoba:
Robson, H.A. "Report of the Commission on Social Vice"

Ontario Archives:
RG 22, 6-2, no. 63279   Clifford Sifton will

Manitoba Archives:
J.W. Sifton will

Athabasca Public Library:
J.D. Edwards interview

Government Documents – Published

Census, 1901 and 1911
House of Commons, Debates, 1896–1915
Senate, Debates, 1896–1914

350

House of Commons, Journals, 1899, vol. 34. "Report of the Select Standing Committee on Agriculture and Colonization. Immigration and Settlement in 1898."

_____ 1903, vol. 38, appendix. "Canadian Immigration in 1902."

_____ 1904, vol. 39, app. 2. "Report of the Select Standing Committee on Agriculture and Colonization."

_____ 1906, vol. 41, app. 3. "Report of the Public Accounts Committee Concerning the Accounts of the North Atlantic Trading Company."

_____ appendix. "Report of the Select Standing Committee on Agriculture and Colonization, Part II, Immigration and Colonization."

_____ 1908, vol. 43. "Report of the Public Accounts Committee Relating to Payments in Connection with Timber Agencies in Edmonton and Calgary."

House of Commons, Sessional Papers, "Annual Report of the Department of the Interior," 1897–1914

_____ "Annual Report of the Northwest Mounted Police," 1897–1914

_____ "Annual Report of the Department of Indian Affairs," 1897–1914

Newspapers

Brandon Independence [Independent], 1898–1902

Brandon Sun, 1896–1900

Calgary Herald, 1896–1914

Edmonton Bulletin, 1896–1906, 1912

Eye Opener (Calgary), 1902–1914

Globe (Toronto), June 1899, January-February 1906

Grain Growers' Guide, 1915

Manitoba Free Press, 1896–1914

Okemah Ledger, March 1911

Regina Leader, 1911–1912

St. Paul Pioneer Press, March 1911

Saskatoon Phenix, 1902–1903

Scarlet and Gold, 1956

Toronto News, 1899, 1908, 1915

Winnipeg Tribune, 1896–1914

Published Primary Sources

Abbott, Edith (ed.). *Immigration: Select Documents and Case Records*. New York: New York Times/Arno Press, 1969.

Ames, Herbert P. *Our Western Heritage and How It Is Being Squandered by the Laurier Government*. N.p., 1908.

Artibise, Alan F.J. *Gateway City: Documents on the City of Winnipeg 1873–1913*. Winnipeg: Manitoba Record Society Publications, vol. 5, 1979.

Beaverbrook, Lord. *Friends*. London: Heinemann, 1959.

Bickersteth, J.B. *The Land of Open Doors*. London: Wells Gardner, Darton, 1914.

Blackburn, J.H. *Land of Promise*. Toronto: Macmillan, 1970.

Borden, Henry (ed.). *Robert Laird Borden: His Memoirs*. Toronto: Macmillan, 1938.

Canada, Department of the Interior. *The Last Best West.* Ottawa: 1907.

Clark, A.F.B. "Winnipeg in 1904," *Canadian Magazine*, vol. 25, no. 2, 1905.

Comer, J.G. *Across the Canadian Prairies.* London: European Mail Ltd., n.d.

Copping, Arthur. *Canada, the Golden Land.* New York: Hodder and Stoughton, 1911.

Crossley, F. Ivan. "My Life with the Barr Colony," *Blackwoods Magazine*, vol. 291, March, 1962.

Curwood, James Oliver. "The American Invasion of Canada," *Overland Monthly,* vol. 41, 1903.

———— "The Effects of the American Invasion," *World's Work*, vol. 10, 1905.

———— *Son of the Forest.* New York: Grosset & Dunlap, 1930.

Davies, Evan, and Vaughan, Aled. *Beyond the Old Bone Trail.* London: Cassell, 1960.

Deane, R.B. *Mounted Police Life in Canada.* London: Cassell, 1916.

Fraser, John Foster. *Canada As It Is.* London: Cassell, 1905.

Gray, James. *The Boy from Winnipeg.* Toronto: Macmillan, 1970.

Griesbach, W.A. *I Remember.* Toronto: Ryerson, 1946.

Hanna, D.B. *Trains of Recollection.* Toronto: Macmillan, 1924.

Hobson, J.A. *Canada To-day.* London: T. Fisher Unwin, 1906.

Homesteader [pseud.]. *Canadian Life As I Found It.* London: Elliott Stock, 1908.

Hough, Emerson. *The Sowing.* Winnipeg: 1909.

Hubbard, Elbert. *A Little Journey to Saskatoon.* New York: Roycrofters, 1913.

Humeniuk, Peter. *The Hardships & Progress of Ukrainian Pioneers.* Winnipeg: Humeniuk, 1977.

Jeffs, Harry. *Homes and Careers in Canada.* London: J. Clarke, 1914.

Kaye, Vladimir J. *Early Ukrainian Settlements in Canada 1895–1900: Dr. Josef Oleskow's Role in the Settlement of the Canadian Northwest.* Toronto: Univ. of Toronto Press, 1964.

Knappen, Theodore M. "Western Canada in 1904," *American Review of Reviews*, vol. 30, 1904.

———— "Winning the Canadian West," *World's Work*, vol. 10, 1905.

Kropotkin, P. "Some of the Resources of Canada," *Nineteenth Century*, March, 1898.

Lowes, F.C. "The Romance of City Building," *Sphere*, 22 February 1913.

Lyle, G.R. "Eye-witness to Courage," *Saskatchewan History*, vol. 20, no. 3, 1967.

McCormick, J. Hanna. *Lloydminster, or 5,000 Miles with the Barr Colonists.* London: Ye Olde St. Brides Press, c.1924.

McNeil, Bill. *Voice of the Pioneer.* Toronto: Macmillan, 1978.

Martin, Sandra, and Hall, Roger (eds.). *Rupert Brooke in Canada.* Toronto: PMA Books, 1978.

Maude, Aylmer. *A Peculiar People.* New York: Funk and Wagnalls, 1904.

Mavor, James. *My Windows on the Street of the World.* 2 vols. Toronto: J.M. Dent, 1923.

Mawson, Thomas. *The Life and Work of an English Landscape Architect.* N.p., n.d.

Meighen, Arthur. *Unrevised and Unrepented.* Toronto: Clarke, Irwin, 1949.

Mountain Horse, Mike. *My People the Bloods.* Calgary: Glenbow-Alberta Institute and Blood Tribal Council, 1979.

Nordegg, Martin. *The Possibilities of Canada Are Truly Great.* Toronto: Macmillan, 1971.

Pick, Harry. *Next Year.* Toronto: Ryerson, 1928.

Piniuta, Harry (ed.). *Land of Pain, Land of Promise.* Saskatoon: Western Producer Prairie Books, 1978.

Pope, Maurice. *Public Servant: The Memoirs of Sir Joseph Pope.* Toronto: Oxford Univ. Press, 1960.

Preston, W.T.R. *My Generation of Politics and Politicians.* Toronto: D.A. Rose, 1927.

Rendell, Alice. "Letters from a Barr Colonist," *Alberta Historical Review*, vol. 11, no. 1, 1963.

A Session's Disclosures: Some Transactions of the Laurier Administration in the Session of 1906. N.d.

Shortt, Adam. "Some Observations on the Great Northwest," *Queen's Quarterly*, vol. 2, 1895.

———— "Some Observations on the Great Northwest II," *Queen's Quarterly*, vol. 3, 1895.

Shepherd, George. *West of Yesterday.* Toronto: McClelland and Stewart, 1965.

Sifton, Clifford. "The Immigrants Canada Wants," *Maclean's*, 1 April 1922.

———— "The Needs of the Northwest," *Canadian Magazine*, vol. 20, no. 5, 1903.

Stewart, Basil. *No English Need Apply, or Canada As a Field for Immigration.* London: George Routledge, 1909.

Stewart, William R. "The Americanization of the Canadian Northwest," *Cosmopolitan*, vol. 34, 1903.

Sykes, Ella C. *A Home Help in Canada.* London: Smith, Elder and Co., 1912.

———— *Through Persia on a Side-Saddle.* London: John MacQueen, 1901.

Talbot, F.A. *Making Good in Canada.* London: Adam and Charles Black, 1912.

Timber Administration. N.d.

Trotter, Beecham. *A Horseman and the West.* Toronto: Macmillan, 1925.

Tweedale, Capt. C. "The Barr Colony," *Maclean's*, 15 May 1938.

Whates, Harry R. *Canada, the New Nation.* London: J.M. Dent, 1906.

Woodsworth, J.S. "Pump Them In – But Whom?" *Christian Guardian*, 27 November 1907.

———— *Report of a Preliminary and General Social Survey on Regina, September 1913 Made by the Department of Temperance and Moral Reform of the Methodist Church and the Board of Social Service and Evangelism of the Presbyterian Church.* N.p., 1913.

———— *Strangers within Our Gates.* Toronto: Univ. of Toronto Press, 1972 (reprint).

———— (ed.) *Ukrainian Rural Communities. Report of the Investigation by the Bureau of Social Research.* Winnipeg: Governments of Manitoba, Saskatchewan and Alberta, 1917.

Secondary Sources

Armytage, W.H.G. *Heavens Below.* Toronto: Univ. of Toronto Press, 1961.

Artibise, Alan F.J. *Town and City: Aspects of Western Canadian Urban Development*. Regina: University of Regina, 1981.

―――― *Winnipeg: A Social History of Urban Growth*. London/Montreal: McGill–Queen's University Press, 1975.

Avery, Donald. "Canadian Immigration Policy and the 'Foreign' Navvy 1896–1914," *Canadian Historical Association Papers*, 1972.

Beard, Geoffrey. *Thomas H. Mawson, a Northern Landscape Architect*. Lancaster: University of Lancaster Visual Arts Centre, 1978.

Bedford, Judy. "Prostitution in Calgary 1905–1914," *Alberta History*, vol. 29, no. 2, 1981.

Bellan, Ruben. *Winnipeg First Century: An Economic History*. Winnipeg: Queenston Publishing House, 1978.

Berton, Pierre. "Edmonton: A Boom at the Crossroads," *Maclean's*, 15 July 1949.

―――― *The Last Spike: The Great Railway 1881–1885*. Toronto: McClelland and Stewart, 1971.

―――― *The National Dream: The Great Railway 1871–1881*. Toronto: McClelland and Stewart, 1970.

―――― *The Wild Frontier: More Tales from the Remarkable Past*. Toronto: McClelland and Stewart, 1978.

Betke, Carl. "The Mounted Police and the Doukhobors in Saskatchewan 1899–1909," *Saskatchewan History*, vol. 27, no. 1, 1974.

Bicha, Karel Denis. *The American Farmer and the Canadian West 1896–1914*. Lawrence, Kansas: Coronado Press, 1968.

―――― "The North Dakota Farmer and the Canadian West 1896–1914," *North Dakota History*, vol. 29, 1962.

―――― "The Plains Farmer and the Prairie Province Frontier," *Proceedings of the American Philosophical Society*, vol. 109, 1965.

Cameron, Ruth. "The Wheat from the Chaff: Canadian Restrictive Immigration Policy 1905–1911." Unpublished M.A. thesis, Concordia University, 1976.

Cashman, Anthony W. (Tony). *The Best Edmonton Stories*. Edmonton: Hurtig, 1976.

―――― *The Edmonton Story: The Life and Times of Edmonton, Alberta*. Edmonton: Institute of Applied Art, 1956.

―――― *More Edmonton Stories: The Life and Times of Edmonton, Alberta*. Edmonton: Institute of Applied Art, 1958.

Chalmers, J.W. "Strangers in Our Midst," *Alberta Historical Review*, vol. 16, Winter, 1968.

Clark, Walter L. "Politics in Brandon City 1899–1949." Unpublished Ph.D. thesis, University of Alberta, 1976.

Coats, R.H., and Maclean, M.C. *The American Born in Canada*. Toronto: Ryerson, 1943.

Cook, Ramsay. *The Politics of John W. Dafoe and the Free Press*. Toronto: Univ. of Toronto Press, 1963.

Cooper, Joy. "Red Lights of Winnipeg," *Historical Society of Manitoba Transactions*, ser. 3, no. 27, 1970–71.

Dafoe, John W. *Clifford Sifton in Relation to His Times*. Toronto: Macmillan, 1931.

―――― "Western Canada, Its Resources and Possibilities," *American Monthly Review of Reviews*, vol. 35, June, 1907.

Dempsey, Hugh (ed.). *The Best from Alberta History.* Saskatoon: Western Producer Prairie Books, 1981.

———— *The Best of Bob Edwards.* Edmonton: Hurtig, 1975.

———— *Indian Tribes of Alberta.* Calgary: Glenbow-Alberta Institute, 1978.

———— (ed.). *Men in Scarlet.* Calgary: Historical Society of Alberta/McClelland and Stewart West, c.1974.

———— *The Wit and Wisdom of Bob Edwards.* Edmonton: Hurtig, 1976.

Donnelly, Murray. *Dafoe of the Free Press.* Toronto: Macmillan, 1968.

Doyle, James (ed.). *Yankees in Canada.* Toronto: ECW Press, 1980.

Drake, Earl G. *Regina, the Queen City.* Toronto: McClelland and Stewart, 1955.

Dunae, Patrick. *Gentlemen Emigrants.* Vancouver/Toronto: Douglas and McIntyre, 1981.

Dutkiewicz, Henry T.K. "Some Aspects of Polish Peasant Immigration to North America from Austrian Poland between the Years 1863 and 1910." Unpublished M.A. thesis, University of Ottawa, 1958.

Elkington, Joseph. *The Doukhobours, Their History in Russia, Their Migration to Canada.* Philadelphia: Ferris and Leach, 1903.

Ewanchuk, Michael. *Pioneer Profiles: Ukrainian Settlers in Manitoba.* Winnipeg: Michael Ewanchuk, 1981.

Foran, Max. "Bob Edwards and Social Reform," *Alberta History*, vol. 21, no. 3, 1973.

———— "The Boosters in Boosterism: Some Calgary Examples," *Urban History Review*, vol. 8, no. 2, 1979.

———— *Calgary: An Illustrated History.* Toronto: James Lorimer/National Museum of Man, 1978.

Fowke, V.C. *Canadian Agricultural Policy: The Historical Pattern.* Toronto: Univ. of Toronto Press, 1947.

———— *The National Policy and the Wheat Economy.* Toronto: Univ. of Toronto Press, 1956.

Fraser, Blair. "The Many, Mighty Siftons," *Maclean's*, 19 December 1959.

———— "The Vast, Turbulent Empire of the Siftons," *Maclean's*, 5 December 1959.

Fraser, W.B. *Calgary.* Calgary: Alberta Teachers' Assoc., 1967.

Fyfe, Hamilton. "The Pure Politics Campaign in Canada," *Nineteenth Century*, October, 1907.

Goddard, P.E. "Notes on the Sun Dance of the Sarsi," *American Museum of Natural History Anthropological Papers*, vol. 16, pt. 4. New York: 1919.

Gray, James. *Booze.* Toronto: Macmillan, 1972.

———— *Red Lights on the Prairies.* Toronto: Macmillan, 1971.

Grover, R., and Moore, Francis Mavor. *James Mavor and His World.* Toronto: Univ. of Toronto Press, 1975.

Hall, D.J. *Clifford Sifton:* vol. 1., *The Young Napoleon 1861–1900.* Vancouver: Univ. of British Columbia Press, 1981.

———— "The Political Career of Clifford Sifton 1896–1905." Unpublished Ph.D. thesis, University of Toronto, 1972.

———— "Clifford Sifton and Canadian Indian Administration 1896–1905," *Prairie Forum*, vol. 2, no. 2, 1977.

Hansen, M.L., and Brebner, J.B. *The Mingling of the Canadian and American Peoples.* Toronto: Ryerson, 1940.

355

Hardy, Dennis. *Alternative Communities in 19th Century England.* London/New York: Longmans, 1979.

Haydon, A.L. *The Riders of the Plains.* Edmonton: Hurtig, 1971.

Heber, E. "Charles Wesley Speers – Dynamic Colonizer of Western Canada," *Historical Society of Manitoba Transactions*, ser. 3, no. 28, 1971–72.

Hedges, James B. *Building the Canadian West: The Land Colonization Policies of the Canadian Pacific Railway.* New York: Macmillan, 1939.

————— *The Federal Railway Land Subsidy Policy of Canada.* Boston: Harvard Univ. Press, 1934.

Holmgren, Eric J. "Isaac M. Barr and the Britannia Colony." Unpublished M.A. thesis, University of Alberta, 1964.

Horrall, S.W. *A Pictorial History of the Royal Canadian Mounted Police.* Toronto: McGraw-Hill/Ryerson, 1973.

Kelly, L.V. *The Range Men.* New York: Argonaut Press, 1965.

Kelly, Nora and William. *The Royal Canadian Mounted Police.* Edmonton: Hurtig, 1973.

Kerr, D.C. "Saskatoon 1910 – 1913: Ideology of the Boomtime," *Saskatchewan History*, vol. 32, no. 1, 1979.

Kesterton, W.H. *A History of Journalism in Canada.* Toronto: McClelland and Stewart, 1967.

Klassen, Henry C. (ed.). *The Canadian West.* Calgary: Univ. of Calgary, 1977.

Kostash, Myrna. *All of Baba's Children.* Edmonton: Hurtig, 1977.

Liddell, Ken. "The Farmers of Amber Valley," *Western Producer*, 1 December 1949.

Longstreth, T. Morris. *The Silent Force.* London: Philip Allan, 1927.

Lyle, G.R. "The Rev. Isaac M. Barr: Apostle of the Canadian Northwest," *American Book Collector*, vol. 17, no. 2, 1966.

Lysenko, Vera. *Men in Sheepskin Coats: A Study in Assimilation.* Toronto: Ryerson, 1947.

McCarthy, D.J. "At Rest But Ready," *Scarlet and Gold*, 38th ed., 1956.

McClung, Nellie. *In Times Like These.* Toronto: Univ. of Toronto Press, 1972 (reprint).

————— *The Stream Runs Fast.* Toronto: Thomas Allen, 1945.

McCormack, A. Ross. "Radical Politics in Winnipeg: 1899–1915," *Historical and Scientific Society of Manitoba Transactions*, ser. 3, no. 29, 1972–73.

McDougall, Duncan M. "Immigration into Canada 1851–1920," *Canadian Journal of Economics and Political Science*, vol. 27, no. 2, 1961.

MacEwan, J.W.G. *Calgary Cavalcade, from Fort to Fortune.* Edmonton: Institute of Applied Art, 1958.

————— *Eye Opener Bob.* Edmonton: Institute of Applied Art, 1957.

MacGregor, J.G. *Edmonton, A History.* Edmonton: Hurtig, 1967.

————— *Vilni Zemli: The Ukrainian Settlement of Alberta.* Toronto: McClelland and Stewart, 1969.

MacInnis, Grace. *J.S. Woodsworth.* Toronto: Macmillan, 1953.

MacIntyre, D.E. *Prairie Storekeeper.* Toronto: Peter Martin Associates, 1970.

Mackintosh, W.A. *Prairie Settlement: The Geographic Setting.* Toronto: Macmillan, 1934.

McLean, John. "Isaac Barr: Missionary Extraordinary," *Canadian Church Historical Journal*, vol. 6, no. 1, 1964.

MacLeod, R.C. *The North-West Mounted Police and Law Enforcement.* Toronto: Univ. of Toronto Press, 1976.

_____ "The North-West Mounted Police 1873–1905: Law Enforcement and Social Order in the Canadian Northwest." Unpublished Ph.D. thesis, Duke University, 1972.

McNaught, Kenneth. *A Prophet in Politics: A Biography of J.S. Woodsworth.* Toronto: Univ. of Toronto Press, 1959.

MacRae, Archibald. *History of the Province of Alberta.* 2 vols. Western Canada History Co., 1912.

Moore, Francis Mavor. "James Mavor: The Doukhobour Papers, Immigration and Settlement." Unpublished paper, 1982.

_____ "James Mavor: The Doukhobour Papers, Preliminary Negotiations." Unpublished paper, 1982.

Morton, W.L. *The Progressive Party in Canada.* Toronto: Univ. of Toronto Press, 1950.

_____ "The Social Philosophy of Henry Wise Wood, the Canadian Agrarian Leader," *Agricultural History*, vol. 22, 1948.

Norrie, K.H. "The Rate of Settlement of the Canadian Prairies 1870–1911," *Journal of Economic History*, vol. 35, June, 1975.

Oliver, Edmund H. "The Coming of the Barr Colonists," *Canadian Historical Association Annual Report*, 1926.

_____ "The Settlement of Saskatchewan to 1914," *Transactions of the Royal Society of Canada*, ser. 3, vol. 20, sec. 2, 1926.

Orlikow, Lionel. "The Reform Movement in Manitoba 1910–1915," *Historical Society of Manitoba Transactions*, ser. 3, no. 16, 1961.

Palmer, Howard. *The Settlement of the West.* Calgary: Univ. of Calgary/Comprint Publishing Company, 1977.

Peel, Bruce. *The Saskatoon Story.* Saskatoon: Melville East, 1952.

Pickett, James. "An Evaluation of Estimates of Immigration into Canada in the Late Nineteenth Century," *Canadian Journal of Economics and Political Science,* vol. 31, 1965.

Raby, Stewart. "Indian Land Surrenders in Southern Saskatchewan," *Canadian Geographer*, vol. 17, no. 1, 1973.

Rasporich, A.W., and Klassen, H.C. (eds.). *Frontier Calgary.* Calgary: Univ. of Calgary/ McClelland and Stewart West, 1975.

_____ (eds.). *Prairie Perspectives.* Toronto: Holt, Rinehart, and Winston, 1973.

Rees, R. "The 'Magic City' on the Banks of the Saskatchewan: The Saskatoon Real Estate Boom 1910–1913," *Saskatchewan History*, vol. 27, no. 2, 1974.

Regehr, T.D. *The Canadian Northern Railway.* Toronto: Macmillan/ Maclean-Hunter, 1976.

Reid, Helen Evans. *All Silent All Damned.* Toronto: Ryerson, 1969.

_____ "The Clerical Con Man Who Helped Settle the West," *Maclean's,* 14 December 1963.

Riddell, W.A. *Regina, from Pile o' Bones to Queen City of the Plains: An Illustrated History.* Burlington: Windsor Publications, 1981.

Roe, Frank G. "The Sod House," *Alberta Historical Review*, vol. 18, no. 3, 1970.

Rolph, William K. *Henry Wise Wood of Alberta.* Toronto: Univ. of Toronto Press, 1950.

Savage, Candace. *Our Nell: A Scrapbook Biography of Nellie McClung.* Saskatoon: Western Producer Prairie Books, 1979.

Schull, Joseph. *Laurier, The First Canadian.* Toronto: Macmillan, 1965.

Sessing, Trevor W. "How They Kept Canada Almost Lily White," *Saturday Night,* September, 1970.

Sharp, Paul. *The Agrarian Revolt in Western Canada.* Minneapolis: Univ. of Minnesota Press, 1948.

–––––– "The American Farmer and the Last Best West," *Agricultural History,* vol. 21, 1947.

–––––– "When Our West Moved North," *American Historical Review,* vol. 55, 1950.

Shortt, S.E.D. *The Search for an Ideal: Six Canadian Intellectuals and Their Convictions in an Age of Transition.* Toronto and Buffalo: Univ. of Toronto Press, 1976.

Skelton, O.D. *The Life and Letters of Sir Wilfrid Laurier.* 2 vols. New York: Century, 1922.

–––––– *The Railway Builders.* Toronto: Glasgow, Brook and Co., 1916.

Sloan, Robert W. "The Canadian West – Americanization or Canadianization?" *Alberta Historical Review,* vol. 16, no. 1, 1968.

Spafford, D.S. "The Elevator Issue, the Organized Farmers and the Government," *Saskatchewan History,* vol. 15, no. 3, 1962.

Sproule, Albert F. "The Role of Patrick Burns in the Development of Western Canada." Unpublished M.A. thesis, University of Alberta, 1962.

Stevens, G.R. *Canadian National Railways.* 2 vols. Toronto: Clarke Irwin, 1962.

Strange, H.G.L. *A Short History of Prairie Agriculture.* Winnipeg: Searle Grain Co., 1954.

Stubbs, Roy St. George. *Lawyers and Laymen of Western Canada.* Toronto: Ryerson, 1939.

Symmes, Natalie. "Nellie McClung of the West," *Canada Monthly,* February, 1916.

Tallant, Clive. "The Break with Barr," *Saskatchewan History,* vol. 6, no. 2, 1953.

–––––– "The North West Mounted Police and the Barr Colony," *Saskatchewan History,* vol. 7, no. 2, 1954.

Thomas, L.C. "The Rancher and the City: Calgary and Cattlemen, 1883–1914," *Transactions of the Royal Society of Canada,* vol. 6, ser. 4, June, 1968.

Timlin, Mabel F. "Canada's Immigration Policy 1896–1910," *Canadian Journal of Economics and Political Science,* vol. 26, 1960.

Troper, Harold M. "The Creek Negroes of Oklahoma and Canadian Immigration 1909–1911," *Canadian Historical Review,* vol. 53, no. 3, 1972.

–––––– "Official Canadian Encouragement of American Immigration 1896–1911." Unpublished Ph.D. thesis, University of Toronto, 1971.

–––––– *Only Farmers Need Apply.* Toronto: Griffin House, 1972.

Turner, Allan R. "Pioneering Farm Experiences," *Saskatchewan History,* vol. 8, no. 2, 1955.

Urquhart, M.C. (ed.). *Historical Statistics of Canada.* Toronto: Cambridge Univ. Press/Macmillan, 1965.

Vandermeulen, E.G. "Mawson – A Landscape Architect at the Turn of the Century," *Architecture Canada,* vol. 43, no. 9, 1966.

Waddell, W.S. "The Honourable Frank Oliver." Unpublished M.A. thesis, University of Alberta, 1950.

Watkins, Ernest. *R.B. Bennett.* Toronto: Kingswood House, 1963.

Wetton, C. *The Promised Land.* Lloydminster: n.d.

Willison, John. *Sir Wilfrid Laurier and the Liberal Party.* London: John Murray, 1903.

Winks, Robin W. *The Blacks in Canada: A History.* Montreal: McGill—Queen's Univ. Press, 1971.

Wood, Louis Aubrey. *A History of the Farmers' Movements in Canada.* Toronto and Buffalo: Univ. of Toronto Press, 1975.

Woodcock, George, and Avakumovic, I. *The Doukhobors.* Toronto: Oxford Univ. Press, 1968.

Wright, J.F.C. *Slava Bohu.* New York: Farrar and Rinehart, 1940.

Young, Charles H. *The Ukrainian Canadians.* Toronto: Thomas Nelson, 1931.

Yuzyk, Paul. "The First Ukrainians in Manitoba," *Historical and Scientific Society of Manitoba Papers,* ser. 3, no. 8, 1953.

Ziegler, Olive. *Woodsworth, Social Pioneer.* Toronto: Ontario Publishing Co., 1934.

Zieman, Margaret K. "Nellie Was a Lady Terror," *Maclean's*, 1 October 1953.

Zubek, John P., and Solberg, Patricia Ann. *The Doukhobours at War.* Toronto: Ryerson, 1952.

Notes

Abbreviations used:

APL   Athabasca Public Library
AR   Annual Report
CH   *Calgary Herald*
EB   *Edmonton Bulletin*
HCD   *House of Commons, Debates*
HCJ   *House of Commons, Journals*
HCSP   *House of Commons, Sessional Papers*
LLM   Legislative Library, Manitoba
MFP   *Manitoba Free Press*
OA   Ontario Archives
PAC   Public Archives of Canada
RL   *Regina Leader*
SAB   Saskatchewan Archives Board
SGIA   Superintendent General of Indian Affairs
TDS   *Toronto Daily Star*
TFL   Thomas Fisher Rare Book Library
WDT   *Winnipeg Daily Tribune*

page	line	**Prologue**
1	33	MacGregor, *Vilni Zemli*, p. 77
2	4	Ibid., p. 79.
3	2	Ibid., p. 82.
3	11	Ibid., p. 81.
3	19	Ibid., 82.
3	26	Ibid., p. 78.
3	39	Ibid., p. 82.
6	7	Kaye, p. 131.

The Young Napoleon of the West

page	line	
9	18	Brandon *Sun*, 26 Nov. 1896.
10	19	Ibid.
10	27	Hall, *Clifford Sifton*, vol. 1, p. 68.
10	33	Ibid.
11	3	Ibid., p. 27.

page	line	
11	14	Dafoe, *Sifton*, pp. 105-6.
11	23	CH, 23 Dec. 1896.
11	28	Hall, *Clifford Sifton*, vol. 1, p. 126.
12	2	Quoted in ibid., p. 35 and Notes p. 312.
12	8	PAC, MG 27 II D15, 19 March 1897, Sifton to Arthur.
12	11	Troper, *Only Farmers*, p. 17.
12	28	PAC, MG 27 II D15, 4 Aug. 1897, Macmillan to Sifton.
12	37	Troper, *Only Farmers*, pp. 26-30 *passim*.
13	11	Fowke, *Canadian Agricultural Policy*, p. 178.
14	18	PAC, MG 27 II D15, 9 Feb. 1904, Sifton to Smart.
14	34	Palmer, p. 77.
14	36	PAC, MG 27 II D15, 10 May 1898, Sifton to Smart.
15	1	Palmer, p. 77.

page	line	
15	*30*	MFP, 1 May 1897.
15	*32*	Timlin, pp. 521-22.
15	*36*	Troper, *Only Farmers*, p. 85.
16	*7*	CH, 8 April 1898.
16	*34*	PAC, MG 27 II D15, 5 July 1897, Sifton to Van Horne.
17	*4*	Shepherd, p.8.
17	*25*	Troper, *Only Farmers*, pp. 94-95.
17	*28*	Ibid.
17	*34*	Hall, *Clifford Sifton*, vol. 1, p. 258.
18	*1*	Troper, *Only Farmers*, p. 90.
18	*3*	Sharp, "When our West," p. 289.
18	*4*	HCSP, 1897, no. 13, 27 Jan. 1897, High Commissioner to Minister of Interior.
18	*5*	HCSP, 1898, no. 13, 15 Jan. 1898, High Commissioner to Minister of Interior.
18	*8*	HCJ, 1899, vol. 34, app. 3, p. 281.
18	*14*	MFP, 5 Jan. 1904.
18	*23*	Curwood, *Son*, pp. 198-201.
18	*32*	PAC, MG 27 II D15, 12 April 1902, Dafoe to Sifton.
18	*39*	McNeil, p. 131.
19	*12*	Fraser, J.F., p. 169.
19	*16*	*Globe* (Toronto), 18 Nov. 1896.
19	*23*	Dafoe, *Sifton*, p. 48.
19	*31*	PAC, MG 27 II D15, 31 July 1897, Sifton to Richardson.
19	*34*	Ibid., 31 July 1897, Sifton to A.G. Rutherford.
20	*3*	Ibid., 7 April 1899, Sifton to Isaac Campbell.
20	*5*	Ibid., 25 Feb. 1902, Sifton to J.W. Greenway.
20	*11*	Ibid., 4 July 1900, Sifton to Willison.
21	*11*	Ibid., 3 March 1897, 22 April 1899, Sifton to his father.
21	*38*	Berton, *National Dream*, p. 243 ff.
23	*9*	Hall, *Clifford Sifton*, vol. 1, p. 95.
23	*19*	PAC, MG 27 II D15, 10 May 1899, Sifton to Willison.
23	*23*	Ibid.
23	*31*	Hall, *Clifford Sifton*, vol. 1, p. 216.
23	*37*	CH, 22 Oct. 1904.
24	*6*	Fraser, Blair, "Many, Mighty Siftons."
24	*22*	PAC, MG 27 II B1, vol. 2, 20 Oct. 1902, note on conversation between Minto and Laurier.
24	*28*	WDT, 4 Oct. 1905.
24	*36*	Quoted in WDT, 30 Sept. 1902.
25	*4*	OA, RG 22, 6-2, no. 63279.
25	*10*	Trotter, p. 192.
25	*28*	PAC, MG 27 II D15, 1 Dec. 1903, Sifton to Smith.
26	*8*	Ibid., 19 Nov. 1903, Sifton to Dafoe.
26	*11*	Ibid., 21 Aug. 1903, Sifton to Harkin.
26	*14*	Ibid., 16 Aug. 1900, Sifton to Greenway.
26	*21*	Ibid., 2 Oct. 1900, Smith to Sifton.
26	*31*	Ibid., 15 Jan. 1897, Sifton to Laurier.
27	*7*	PAC, MG 27 II B1, vol. 2, 20 Oct. 1902, note on conversation between Minto and Laurier.
27	*15*	PAC, MG 27 II D15, 5 Feb. 1897, Sifton to Borden.
27	*26*	Ibid., 24 July 1897, Sifton to Shaughnessy.
27	*32*	Ibid.
28	*9*	Ibid., 28 Feb. 1898, Sifton to McCreary.
28	*21*	Ibid., 18 Feb. 1897, Sifton to Paterson.
28	*23*	Ibid., 9 Sept. 1901, Sifton to Smith.
28	*27*	Ibid., 13 March 1897, Sifton to Burgess.
28	*33*	Ibid., 18 Aug. 1897, Sifton to Campbell.
28	*40*	Ibid., 24 Oct. 1898, Sifton to Willison.
29	*20*	Hall, *Clifford Sifton*, vol. 1, p. 57.
29	*21*	Ibid.
29	*27*	Ibid., pp. 215-16.
29	*35*	PAC, MG 27 II D15, 9 Nov. 1898, Sifton to Campbell.
30	*2*	Ibid., 14 Nov. 1898, Sifton to Rutherford.
30	*3*	Ibid., 16 Nov. 1898, Sifton to Husband.
30	*8*	Ibid., 19 Jan. 1899, Sifton to Gregory.
30	*13*	WDT, 13 Jan. 1899.
30	*19*	PAC, MG 27 II D15, 20 Aug. 1898, Sifton to Smart.
30	*21*	Ibid., 7 Nov. 1898, Sifton to Young.

page line   page line

30	27	Undated clipping, WDT.
31	16	CH, 22 Oct. 1904.
31	36	Orlikow, pp. 57-58.
32	13	Fyfe.
32	21	Hall, *Clifford Sifton*, vol. 1, p. 133.
32	26	WDT, 13 Nov. 1901, 23 April 1904, 4 Feb. 1902, 28 Sept. 1904.
32	27	WDT, 23 April 1904.
32	29	Ibid., 4 Feb. 1903.
32	30	Ibid., 4 Feb. 1902.
32	35	Ibid., 28 Sept. 1904.
34	9	PAC, MG 27 II D15, 27 July 1900, Sifton to Macklin.
34	24	Donnelly, p. 43.
34	37	Ibid., pp. 12-13.
35	11	PAC, MG 27 II D15, 29 March 1901, Sifton to Dafoe.
35	15	WDT, 30 Jan. 1902.
35	18	PAC, MG 27 II D15, 27 Nov. 1901, Dafoe to Sifton.
36	11	Ibid., 30 March 1904, Sifton to Dafoe.
36	18	Ibid., 28 Sept. 1904, Sifton to Dafoe.
36	22	Ibid.
36	31	Clark, Walter L., p. 34n.
36	34	PAC, MG 27 II D15, 9 Jan. 1902, Dafoe to Sifton.
36	36	Ibid., 1 Oct. 1902, Dafoe to Sifton.
36	38	Ibid., 18 Oct. 1901, Dafoe to Sifton.
37	3	Ibid., 27 Dec. 1902, Dafoe to Sifton.
37	13	Ibid., 27 Nov. 1901, Dafoe to Sifton.
37	19	Ibid., 22 Jan. 1904, Dafoe to Sifton.
37	31	Ibid., 7 April 1904, Dafoe to Harkin.
38	26	Ibid., 9 Jan. 1912, Sifton to Dafoe.

The Sheepskin People

42	13	MacGregor, *Vilni Zemli*, p. 1.
42	21	Kaye, p. 10.
42	26	Humeniuk, p. 10.
42	35	Sifton, "Immigrants."

43	35	Humeniuk, pp. 29-30.
44	18	Dutkiewicz, p. 78.
44	25	Ibid., pp. 78-79.
44	28	Ibid., p. 79.
44	31	Ibid.
45	3	Kaye, p. 281.
45	11	Ibid., p. 282.
45	23	Ibid., pp. 282-84.
47	15	Abbott, pp. 86-90 *passim*.
47	35	Ibid., p. 86.
48	20	MacGregor, *Vilni Zemli*, p. 96.
48	34	Kaye, pp. 192-93.
48	40	Shepherd, pp. 11-12.
49	4	Davies and Vaughan, p. 13.
49	11	Abbott, p. 92.
49	31	Piniuta, pp. 55-56.
50	6	Quoted in MFP, 1 Feb. 1904.
50	17	Piniuta, p. 99.
50	28	MacGregor, *Vilni Zemli*, p. 92.
50	32	Humeniuk, p. 42.
50	35	Piniuta, p. 56.
51	3	Kaye, pp. 105-6.
51	10	CH, 19 July 1897.
51	19	Piniuta, p. 57.
51	26	Ibid.
51	39	Kaye, p. 160, 14 May 1897, McCreary to Smart.
53	3	Humeniuk, p. 43, and conversation with author.
53	15	Griesbach, p. 204.
53	30	Lysenko, pp. 55-56.
53	39	Kaye, p. 67, 28 May 1896, Van Horne to Burgess.
54	1	HCSP, no. 28, 1903, AR NWMP p. 27.
54	3	Kaye, p. 73.
54	6	WDT, 5 Nov. 1898.
54	10	Kaye, p. 365.
54	14	Ibid., p. 366.
54	20	MFP, 14 Sept. 1901.

page	line	
_54_	_25_	Quoted in MFP, 1 Feb. 1904.
_54_	_26_	_Brandon Independent_, 23 June 1898.
_54_	_28_	Quoted in MFP, 1 Feb. 1904.
_54_	_32_	EB, 14 Dec. 1896, 7 June 1897.
_54_	_37_	MFP, 18 Jan. 1899.
_55_	_3_	MFP, 1 Feb. 1904.
_55_	_4_	MFP, 4 July 1903.
_55_	_6_	MFP, 8 Feb. 1904.
_55_	_11_	MFP, 1 Feb. 1904.
_55_	_19_	MFP, 27 Feb. 1900.
_55_	_25_	WDT, 27 June 1899.
_55_	_26_	WDT, 24 Feb. 1902.
_56_	_3_	Quoted in MFP, 1 Feb. 1904.
_56_	_6_	Ibid.
_56_	_13_	PAC, MG 27 II D15, 13 July 1900, Magurn to Sifton.
_56_	_19_	Quoted in MFP, 3 Feb. 1904.
_56_	_28_	MFP, 8 Feb. 1904.
_56_	_33_	Ibid.
_57_	_10_	Piniuta, p. 114.
_57_	_14_	Ibid.
_57_	_32_	MacGregor, _Vilni Zemli_, pp. 235-36.
_57_	_38_	EB, 7 June 1897.
_57_	_39_	CH, 22 April 1901.
_58_	_1_	Ibid.
_58_	_21_	MacGregor, _Vilni Zemli_, p. 192.
_58_	_34_	Griesbach, pp. 216-17.
_58_	_40_	MacGregor, _Vilni Zemli_, pp. 190-91.
_59_	_3_	Ibid., p. 194.
_59_	_35_	EB, 30 March 1899.
_60_	_3_	Quoted in MFP, 15 July 1898.
_60_	_10_	MFP, 3 Aug. 1897.
_60_	_13_	CH, 9 Oct. 1897.
_60_	_27_	Dafoe, "Western Canada," p. 703.
_60_	_39_	Woodsworth, _Strangers_, p. 112.
_61_	_6_	Ibid., p. 8.
_62_	_4_	Ibid., p. xix.
_62_	_12_	MFP, 15 Nov. 1898.
_62_	_21_	Woodsworth, _Strangers_, p. 256.

page	line	**The Spirit Wrestlers**
_68_	_17_	Kropotkin, pp. 498-507 _passim_.
_68_	_34_	Ibid., pp. 504-5.
_70_	_1_	Armytage, p. 349.
_70_	_2_	Hardy, p. 187.
_70_	_6_	Ibid.
_70_	_10_	Ibid.
_71_	_16_	PAC, MG 29 C16, 10 July 1898, Kropotkin to Mavor.
_71_	_22_	Shortt, S.E.D., p. 121.
_71_	_32_	Ibid.
_71_	_35_	Ibid.
_72_	_4_	Moore, "Preliminary Negotiations," p. 5.
_72_	_20_	Ibid., p. 15.
_72_	_24_	Maude, p. 47.
_72_	_34_	Armytage, p. 352.
_72_	_36_	Moore, "Preliminary Negotiations," p. 21; Maude, p. 46.
_73_	_3_	TFL, Mavor Papers, notes of conversation with Planedin, Nov. 1902.
_73_	_15_	Moore, "Preliminary Negotiations," p. 15.
_73_	_20_	Ibid., p. 17.
_73_	_28_	Ibid., pp. 29 and 31.
_73_	_37_	Moore, "Immigration and Settlement," p. 12.
_74_	_7_	Moore, "Preliminary Negotiations," p. 33.
_74_	_11_	Ibid., pp. 38-41.
_74_	_25_	Ibid., p. 42.
_75_	_26_	Wright, p. 128.
_76_	_20_	Ibid., pp. 128-30; Ottawa _Journal_, 25 Jan. 1899; Chicago _Sunday Tribune_, 5 Feb. 1899.
_76_	_26_	Wright, p. 131.
_76_	_37_	PAC, RG 76/65101, memo re Doukhobors.
_76_	_39_	Ibid.
_77_	_7_	Ibid., 14 Oct. 1898, McCreary to Smart.
_77_	_17_	Ibid., 14 Dec. 1898, McCreary to Smart.
_77_	_28_	PAC, RG 76/65101, memo re Doukhobors.
_77_	_34_	Ibid.

page	line	
78	1	PAC, MG 27 II D15, 29 April 1899, McCreary to Sifton.
78	6	PAC, MG 27 II D15, 13 Jan. 1899, McCreary to Whitla.
78	14	PAC, RG 76/65101, 5 Jan. 1899, McCreary to Smart.
78	22	Ibid.
78	32	PAC, RG 76/65101, 28 Jan. 1899, McCreary to Smart.
78	40	Ibid.
79	5	Ibid., Toronto *Evening News*, 2 Feb. 1899.
79	14	Ibid.
79	16	PAC, RG 76/65101, 28 Jan. 1899, McCreary to Smart.
79	31	Ibid., 9 Feb. 1899, McCreary to Smart.
79	39	Ibid., 31 Jan. 1899, McCreary to Smart.
80	16	Ibid., 31 Jan. 1899, 9 Feb. 1899, McCreary to Smart.
80	20	Ibid., 9 Feb. 1899, McCreary to Smart.
80	24	Ibid., 16 Feb. 1899, McCreary to Smart.
80	33	Moore, "Immigration and Settlement," p. 20.
81	4	Ibid., p. 27.
81	32	PAC, RG 76/65101, 31 Jan. 1899, McCreary to Smart.
83	22	Mavor, *My Windows*, vol. 2, pp. 7-8.
83	30	MFP, 28 Aug. 1902.
83	41	PAC, RG 18/1447/199, 14 Aug. 1899, Insp., Duck Lake, to Commissioner.
84	4	PAC, RG 76/65101, 1 Feb. 1899, ? to Pedley.
84	9	PAC, RG 18/295/263, 21 Nov. 1902, Strickland to OC, Regina.
85	7	MFP, 1 March 1902.
85	27	Ibid., PAC, RG 76/65101, pt.6, 25 Oct. 1902, Pedley to Sifton.
86	12	London *Free Press*, 31 Jan. 1899.
86	14	*Halifax Herald*, 16 Dec. 1899.
86	15	*Ottawa Citizen*, 22 Jan. 1899.
86	24	Ibid., 29 Jan. 1899.
87	11	WDT, 31 Oct. 1902; PAC, RG 76/65101, pt.6, 26 Nov. 1902, Speers to Pedley.
87	40	PAC, RG 76/65101, pt.6, 26 Nov. 1902, Speers to Pedley.
88	16	Ibid.; WDT, 31 Oct. 1902.
88	32	PAC, RG 76/65101, pt.6, 10 July 1902, Speers to Pedley.
88	33	Ibid., 9 Aug. 1902, Smith to Pedley.
88	38	Ibid., 11 Aug. 1902, Speers to Pedley.
89	4	HCD, 26 March 1903, p. 542.
89	37	Quoted in Woodcock and Avakumovic, pp. 176-77.
90	20	WDT, 30 Oct. 1902; PAC, RG 76/65101, pt.6, 26 Nov. 1902, Speers to Pedley.
90	29	Ibid.
91	5	WDT, 3 Nov. 1902.
91	16	WDT, 6 Nov. 1902.
91	21	Ibid.
91	30	WDT, 10 Nov. 1902.
92	8	Ibid.
93	5	Ibid.
93	11	PAC, RG 18/295/263, 21 Nov. 1902, Strickland to OC Regina.
93	23	Quoted in WDT, 4 Nov. 1902.
93	40	EB, 14 Nov. 1902.
94	11	WDT, 10 Nov. 1902.
95	11	MFP, 23 Dec. 1902.
95	36	PAC, RG 76/65101, pt.7, 27 Dec. 1902, Archer to Moffat.
96	7	PAC, RG 18/295/203, 19 Jan. 1903, Junget weekly report.
96	23	Zubek and Solberg, p. 70.
96	34	PAC, RG 76/65101, pt.7, 13 April 1903, Speers to Scott.
97	4	TDS, 15 April 1903; PAC, RG 76/65101, pt.7, 31 March 1903, Harley to Smith.
97	10	Mavor, *My Windows*, vol. 2, p. 24.
98	3	PAC, RG 18/295/263, 14 May 1903, Spalding to Parker; statement of Cons. Glisby; statement of Cons. Melanson.
98	7	PAC, RG 18/295/263, 5 May 1903, Spalding to Parker.
99	33	WDT, 3 June 1907.
99	40	WDT, 4 June 1907.

page	line	
118	*33*	SAB, interview with P.S. Hordern; Wetton, p. 17.
119	*25*	TFL, Mavor Papers, interview with Ivan Crossley.
119	*26*	SAB, interview with P.S. Hordern.
120	*3*	*Ottawa Citizen*, 14 April 1903.
120	*4*	*Globe*, 13 April 1903.
120	*5*	WDT, 7 April 1903.
120	*6*	MFP, 7 April 1903.
120	*12*	Toronto *News*, 14 April 1903.
120	*19*	HCSP, 1904, no. 25, 1 Aug. 1903, Speers to Supt. of Immigration.
120	*30*	SAB, Rackham diary, 16 April 1903.
121	*13*	Ibid., 17 April 1903.
121	*19*	TDS, 22 April 1903.
121	*23*	Lyle, p. 87.
121	*31*	SAB, interview with P.S. Hordern.
121	*34*	Lyle, p. 89.
122	*27*	McCormick, pp. 39-40; Toronto *News*, 27 April 1903.
123	*35*	Toronto *News*, 24 and 25 April 1903.
124	*15*	PAC RG 76/255/194804, pt.2, 27 May 1903, Speers to Scott; Minneapolis *Journal*, 23 April 1903.
124	*24*	TDS, 18 April 1903; 23 April 1903.
124	*30*	CH, 29 May 1903.
124	*36*	Oliver, "Coming of Barr Colonists," p. 73.
125	*6*	Saskatchewan *Herald*, 6 May 1903; Toronto *News*, 28 April 1903.
125	*11*	Pick, p. 42.
125	*12*	PAC, RG 76/255/194804, pt.2, 23 April 1903, Speers to Smith.
125	*18*	Ibid., 27 May 1903, Speers to Smart.
125	*27*	Toronto *News*, 28 April 1903.
125	*36*	Toronto *News*, 27 April 1903.
125	*40*	TDS, 27 April 1903.
126	*7*	SAB, interview with P.S. Hordern.
127	*19*	TDS, 27 April 1903.
127	*23*	Ibid.
127	*24*	Ibid.
127	*27*	Ibid.
127	*31*	Toronto *News*, 27 April 1903.
127	*33*	Oliver, "Coming of Barr Colonists," p. 70.
127	*38*	TDS, 16 April 1903.
128	*3*	Ibid.
129	*10*	SAB, Rackham diary, 24 April 1903.
129	*29*	Lyle, pp. 92-93.
130	*15*	SAB, Donaghy reminiscences, section 1.
130	*29*	SAB, Holtby diary, trekking (written 22/23 July 1903).
130	*34*	SAB, Rackham diary, 1 and 3 May 1903.
131	*17*	Lyle, p. 95.
131	*22*	SAB, Holtby diary, trekking.
131	*37*	Ibid.
132	*29*	Tallant, "Break with Barr," p. 42.
133	*5*	PAC, RG 76/255/194804, pt.2, 27 May 1903, Speers to Scott.
133	*12*	SAB, Holtby diary, trekking.
134	*6*	Tweedale.
134	*21*	Lyle, p. 104.
134	*26*	Crossley, p. 241.
134	*34*	SAB, E.J. Ashton reminiscences.
135	*3*	PAC, RG 76/255/194804, pt.2, 20 May 1903, Speers to Smart; 6 June 1903, Smart to Preston; 6 June 1903, Smart to Speers; 27 May 1903, Speers to Smart.
135	*11*	CH, 19 May 1903.
135	*19*	PAC, RG 76/255/194804, pt.4, 31 May 1904, Smart to Sifton.
135	*26*	Reid, *All Silent*, pp. 119, 123.

The Problem of the English

page	line	
138	*14*	Senate, Debates, 15 April 1903.
138	*23*	HCSP, no. 13, 1898, pp. 40-44, 25 Dec. 1897, Fleming to High Commissioner.
139	*12*	Quoted in Hall, *Clifford Sifton*, vol. 1, p. 268.
139	*28*	Stewart, Basil, p. 1.
139	*32*	Ibid., p. 7.
139	*38*	Ibid., p. 85.
140	*40*	HCD, 13 July 1905, p. 9461.

141	4	Timlin, p. 523.
141	10	Woodsworth, *Strangers*, p. 9.
141	12	Ibid., p. 46.
141	17	Ibid., p. 51.
141	20	Ibid., p. 54.
141	24	Ibid., p. 240.
141	29	Whates, p. 51.
141	35	Stewart, Basil, p. 7.
141	39	HCD, 13 July 1905, p. 9461.
142	2	Ibid.
145	4	Homesteader, p. 117.
145	10	1911 Census.
145	33	Davies and Vaughan, p. 23.
146	12	Ibid., p. 89.
146	22	Ibid.
146	41	MFP, 19 Feb. 1902.
147	25	*Eye Opener*, 24 Oct. 1903.
147	40	Boston *Globe*, 11 March 1906.
148	11	Kennedy, Howard, *New Canada and the New Canadians* (London: Horace Marshall, 1907), p. 100.
148	28	*Eye Opener*, 2 Dec. 1905.
148	35	Dempsey, *Best of Alberta History*, p. 46.
148	39	Ibid., p. 47.
149	8	Ibid.
149	31	Cashman, *Edmonton Story*, pp. 204-5.
150	16	PAC, RG 76/255/194804, pt.3, 31 July 1903, Langley to Smith.
150	16	SAB, J.A. Donaghy reminiscences.
150	29	Toronto *News*, 14 April 1903.
150	34	Copping, p. 75.
151	2	PAC, RG 76/255/194804, pt.3, 15 July 1903, Langley to Smith.
152	9	Crossley, p. 242.
152	24	PAC, RG 76/255/194804, pt.3, 6 July 1903, Snow to Commissioner of Immigration.
153	8	*Scarlet and Gold*, 38th ed., 1956, p. 44.
153	26	SAB, Rendell MSS., 19 Jan. 1904, Alice Rendell to friends.

153	33	PAC, RG 76/255/194804, pt.3, 30 Oct. 1903, Speers to Scott.
153	39	Ibid.
154	5	Ibid., 30 Oct. 1903, Speers to Smith.
154	8	Ibid., 30 Oct. 1903, Speers to Scott.
154	16	Boston *Evening Transcript*, 21 Nov. 1903.
154	21	PAC, RG 76/255/194804, pt.4, 4 April 1904, Speers to Scott.
154	33	Ibid., 13 June 1904, Speers to Scott.
155	11	Ibid., 3 July 1905, Speers to Cory.
155	13	TFL, Mavor Papers, Box 41, 18 Nov. 1905, Speers to Mavor.
155	19	Ibid., 2 Feb. 1907, Riddington to Mavor.
155	21	Ibid., 8 Jan. 1906, Jemmett to Mavor, encl.
155	26	SAB, E.J. Ashton reminiscences.
155	29	PAC, RG 76/255/194804, pt.4, *Weekly Telegraph*, Sheffield, 19 March 1904 and other issues.
155	32	SAB, Rackham diary, introduction.
156	7	Crossley, pp. 251-53.
156	16	Sykes, *Home Help*, p. vii.
156	27	Sykes, *Through Persia*, p. 3.
157	3	Sykes, *Home Help*, p. viii.
157	6	Ibid., p. ix.
157	29	Ibid., pp. 7 and 8.
157	41	Ibid., p. 20.
158	6	Ibid.
159	8	Ibid., p. 29.
159	21	Fraser, John, p. 111.
160	6	Sykes, *Home Help*, p. 55.
160	18	Ibid., p. 97.
160	27	Ibid., p. 99.
160	34	Ibid., p. 100.
161	24	Ibid., p. 124.
161	37	Ibid., pp. 124-25.
162	14	Ibid., pp. viii, xi.
163	6	Shepherd, pp. 2-6 *passim*.
163	25	Ibid., p. 9.
164	14	Ibid., pp. 15-18.
164	18	Ibid., p. 18.

165   10   Ibid., pp. 18-21.

166   10   Ibid., pp. 24-27.

166   34   Ibid., pp. 30-34.

166   41   Ibid., p. 45.

167   11   Ibid., p. 46.

167   14   Ibid.

The American Invasion

170   3   Hall, *Clifford Sifton*, vol. 1, p. 132.

170   20   Bicha, *American Farmer*, p. 80.

170   25   1901 and 1911 Census.

171   19   Brandon *Sun* Centenary issue, January 1982.

171   26   Bicha, *American Farmer*, p. 64.

171   30   Troper, *Only Farmers*, p. 62.

172   16   Bicha, *American Farmer*, pp. 68-69.

172   21   Troper, *Only Farmers*, pp. 48-49; Hedges, *Building*, p. 140.

172   38   Bicha, *American Farmer*, p. 72; Troper, *Only Farmers*, p. 93.

173   10   Troper, *Only Farmers*, p. 81.

173   15   Sharp, "When our West," p. 297.

173   17   Ibid.

173   25   Troper, *Only Farmers*, p. 108.

173   27   Ibid., pp. 109-11.

173   36   Ibid.

173   41   Ibid., p. 110.

174   17   WDT, 28 Jan. 1904.

174   22   Troper, *Only Farmers*, p. 111.

174   41   MFP, 23 Oct. 1903.

175   8   MFP, 13 April 1904.

175   17   1911 Census.

175   26   CH, 7 June 1912.

176   19   WDT, 26 Feb. 1906.

176   28   Quoted in Regina *Standard*, 10 May 1905.

177   5   CH, 9 March 1906.

177   8   CH, 12 March 1906.

177   12   Ibid.

177   20   CH, 9 March 1906.

177   24   CH, 19 March 1906.

177   33   CH, 12 March 1906.

177   40   CH, 10 March 1906.

180   8   *Grain Growers' Guide*, 27 Oct. 1915.

180   24   Knappen, "Winning Canadian West."

180   38   Ibid.

181   1   Ibid.

181   6   Ibid.

181   18   Troper, *Only Farmers*, p. 87.

181   20   Laut, "The Last Trek to the Last Frontier," *Century Magazine*, vol. 78, 1909.

181   36   WDT, 6 Jan. 1903.

182   6   Woodsworth, *Strangers*, p. 158.

182   8   Ibid.

182   25   Troper, *Only Farmers*, p. 124.

182   29   Ibid., p. 130.

182   35   Sessing, pp. 31-32.

183   1   Quoted in Troper, *Only Farmers*, p. 126.

183   6   Ibid., pp. 125-26.

183   15   Troper, "Creek Negroes," p. 284 and note.

183   24   Winks, p. 309.

183   26   Ibid., p. 310.

184   8   Ibid., p. 303; "Between the Rivers," (Maidstone, Sask., Jubilee Committee, 1955), p. 19.

184   19   Winks, p. 306.

184   30   Ibid.; Liddell, *Farmers*.

184   32   APL, J.D. Edwards interview.

184   39   *St. Paul Pioneer Press*, 21 and 23 March 1911.

185   15   Ibid., 22 March 1911.

185   21   *Okemah Ledger*, 23 March 1911; *St. Paul Pioneer Press*, 23 March 1911.

185   29   Blackburn, p. 24.

185   37   *Okemah Ledger*, 23 March 1911; *St. Paul Pioneer Press*, 23 March 1911.

186   3   *Okemah Ledger*, 23 March 1911.

186   5   Sessing.

186   6   Troper, *Only Farmers*, pp. 135-36.

186   12   Ibid., p. 134.

The Passing of the Old Order

page	line	
211	16	McNeil, p. 17.
211	28	Hall, "Indian Administration," p. 128.
211	32	Quoted in Hall, "Indian Administration," p. 138.
211	34	HCSP, no. 27, 1906, p. 153, 4 Sept. 1905, McNeill to Pedley.
211	40	Ibid.
212	3	Hall, "Indian Administration," p. 141.
212	5	HCSP, no. 27, 1903, 4 Sept. 1902, Swinford to SGIA.
212	12	CH, 23 June 1908.
212	36	Mountain Horse, pp. 15-16.
213	8	HCSP, no. 27, 1902, 24 Sept. 1901, Semmens to SGIA.
213	9	HCSP, no. 27, 1904, 2 Sept. 1903, Swinford to SGIA.
213	10	Quoted in Raby, p. 2.
213	12	HCSP, no. 27, 1906, 30 June 1905, Semmens to Insp. of Indian Agencies.
213	14	CH, 16 Sept. 1902.
213	31	HCSP, no. 14, 1899, p. xxi, 31 Dec. 1898, Smart to SGIA.
213	36	HCSP, no. 27, 1905, 17 Aug. 1904, Semmens to SGIA.
213	38	HCSP, no. 27, 1901, 1 Dec. 1900, Laird to SGIA.
213	40	HCSP, no. 27, 1901, 12 Oct. 1900, Swinford to SGIA.
214	5	HCSP, no. 27, 1903, 4 Sept. 1902, Swinford to SGIA.
214	11	HCSP, no. 14, 1898, 31 Dec. 1897, Smart to SGIA.
215	32	Goddard, *passim*.
216	12	HCSP, no. 27, 1903, 15 Oct. 1902, Laird to SGIA.
216	20	HCSP, no. 27, 1903, 12 Aug. 1902, Begg to SGIA.
216	31	HCSP, no. 27, 1909, 30 June 1908, Laird to Pedley.
216	38	HCSP, no. 27, 1901, 18 Aug. 1900, Mackenzie to SGIA.
217	3	Ibid., 1 Oct. 1900, Marlatt to SGIA.
217	7	HCSP, no. 27, 1902, 31 July 1901, Gibbons to SGIA.
217	16	EB, 28 Oct. 1907.
217	27	Dempsey, *Indian Tribes*, p. 34.
217	29	Ibid., p. 41.
218	10	HCSP, no. 27, 1908, 31 March 1907, Semmens to Pedley.
218	20	CH, 22 Jan. 1902.
218	23	Ibid.
218	31	HCSP, no. 15, 1899, 20 Dec. 1898, Herchmer to Laurier.
218	34	HCSP, no. 15, 1900, 30 Nov. 1899, Deane to Commissioner.
219	1	HCSP, no. 28, 1901, 20 Dec. 1900, Perry to Laurier.
219	4	HCSP, no. 28, 1904, 30 Nov. 1903, Sanders to Commissioner.
219	14	Quoted in Longstreth, p. 175.
219	21	Berton, *Wild Frontier*, p. 220.
219	28	HCSP, no. 15, 1899, 20 Dec. 1898, Herchmer to Laurier; 30 Nov. 1898, Constantine to Commissioner; 30 Nov. 1898, Deane to Commissioner.
219	31	HCSP, no. 15, 1899, 20 Dec. 1898, Herchmer to Laurier.
219	32	Ibid.
219	33	HCSP, no. 28, 1902, 17 Jan. 1902, Perry to Laurier.
219	36	HCSP, no. 28, 1904, 1 Dec. 1903, Primrose to Commissioner.
219	39	HCSP, no. 28, 1898, 17 Dec. 1897, Herchmer to Laurier.
220	1	HCSP, no. 28, 1902, 17 Jan. 1902, Perry to Laurier.
220	7	HCSP, no. 28, 1912, 31 Oct. 1911, Perry to Borden.
220	12	Longstreth, p. 240; MacLeod, *North-West Mounted Police*, p. 111; HCSP, no. 28, 1905, 3 Jan. 1905, Commissioner to Laurier.
220	22	Berton, *Wild Frontier*, pp. 113-14.
220	26	MacLeod, *North-West Mounted Police*, pp. 98-99.
220	27	Ibid., p. 99.
220	35	Deane, p. 93.
220	41	RCMP Archives, interview with Junget; CH, 16 May 1902.

page line

221 15 MacLeod, *North-West Mounted Police*, p. 74.

221 19 HCSP, no. 28, 1908, 1 Nov. 1907, Sanders to Commissioner.

221 27 HCSP, no. 28, 1904, 25 Jan. 1904, Perry to Laurier.

221 40 HCSP, no. 15, 1897, 30 Nov. 1896, Herchmer to President of Privy Council.

222 1 Ibid.

222 5 HCSP, no. 15, 1899, 20 Dec. 1898, Herchmer to Laurier.

222 15 MacLeod, *North-West Mounted Police*, pp. 154-55.

223 29 PAC, RG 18/3407/3156, file on Henry Lett.

The Sifton Scandals

226 4 Dafoe, *Sifton*, p. xi.

228 21 Senate Journals, 1901, vol. 36, p. 41.

228 25 Toronto *World*, 28 June 1899.

228 37 Ibid.

229 2 Ibid.

229 5 HCD, 4 June 1906, p. 4503.

229 10 Ibid., p. 4502.

229 21 HCJ, 1906, vol. 41, app., Report of Public Accounts Committee; HCJ, 1906, vol. 41, app., Report of Select Standing Committee on Agriculture and Colonization.

229 30 HCJ, 1906, vol. 41, app., Report of Select Standing Committee on Agriculture and Colonization, p. 410.

230 9 PAC, RG 76/225/113228, pt. 11, 23 Oct. 1899, Preston to Smart (copy).

230 12 HCJ, 1906, vol. 41, app., Report of Public Accounts Committee, pp. 322-23; Report of Select Standing Committee on Agriculture and Colonization, p. 315.

230 17 PAC, RG 76/223/113228, pt. 1, 24 Sept. 1900, Min. of Interior to Gov. Gen. in Council.

230 23 HCJ, 1906, vol. 41, app., Report of Public Accounts Committee, pp. 331-38.

230 27 Ibid., p. 115; PAC, RG 76/225/113228, 25 June 1900, Pedley to Smart; 23 Oct.

page line

1900, Preston to Smart; PAC, RG 76/223/113, 24 Sept. 1900, Sifton to Gov. Gen. in Council; PAC, RG 76/224/113228, pt. 3, 21 April 1902, Order in Council.

230 29 Ibid.

230 33 PAC, RG 76/223/113228, pt. 1, 24 Sept. 1900, Smart to Preston.

230 35 PAC, RG 76/113228, pt. 6, 4 Nov. 1903, Smart to Preston.

230 37 HCJ, 1906, vol. 41, app., Report of Public Accounts Committee, p. 79.

231 11 HCD, 3 July 1906, pp. 6881-83.

231 15 PAC, Mavor Papers, 11 March 1922, Mavor to Maclean.

231 18 HCD, 8 Oct. 1903, p. 13372.

231 20 HCJ, 1906, vol. 41, app., Report of Select Standing Committee on Agriculture and Colonization, p. 396.

231 22 Ibid., p. 408.

231 24 PAC, RG 76/223/113228, pt. 1, 17 Aug. 1900, NATC to Smart, is an example.

231 32 HCJ, 1906, vol. 41, app., Report of Select Standing Committee on Agriculture and Colonization, pp. 60-61.

231 35 HCJ, 1906, vol. 41, app., Report of Public Accounts Committee, p. 106.

232 6 HCJ, 1906, vol. 41, app., Report of Select Standing Committee on Agriculture and Colonization, pp. 60-61.

232 16 Ibid.

232 24 PAC, RG 76/224/113228, pt. 7, 19 Aug. 1904, Sifton to Gov. Gen. in Council.

232 38 HCJ, 1906, vol. 41, app., Report of Public Accounts Committee, pp. 238-39.

232 39 Ibid., p. 239.

233 5 HCD, 4 June 1906, p. 4493.

233 17 HCJ, 1906, vol. 41, app., Report of Public Accounts Committee, pp. 65, 171-73.

233 23 PAC, RG 76/255/113228, pt. 11, 27 Oct. 1899, Preston to Smart.

233 31 HCJ, 1906, vol. 41, app., Report of Public Accounts Committee, p. 305.

233 35 PAC, RG 76/225/113228, pt. 9, 2 June 1906, NATC to Strathcona.

233　*40*　HCJ, 1906, vol. 41, app., Report of Public Accounts Committee, pp. 202-3.

234　*4*　Ibid.

234　*7*　HCJ, 1906, vol. 41, app., Report of Public Accounts Committee, pp. 203-6, 405, 437.

234　*12*　HCJ, 1906, vol. 41, app., Report of Select Standing Committee on Agriculture and Colonization, p. 404.

234　*18*　HCD, 3 July 1906, pp. 6874-75.

234　*25*　*Ottawa Citizen*, 24 Sept. 1903; HCD, 3 July 1906, pp. 6877-78.

234　*29*　HCD, 21 July 1904, p. 7310.

234　*34*　HCJ, 1906, vol. 41, app., Report of Public Accounts Committee, pp. 431-32.

234　*36*　HCD, 3 July 1906, pp. 6877-78.

235　*8*　PAC, RG 76/225/113228, pt. 10, 7 Jan. 1907, Beddoe to Oliver; ibid., statement of money paid to NATC, n.d.; PAC, RG 76/225/113228, pt. 10, statement of monies paid to NATC to 1 Nov. 1906.

235　*15*　HCD, 4 June 1906, p. 4504; HCJ, 1906, vol. 41, app., Report of Public Accounts Committee, p. 323.

235　*17*　HCJ, 1906, vol. 41, app., Report of Public Accounts Committee, p. 446; Preston, p. 261.

235　*22*　PAC, MG 26G, 11 Jan. 1905 (misdated?), Sifton to Laurier.

235　*24*　Preston, p. 262.

235　*25*　Ibid., p. 261.

235　*27*　HCD, 3 July 1906, p. 6928.

235　*31*　PAC, RG 76/194/73989, pt. 2, 5 Oct. 1906, O'Hara to Deputy Minister of the Interior.

235　*33*　PAC, MG 27 II D15, 14 Aug. 1897, Sifton to Campbell.

236　*3*　Ibid., 19 Aug. 1899, Sifton to Calvert.

236　*11*　HCD, 19 May 1908, pp. 8715-16.

236　*13*　HCJ, 1908, Report of Public Accounts Committee, payments in connection with timber agencies, *passim*.

236　*17*　HCD, 19 May 1908, pp. 8715-16; HCJ, 1908, op. cit., *passim*.

236　*21*　Toronto *News*, 20 May 1908.

236　*31*　Ames, pp. 85-86.

236　*35*　Ibid.

236　*37*　Ibid., p. 87.

237　*5*　Ibid., p. 88.

237　*13*　HCJ, 1908, op. cit., pp. 487-88.

237　*21*　Ibid., *passim*; HCD, 19 May 1908, pp. 8716-17.

237　*24*　HCJ, 1908, op. cit., pp. 573-75.

237　*38*　HCD, 19 May 1908, pp. 8716-17; HCJ, 1908, op. cit., pp. 513-15.

238　*5*　HCD, 19 May 1908, pp. 8720-21; HCJ, 1908, op. cit., pp. 515-21, 582-83.

238　*15*　HCD, 19 May 1908, pp. 8720-21; HCJ, 1908, op. cit., pp. 528, 537-38, 539-41, 547.

238　*25*　HCD, 19 May 1908, pp. 8725-27; HCJ, 1908, op. cit., pp. 485-98, 525, 538-39, 589.

238　*30*　HCD, 19 May 1908; HCJ, 1908, op. cit., *passim*.

238　*33*　HCJ, 1908, op. cit., p. 525.

238　*33*　Ibid.

238　*40*　Ibid., *passim*.

239　*7*　HCD, 19 May 1908, pp. 8730-31; HCJ, 1908, op. cit., pp. 525-30, 537-41, 547.

239　*30*　HCD, 19 May 1908, p. 8733.

239　*37*　Ibid.

240　*14*　*A Session's Disclosures*, p. 59; Dempsey, *Men in Scarlet*, p. 130 ff.

241　*6*　HCD, 5 Feb. 1907, p. 2514; Berton, *Wild Frontier*, pp. 113-14; MG 27 II D15, vol. 84, 19 June 1900; McGregor to Smart.

241　*13*　*A Session's Disclosures*, p. 59; HCD, 5 Feb. 1907, p. 2515; PAC, RG 15, vol. 1211/145330/4, 15 June 1905, Ryley to Oliver.

241　*15*　PAC, MG 27 II D15, 10 Dec. 1904, Philp to Sifton; 21 Jan. 1905, Philp to Sifton.

241　*17*　PAC, RG 15/1211/145330/4, 15 June 1905, Ryley to Oliver; HCD, 5 Feb. 1907, p. 2492.

241　*18*　HCD, 5 Feb. 1907, p. 2499.

241　*24*　Ibid., p. 2513.

241　*25*　Ibid., p. 2495; *A Session's Disclosures*, p. 59.

241　*28*　HCD, 5 Feb. 1907, p. 2495.

241　*37*　Ibid., p. 2421, 2495.

page	line	
242	3	HCD, 5 Feb. 1907, p. 2591; PAC RG 2, series 1, Privy Council Office, Order in Council 1269, 25 June 1906.
242	3	HCD, 5 Feb. 1907, pp. 2543-46; *A Session's Disclosures*, p. 59.
242	14	HCD, 5 Feb. 1907, pp. 2515, 2543.
242	24	Ibid., p. 2492.
242	27	Ibid., p. 2495.
242	32	Ibid., p. 2548.
243	3	Ibid., p. 2495.
243	6	*A Session's Disclosures*, p. 59.
243	20	HCD, 21 Feb. 1907, p. 3490.
243	28	PAC, RG 15/1245/4234891: 12 June 1903, 27 July 1903, 14 Jan. 1904, 13 April 1904, 26 May 1904, 7 Jan. 1905, Keyes to Brown; 6 Dec. 1904, Campbell to Ryley; 28 March 1905, Campbell to Ryley; 7 June 1905, Mitz to Ryley; 6 July 1905, Ryley to Corey.
243	29	PAC, RG 15/1245/4234891: 12 June 1903, Keyes to Brown; HCD, 21 Feb. 1907, p. 3504; HCD, 14 April 1915, pp. 2558, 2595-96.
243	30	PAC, RG 15/1245/4234891, 7 Jan. 1905, Keyes to Brown.
243	32	PAC, RG 15/1245/4234891, petition to Dept. of Interior, 28 June 1905; 30 April 1903, Campbell to Ryley; HCD, 6 Feb. 1907, p. 3478.
243	40	HCD, 21 Feb. 1907, pp. 3470, 3480; PAC, RG 15/1245/4234891, 28 July 1905, Corey to Adamson; 28 July 1905, Keyes to McCarthy; 4 Aug. 1905, Keyes to Adamson.
244	20	HCD, 21 Feb. 1907, p. 3481.
244	24	Ibid., p. 3482; PAC, RG 15/1245/4234891, 27 Feb. 1906, Oliver to Campbell.
244	28	PAC, RG 15/1245/4234891, 19 May 1906, Keyes to Dep. Minister of Public Works; HCD, 6 Feb. 1907, pp. 3470, 3487.
245	8	HCD, 14 April 1915.
245	27	PAC, MG 27 II D15, 12 Nov. 1898, Smart to Sifton.
245	33	PAC, RG 10/3839/69-244-1, 3 Dec. 1898, Smart to McLean.
246	9	HCSP, 1901, no. 27, 7 Aug. 1900, McGibbon to SGIA.
246	16	PAC, RG 10/3839/69-244-1, 25 Jan. 1899, Halpin to Laird; 3 Dec. 1898, Smart to McLean.
246	19	PAC, RG 10/3839/69-244-1, 23 June 1899, Smart to McLean.
246	29	Ibid., 5 March 1901, Smart to Sifton.
246	38	*Brandon Independence*, 2 Feb. 1900.
246	40	PAC, RG 10/3839/69-244-1, 5 March 1901, Smart to Sifton.
247	13	PAC, RG 10/3839/69-244-1, 3 Aug. 1901, Laird to Sifton.
247	14	PAC, MG 27 II D15, 10 May 1901, Madill and Bainbridge to Sifton; 14 May 1901, Bainbridge to Sifton.
247	17	PAC, RG 10/3839/69-244-1, 4 and 5 June 1901, Smart to McLean.
247	32	Ibid., 2 and 7 Oct. 1901, Smart to McLean.
247	35	Ibid., 17 Oct. 1901, Smart to McLean.
247	37	Ibid., 6 Sept. 1901, Lash to Laird.
247	38	Ibid., 17 Oct. 1901, Smart to McLean.
247	40	TDS, 14 April 1915.
248	8	MFP, 25 Oct. 1901; *l'Echo de Manitoba*, 7 Nov. 1901; Moosomin *Spectator*, 7 Nov. 1901 et seq.; *l'Echo de Manitoba*, 14 Nov. 1901; Moosomin *Spectator*, 21 Nov. 1901.
248	15	TDS, 14 April 1915.
248	24	Ibid; Toronto *Daily News*, 14 April 1915; HCD, 14 April 1905, p. 2560.
248	31	TDS, 14 April 1915.
248	33	Toronto *Daily News*, 14 April 1905.
248	38	Ibid.
250	10	PAC, MG 27 II D15, 21 Jan. 1905, Philp to Sifton.

The Spirit of the West

page	line	
252	13	Quoted in CH, 15 Feb. 1906.
252	37	Sproule, p. 111.
253	6	Quoted in CH, 12 Aug. 1904.
253	9	CH, 23 Nov. 1896.
253	13	Quoted in WDT, 19 June 1899.
253	14	Ibid.
253	18	Ibid.

373

page	line	
253	26	Ibid.
253	29	Ibid.
254	4	Quoted in CH, 6 Sept. 1958.
254	12	Ibid.
254	35	CH, 5 May 1902.
254	40	CH, 14 Feb. 1901.
255	2	CH, 21 Feb. 1905.
255	7	CH, 23 Aug. 1905.
255	9	CH, 8 May 1905.
255	12	Ibid.
255	16	CH, 4 May 1905.
255	19	Ibid.
255	25	CH, 10 Nov. 1905.
256	7	CH, 16 May 1905.
256	14	CH, 20 Aug. 1910.
256	32	Piniuta, p. 53.
256	34	Shepherd, p. 10.
257	1	Davies and Vaughan, p. 14.
257	3	Shepherd, p. 14.
257	6	Shepherd, p. 16.
258	39	Whates, pp. 121-41 *passim*.
259	22	McNeil, p. 132.
259	31	Piniuta, p. 308.
259	33	Davies and Vaughan, pp. 40-41.
259	36	McNeil, p. 40.
261	17	Quoted in Sproule, p. 106.
261	25	Rasporich and Klassen, *Frontier Calgary*, pp. 231-32.
261	31	Sproule.
261	37	Ibid.
262	14	Ibid.
262	21	Ibid.
262	24	Rasporich and Klassen, *Frontier Calgary*, p. 231.
262	33	Sproule.
262	38	Sproule, p. 42; Rasporich and Klassen, *Frontier Calgary*, pp. 224-25.
263	6	Sproule, p. 121.
263	24	Quoted in WDT, 29 Feb. 1904.
263	28	Whates, p. 57.
263	31	Bickersteth, p. 93.
263	33	Sykes, *Home Help*, p. 128.
264	14	Klassen, p. 52.
264	17	HCSP, no. 28, 1909, 1 Nov. 1908, Sanders to Commissioner, pp. 41-43.
264	21	CH, 16, 23, 24, 30 April 1908.
265	8	Fraser, J.F., p. 168.
265	10	Hobson, p. 17.
265	12	Quoted in CH, 25 Aug. 1910.
265	16	CH, 14 Sept. 1906.
265	18	Ford, p. 230.
266	18	Stubbs, *Lawyers*, p. 190.
266	21	Dempsey, *Best of Bob Edwards*, p. 21.
266	31	Stubbs, *Lawyers*, p. 189.
267	13	Fraser, W.B., p. 318.
267	39	*Eye Opener*, 6 Oct. 1906.
268	19	MacEwan, *Eye Opener Bob*, pp. 102-3.
269	15	*Eye Opener*, 2 Dec. 1905.
269	18	Stubbs, *Lawyers*, p. 180.
269	25	*Eye Opener*, 22 May 1915.
269	34	Stubbs, *Lawyers*, p. 195.
270	11	Ibid., pp. 192-93.
270	21	Dempsey, *Best of Bob Edwards*, p. 17.
270	31	MacEwan, *Eye Opener Bob*, p. 111.
271	5	Ibid., pp. 111-14.
271	16	Ibid., p. 116.
271	38	Stubbs, *Lawyers*, p. 191.
271	40	Ibid., p. 197.
273	5	Knappen, "Winning Canadian West."
274	19	WDT, 27 Nov. 1902.
274	27	PAC, MG 27 II D15, 14 Jan. 1897, Sifton to Watson.
274	37	WDT, 25 Nov. 1899.
275	26	Sharp, *Agrarian Revolt*, p. 64.
275	38	Quoted in ibid., p. 61.
275	40	Ibid.
276	3	Ibid., p. 55.
276	11	PAC, MG 27 II D15, 30 Aug. 1903, Dafoe to Sifton.
277	16	Skelton, *Life*, vol. 2, p. 371.

277   28   Cook, p. 51.

278   4   Sharp, *Agrarian Revolt*, p. 48.

278   7   Ibid., p. 51.

279   41   Beaverbrook, p. 18.

280   4   Stubbs, *Lawyers*, p. 184.

281   18   Beaverbrook, p. 7.

281   28   *Eye Opener*, 13 July 1907.

281   37   Stubbs, *Lawyers*, p. 159.

282   8   Ibid., p. 163.

282   12   Rasporich and Klassen, *Frontier Calgary*, p. 232.

282   16   Watkins, p. 40.

282   30   CH, 6 Sept. 1958.

284   15   CH, 20 and 21 March 1901.

284   28   Watkins, pp. 44-45.

284   34   Ibid., p. 44.

285   16   Ibid., p. 46.

The Dark Side of Boosterism

288   18   Martin and Hall, p. 98.

288   28   Ibid.

288   32   Bickersteth, pp. 130-31.

289   2   Quoted in Riddell, p. 149.

289   6   MFP, 16 March 1904.

289   9   Ibid.

289   18   CH, 10 Jan. 1907.

289   20   Rees, p. 52.

289   23   Quoted in Kerr, p. 18.

289   24   Ibid.

289   25   Rees, p. 52.

289   25   CH, 13 April 1912.

289   26   Rees, p. 52.

290   2   Hubbard, p. 22.

290   4   Artibise, *Winnipeg*, p. 115.

290   10   Ibid., p. 339 n.1.

290   15   CH, 27 July 1906.

290   17   CH, 10 Jan. 1907.

290   23   CH, 15 March 1909.

290   25   CH, 18 Oct. 1911.

290   28   Rees, p. 54.

290   32   Kerr, p. 17.

290   36   Ibid., p. 18.

291   5   CII, 1 and 9 Nov. 1906.

291   12   Talbot, p. 136.

291   17   Rees, p. 53.

291   21   Kerr, p. 19.

291   30   CH, 11 Jan. 1913.

291   38   Artibise, *Town and City*, p. 218.

292   7   Ibid., pp. 218-19.

292   15   Artibise, *Winnipeg*, p. 118.

292   17   Ibid.

292   18   Ibid., p. 119.

292   24   MacEwan, *Calgary Cavalcade*, p. 161.

293   2   Gray, *Red Lights*, p. 125.

293   7   Ibid., pp. 125-26.

293   13   CH, 16 May 1908.

293   17   Rasporich and Klassen, *Frontier Calgary*, p. 137.

293   19   CH, 25 July 1910.

293   23   CH, 6 Nov. 1911.

293   26   Gray, *Red Lights*, p. 141.

293   30   Rasporich and Klassen, *Frontier Calgary*, p. 209.

293   31   Gray, *Red Lights*, p. 9.

294   1   WDT, 15 Oct. 1909.

294   3   Ibid.

294   4   Riddell, p. 155.

294   8   Drake, p. 138.

294   20   Woodsworth, *Report*, pp. 36-38.

294   27   CH, 8 July 1913.

294   40   Ibid.

295   11   CH, 18 Jan. 1913.

295   19   Woodsworth, *Report*, p. 36.

295   27   Ibid., p. 47.

295   29   Ibid., p. 28.

295   32   Gray, *Boy*, p. 8.

295   40   Woodsworth, *Report*, p. 28.

296   5   CH, 3 Nov. 1910.

296   14   Gray, *Red Lights*, p. 12.

page line

296   19   Bedford, p. 4.

296   21   Ibid.

296   27   Ibid., p. 5.

296   38   Artibise, *Winnipeg*, p. 254.

297   7   Ibid., pp. 254-55.

297   15   LLM, Robson, "Report of Commission on Social Vice," *passim*.

298   5   Ibid., testimony of Mrs. Bradley, pp. 608-12.

298   11   Artibise, *Winnipeg*, p. 258.

298   13   Ibid., p. 259.

298   27   Ibid., p. 262.

298   31   Ibid., p. 263.

299   6   Artibise, *Winnipeg*, p. 27.

299   18   Riddell, p. 139.

299   22   Woodsworth, *Report*, p. 11.

299   24   Ibid.

299   29   Ibid., p. 4.

300   11   Rasporich and Klassen, *Frontier Calgary*, p. 221 ff.

300   24   Riddell, p. 138.

302   5   McNaught, p. 25.

302   9   Ibid., p. 24.

302   36   Unpublished MSS of Charles Woodsworth.

302   37   Ibid.

303   5   Letter, Grace MacInnis to author, 10 Jan. 1984.

303   17   Ibid.

303   40   Woodsworth, *Report*, p. 26.

305   2   McClung, *In Times*, p. vii.

305   8   Zieman.

305   16   Ibid.

305   36   Savage, p. 49.

305   38   Ibid.

306   19   McClung, *Stream*, p. 112.

308   12   Savage, pp. 72-74.

308   18   McClung, *Stream*, p. 114.

308   26   Ibid., pp. 115-16.

309   10   Savage, p. 89.

309   15   Ibid., p. 93.

309   17   Ibid., p. 105.

Boom and Bust

312   1   Peel, p. 44.

312   11   Regehr, p. 196.

312   27   Talbot, p. 132.

312   36   Ibid., p. 134.

313   6   Regehr, p. 210.

313   9   Ibid., pp. 210-11.

314   2   Hanna, p. 269.

314   27   Nordegg, pp. 218-19; Regehr, p. 29.

314   31   Regehr, p. 29.

314   39   Ibid., p. 31.

315   22   Hanna, p. 174.

316   39   Cashman, *Best Edmonton Stories*, pp. 68-70.

317   17   Regehr, p. 238.

318   18   Ibid., p. 193.

319   14   Skelton, *Life*, vol. 2, pp. 81-82.

319   26   Schull, p. 426.

320   15   PAC, MG 27 II D15, 20 March 1903, Sifton to Laurier; 9 Jan. 1912, Sifton to Dafoe.

320   38   Skelton, *Life*, vol. 2, p. 81.

321   14   Skelton, *Railway*, p. 213.

321   35   Bellan, pp. 99-100.

322   3   Ibid., p. 108.

322   5   Ibid.

322   6   Ibid.

322   9   Ibid., p. 104.

322   10   Ibid., p. 103.

322   14   Ibid., p. 105.

322   23   Hubbard, p. 7.

322   31   Bellan, pp. 103-4.

322   39   CH, 3 Feb. 1906.

323   5   Rees, p. 53.

323   8   Rasporich and Klassen, *Frontier Calgary*, p. 213.

page line

323 10 MacEwan, *Calgary Cavalcade*, p. 162.

323 20 MacIntyre, p. 84.

323 24 Cashman, *Edmonton Story*, p. 156.

323 31 MacRae, vol. 2, p. 873.

323 33 Ibid., p. 872.

323 37 Dempsey, *Best from Alberta History*, p. 153.

324 9 RL, 4 May 1912.

324 14 Talbot, p. 159.

324 19 CH, 14 Jan. 1913.

324 20 RL, 18 Nov. 1910.

324 23 CH, 21 Nov. 1911.

324 29 CH, 12 June 1912.

324 35 Cashman, *Edmonton Story*, p. 158.

324 36 Rasporich and Klassen, *Frontier Calgary*, p. 212.

324 40 Ibid., p. 214.

325 4 Ibid.

325 8 Ibid., p. 213.

325 12 Ibid.

325 27 Lowes, p. 21.

325 39 MacEwan, *Calgary Cavalcade*, p. 161.

326 8 CH, 2 July 1950.

326 10 Calgary *News-Telegram*, 16 Oct. 1911.

326 18 Lowes, p. 21.

326 37 Bickersteth, p. 103.

327 15 Kerr, p. 21.

327 18 Ibid.

327 20 Hubbard, p. 26.

327 26 Ibid., pp. 27, 31, 32.

327 30 MacEwan, *Calgary Cavalcade*, p. 159.

327 32 MacIntyre, p. 85.

327 34 Cashman, *Edmonton Story*, p. 157.

327 36 Dempsey, *Best from Alberta History*, p. 155.

327 39 MacEwan, *Calgary Cavalcade*, p. 160.

327 41 Ibid.

329 1 CH, 27 April 1910.

329 13 Ibid.

329 29 RL, 3 Jan. 1912.

329 34 MFP, 3 June 1911.

330 2 CH, 6 Aug. 1912.

330 8 CH, 20 April 1910.

330 13 RL, 13 April 1912.

333 15 RL, 25 March 1912.

333 19 MacEwan, *Calgary Cavalcade*, p. 160.

333 23 Rasporich and Klassen, *Frontier Calgary*, p. 210.

333 24 Ibid., p. 213.

333 28 Rees, p. 53.

333 32 Cashman, *Edmonton Story*, p. 155.

333 37 CH, 4 Jan. 1911.

334 1 Rasporich and Klassen, *Frontier Calgary*, pp. 214-15.

334 12 RL, 3 July 1912.

334 20 Dempsey, *Best from Alberta History*, p. 154.

334 28 Rasporich and Klassen, *Frontier Calgary*, p. 213.

334 32 Bickersteth, pp. 111-12.

335 21 EB, 13 May 1912.

336 12 EB, 13 May and 14 May 1912.

337 33 Ibid.

338 1 EB, 14 May 1912.

338 13 Ibid.

338 21 Ibid.

339 4 MacEwan, *Calgary Cavalcade*, p. 162.

340 2 Berton, *Last Spike*, pp. 52-82.

340 6 Rees, p. 57.

340 11 Kerr, p. 17.

340 15 Ibid., p. 20.

340 17 Rees, p. 54.

340 19 Kerr, p. 27.

340 22 Ibid., p. 17.

340 29 CH, 10 June 1913.

340 31 Rees, p. 58.

340 35 PAC, MG 27 II D15, 19 Feb. 1913, Turriff to Sifton.

340 40 CH, 2 July 1913.

341 4 CH, 13 Aug. 1913.

page	line	
341	*16*	Kerr, p. 26.
341	*25*	Skelton, *Railway*, p. 238.
341	*27*	Ibid.
342	*9*	Regehr, p. 198.
342	*31*	Kerr, p. 16.
342	*32*	Berton, "Edmonton."
342	*37*	Ibid.

page	line	
342	*38*	Rasporich and Klassen, *Frontier Calgary*, p. 211.
343	*8*	*Eye Opener*, 24 Aug. 1912.
343	*14*	Dempsey, *Best from Alberta History*, p. 158.
343	*19*	Rees, pp. 56-57.
343	*33*	Vandermeulen, p. 198.
346	*26*	MFP, 17 Aug. 1914.

Index

Galway Horse and Cattle Co., 243
Gazette (Midnapore), 267
Germans, as immigrants, 14, 60, 84
Germany, 45-46, 47, 230, 233
Gidley, Job, 75, 76
Girvin, Sask., 164-66
Globe (St. Paul, Minn.), 174
Globe (Toronto), 190; *quoted*, 120, 205
Golubova, Anastasia, 97
Gordon, Rev. Charles W. (Ralph Connor), 303
Gourley, Seymour, 109
Grain Growers' Assoc., 167, 180, 275, 301
Grain Growers' Guide, 167, 275-76, 301; *quoted*, 278
Grand Trunk Ry., 317-21
Grand Trunk Pacific Ry., 37, 38, 53, 139, 317, 318, 341, 342; and Oliver, 207
Grange movement, 273
Grant, B.L., *quoted*, 188
Grant-Armstrong Land Co., 188
Great Northern Ry., 174
Great War, 344
Great West Saddlery strike, 304
Greenway, Thomas, 170; *quoted*, 274
Grey, Lord, 192-93, 209
Griesbach, W.A., 53, 58
Griffin, F.T., *quoted*, 188
Grip, 181
Gubanova, Lukeria Vasilevna, 81
Guernsey, Isle of, 232

Hag, V.D., 177
Halbrite, Sask., 223
Hale, Jim, 164
Halifax, N.S., 49, 75
Halifax Herald, *quoted*, 86
Halpin, H.R., 246
Hanna, David Blythe, 315
Hardisty family, 281
Harkin, J.B., 26
Harper, Jessie, 100
Harriman, E.H., 174
Haultain, Frederick, 190, 209, 276, 282-84
Hayes, Joseph, 184
Hayes, Mattie (Mammy), 184
Hays, Charles, 318, 319, 320
Healy, John J., 222
Helgerson, O.M., 327

Herald (Calgary), 11, 31, 124, 253-56, 266, 274, 298; *quoted*, 23, 192-93, 200-201, 207, 213, 218, 254, 255-56, 265, 290, 322, 333, 340-41
Herald (Lethbridge), *quoted*, 176
Herald (Montreal), 35
Herchmer, Lawrence, 220; *quoted*, 218, 219, 221-22
Herz, Simon, 44
Hilkoff, Dmitri Alexandrovich, 69, 70, 72, 74, 75-76, 77, 83, 85
Hill, James Jerome, 174-75; *quoted*, 174
Hitchcock, A.E., 241
Holtby, Robert, 114, 115, 130, 131, 155; *quoted*, 118
Holtby family, 133, 155
Home of Welcome (Winnipeg), 157-58
Homestead Act [Free Land Homestead Act, 1872], 74, 98, 110
Hopewell Cape, N.B., 280
Hordern, Paul Sylvester, 115, 119, 121, 126
Hordern family, 115, 119, 126
Howard, Henry, 340
Hubbard, Elbert, *quoted*, 322, 327
Hudson's Bay Co., 13, 335, 338
Humeniuk, Petryk (Peter), 43
Humeniuk family, 43, 52-53
Hutchings, E.F., 26
Hutchison, Bruce, 39
Hutchison, Ted, 129, 134
Hutchison, William, 117-18, 129, 131, 134, 155

Icelanders, 26
Idaho Kid (Brandenburger), 222-23
Immigrants, exploitation of, 44, 46-47, 50-51, 53
Immigration Department, 16, 22, 73, 74-75, 95, 182, 185, 186, 230, 234
Immigration: policy, 14-15, 181, 206, 234; promotion of, 15-19, 170-75, 227-35 *passim*; unrestricted, 5, 54, 59, 183
Imperial Order Daughters of the Empire, 186
Imperial Pulp Co., 238, 239, 249
Independent (Bobcaygeon), *quoted*, 253
Independent (Brandon), *quoted*, 54
Independent Order of Foresters, 317

Rivers-Wilson, Sir Charles, 318
Robbins, Rev. John, 112, 113, 121
Roberts, J.H., 187
Robertson, Rev. Dr. James, 62
Robins, Guy Tracy, 241, 242
Roblin, Rodmond, 35, 55, 56-57, 274, 306-9, 317
Roe, Frank G., *quoted*, 148-49
Romanchych, Dmytro, 50, 57
Rosthern, Sask., 37, 84
Rosthern colony, 82, 97, 99
Rowan, John M., 177
Roxborough Place (Calgary), 326
Russia, 67-68
Russian Carpet Co., 70
Ruthenia, 1-2, 4; immigrants from, 3
Ruthenian Population Society, *see* Provista
Ruttan, R.A., *quoted*, 54

Saint John, N.B., 76, 118
St. Paul, Minn., 174, 184-85
Saltcoats, Sask., 45
Salteaux Indians, 246
Sanders, Supt. G.E., 220; *quoted*, 219, 221
Sarcee Indians, 214, 217, 219
Saskatchewan, 99-100, 196, 252; Americans in, 170, 175. *See also* Doukhobors, Barr colonists
Saskatchewan rebellion, 107, 171
Saskatchewan Valley Land Corp., 188
Saskatoon, Sask., 2, 111, 113, 121-22, 142, 146, 257-58, 289, 290, 292, 323, 327, 333, 342, 343
Saturday Evening Post, *quoted*, 190
Saunders, William, 81
Scandinavians, as immigrants, 14, 60, 84
School legislation, 197-98, 204
Sclanders, F. McClure, *quoted*, 341
Scots, as immigrants, 14, 141
Scotsman (Edinburgh), *quoted*, 263
Scott, Walter, 205-6
Seattle, Wash., 175
Second Chance, 304
Secord, Richard, 58
Selkirk, Man., 77, 80
Semmens, John, *quoted*, 217-18
Sentinel (Shelby, Ky.), 17
Sharpe, James, 264
Shaughnessy, Thomas, 27

Shearer, Rev. J.G., *quoted*, 298
Shepherd, Charlie, 163, 165-66
Shepherd, Geoff, 165
Shepherd, George, 163-64, 165-66; *quoted*, 210
Shepherd, Harry, 165, 346
Shepherd, Kit, 164, 165
Shepherd, Will, 163, 165-66
Shepherd, William John, 162, 163-64, 165, 166
Shepherd, Mrs. William J., 163, 164-67
Shoal Lake, Man., 91
Shunks, W.J., *quoted*, 312
Sifton, Arma, 20
Sifton, Arthur, 21, 22, 203, 267
Sifton, Clifford, 5, 8, 12, 61, 72, 74, 98, 171, 220, 270, 277; described, 9, 19-25, 206, 226; and Manitoba school question, 10; and promotion of immigration, 13-19; as politician, 22-23, 25-33, 59; and *Free Press*, 29-30, 36-38; and Barr colonists, 112-13; immigration policy, 138-39, 170, 205, 234; and land deals, 188; resignation, 196-205; and Indians, 211-12; and profiteering, 226-27, 235-36, 240-43, 246-47, 249-50; and railways, 320; *quoted*, 42, 202, 274
Sifton, J.D., 236
Sifton, J.W., 21-22
Sinclair, Upton, 272
Sioux Indians, 245
Sisley, Laura, 115-16
Smart, James Allan, 9, 22, 73, 75, 171, 249; described, 11-12; and patronage, 27-28; and Barr, 109, 110, 112, 113; and Indians, 211, 213; and Indian lands, 226-27, 245-48; and North Atlantic Trading Co., 229-35; and timber leases, 237
Smith, Donald, *see* Strathcona, Lord
Smith, J. Obed, 25, 96, 112-13, 120, 292
Sneed, Henry, 184-86
Snow, Matthew, 129, 152
Social Credit, 278
Social Gospel, 275, 300, 303
Society of Equity, 273
Society of Friends, 69. *See also* Quakers
Somerville, Roy, 234
Sons of Freedom, *see* Freedomites
Sons of God, 87, 89-93
Soulerkitsky, Leopold, 79
South Africa, 104

386

South African War, *see* Boer War
South Alberta Cattle Co., 242
South Colony, 82, 97
Sowing Seeds in Danny, 304
Sparling, A.J., 324
Sparling, J.W., 60-61; *quoted*, 61
Speers, Charles Wesley, 12, 55; and Doukhobors, 86-94, 96, 98; and Barr colonists, 113, 121, 124, 125, 126-27, 153-55; and Blacks, 186; and land deal, 189; *quoted*, 150, 154, 155
Sphere, *quoted*, 325
Star (Shoal Lake), 55
Steele, Sam, 220, 241, 346
Steffens, Lincoln, 272
Stevenson, J.E., *quoted*, 275
Stewart, Basil, *quoted*, 139, 141
Stoney Indians, 219
Stony Plain Indian Reserve, 217
Strangers within Our Gates, 60, 141, 182, 303
Strathcoholic (Leduc), 267
Strathcona, Lord, 29, 174, 230, 233, 267-68
Strathcona, Alta., 179, 290, 316
Strickland, Insp. Darcy, *quoted*, 84
Stringer, Arthur, 323
Stringer, Bert A., 323, 343
Stuart, C.A., 283-84
Stuartburn, Man., 52-53
Stubbs, Roy St. George, *quoted*, 266, 269
Studies in Rural Citizenship, 301
Sun (Brandon), 170, 171; *quoted*, 9
Sun Dance, 214-16
Svobodniki, *see* Freedomites
Sykes, Ella Constance, 156-62, 187
Sykes, Brig. Gen. Sir Percy Molesworth, 162
Sylvan Lake, Alta., 264

Tarbell, Ida M., 272
Tarte, Israel, 21, 36, 77
Tasiv, Vasyl, 3
Tchertkoff, Vladimir, 69, 70, 71, 81, 89, 95
Teeswater, Ont., 104
Telegram (Winnipeg), *quoted*, 55-56
Telegraph (New York), 202
Telegraph (Saint John), *quoted*, 265
Tellenius, Mrs. Carl, 259
Temperance, 21, 295, 300

Terpenie, Sask., 84-85
Territorial Grain Growers' Assoc., 273
Thomson, E.W., *quoted*, 154
Thomson, Dr. W.A., 299
Through Persia on a Side Saddle, 156
Times (Hamilton), *quoted*, 59-60
Times (London), 268; *quoted*, 252
Times (Seattle), 175
Tolstoy, Leo, 66, 68, 69, 70, 71, 73, 95
Tolstoy, Sergius, 74
Toronto, 85
Toronto Star, 124, 127; *quoted*, 253, 298
Trade union movement, 275, 300
Tribune (London), 233
Tribune (New York), *quoted*, 253
Trochu colony, 264
Trotter, Beecham, *quoted*, 25
Tulsa, Okla., 183
Turkestan, 162
Turriff, John Gillanders, 189, 237, 244, 249
Tweedale, Charles, 198
Twelve Apostles, 135

Underhill, William, 247
Unemployed Workmen's Act (U.K.), 140
Union Trust Co., 317
United Farmers of Alberta, 180, 273-74, 275, 278
United States, 15. *See also* Americans
University of Saskatchewan, 291
University of Toronto, 71, 291
Utopia subdivision (Saskatoon), 340

Van Horne, William Cornelius, 15-16, 29, 59, 318; *quoted*, 16, 53, 54
Verigin, Anna, 94-95
Verigin, Peter Vasilivich (the Lordly), 73, 81, 82-83, 89, 94-100
Victoria, B.C., 162
Victoria College, 22
Voisey, Paul, 300

Walker, Sir Edmund, 277
Walsh, James, 338
Warman, Cy, *quoted*, 189
Warner, Daniel Webster, 179-80, 277
Wascana Park (Regina), 343
Washington State, 104
Wausau, Wisc., 173